THE CAMBRIDGE COMPANION TO
IGNATIUS SANCHO

One of the largest archives of writing by an eighteenth-century Black individual, this volume not only connects the letters of Ignatius Sancho to their social and historical contexts but also highlights their cultural and aesthetic significance. Offering an interdisciplinary range of perspectives on Sancho and his letters from across literary, historical, and cultural studies, and authored by scholars, archivists, and performers alike, it provides the first authoritative, accessible resource focused exclusively on Sancho's life and writing. Building on established connections to abolitionism and the aesthetics of sentiment, it breaks new ground by considering Sancho's continuing significance for Black British society specifically, and UK literature and history generally.

NICOLE N. ALJOE is Professor of English and Africana Studies at Northeastern University in Boston. She is Co-Director of The Early Caribbean Digital Archive and Mapping Black London, and Director of the Early Black Boston Digital Almanac. She is the author of *Creole Testimonies: Slave Narratives from the British West Indies, 1709–1836* (2012) and co-editor of *Journeys of the Slave Narrative in the Early Americas* (2014), as well as *A Literary History of the Early Anglophone Caribbean: Islands in the Stream* (2018).

KRISTINA HUANG is Assistant Professor of English at the University of Wisconsin–Madison. She specializes in African diasporic literatures from the vantage point of the eighteenth-century transatlantic world. As an interdisciplinary scholar and educator, her work centers on historical representations of subaltern, enslaved, and minoritized lives and how those representations inform critical theory, literary study, and political practice. Her articles have appeared in *African and Black Diaspora: An International Journal*, *Eighteenth-Century Fiction*, *European Romantic Fiction*, and *Studies in Romanticism*.

A complete list of books in the series is at the back of the book.

THE CAMBRIDGE COMPANION TO IGNATIUS SANCHO

EDITED BY

NICOLE N. ALJOE
Northeastern University, Boston

KRISTINA HUANG
University of Wisconsin–Madison

CAMBRIDGE
UNIVERSITY PRESS

Shaftesbury Road, Cambridge CB2 8EA, United Kingdom

One Liberty Plaza, 20th Floor, New York, NY 10006, USA

477 Williamstown Road, Port Melbourne, VIC 3207, Australia

314–321, 3rd Floor, Plot 3, Splendor Forum, Jasola District Centre,
New Delhi – 110025, India

Cambridge University Press is part of Cambridge University Press & Assessment,
a department of the University of Cambridge.

We share the University's mission to contribute to society through the pursuit of
education, learning and research at the highest international levels of excellence.

www.cambridge.org
Information on this title: www.cambridge.org/9781009280648

DOI: 10.1017/9781009280631

© Cambridge University Press & Assessment 2026

When citing this work, please include a reference to the DOI 10.1017/9781009280631

First published 2026

Cover image: Joy Labinjo, *Portrait of Ignatius Sancho* (2022). Image: UK Government Art
Collection. © Crown copyright: UK Government Art Collection

A catalogue record for this publication is available from the British Library

A Cataloging-in-Publication data record for this book is available from the Library of Congress

ISBN 978-1-009-28064-8 Hardback
ISBN 978-1-009-28060-0 Paperback

For EU product safety concerns, contact us at Calle de José Abascal, 56, 1°, 28003 Madrid, Spain,
or email eugpsr@cambridge.org

Contents

v

Figures

Maps

Contributors

NICOLE N. ALJOE is Professor of English and Africana Studies at Northeastern University in Boston. She is co-founder and current conference co-chair of the Women of Color in the Academy Initiatives in Boston. She is also co-Director of *The Early Caribbean Digital Archive* and *Mapping Black London* digital projects, and Director of the *Early Black Boston Digital Almanac*. Her research and teaching focuses on eighteenth- and early nineteenth-century Black Atlantic and Caribbean literatures as well as Digital Humanities. The author of *Creole Testimonies: Slave Narratives from the British West Indies, 1709–1836* (Palgrave, 2012), Aljoe has edited several collections, including *The Cambridge Companion to Mary Prince* (2025) and the forthcoming *Oxford World Classics* edition of *The Letters of the Late Ignatius Sancho*. Her work has been published in a variety of venues, including *African American Review, American Literary History, Eighteenth-Century Fiction, The Journal of Early American Literature*, and *Women's Studies*.

OLIVER AYERS is Associate Professor in History at Northeastern University of London, where he also leads the research cluster focused on Cities: Past, Present and Future. His research centers on themes of race, urban space, and digital historical analysis. His first monograph, *Laboured Protest*, was published by Routledge in 2019 and examined Black civil rights activism in the United States during the 1930s and 1940s. He has written numerous articles on racial protest in American cities in the first half of the twentieth century for journals including *The Journal of Urban History* and *The Journal of American Studies*. Dr. Ayers co-leads the multiyear digital history project Mapping Black London, alongside Professor Nicole Aljoe.

BRYCCHAN CAREY is Professor of Literature, Culture, and History at Northumbria University. He is the author or editor of nine books and numerous articles on slavery, abolition, and the environmental humanities including *The Unnatural Trade: Slavery, Abolition, and Environmental Writing, 1650–1807* (Yale University Press, 2024), *From Peace to Freedom: Quaker Rhetoric and the Birth of American Antislavery, 1658–1761* (Yale University Press, 2012), and *British Abolitionism and the Rhetoric of Sensibility: Writing, Sentiment, and Slavery, 1760–1807* (Palgrave, 2005).

VINCENT CARRETTA is Professor Emeritus of English at the University of Maryland. His recent publications include *The Life and Letters of Philip Quaque: The First African Anglican Missionary* (2010), co-edited with Ty M. Reese; an edition of *Letters of the Late Ignatius Sancho, an African* (2015); *Olaudah Equiano: The Interesting Narrative and Other Writings* (1995; rev. eds. 2003, 2020); *Equiano, the African: Biography of a Self-Made Man* (2005; rev. ed. 2022); *Phillis Wheatley Peters: Biography of a Genius in Bondage* (2011; rev. eds. 2014, 2023); and *The Writings of Phillis Wheatley Peters* (2019; rev. ed. 2024).

DAVID MARK DIAMOND is an assistant professor in the Department of English and the Institute for African American Studies at the University of Georgia. He teaches and writes about eighteenth-century British and Black Atlantic writing, with a focus on the role religion plays in shaping global imaginaries. He is the author of *Reading Character after Calvin: Secularization, Empire, and the Eighteenth-Century Novel* (University of Virginia Press, 2024) and essays in *ELH, Eighteenth-Century Fiction*, and *Eighteenth-Century Studies*.

MARKMAN ELLIS is Professor of Eighteenth-Century Studies at Queen Mary University of London. He is the author of *The Politics of Sensibility: Race, Gender and Commerce in the Sentimental Novel* (1996), *The History of Gothic Fiction* (2000), and *The Coffee-House: A Cultural History* (2004), and co-author of *Empire of Tea* (2015). He co-edited *Discourses of Slavery and Abolition: Writing in Britain and Its Colonies 1660–1832* (2004) and has published essays on Ignatius Sancho, slave narratives, and eighteenth-century Caribbean poetry. He is currently editing, with Nicole Aljoe and Oliver Ayres, *The Letters of Ignatius Sancho, an African* (1782) for Oxford University Press.

LAWRENCE EVALYN is the Text Mining Specialist at Northeastern University Library, where he supports research in the digital humanities and computational social sciences. He is interested in digital infrastructure and book history, always through the lens of eighteenth-century English literature. His dissertation at the University of Toronto examined the uneven digitization of women's writing. He has published in *Digital Humanities Quarterly*, *Eighteenth-Century Fiction*, and computer science venues. His current projects focus on authorless works in digital archives, and subscription publishing.

CHARLOTTE GRANT is Associate Professor in English at Northeastern University London. She is co-editor of *Cultures of London: Legacies of Migration* (Bloomsbury, 2024), *Imagined Interiors: Representing the Domestic Interior since the Renaissance* (V&A, 2006), and *Women, Writing and the Public Sphere* (Cambridge University Press, 2001).

SÖREN HAMMERSCHMIDT is Residential Faculty in English at GateWay Community College in Phoenix, AZ, where he teaches courses in composition and literature. He also moonlights as a scholar of eighteenth-century media ecologies, portraiture, and epistolary culture in Britain and the Atlantic world, with articles in *Eighteenth-Century Fiction*, *Word & Image*, *Journal for Eighteenth-Century Studies*, and *European Romantic Review* as well as contributions to two collected volumes, *Samuel Richardson in Context* and *Making Stars: Biography and Celebrity in Eighteenth-Century Britain*. He recently completed work (as co-editor) on volume 9 of the *Cambridge Edition of the Correspondence of Samuel Richardson*.

KRISTINA HUANG specializes in African diasporic literatures from the vantage point of the eighteenth-century transatlantic world. Her research and teaching engage with methods from Caribbean Studies, Black Studies, Cultural Studies, and social movement histories through the Black Atlantic world. As an interdisciplinary scholar and educator, her work centers on historical representations of subaltern, enslaved, and minoritized lives and how those representations inform critical theory, literary study, and political practice. She has also published a range of short essays (from reviews of academic work and contemporary fiction to short-form pieces about race and the university) alongside interviews with artists on how their research on Caribbean History and Black History in Britain informs their creative practices. These texts have appeared in various online and print publications: *Small Axe Salon*, *The Los Angeles Review of Books*, *The Asian American Writers' Workshop*, the Lincoln Center Theatre Blog, *Social Text Online*, *Warscapes*, *Restoration and 18th Century Theatre Research*, *Eighteenth-Century Studies*, and *Early Modern Women: An Interdisciplinary Journal*.

PATERSON JOSEPH has performed extensively on the British stage in venues large and small. He has also been working on TV since the late 1980s in both UK and US shows. He has also performed in a number of films, including *In the Name of the Father, Aeon Flux, The Beach*, and *Wonka*. In addition to directing, Joseph has more recently written several one-act plays, including *Sancho: An Act of Remembrance* and *Sancho & Me – For One Night Only*, as well as essays, including "Sancho: An Act of Remembrance," "Julius Caesar and Me: Exploring Shakespeare's African Play," and a chapter on Sancho in *Britain's Black Past* entitled "Staging Sancho." *The Secret Diaries of Charles Ignatius Sancho* is his debut novel. His most recent work is the children's book *TEN: Children Who Changed the World* (2025).

DEVIN LEIGH is an educator and researcher who lives and works in the San Francisco Bay Area. He currently teaches African History at the University of San Francisco and Global Studies at the University of California, Berkeley. His scholarship focuses on connections between West Africa, Western Europe, and the Caribbean in the eighteenth century. His research has appeared in such journals as *Eighteenth-Century Studies, Slavery & Abolition*, and *History in Africa*.

ATESEDE MAKONNEN is an assistant professor in Literary and Cultural Studies in the Department of English at Carnegie Mellon University. Her research focuses on eighteenth- and nineteenth-century Britain and investigates how the approaching end of slavery sparked new consideration and wariness of Black subjects and gave birth to persistent forms of anti-blackness. She works across periods and media to paint a picture of how cultural objects contribute to and bolster ideas about race. Her current book project, *Sensing Blackness in the 19th Century Britain*, explores how the languages of sight, smell, sound, taste, and touch were employed to preserve racial boundaries.

MONTAZ MARCHÉ is a historian, writer, and theatre director, completing her PhD at the University of Birmingham, examining black women's lives in eighteenth-century London. She works as the Project Lead on the This Is Black Britain project at University College London and is the artistic director of the Ruckus Theatre Company. She regularly works in historical consultancy, media, television, and public engagement and has recently featured on television and radio projects with the BBC and Channel 4.

CRISPIN POWELL has been archivist to the Buccleuch Living Heritage Trust and to the Duke of Buccleuch and Queensberry and his family for twelve years. He cares for and makes accessible to research the Duke's ancestral family and estate archives. These embrace three ducal lines: Montagu, Queensberry, and Buccleuch, created for the Montagu, Douglas, and Scott dynasties at Boughton House, Northamptonshire, Drumlanrig Castle, Dumfriesshire, and Bowhill House, Scottish Borders. Before working for Buccleuch, he was an archivist at the Northamptonshire Record Office for twenty-two years.

AMIT S. YAHAV teaches at the University of Minnesota, Twin Cities. She is the author of *Feeling Time: Duration, the Novel, and Eighteenth-Century Sensibility* (University of Pennsylvania Press, 2018) and of a range of articles on the intersections of nationalism, liberalism, phenomenology, and early novels.

Chronology

<table>
<tr><td>1729?</td><td>Though the Jekyll "biography" claims he was born on a slave ship in 1729, Sancho himself claims in a letter that he was "born in Afric."[1]</td></tr>
<tr><td>1730s</td><td>In a letter to novelist Laurence Sterne in 1776, Sancho writes "The first part of my life was rather unlucky, as I was placed in a family who judged ignorance the best and only security for obedience." This family might have been the three Legge sisters, related to the Duke of Dartmouth, who lived near the Montagues in Greenwich.</td></tr>
<tr><td>1749</td><td>Sancho aged c. 20 years.
26 April 1749. First documented reference to Sancho in the Montagu archives on a receipt mentions a journey in a water taxi on the Thames.</td></tr>
<tr><td>1751</td><td>Duchess of Montagu's will bequeaths Sancho a year's salary and an annuity of £30. Aged 22.</td></tr>
<tr><td>1750s?</td><td>March 1756, Sancho is witness to a bond for Lord Cardigan.</td></tr>
<tr><td>1758</td><td>Marries Anne Osborne in St. Margaret's Church Westminster, 17 December 1758. Sancho is identified as being in his "mid-thirties" on the marriage license. Between 1761 and 1775, they have six daughters and two sons.</td></tr>
<tr><td>1759</td><td>Birth of Mary Ann (d. 1805).</td></tr>
<tr><td>1760</td><td>Receipt for a suit of clothes purchased for Sancho.</td></tr>
<tr><td>1761</td><td>Frances "Fanny" Joanna born (d. 1815).</td></tr>
<tr><td>1763</td><td>Ann Alice born (d. 1766).</td></tr>
<tr><td>1766</td><td>Elizabeth (Betsy, Elizabeth or Lizzie) born (d. 1837).</td></tr>
<tr><td>1766</td><td>Employed as a valet to the newly created Duke of Montagu (Duke John's son in law).
Initiates correspondence with Irish cleric and novelist Laurence Sterne.
Between 1766 and 1768 stops using Charles as first name.</td></tr>
</table>

1767   Music published: *Minuets Composed by an African* and *A Collection of New Songs*.

1768   Gainsborough paints his portrait at Bath.

1768   Jonathan William born (d. 1770).

1768   Resident in Richmond to 1771.

1770   Jonathan William dies (b. 1768).
       Visits Dalkeith, Scotland and tours the Highlands.

1771   Lydia born (d. 1776).

1772   Letters to Soubise.

1773   C/Katherine Margaret (Kitty) born (d. 1779).

1773   Writes about plans to open a grocery shop in Westminster.

1774   Saturday 29 January 1774 Sancho's shop opens.
       Sancho's vote is recorded for the General Election in Westminster.

1775   William Leach Osborne (Billy) born (d. 1810).

1776   Lydia dies (b. 1771).

1776   Music published: *Cotillions Dedicated to the Princess Royal*.

1777   Satire published: *The General Advertiser*, signed "Africanus."

1778   Publishes articles and letters in newspapers: *The General Advertiser*, *The Public Advertiser*, and *The Morning Post*.

1779   Kitty (Catherine) dies (b. 1773).
       Music published: *Twelve Country Dances for the Year 1779. Set for the Harpsichord*. London: S. and A. Thompson, 1779.
       Edmund Rack, *Letters of Friendship*, 1779, proposes to publish two Sancho letters by permission, but evidently never does so.

1780   Votes in General Election.
       Dies 14 December of complications from gout.
       Buried 17 December in St Margaret's burying ground, Westminster.

1782   *Letters of the Late Ignatius Sancho* published in London with over 1,200 subscribers. Ann Sancho receives over £500.

1783   *Letters* is reviewed in the press.
       Letters, 2nd edition, published.

1783   *Letters*, 3rd edition (Dublin "pirate" edition).
       Letters, 3rd [4th] edition (London counter-piracy).

1803   *Letters*, 5th [4th] "deluxe" edition, published by William and Anne Sancho.

Notes

1. Ignatius Sancho to John Spink, 6 June 1780, Letter LXVII, *Letters of the Late Ignatius Sancho: An African*, ed. Vincent Carretta (Peterborough, Ontario: Broadview Editions, 2015), p. 272.

Introduction

Kristina Huang and Nicole N. Aljoe

Ignatius Sancho's (c. 1729–80) public presence as a free Black writer countered prevailing racist beliefs about Africans and their descendants in the eighteenth-century Atlantic world. The popularity of *Letters of the Late Ignatius Sancho, an African* (1782) was immediate and led to the publication of a second edition the following year. Sancho's public renown began in 1775, when the daughter of novelist Laurence Sterne (1713–68) published her father's letters, including Sancho's 1766 epistolary exchange with Sterne. Many newspapers reprinted Sancho's letter to Sterne as a curiosity but also as an emulative example of the *belles lettres* tradition. Indeed, four years after the Sterne letters appeared, Sancho's permission was requested to publish two of his letters for a proposed collection of *Letters of Friendship* (*Letters* 335). Sadly, that collection seems not to have appeared. But nevertheless, the corpus of 161 extant letters and his musical compositions, alongside his contemporaries' documentations of his presence, establish a different vector for the study of Black life during the eighteenth century.

The story behind Sancho's ascendancy as a notable writer is an exceptional one in contrast to ordinary people of his time. In relation to many members of the laboring classes in the British empire, Sancho experienced relative social mobility as he shifted from working as a servant in wealthy households to acquiring property as a shopkeeper in London. In a number of his published letters, Sancho emphasizes the extraordinary circumstances of his life in relation to other people of the African diaspora. There are three interrelated historical circumstances that paved the way for Sancho's celebrity in the eighteenth century and his subsequent legacy. First, Sterne's prominence as a novelist helped popularize understandings of Sancho as a "man of letters" who not only appreciated literary value, but was an exceptional practitioner himself. The exchange also showcased their mutual respect for one another while centering their shared investments in the persuasive potentialities of sympathetic literary representations of enslaved Africans. Second, public campaigns focused on liberty and political enfranchisement were gaining momentum and shifting British imperial and domestic law. The reprintings of the Sancho–Sterne correspondence coincided with the American revolutionary era, when Britain lost thirteen colonies that would subsequently establish themselves as a competing empire also built on slavery. In the final decades of the eighteenth century, the published volume of Sancho's letters and his personal visibility became intimately entangled with the literary establishment's participation in transatlantic public debates around the relationships between freedom and race.

The transformation of the literary establishment in the English-speaking world forms the third context for Sancho's renown. With the developments in print technology, more and new classes of people were involved in the production and circulation of written information. Alphabetic literacy in the eighteenth century became a prerequisite skill for participating in an expanding middling class of merchants, traders, and others involved in the commercial activities of empire.[1] Although Sancho worked in the households of elite families for much of his life, his position as an upper-level servant certainly provided the foundation for his movement into the middle class as a business owner of a grocery shop at 19 Charles Street in Westminster. The middling status that he secured for himself and his family was bolstered by his connections to the elite Montagu family, as well as his abilities to read and write.

Sancho's early interests in the literary arts were thwarted by the first household he lived in. Despite this, Sancho pursued the pleasure he found in reading and writing and continued to nurture his talents throughout his life. In his letter to Sterne, Sancho informs that the first family he worked for "judged ignorance the best and only security for obedience.– A little reading and writing I got by unwearied application" (*Letters* 128). Although advancements in print technology created conditions for more widespread text-based communication by the eighteenth century, alphabetic literacy was still circumscribed within privileged groups as a marker of social status.

As Sancho conveys in his letter to Sterne, the circumscription of alphabetic literacy was an enforced mode of social control. Over the course of the eighteenth century, alphabetic literacy was also weaponized in European cultures to justify hierarchical ideas about human difference.[2] Assumptions that non-Europeans lacked literary cultures satisfied the pretensions of the ruling classes that some people were more human than others.[3] Sancho's writings and the records of his presence generated by his contemporaries tell a different story. His oeuvre testifies to the myriad ways that within and beyond the literary establishment, Black creativity and art-making persist.

One of the ironies surrounding Sancho's afterlife is that the very political networks that promoted his work also constrained the terms of his remembrance. Sancho's image and posthumous publication became affiliated with British anti-slavery campaigns and, more broadly, transatlantic debates over holding Africans captive for European trade and industry. The letters in the posthumous publication, however, predate the beginnings of the formal abolitionist movement in Britain. The formal beginnings are often associated with the founding of the Committee on the Slave Trade by the Quakers in 1783, a year after the initial publication. While Sancho's letters harbored critiques of empire and slavery, his writings and body of work covered a range of topics that were largely grounded in his everyday life. And yet, despite the diversity of topics addressed in the letters, transatlantic debates around racial slavery continue to affect the reception of Sancho's life and published letters.

Sancho's embodied presence was documented across print and visual media, as Charlotte Grant illuminates further in Chapter 13 in this volume. Notably, Sancho was a portrait sitter for one of the most famous British painters of the eighteenth century, Thomas Gainsborough (1727–88). Sancho was talked about by his contemporaries, and their representations of him continue to exert a great deal of influence on his legacy. In addition to sitting for Gainsborough, for instance, Sancho is potentially a figure in the Montagus' commissioned "conversation piece" by William Hogarth (1697–1764).

Sancho's Biography: What We Know Now

Although it is often assumed that Sancho himself was enslaved, there are currently no corroborating documents to support that presumption. Concrete evidence of Sancho's enslavement, whether and when he might have been manumitted, has not yet appeared in recent archival searches. The popular assumption that Sancho was enslaved from birth is based on the biography that prefaces the posthumous publication *Letters*. That biography was written by Joseph Jekyll (1753–1837), a self-styled writer, Member of Parliament, and lawyer who had never actually met Sancho. Jekyll writes that Sancho was born on a slave ship on the way to Cartagena, Columbia. However, Sancho himself writes in a letter that he had been "born in 'Afric'" (*Letters* 272). As Bryrchan Carey has demonstrated, many of the details in Jekyll's biography are not accurate and cannot be corroborated, and further, it's even possible that the biography might have included some fabrications.[4] Though Jekyll's oft-cited biography is not entirely reliable, it is one of the few contemporary accounts of Sancho that is not a conversational fragment but instead offers a semi-panoramic representation of Sancho's life.

According to Jekyll's "biography," Sancho might have been born around 1729–31. However, the recently recovered 1758 marriage certificate of Ignatius and Anne identifies Sancho as being in his "mid-thirties," which might place his birth as early as 1721.[5] Jekyll goes on to claim that Sancho's earliest years were spent with "three maiden sisters, resident at Greenwich" (*Letters* 49). Recent research suggests that the three sisters might have been Elizabeth, Susanna, and Barbara Legge, relatives of the Duke of Dartmouth; the sisters lived very close to the Duke of Montagu's house in Greenwich, and rented a stable from the Montagus.[6] Yet, much of this early history is speculative: for instance, at least one of the Legge sisters was in fact married. Brycchan Carey's chapter in this volume attempts to fill out much of the documented history behind Jekyll's "biography." To date, the first documented evidence of Sancho's existence in the Montagu archives is a 26 April 1749 receipt from a water taxi journey on the Thames.[7] This definitively puts Sancho in connection to the Montagu family at least two months before the death of John, the 2nd Duke of Montagu (b. 1690) in July 1749.

That Sancho would have captured the Duke's attention is not surprising. Duke John was known to have employed and sponsored several young Black and African men and women in London, including Fulani-born Ayuba Suleiman Diallo (1701–73) and Francis Williams of Jamaica (c. 1697–1762). The Montagu family also had at least six Black servants or enslaved people working in their household since the late seventeenth century.[8] Consequently, we also know that Sancho's earliest years were not spent in complete racial isolation, but rather that he came of age around and worked with other Black people in the Montagu household. Soon after the Duke's death, Sancho became more formally associated with the Montagu family and began working in service as the butler – the highest-ranking male servant in the household – for the Duke's widow, Mary Churchill (1689–1751), the Duchess of Montagu. When Mary Churchill, the Duchess of Montagu (b. 1689), died in 1751, she left Sancho an annuity of £30 per year (roughly equivalent to $700 in 2024). Although Jekyll's biography claims that Sancho squandered his inherited money on women, gambling, and theater, this is not supported by any documentary or archival evidence. Sancho not only married, but also continued to work for the Montagus during this time, eventually becoming the valet for the Montagus' son-in-law and heir to the Duke of Montagu title, George Brudenell (1712–90). He also accompanied Duke George when he had to stay at Windsor Castle for George's work as Master of the Horse – where "Mr. Sancho," as he is identified on the receipt, had his own furnished room. Sancho also signed as witness to several legal documents created by Duchess Mary and Duke George.[9] It seems hardly likely that the Montagus would have continued to employ an inveterate gambler for so long, and in such an intimate position, as butler and valet.

Because much is not definitively known of Sancho's earliest years, we often have to work from the contexts generated by the extant letters that were written in his adult years. In those letters, he frequently referenced his experiences as a father, husband, friend, and grocery shopkeeper. While providing retrospective glances of his former life as a servant, his *Letters* center on Sancho's family life and his grocery shop. For instance, Sancho playfully and affectionately documents traces of his wife Anne Osborne (1733–1817), whose authorial presence appears, albeit fleetingly, in the published letters.[10] Sancho married the London-born, Black British woman in 1758 at St. Margaret's Church in Westminster, where the family were active members of the congregation. The congregation also included Olaudah Equiano (1745–97), who was baptized at the same church in the following year, 1759. All eight of the Sancho children were also baptized at St. Margaret's. In addition to writing about his wife and their children, Sancho wrote about and corresponded with his wife's family network, which, in addition to her parents, included the families of her brother and sister, whom they visited frequently.

During Sancho's time in the household of the Montagus, they were well known as supporters of the arts. It is likely that Sancho's proximity to this family provided him access to resources that cultivated his lifelong creative pursuits. His deep appreciation of the arts was not limited to literature. As his letters illustrate, he frequently referenced the performing arts. In fact, Sancho's initial publications were in music: in 1766 and 1768 he published two collections of musical compositions and lyrics. Sancho's musical pursuits add another valence to his published letters: letters were often read aloud and thus featured qualities designed for aural social experiences of epistolary culture. Not only are Sancho's letters peppered with references to other artists; they are among his correspondents as well: the painter John Meheux (1751–1839); amateur violinist Julius Soubise (c. 1754–98), who worked as a servant for the Duchess of Queensberry; army musician Charles Lincoln, who, like Soubise, was also Black. The letters also suggest that Sancho was well acquainted with the sculptor Joseph Nollekens (1737–1823) and the actor David Garrick (1717–79).

In 1773, Sancho stopped working as a valet, likely because of increasing health problems due to gout. About a year later, on Saturday 29 January, Sancho opened his grocery shop at 19 Charles Street in Westminster, which served as the backdrop to many of his published letters. The shop sold a variety of goods, including products from plantations such as tea, sugar, coffee, rum, and tobacco. The shop's location was ideal; its proximity to the docks made inventory easy. The shop was also close to wealthy customers of the Montagus in Privy Gardens, as well as the center of British political power in Downing Street. As a business owner, Sancho was eligible to vote in local and national Parliamentary elections, and he is recorded as doing so in 1774 and 1780.

The Genre of the Letter Form

Although the slave narrative is frequently the genre of writing most associated with early accounts of Black life, Sancho's epistolary writings unsettle any facile conflation of early Black writing, auto/biographical life writing, and narratives of enslavement. The slave narrative genre is often characterized by complex yet asymmetrical relationships of power between narrators and those who assumed authority over the written formats of their lives. By contrast, the epistolary form was a widely used genre not inherently associated with documenting the horrors of slavery. *Letters* reveals a variety of formal articulations of the genre of the familiar letter. The posthumous publication displays Sancho's experimentations in the epistolary genre with a number of tones and styles, from essay-like meditations to gossipy harangues and observational reportage. Through his use of the familiar letter, Sancho prompts his addressees and future readers to converse with him through the varied idioms of everyday life.

Frequently referred to as an "African man of letters," Sancho's achievements are often associated with the fact that Duke John supposedly provided Sancho with unfettered access to his library. At a time when books were costly and extensive personal libraries often the sole preserve of the wealthy, Sancho's access to the resources of a wealthy household was no minor matter. But solely focusing on Sancho's literary achievements in relation to the Montagu family can inadvertently celebrate the prestige and influence of those in power. Literary scholar John Sekora mobilized the metaphor of a "white envelope" that often "sealed" records of Black subjects recounting their experiences in the eighteenth and nineteenth centuries.[11] The metaphor refers to Anglo-American institutions' practices of using white voices to authenticate or corroborate the writings associated with enslaved people, particularly their testimonies of enslavement. Sancho was also alert to the racialized practices that presumed authority over Black lives and writing. In his 1778 letter to a Quaker from Philadelphia, Sancho thanks him for sending a copy of Wheatley Peters's *Poems on Various Subjects, Religious and Moral* (1773). He celebrates Wheatley Peters's poetry while criticizing her enslavers and the paratextual materials accompanying her book. Sancho draws attention to "the list of splendid–titled–learned names" that ultimately insults her genius with its intended function as "confirmation of her being the real authoress" (*Letters* 166). Rituals of approval, or the "white envelope," were exercises of racial control and containment employed by the ruling classes.

To avoid the slippage of seeing Sancho's artistic accomplishments as a sole reflection of his benefactors, we might take a cue from this same letter, where he describes Wheatley Peters as a "Genius in bondage" (*Letters* 166). Sancho asserts that her talent "reflects nothing either to the glory or generosity of her master" (*Letters* 166). In a similar vein, we can focus on Sancho's artistry and his fluency in the literary tastes of the elite as a reflection of the complex social system that he was forced to navigate as a Black British subject. *Letters* was published in part to support his family, as the compiler of the letters, Frances Crewe (1759–1834), states in her editorial note that her intent was "the still superior motive, of wishing to serve his worthy family" (*Letters* 47). Sold primarily by subscription, the two volumes of *Letters* proved popular and garnered over £500 for Sancho's surviving family. The text went through five editions that were widely reviewed in a variety of venues.[12] The fourth and fifth editions were published by his widow, Anne, and their only surviving son, William Leach Osbourne Sancho (1775–1810).

The formal and aesthetic structure of the letter form destabilizes the "white envelope" that often frames accounts of Black life prior to the nineteenth century. Sancho's self-representation through the familiar letter displaces the asymmetrical relationship implied by a subaltern subject's need to make their life legible to a person of privilege. Not only does Sancho's use of the familiar letter de-center the grammar of violence often shaping historical accounts of Black life, but his experimentation with the genre is also revealing. His reflections on the current events of his day illustrate his fluencies in the topics meaningful to other men of middling social status. The range and heterogeneity of Sancho's correspondents, as well as the intertextual references within the letter, speak to his negotiations with the various spaces and hierarchies of a seemingly rigidly stratified and racialized society. While maintaining authorial control over how he represents his everyday life, Sancho manifests how his skills were intimately tied to his struggles to secure financial independence and security for himself and his family.

While the volume of *Letters* does not precisely accord with the conventions of testimonies of the enslaved and the formerly enslaved, the list of subscribers for *Letters* does seem to echo the tradition of the "white envelope," wherein Sancho's writings are subjected to the racializing gaze of a predominantly white readership. Philanthropic recognition and inclusion of subordinated, exploited members of a society can, unintentionally or not, reproduce hierarchical ideas about human difference. Like the poetry of Wheatley, Sancho's volume of *Letters* was celebrated as "evidence" of the humanity of African-descended peoples. Before one even encounters the actual letters, an editorial note instructs us in the importance of displaying "before the publick" that "an untutored African may possess abilities equal to an European" (*Letters* 47). Here, racial condescension is smuggled under a seemingly benevolent statement.[13]

Sancho's letters – collectively as the publication and individually – shift the literary contexts for considering African diasporic experiences in the early transatlantic world in a few ways. First, as one might gather from his use of the familiar letter, Sancho's epistolary writing provides rare representations of eighteenth-century Black life across a variety of domestic and public spaces, beyond the terms of servitude and enslavement. More specifically, as demonstrated by Montaz Marché's contribution to this volume in Chapter 2, *Letters* provides a unique literary portrait of a Black family in the eighteenth century, one that is caringly represented by the head of the household. With his grocery store on Charles Street as one of the central settings of his writings, Sancho foregrounds the pleasures and challenges he faced in the struggle of securing his loved ones' independence and financial security for the future. Through his textured depictions of his family life, Sancho's epistolary writing publicized alternative scenes of Black life beyond the sentimental and political debates around antislavery. In addition to painting vibrant scenes of his family life, Sancho documented traces of his wife as possible co-author of some of his letters.

Second, Sancho's epistolary writing identifies additional spaces where early Black women's literary contributions might be located, in and beyond the public eye. Just as race and class shaped how citizenry was imagined, so did gender. Besides Wheatley Peters, most of the Black writers who were in the spotlight, like Sancho, were men like the poet

Jupiter Hammon (1711–1806) or the evangelist John Marrant (1755–91). Because letters shaped conversations across the gendered spaces of public and private spheres of experience, epistolary culture invites a more expansive, textured mapping of Black literary production in the eighteenth century. For example, in his correspondence with Thomas Jefferson in 1791, mathematician and astronomer Benjamin Banneker (1731–1806) identified the Secretary of State's hypocritical stance on freedom. The Banneker–Jefferson exchange was reprinted, like the Sancho–Sterne exchange, and their correspondence intervened directly in public discourse. Other epistolary writings were established away from the limelight: the extant letters of Boston-based poet Wheatley Peters to her friend Obour Tanner of Newport, Rhode Island, testify to a shared intimate and spiritual language between two enslaved women.[14]

Sancho's participation in the public sphere through his letter-writing is an example of how eighteenth-century Black epistolary writing not only intervened in transatlantic debates over racial slavery but also spoke to Black life-worlds beyond the political terms of debates on equality and abolition. Rather than attesting to the "facts" of slavery, *Letters* exhibits a mosaic of topics that reflect Sancho's particular diasporic experiences as an African raised in eighteenth-century England. From libertine to sentimental writing, from devotional to humorous tones, Sancho's vivid writing reflects his omnivorous reading habits and interests.[15] In addition to the varied contents of his letters – solicitations, family updates, recommendations, theatrical commentary – Sancho's epistolary writing reflects his embeddedness in various social networks. The heterogeneity of topics and addressees reflected in Sancho's letters reveals a complex discourse with a range of people across Britain's class structure, from the upper-class gentry to their servants, including white and Black correspondents.[16] Embedded in Sancho's integrated networks of correspondents, his letters also offer a vivid testimony of extensive Black social networks. These networks are often overlooked because racial designations were not always included in eighteenth-century archival materials.

Volume Organization

Prior to the developments in print technology that were co-extensive with rising rates in alphabetic literacy, there was a sharp imbalance of representations of Black life. Print and visual representations of Africans in England were overwhelmingly produced by those who assumed authority over their lives.[17] This asymmetry is exacerbated by the fact that the visual arts of the elite often, though not exclusively, displayed a tradition of exoticizing Black people as domestics and symbols of wealth and affluence.[18] That Sancho's epistolary writing provides alternative representations of Black life beyond the terms of servitude is significant. Sancho's counter-representations of Black life in eighteenth-century England through his oeuvre provide a useful tension with the visual and written documentation that his contemporaries generated about Sancho. The former set reveals the intricate forms of affiliation, intimacy, and joy created despite the constrained, uneasy freedom that Black people experienced in eighteenth-century London. The latter illustrates how an individual life can be absorbed into broader narratives of power and prestige of empire. The volume and its organization are intended to explore the myriad and multidisciplinary aspects of Sancho, his contexts, and his legacies.

The first section, "Archival Contexts and Networks" offers new archival evidence and provides new methods for interpreting the sometimes fragmentary information surrounding Sancho's life and career, including the earliest years and those with the Montagu family. Archival ambiguities reveal a broader terrain of the institutions of power and prestige that Sancho had to navigate. For instance, the uncertainty around whether or not Sancho was enslaved speaks to his precarious social status, as well as larger ambiguities about enslavement in eighteenth-century England. During Sancho's lifetime, Britain's legal system, which refined and expanded the institution of enslaving Africans and their descendants, also asserted that slavery was "incompatible" with its domestic law through the 1772 *Somerset vs. Stewart* case. This decision was handed down by Lord Chief Justice Mansfield, who claimed that the air in Britain was too pure for enslavement.[19] While this case secured the impression that Britain was a zone of inherent freedom, printed advertisements for enslaved persons brought to Britain who "ran away" from their captors between 1772 and 1807 point to the contradictory and byzantine systems policing Black life.[20]

In other words, Britain had an ambivalent relationship with the diverse populations of Black diasporic peoples who worked and lived primarily, but not exclusively, in its major cities and port towns.[21] From liveried servants to musicians, from craftsmen to seamen, the "diverse black community fluctuated with the demands of economics and trends of fashion" but "the uncertainty about their status remained constant."[22] At a time when records pertaining to domestic servants were usually registered as transactional information in account books or documented as spectacle in the visual art of the nobility and ruling classes, Sancho contributed alternative images of his life and communities that exceeded the stereotypes and social categories that were projected onto him and his work.

While Sancho's earliest years and social status remain speculative, the first four chapters all provide some of the most recent archival findings about Sancho's life. Chapter 1 by Brycchan Carey begins the volume by analyzing Joseph Jekyll's biography of Sancho that was included in every edition of the *Letters*. Rather than merely focusing on the archival corroborations of and gaps within Jekyll's biography, Carey instead offers the possibility of reading the Jekyll biography as offering a kind of moral and rhetorical meditation on Sancho's life. Chapter 2 by Montaz Marché and Chapter 3 by Oliver Ayers situate Sancho and his family within the social geographies of eighteenth-century domestic life and London. Chapter 4 is written by the current archivist to the Buccleuch/Montagu family and elaborates on the documentary evidence of Sancho found within the family's archives. The final two chapters in this section, by Lawrence Evalyn and Vincent Carretta, focus on different approaches to Sancho's social networks. Evalyn analyzes the unique social and aesthetic dynamics of the subscriber list of *The Letters* by drawing on Digital Humanities techniques, while Carretta's chapter offers details about some of Sancho's key correspondents.

Sancho's prominence in visual and print media at the end of the eighteenth century was in part the result of the historical conjuncture described at the beginning of this introduction: the reprintings of his correspondence with a popular novelist; growing anti-slavery sentiment in British public opinion; and the surge of alphabetic literacy among middling people. To deepen our understandings of Sancho's alternative images of himself and his life that compete with the stereotypes projected onto him, the second section, "Social Contexts," elaborates on the aesthetic terms that he utilized and explores the myriad cultural milieus that he was in dialogue with. The contents of his letters not only reflect various dimensions of Sancho's quotidian experiences, but also manifest his extensive reading. Sancho's reverence for Sterne, which he directly states in his 1766 correspondence with the novelist, is evidenced through the reference and stylistic techniques employed in some of his epistolary writings.[23] He also drew on a variety of literary texts and traditions in his epistolary writings. Among these traditions, Sancho included ancient Roman mythology and often used such myths as metaphors or foundations for reflections on history and contemporary politics. In Sancho's letters, references to the Bible are ubiquitous. He commented on the works of his contemporaries in novels, poetry, and plays, as well as historical and philosophical texts.

The chapters in "Social Contexts" provide models for reading Sancho's epistolary writing in close relation to the prevailing discourses and aesthetic trends of his time. In Chapter 7, Markman Ellis illuminates the very nuanced and unique manner in which Sancho both appropriated and re-styled eighteenth-century literary motifs associated with sentiment. Sören Hammerschmidt's following chapter offers a reading of the abolitionist import of Sancho's letters by focusing on how Sancho used key aesthetic strategies to critique slavery while rejecting and undermining emerging concepts of "race." Like most members of his eighteenth-century world, Sancho's letters reveal an abiding engagement with religious spirituality and morality. Focusing on Sancho's articulations of the afterlife in his letters, David Diamond's chapter highlights the parameters of an ideal religious collective focused on notions of divine love and salvation that exist across various spiritualities – American Quakers, enslaved West Africans, Roman Catholics, Hindus, and Muslim clerics, as well as fellow Anglican Protestants. Finally, in this section, Amit Yahav's chapter explores the ways that Sancho uses specific strategies of humor and comedy in his letters: farce to create internal tiers of closeness within his group of affiliates, parody to forge pathways for bonding with strangers, and satire to criticize society while also promoting recognition of commonalities. The intertextual connections and references embedded in his letters reveal Sancho's nimble navigation through his social world and his artistic experimentations therein.

The closing section, "Performance, Visual Cultures, and the Afterlives," brings into sharp focus Sancho's cultural impact across various genres and media forms. This final set of chapters continues to trace alternative ways of reading Sancho's oeuvre through the aesthetic terms generated by his work. As Devin Leigh reminds us in Chapter 11, while *Letters* is a posthumous publication, Sancho self-published his musical compositions during his lifetime. That Sancho prioritized publishing his music invites us to read Sancho's letters in concert with other modes of artistic experience – dramatic, visual, and aural. Atesede Makonnen's chapter explores the tensions between the apocryphal story that Jekyll relates in his biography of Sancho that he failed at performing on the stage alongside the historical popularity of eighteenth-century theater, of which Sancho was an avid audience member. In Chapter 13, Charlotte Grant explores Sancho's relationship to eighteenth-century London's visual culture not only through images by Gainsborough and Hogarth, but also through Sancho's own rhetorical style, his networks, and his relationships with artist correspondents. She reminds us that Sancho was not only a subject in eighteenth-century British visual culture; he was an agent in that world as well. It is by juxtaposing the various aesthetic arenas that the writer was immersed in that readers of Sancho can reconstruct a more textured portrait of his life and times.

Sancho's Letters as Diasporic Dialogues, Past and Present

The final chapter in the volume, by actor and writer, Paterson Joseph, highlights the way that Sancho remains an integral figure in accounts of Britain's multicultural, multiethnic past. Joseph's chapter speaks of Sancho's meaning to contemporary Black Britons and his general place in the pantheon of Black British figures. Joseph explores the theme of national belonging across his motivations for studying and writing about Sancho's life. He emphasizes that learning about Sancho and his eighteenth-century world can impact on Black lives lived in the UK today. One of Sancho's legacies is his direct engagement with the world he was immersed in, and his life invites us to directly engage in ours.

The longstanding scholarly and popular interest in Ignatius Sancho is a product of decades-long creative and archival labor in reconstructing the history of Black people in Britain and the African diaspora in Europe.[24] These accounts weave Sancho's biography alongside others into a more complex global story about the African diaspora.[25] Much like his public presence in the print networks of the English-speaking world, Sancho's cultural impact today is commemorated across media forms, across scholarly and popular interests. Sancho's documentation of his life through the epistolary form has served as the inspiration for contemporary historical fiction and children's literature. In addition to contemporary theatrical work inspired by Sancho's life, like Joseph's monodrama *Sancho: An Act of Remembrance*, modern-day musicians have also recorded their performances of Sancho's musical compositions, making those recordings available on YouTube.

Sancho's life and legacy maps onto a broader transatlantic story about the "difficult miracle" of Black writing in English-speaking publics of the eighteenth century.[26] The "difficult miracle" of early Black writing prevailed, despite the legal and cultural regimes of racialization. Sancho's oeuvre forms a crossroads of African diasporic connections, from the eighteenth century into the present, inviting contemporary readers to develop what some scholars have termed "diaspora literacy," a mode of cultural engagement where readers consider African diasporic writing "from indigenous, cultural perspectives beyond the field of Western or westernized signification."[27] The "white envelope" of cultural references and contexts that were meaningful to the patrons who sponsored early African diasporic publications can easily reproduce seemingly isolated stories of philanthropic families and imperial benevolence. Sancho's range of social connections breaks the "seal" of that envelope, and his correspondence about or addressed to others of the eighteenth-century African diaspora points to the range of Black diasporic worlds.

Notes

1. Bannet, E., *Empire of Letters: Letter Manuals and Transatlantic Correspondence, 1688–1820* (Cambridge: Cambridge University Press, 2005).
2. Parekh, S., *Black Enlightenment* (Durham, NC: Duke University Press, 2023).
3. Gates, H. L., Jr., *Figures in Black: Words, Signs, and the "Racial" Self* (Oxford: Oxford University Press, 1987).
4. Carey, B., "'The extraordinary Negro': Ignatius Sancho, Joseph Jekyll, and the problem of biography," *Journal for Eighteenth-Century Studies* 26.1 (2003), 1–13.
5. Ayers, O. and Collard, L., Lambeth Palace.
6. Dingsdale, A. *Ignatius Sancho: (1729–1780) Life and Times* (London, 1998), Teaching Pack, section 2.4. Greenwich Education Services; Carey, B., Chapter 1 in this volume, page 19–36.
7. Powell, C., Chapter 4 in this volume, page 74–87.
8. Ibid., page 74–87.
9. Ibid., page 74–87.
10. Anim-Addo, J., *Touching the Body: History, Language, and African-Caribbean Women's Writings* (Miami, FL: Mango Publishing, 2007), 71–81; Huang, K., "Beyond the nation, traces of Anne Sancho," *Studies in Romanticism* 61.1 (2022), 101–11.
11. Sekora, J., "Black message/white envelope: Genre, authenticity, and authority in the Antebellum slave narrative," *Callaloo* 32 (Summer 1987), 482–515, 502.
12. *The Gentleman's Magazine: and Historical Chronicle* 51 (May 1781), 219–20; *The Public Advertiser, 9 August 1782; A New Review with Literary Curiosities, and Literary Intelligence* 2 (1782), 168; *The Gentleman's Magazine* 2 (September 1782), 437–9; *The European Magazine and London Review* 2 (September 1782), 199–202; *The New Annual Register, or General Repository of History, Politics, and Literature, for the year 1782* (London, 1783), 245–6; *The Monthly Review: or, Literary Journal* 49 (December 1783), 492–7; *The Critical Review: or Annals of Literature* 57 (January 1784), 43–8; *Town and Country Magazine, or Universal Repository of Knowledge, Instruction, and Entertainment* 16 (February 1784), 99–100.
13. Tita, C., "Ignatius Sancho's *Letters of the Late Ignatius Sancho, an African* (1782): Race and nation as a rhetoric of resistance," *Studies in Religion and the Enlightenment* 3.1 (2023), 53–67.
14. Bynum, T., "Phillis Wheatley on friendship," *Legacy* 31.1 (2014), 42–51, 43.
15. Ellis, M., "Ignatius Sancho's letters: Sentimental libertinism and the politics of form," *Genius in Bondage: Literature of the Early Black Atlantic*, ed. V. Carretta and P. Gould. (Lexington, KT: The University Press of Kentucky, 2001), 199–217; Salliant, J., "The invisible man of indecency: Profanity and the *Letters of the Late Ignatius Sancho, an African* (1782)," *Journal for Eighteenth-Century Studies* 43.2 (2020), 221–38; Pawluk, C., "'Almost a savage': The rhetoric of comic violence in Ignatius Sancho's *Letters*," *Eighteenth-Century Studies* 55.1 (2021), 1–19.
16. Gikandi, S., *Slavery and the Culture of Taste* (Princeton, NJ: Princeton University Press, 2011).

17. Hall, K. F., *Things of Darkness: Economies of Race and Gender in Early Modern England* (Ithaca, NY: Cornell University Press, 1995).

18. Dabydeen, D., *Hogarth's Blacks: Images of Blacks in Eighteenth Century English Art* (Athens, GA: University of Georgia Press, 1987).

19. Fryer, P., *Staying Power: The History of Black People in Britain* (London: Pluto Press, 2018), 115.

20. "Runaway slaves in Britain: Bondage, freedom and race in the eighteenth century," www.runaways.gla.ac.uk.

21. Brown, C. L., *Moral Capital: Foundations of British Abolitionism* (Durham, NC: University of North Carolina Press, 2006), 285.

22. Miller, M. L., *Slaves to Fashion: Black Dandyism and the Styling of Black Diasporic Identity* (Durham, NC: Duke University Press, 2009), 56.

23. Sandhu, S. S., "Ignatius Sancho and Laurence Sterne," *Research in African Literatures* 29.4 (1998), 88–105.

24. Edwards, P. and Dabydeen., D., *Black Writers in Britain 1760–1890: An Anthology* (Edinburgh: Edinburgh University Press, 1991); Phillips, C., *Extravagant Strangers: A Literature of Belonging* (New York, NY: Vintage International, 1997).

25. Fryer, P., *Staying Power: The History of Black People in Britain* (London: Pluto Press, 2018); Sandhu, S., *London Calling: How Black and Asian Writers Imagined a City* (New York, NY: Harper Perennial, 2003); Adi, H. (ed.), *Many Struggles: New Histories of African and Caribbean People in Britain* (London: Pluto Press, 2023).

26. Jordan, J., "The difficult miracle of Black poetry in America or something like a sonnet for Phillis Wheatley," *The Massachusetts Review* 27.2 (1986), 252–62.

27. Clark, V., "Developing diaspora literacy and Marasa consciousness," *Theatre Survey* 50.1 (2009), 9–18, 10.

Further Reading

"Runaway slaves in Britain: Bondage, freedom and race in the eighteenth century," www.runaways.gla.ac.uk.

Adi, H. (ed.), *Many Struggles: New Histories of African and Caribbean People in Britain*. (London: Pluto Press, 2023).

Anim-Addo, J., *Touching the Body: History, Language, and African-Caribbean Women's Writings* (Miami, FL: Mango Publishing, 2007).

Bannet, E., *Empire of Letters: Letter Manuals and Transatlantic Correspondence, 1688–1820* (Cambridge: Cambridge University Press, 2005).

Brown, C. L., *Moral Capital: Foundations of British Abolitionism* (Chapel Hill, NC: University of North Carolina Press, 2006).

Bynum, T., "Phillis Wheatley on friendship," *Legacy* 31.1 (2014), 42–51.

Carey, B., "'The extraordinary Negro': Ignatius Sancho, Joseph Jekyll, and the problem of biography," *Journal for Eighteenth-Century Studies* 26.1 (2003), 1–13.

Ellis, M., "Ignatius Sancho's letters: Sentimental libertinism and the politics of form," *Genius in Bondage: Literature of the Early Black Atlantic*, ed. V. Carretta and P. Gould (Lexington, KT: The University Press of Kentucky, 2001), 199–217.

Dabydeen, D., *Hogarth's Blacks: Images of Blacks in Eighteenth Century English Art* (Athens, GA: University of Georgia Press, 1987).

Gates, H. L., Jr., *Figures in Black: Words, Signs, and the "Racial" Self* (Oxford: Oxford University Press, 1987).

Hall, K. F., *Things of Darkness: Economies of Race and Gender in Early Modern England* (Ithaca, NY: Cornell University Press, 1995).

Hanley, R., *Beyond Slavery and Abolition: Black British Writing, c. 1770–1830* (Cambridge: Cambridge University Press, 2018).

Huang, K., "Beyond the nation, traces of Anne Sancho," *Studies in Romanticism* 61.1 (2022), 101–11.

Fryer, P., *Staying Power: The History of Black People in Britain* (London: Pluto Press, 2018).

Gikandi, S., *Slavery and the Culture of Taste* (Princeton, NJ: Princeton University Press, 2011).

Joseph, P., "Staging Sancho," *Britain's Black Past*, ed. G. H. Gerzina (Liverpool: Liverpool University Press, 2020), 197–214.

Miller, M. L., *Slaves to Fashion: Black Dandyism and the Styling of Black Diasporic Identity* (Durham, NC: Duke University Press, 2009).

Parekh, S., *Black Enlightenment* (Durham, NC: Duke University Press, 2023).

Pawluk, C., "'Almost a savage': The rhetoric of comic violence in Ignatius Sancho's *Letters*," *Eighteenth-Century Studies* 55.1 (2021), 1–19.

Sandhu, S. S., "Ignatius Sancho and Laurence Sterne," *Research in African Literatures* 29.4 (1998), 88–105.

   London Calling: How Black and Asian Writers Imagined a City (New York, NY: Harper Perennial, 2003).

Salliant, J., "The invisible man of indecency: Profanity and the *Letters of the Late Ignatius Sancho, an African* (1782)," *Journal for Eighteenth-Century Studies* 43.2 (2020), 221–38.

Tita, C., "Ignatius Sancho's *Letters of the Late Ignatius Sancho, an African* (1782): Race and nation as a rhetoric of resistance," *Studies in Religion and the Enlightenment* 3.1 (2023), 53–67.

PART I

Archival Contexts and Networks

CHAPTER I

Joseph Jekyll's "Life of Ignatius Sancho"

Brycchan Carey

Everything we know about Ignatius Sancho's early life, and much about his adult life, comes to us from a short biographical sketch written by the lawyer Joseph Jekyll (1754–1837) as a preface to *Letters of the Late Ignatius Sancho, an African, to which are Prefixed, Memoirs of his Life* (1782). Jekyll tells us how Sancho was born on a slave ship in the mid-Atlantic, how his mother died from an infection and his father committed suicide, how he was baptized by the Bishop of Cartagena, how he was brought to Greenwich and given to "three maiden sisters" who treated him badly, and how he claimed his freedom by seeking the protection of the powerful Montagu family. The narrative is familiar to everyone who has heard of Sancho, even if they have not read any of his letters. It is a powerful and moving story which epitomizes the barbarity of the slave trade and reveals the cruelty of slaveholding at the heart of British society. It has been reproduced hundreds of times since it was published in 1782, sometimes in paraphrase but often verbatim, and even today is frequently presented uncritically as an established historical narrative. Some of it can be independently verified. Sancho's lifelong connection with the Montagu family, for example, is well documented. It contains much, however, that is unsubstantiated and some which, on closer inspection, appears improbable, exaggerated, or even invented. This chapter offers, therefore, a critical reassessment of Jekyll's "Life of Ignatius Sancho." It attempts to reconstruct the details of Sancho's early life by reading surviving records in the context of recent research and offers a possible version of events that fits with Jekyll's account. It argues, however, that the challenge of verifying much of "The life" remains insurmountable at present. Although Jekyll betrays his racial prejudices at times, we can better understand "The life" as a rhetorical intervention in the early phase of the British abolition campaign rather than as an unproblematic record of historical events. Sancho's celebrity, both as a noted associate of artists, writers, and the nobility and as a writer and composer, made him the ideal figure through whom to publicize the inhumanity of slavery. Jekyll's "Life" offers the reader, this chapter concludes, a moral rather than a literal truth.[1]

The 1,245 words of "The life of Ignatius Sancho" have been included in every edition of Sancho's letters.[2] It is divided into three sections. The first and longest tells Sancho's life story in chronological order from birth to death. The second and shortest expands on his networks and cultural achievements. The final section generalizes from Sancho's example to assert the intellectual equality of Africans and Europeans. Its authorship was unattributed in the first four editions (1782–4), but the final part of the title of the 1803 fifth edition was amended to *Memoirs of His Life by Joseph Jekyll, Esq., M.P.*, revealing the author for the first time. In 1782, Jekyll was an unknown lawyer who was gaining a reputation as a witty, if not especially substantial, speaker and dinner companion who also contributed light satirical sketches and poems to Whig newspapers. By 1803, he had come to wider public attention as the Member of Parliament (MP) for the pocket borough of Calne in Wiltshire and, while his reputation was as a political lightweight prone to gaffes and errors, he was nevertheless well enough known for William Sancho (1775–1810), Ignatius's only surviving son, who printed the fifth edition, to consider it worthwhile advertising his authorship. Jekyll was not, however, the first choice to write Sancho's biography. A handwritten note in Jekyll's own copy of the fifth edition states that "Dr Johnson had promised to write the Life of Ignatius Sancho, which afterwards he neglected to do." As Vincent Carretta has noted, however, in a letter written to Sir Martin Brown Folkes (1749–1821) shortly after Sancho's death in 1780, the Rev. Thomas Lord (d. 1788) mentioned that "Johnson refused to write Sancho's biography."[3] Lord had been the personal chaplain of John, 2nd Duke of Montagu (1690–1749) in 1744–6, so he may well have been among those consulted by Francis Crewe (1759–1834), who collected and edited Sancho's letters.[4] He might even have been one of Jekyll's sources. Either way, Jekyll was a stand-in, and the reasons for his appointment remain obscure. We have no evidence that he had ever met Sancho or that he was close to any of Sancho's friends and correspondents. To date, no one has identified any notes or other records that show how Jekyll researched "The life," and we do not even know whether he met with Sancho's widow Anne Osborne (1733–1817), with Crewe, or with anyone else in Sancho's circle. The circumstances and manner of composition of the "The life" remain entirely mysterious.

Jekyll's opening sentence asserts one of the most often-repeated claims about Sancho's early life: that he was born aboard a slave ship. It also reveals something of his writing method, reminding us that we should read "The life" both as a historical and as a literary document. He begins:

> The extraordinary Negro, whose Life I am about to write, was born A.D. 1729, on board a ship in the Slave-trade, a few days after it had quitted the coast of Guinea for the Spanish West-Indies, and at Carthagena, he received from the hand of the Bishop, Baptism, and the name of Ignatius. (*Letters* 49)

The phrase "whose Life I am about to write," in the future tense, provides a glimpse of an author at work, conscious of the task he is undertaking, but also keen, despite publishing anonymously, to assert his authorial presence. The effect is appropriately Shandean, offering a brief nod to Sancho's celebrated correspondent Laurence Sterne (1713–68). It also reminds the alert reader that biography is always a literary production, a species of creative nonfiction, in which the author makes choices about the order and content and may sometimes even embellish or invent where the historical narrative is thin. By foregrounding the act of creation in the opening line, Jekyll raises questions about the tension between narrative convenience and unvarnished truth in a document that is both historical and literary. Recognizing this tension offers us an important way of understanding the competing factual and aesthetic claims of "The life."

Jekyll's opening sentence raises significant questions, including whether the date of 1729 is accurate, whether Sancho was indeed born on a slave ship, whether that ship in fact took him to Cartagena, and whether he was actually baptized by a bishop. One might also ask how Jekyll came to be in possession of this information, indeed, whether it was even possible for him to know any of this, and whether it contradicts Sancho's own accounts of his early life. There is no record of what research, if any, Jekyll undertook in preparing "The life," although his confession that "there are but slender anecdotes to animate the page of the biographer" suggests that, while he might have talked to a few of Sancho's circle and family, he did not otherwise research deeply. Nevertheless, it is vanishingly unlikely that the specific information he relates at this point would have been available to him. Sancho was too young to have any memories of these events himself. An enslaved orphan child, as the infant Sancho was, would not have traveled with a portfolio of documents recording his origins and identity. His value to his enslavers would have been entirely economic rather than personal, but, given the brutal realities of both infant and plantation mortality in the eighteenth century that would have given him a low chance of surviving into adulthood, that value would not have been high. It is possible that the slave-ship birth story could have been transmitted orally from one of his former enslavers to another, perhaps as a means of increasing the infant's purchase price in Europe, where the story might have piqued the interest of an aristocratic buyer. The story might then have passed orally from seller to buyer and through them to Jekyll, but, if that were the case, we would expect Sancho to have been aware of it. In fact, not only does Sancho never mention this account of his birth, but on two occasions he offers a contradictory account. In a letter written to John Spink (1729–94) at the height of the Gordon Riots that convulsed London in June 1780, Sancho explicitly declares that "I am not sorry I was born in Afric" (*Letters* 272). He does not say that he was born in a ship *en route* from Africa to elsewhere. On another occasion, however, he suggests that he simply has no knowledge of his origins. In a letter to the Philadelphia Quaker Jabez Fisher (1717–1806), who lent Sancho some books about the slave trade in January 1778, Sancho laments that "my heart was torn for the sufferings – which, for aught I know – some of my nearest kin might have undergone" (*Letters* 165). This suggests that Sancho himself claimed complete ignorance of the circumstances of his birth, even to the extent of not knowing whether he, his parents, or his grandparents had experienced the middle passage or had arrived in Europe by some other route. Of course, he might have feigned ignorance in this letter as a rhetorical construction, but there was little reason for him to have done so. If Sancho was ignorant of his own origins, it is doubtful that Jekyll would have known anything more.

Nevertheless, if the slave-ship story is true, it might be possible to verify it, or at least find evidence that supports it circumstantially. Jekyll confidently gives Sancho's birth year as 1729, although this is likely to be an approximation based on the child's appearance and the date of his arrival in Greenwich. Nevertheless, this allows us to look for ships that made the journey from West Africa to Cartagena in or around that year and these turn out to have been surprisingly few in number. Today a substantial city in Colombia, Cartagena was at that time a port in the Spanish colony of New Granada. It had previously been one of the main receiving ports for enslaved people being taken directly from Africa to the Spanish Empire but by the 1720s, under the terms of the *Asiento* negotiated as part of the Treaty of Utrecht in 1713, the majority of enslaved people arriving there came in small British sloops and packet boats after first having been disembarked from large transatlantic ships in Barbados or Jamaica.[5] The year 1729 was a low point for trade between Great Britain and Spain in the Caribbean. Tensions between the two countries, particularly over Gibraltar, had boiled over into war in 1727 and, although a truce had been called in

1728, there was no formal peace treaty until November 1729 and consequently very little trade. With the normal trade route via the British Caribbean disrupted, it is possible that Spanish, French, or Dutch ships brought enslaved people directly from Africa to Cartagena, but there is no evidence for this. The online Slave Voyages database lists only three possible voyages between 1726 and 1731 – all in 1729. The British ship *Ferrett* of Bristol, which was captured by a Spanish warship, was forced to disembark approximately 200 captive Africans in Santa Marta, a port approximately 180 km (110 miles) east of Cartagena. Another British ship, the *Italian Galley* of London, disembarked 353 captives in Portobelo, today a small town in Panama about 470 km (290 miles) west of Cartagena, after having first called at Kingston, Jamaica. Neither of these ships went directly to Cartagena, although it is possible that the captives they brought to New Grenada were later taken there by local traders. A third ship, the *Argyle* of London, is recorded in the database as having disembarked approximately 430 captives in an area which it describes as "Spanish Circum-Caribbean, unspecified." Whether or not this area included Cartagena is not known, but it is possible. If Sancho was indeed born on a slave ship at sea and taken directly to Cartagena, this voyage is a plausible candidate.[6]

If the infant Sancho was disembarked in Cartagena during 1729, on this ship or any other, it is very likely that he would have been baptized. As far back as the end of the fifteenth century, the Catholic church had made baptism of captive Africans and others obligatory. Despite having a population of just a few thousand in the early eighteenth century, Cartagena had many churches, including the church today known as L'Iglesia de San Pedro Claver, named for St. Peter Claver (1580–1664), who, in the words of *The Catholic Encyclopedia*, "baptized and instructed in the Faith more than 300,000 negroes" and, somewhat egregiously, became "the patron saint of slaves."[7] Before Claver's canonization by Pope Leo XIII in 1888, his church was dedicated to the founder of the Jesuits, Saint Ignatius of Loyola (1491–1596), after whom, Jekyll asserts, Sancho was named. Jekyll also claims that Sancho was baptized by the bishop of Cartagena. In 1729, this was Don Gregorio de Molleda y Clerque (1692–1756), although Jekyll does not name him. Eighteenth-century bishops of Cartagena tended, however, to leave the spiritual care of enslaved people to the Jesuits.[8] Whether in the cathedral, the Church of Saint Ignatius of Loyola, or elsewhere, if the infant Sancho had arrived in Cartagena he almost certainly would have been baptized, although probably not by the bishop himself. The story of the slave-ship birth and journey to Cartagena is plausible, therefore, even if the bishop was unlikely to have been involved. It is, however, essentially unverifiable, it remains difficult to imagine how Jekyll could have got the information, and we should remember that Sancho himself appeared to know nothing of it.

The second sentence of "The life" is also impossible to verify independently and may have been constructed on aesthetic rather than historical grounds. Jekyll asserts that "A disease of the new climate put an early period to his mother's existence; and his father defeated the miseries of slavery by an act of suicide" (*Letters* 49). This double tragedy is, of course, entirely plausible. There is absolutely no question that mortality rates for enslaved people across the Caribbean region were shockingly high and that "suicide by enslaved people was particularly acute during the initial years of enslavement."[9] Nevertheless, in his own writings Sancho shows no awareness that these tragic events took place, it is unlikely that Sancho's parents and the child would have made it together as a family unit from Africa to New Granada, and in any case it is unclear how Jekyll might have found out about it. There is, of course, the possibility that this story was told to Sancho's purchasers by his seller in the 1730s, either because he thought it was true or because he thought the pathos would raise the price of the enslaved child. It seems highly likely, however, that Jekyll introduced this element of Sancho's biography to meet his readers' narrative expectations. In the early 1780s, many literary representations of Africans depicted their actual or attempted suicide. Readers and theatergoers would have been familiar with the characters of Othello and Oroonoko, and, indeed, Jekyll tells us that Sancho attempted to play both roles on the London stage. More recently, John Bicknell and Thomas Day had published an influential poem, *The Dying Negro, a poetical epistle, supposed to be written by a black, (who lately shot himself on board a vessel in the river Thames;) to his intended wife*, which went through three increasingly lengthy and popular editions between 1773 and 1775. The poem, which was based on a true story that had appeared in several newspapers, alerted the British reading public to the scandal of enslaved people in London being forced out of the country against their will – a practice which had recently been outlawed in the celebrated Mansfield Decision of 1772. It was one of several literary interventions in this period that boosted the increasingly anti-slavery mood of the nation, but it also reinforced the literary formula in which suicide was seen as an appropriate resolution for a tragedy depicting an enslaved protagonist.[10] The passage also prefigures another later in "The life" in which the young Sancho, Jekyll tells us, "procured an old pistol for purposes which his father's example had suggested as familiar, and had sanctified as hereditary" (*Letters* 50). This threatened suicide might well have taken place and might have been recounted to Jekyll by someone who had witnessed it or who had heard about it from a reliable source. The parallel with the father's suicide, which there is little possibility Jekyll could have known about directly, appears more likely to be a convenient and introduced unifying narrative structure.

The third sentence of "The life" brings the infant Sancho from the Spanish colony of New Grenada to England, where Jekyll tell us that "At little more than two years old, his master brought him to England, and gave him to three maiden sisters, resident at Greenwich" (*Letters* 49). This was a complex, hazardous, and highly unusual journey of more than 8,000 km (5,000 miles), which would have taken two to three months to complete even with a direct voyage, which was itself a rarity. Relationships between Great Britain and Spain were often fractious in this period, but were also highly regulated. While corruption, smuggling, and piracy continued to be significant law and order issues in the early eighteenth-century Caribbean, most traffic between the two nations and their empires was conducted legally through a small number of ports under rules that had been agreed in the Treaty of Utrecht. As we have seen, captive Africans were taken *to* New Grenada from British territories, not normally the other way round, and there were few ships trading directly between the Spanish Caribbean and Great Britain. There are, therefore, three plausible scenarios to explain Sancho's journey. The first is that he was never in Cartagena at all and arrived from Africa via a British colony or was even born in England. The second is that he came from Cartagena in a British ship, or ships, taking an indirect route through the British Americas, perhaps via Jamaica, Barbados, or Virginia. The third is that he came from Cartagena to Spain in a Spanish ship, before traveling onwards to London.

Occam's razor would suggest that the first option, as the simplest, is the most likely, especially given that nothing Jekyll asserts about Sancho's birth and arrival in Cartagena can be independently verified. It too is almost certainly unverifiable but, given that, in 1731 and the two years around it, several hundred slave ships made the triangular journey from Britain to Africa, from Africa to the British American and Caribbean colonies, and then back to Britain, it is statistically overwhelmingly likely. It would, however, require us to reject all of Jekyll's account of Sancho's life before he arrived in England.

The second option, that Sancho was brought from Cartagena in a British ship, is plausible in general terms, since there was a clear reason why an enslaver might bring an African child to Europe. The trade in captive children was a relatively small one, but there certainly was a market at this time for enslaved child servants. Portraits of aristocratic women from across the continent in this period abound with images of African children as young as two or three years of age in attendance, often dressed in exotic outfits. An attractive, healthy child might have fetched a good enough price in London to justify the risk and expense of a long sea journey. While possible, however, this scenario is not highly probable. As we have seen, only a tiny number of British slave-trading ships were involved, willingly or otherwise, in trading captives direct to New Granada. It is, of course, remotely possible that the child Sancho was born on one of these few ships, mostly likely the *Argyle*, was landed in Cartagena, and then taken back to the ship before it visited British colonies on its way back to Great Britain. It does not seem plausible, however, that a British, Protestant slave-ship crew would disembark a new-born baby solely for the purpose of having him baptized in the Roman Catholic faith. Nor does it seem likely that the disembarked child, once his parents had died, or for any other reason, would be returned to the slave ship. Had the ship's captain intended to sell Sancho in Britain, he would almost certainly have kept him on board for the duration of the voyage. In any case, as we have seen, the transatlantic ships rarely went to Spanish ports. Instead, slave traders based in the islands "would hire sloops or packet boats locally in Jamaica or Barbados for the short onward journey to the Spanish ports" and for the enslaved passengers this was a journey in one direction only.[11] This version of events also contradicts a detail of Jekyll's account, which is that Sancho was given to the Greenwich sisters by his master; a circumstance that does not suggest he was brought to England purely for commercial gain. The suggestion that Sancho was brought from Cartagena in a British ship only makes sense if we reject parts of Jekyll's account.

A third possibility is that Sancho arrived or was born in Cartagena and was the property of a Spanish colonist who two years later took him to Spain, from where he was subsequently taken to England. While on the face of it this seems unlikely, there are in fact several pieces of circumstantial evidence to suggest that it is possible. Spanish merchant ships generally traveled in convoy, accompanied by warships, and the movements of such valuable convoys were closely observed by traders and investors and reported in newspapers across Europe. Throughout the summer and autumn of 1731, numerous newspapers in London printed reports from correspondents in Cádiz and Jamaica that a huge convoy crammed with gold and other precious metals was preparing in the Caribbean. Over the coming months, further details emerged, revealing that some of the ships had succumbed to storms while others had been ravaged by disease. On 11 November, after months of speculation, the London *Daily Journal* at last published a letter from Cádiz reporting that, between 27 and 29 October, the convoy of more than a dozen merchant ships and four warships had arrived from Cartagena, of which just one, "the Almirante, brings about five millions of Pieces of Eight, being near one half the Galleons Treasure."[12] Such a large convoy would have brought hundreds, perhaps thousands, of people with it, including crew members of all ranks, colonial officials, priests, merchants, and, in some cases, their families and servants – including those held in slavery. It is entirely possible that Sancho was among them, perhaps having been brought to Cádiz with the intention of selling him to a wealthy Spanish family in accordance with the fashion for African child attendants. If this was the case, the child might instead have been sold on to one of the many British merchants in Cádiz, who then took, or sent, him as a gift to the sisters in Greenwich, about two weeks' sail away.

At this point, knowing the identity of the sisters becomes an important piece of information in the attempt to understand Sancho's journey. In the 1990s, the archivist Ann Dingsdale conjectured that the three women may have been the sisters of William Legge, 1st Earl of Dartmouth (1672–1750), who lived directly opposite Montagu House in Blackheath, a fashionable area of Greenwich.[13] In fact, George Legge, 1st Baron Dartmouth (c. 1647–91), had seven daughters in addition to his son William, two of whom died in infancy and one of whom was married, leaving four unmarried sisters, Elizabeth, Barbara, Susanna, and Anne, in Blackheath. It appears that only three survived as late as 1731, which, if we accept the 1729 birth date, is the year that Sancho most likely arrived in Greenwich. The Blackheath location is confirmed by Jekyll shortly after in "The life," which further supports Dingsdale's identification. As aristocratic neighbors, the Montagus and the Legges were undoubtedly well acquainted. As Crispen Powell points out, "The tale of Sancho's origins in the ownership of three ladies of the Earl of Dartmouth's family at Blackheath is supported a little by the fact that the 2nd Duke paid a ground rent to the Earl of Dartmouth for the stables he kept there."[14] The two families were later directly connected by marriage. Sancho himself celebrates the connection in the dedication of his c. 1769 *Collection of New Songs Composed by An African Humbly Inscribed to the Honble. Mrs James Brudenell by her most humble Devoted & Obedient Servant, The Author*. The "Mrs James Brudenell" to whom Sancho dedicates the work was by birth Ann Legge (1723–80), the daughter of George Legge (1704–32), himself the son of William Legge, 1st Earl of Dartmouth, and thus a nephew of the three Legge sisters whom Dingsdale conjectures may have held Sancho in slavery. Ann Legge's husband James Brudenell, 5th Earl of Cardigan (1725–1811), was the brother of George Brudenell Montagu (1712–90), the 1st Duke of Montagu of the second creation, and Sancho's employer. Dingsdale's identification of the "three maiden sisters" as the sisters of William Legge looks secure.

By coincidence, two nephews of the Legge sisters were independently in the Cádiz area at around the time the Cartagena convoy arrived. The first was Henry Legge (1708–64), who is today best remembered as Henry Bilson-Legge, the politician who was three times Chancellor of the Exchequer. In 1731, he was a midshipman aboard HMS *Hampton Court* in the Mediterranean. With the war over, Great Britain and Spain resumed their alliance, and, in the summer and autumn of 1731, an Anglo-Spanish fleet that included HMS *Hampton Court* cooperated in ferrying Spanish troops to the Habsburg possessions in Italy, traveling via Cádiz and Gibraltar. Mystery surrounds Henry Legge's movements, however. He disappears from the ship's muster roll in September and appears to have left the Navy, possibly, according to Patricia Kulisheck, disembarking in Barcelona and thereafter maybe traveling to Rome overland.[15] It seems unlikely that he was in a position to travel with a small child, especially one that did not arrive in Cádiz until early November – unless, of course, Kulisheck's analysis is incorrect and he in fact returned by the well-established sea route via Cádiz, which would have put him in the city at precisely the right moment.

At the same time, however, Henry's younger brother Edward Legge (1710–47), a young midshipman, was also in the region. Legge is today best remembered for having been elected in absentia as MP for Portsmouth even though, unbeknown to the electorate, he had died three months earlier in the Caribbean. The young Legge was aboard HMS *Kinsale* as it cruised the Mediterranean in the summer and autumn of 1731, identified as the "Hon[bl] Edw[d] Legg, Midsp" in the ship's muster roll and present throughout its voyage from 1 June to 31 December 1731, which began and ended at Portsmouth.[16] The ship's log suggests that Legge may have had several opportunities to strike deals with Spanish traders. The *Kinsale* was "Moor'd in Cadiz Bay" for almost three weeks between 2 and 21 August, during which time the crew traded with Spanish merchants for water and for wine on numerous occasions. As a midshipman, Legge would have been among those expected to take command of the ship's longboat as it went on shore or alongside other ships for provisions and other purposes. These included taking people as well as produce on board. On 21 August, as the Kinsale prepared to leave Cádiz, the log notes that they "Weigh'd and Came to Sail at the same time Came on board 16 English Men Which Were Discharged from the Spanish Service and 4 Barbary Slaves at 7pm." The log does not say whether these four individuals had been emancipated or were continuing in bondage, but the fact that they are not identified as being among the "16 English Men" suggests the latter. Legge's precise part in these transactions is not recorded, but he had ample opportunity to form business relationships during the three weeks the *Kinsale* remained in Cádiz Bay. He might well have made enquiries about purchasing an enslaved child. The ship then sailed for Leghorn (Livorno) and Barcelona before returning to Great Britain. Before it did, however, there was one more port of call. On 17 November 1731, on the return journey, the *Kinsale* "Moor'd in Cadiz Bay," where, late in the afternoon, the captain "sent the Long boat ashoar for Watter" and was also attended by "a Spanish Launch to Watter Us." Early the next morning, "the Long b^t: and Launch return with Watter at ½ past 4 am," the longboat was hoisted in, and the ship set sail for England. Whether the longboat and the launch brought more than just water is not recorded but, at this point just two weeks after the convoy from Cartagena arrived in Cádiz, this transaction may well have provided an opportunity for Legge to take possession of an enslaved child who had recently been brought from Cartagena to Spain.[17]

The *Kinsale* returned home, mooring at Portsmouth on 20 December. The remainder of the log is in a different hand, with a poorer quality of writing, suggesting that the captain and perhaps other officers had gone ashore, although it was not until 28 December that "this Day our men wass order a Shore to be Payd." Either way, if Legge had indeed brought the young Sancho with him, he might have got to Blackheath in time to present the child as a Christmas gift to his aunts Barbara, Elizabeth, and Susanna, since eighteenth-century gift giving extended across the twelve days of Christmas. Of course, it may never be possible to unambiguously verify this story, but we can assert with confidence that Legge had the motive, means, and opportunity to purchase an enslaved child at Cádiz at the precise moment when the city had received a substantial convoy from Cartagena. Moreover, if he had in fact brought Sancho from Cádiz, he would not have been the only naval officer of the eighteenth century to have traveled with an enslaved child. Twenty-five years later, for example, Michael Pascal (d. 1787). bought an enslaved African child in Virginia, whom he renamed Gustavus Vassa. The young Vassa, better known today as Olaudah Equiano (c. 1745–97), served aboard Royal Navy warships under Pascal's command until Pascal sold him in 1762.

Once in Blackheath, Sancho's own sparse comments about his early life begin to align more closely with Jekyll's account. Sancho's celebrated 1766 letter to Laurence Sterne, the only time when Sancho explicitly described his childhood, is clearly one of Jekyll's sources. Jekyll tells us that Sancho was given to three sisters "whose prejudices had unhappily taught them, that African ignorance was the only security for his obedience," which paraphrases Sancho's statement that "I was placed in a family who judged ignorance the best and only security for obedience" (*Letters* 128). Sancho is, however, silent both on the family's name and on his own. According to Jekyll, "The petulance of [the sisters'] disposition surnamed him Sancho, from a fancied resemblance to the 'Squire of Don Quixote" (*Letters* 49). The first name "Sancho" is common and widespread in the Spanish-speaking world. When it occurs as a surname it is usually in the form "Sánchez," which tends to corroborate the claim that it was given to him by English rather than Spanish speakers. That the sisters thought a Spanish name was fitting perhaps supports the claim that he had recently come from New Granada and, if he had, presumably he would have spoken Spanish rather than English, albeit at the basic level of a two-year-old. Either way, Jekyll did not know, or did not think it worth mentioning, that Sancho's first name, which Sancho himself appears to have used only very rarely, was Charles. It may have originally been in the Spanish form, Carlos.

Jekyll next tells the story of how Sancho freed himself from the three sisters, and from enslavement, first by attracting the attention of John Montagu, 2nd Duke of Montagu (1690–1749), who encouraged him to read and write, then by absconding and appealing to the late Duke's widow, Mary Montagu, née Churchill, Duchess of Montagu (1689–1751), and, when that was unsuccessful, seizing "an old pistol for purposes which his father's example had suggested as familiar, and had sanctified as hereditary" (*Letters* 50). There is no reason to doubt the outline of this sequence of events, which must have been well known both within and beyond the Montagu family. As Powell shows, Sancho's relationship with the Montagu family was genuine, sustained, and well attested. In the letter to Sterne, Sancho downplays the duke's encouragement, instead relating that "A little reading and writing I got by unwearied application," but this flattering self-representation is understandable in a letter in which Sancho was eager to represent himself well to his literary hero (*Letters* 128). We should be cautious about the threatened suicide, however. As well as the parallel Jekyll draws with Sancho's father, he also notes that Sancho considered suicide after the sisters "threatened on angry occasions to return Ignatius Sancho to his African slavery" (*Letters* 49). This was also the circumstance of James Somerset (c. 1741–after 1772), whose case led to the 1772 Mansfield Decision, as well as that of the unknown African whose suicide in 1773 inspired Day and Bicknell to write *The Dying Negro*. As we saw earlier, the threatened suicide episode, whether embellished or invented, was probably added to "The life" to meet readers' narrative expectations.

Sancho's career with the Montagu family and his later occupation as a shopkeeper are increasingly well understood, as Powell shows. We know that at her death in 1751, the Duchess of Montagu left Sancho a year's salary and an annuity of £30. In Jekyll's account, Sancho then spent a few years living beyond his means. Displaying his racial prejudices, and implying that without an overseer Africans are incapable of self-discipline, Jekyll relates that "Freedom, riches, and leisure, naturally led a disposition of African texture into indulgences." Sancho is alleged to have spent his time in womanizing and gambling: a "propensity which appears to be innate among his countrymen." More attractively, he became a fan of the theater and even attempted to play Othello and Oroonoko, although, says Jekyll, "a defective and incorrigible articulation rendered it abortive" (*Letters* 50). Like so much in "The life," this account of Sancho's youthful gallivanting is largely unverifiable and even contradicts other accounts. The "incorrigible articulation," for example, has often been interpreted as some sort of speech disorder, but may have been no more than poor projection or even a residual Spanish accent. None of these were noted by others who described Sancho. Indeed, in a "Letter concerning Ignatius Sancho" published in 1812, Sancho's friend William Stevenson (1741–1821) described Sancho as having "a thundering voice."[18] Likewise, although people do change as they age, it is nonetheless hard to square the account of Sancho as a gambling libertine with the numerous later accounts of him as a faithful husband, devoted father, and sage advisor to wayward youth. Some time later, according to Jekyll, Sancho "was retained a few months by the Chaplain at Montagu-house" ("The life" 50). The new Duke appears to have had no fewer than nine chaplains over the 1750s, none of whom are among Sancho's published correspondents, which makes identification difficult, but, given that Sancho was married to Anne Osborne (1733–1817) on 12 December 1758, after what Jekyll describes as a period of "habitual regularity of life," it may have been the Rev. Phillip Lloyd (1729–90), later Dean of Norwich Cathedral, who was Montagu's chaplain from March 1756 to November 1766 and Sancho's exact contemporary.[19] The Duke himself shortly after employed Sancho, says Jekyll, but the reason for the chaplain taking Sancho on in the first place remains obscure. Although Montagu's chaplain may possibly have considered Sancho in his mid twenties as a young man in need of reformation and salvation, in reality it is unlikely that an ambitious young clergyman would want to associate himself with a known rake and gambler. Again, the suspicion is that Jekyll has invented or exaggerated Sancho's youthful indiscretions to enliven his narrative. Indeed, as Buccleuch archivist Crispen Powell has noted, Sancho witnessed documents signed by the duchess during this period, which suggests both that he remained in close proximity to the Montagu family and that the duchess considered him reliable enough to undertake this important legal service.[20]

Jekyll's chronological account of Sancho's life is rounded off with a short description of his illness, retirement, and death, which accords with what we can glean from other sources including Sancho's own letters. The second and shortest section of "The life" expands on Sancho's network of friends and acquaintances as well as his cultural activities. The names mentioned are public figures whose relationships with Sancho are often easy to verify. In the final sentence, however, Jekyll makes a number of claims about Sancho's creative output, asserting that "the Poets were studied, and even imitated with some success; – two pieces were constructed for the stage; – the Theory of Music was discussed, published, and dedicated to the Princess Royal; – and Painting was so much within the circle of Ignatius Sancho's judgement and criticism, that Mortimer came often to consult him." John Thomas Smith (1766–1833), who met Sancho in June 1780, remarked that Sancho was "extremely intimate" with the artist John Hamilton Mortimer (1741–79) and, since Smith did not publish this anecdote until the 1820s, we can be confident that Jekyll is reporting something that was well known at the time.[21] Sancho is identified only as an art critic, not as an artist himself, but the other claims are that Sancho wrote poetry, two plays, and a *Theory of Music*. The difficulty with these is not merely that they no longer exist, but that there is no evidence that they ever existed. A short story attributed to Sancho in 1789, *The History of Otang, an Indostan Slave*, is accompanied by a poem called "Otang's Complaint," but these are almost certainly the creations of the anonymous author of *Fortescue; or, the soldier's reward*, the mildly satirical epistolary novel in which they appear, rather than by Sancho himself.[22] No trace of the plays or the *Theory of Music* has ever been located, nor are they mentioned by Sancho or anyone other than Jekyll. Jekyll should have known, however, that Sancho published at least five collections of songs and dances in his own lifetime. The fact that he neglects to mention these important achievements is further evidence that either Jekyll's research method was inadequate or he was highly selective in what he chose to share with his readers.

Despite Jekyll's prejudiced opinions on the innate propensities of the "African texture," the final section of "The life" argues powerfully that Sancho's life and writings are evidence for the intellectual equality of Africans and Europeans. "Such was the man," argues Jekyll, "whose species philosophers and anatomists have endeavoured to degrade as a deterioration of the human" (*Letters* 51). To this, "oppressions political and legislative have been added; and such are hourly aggravated towards this unhappy race of men by vulgar prejudice and popular insult" (*Letters* 52). Although this section adds nothing further to Jekyll's account of Sancho's life and works, its stance makes "The life" one of the key documents of the emerging anti-slavery sentiment of the 1780s that would lead to the establishment of the Society for Effecting the Abolition of the Slave Trade just five years later. Jekyll was a lawyer with political ambitions, who is making a case for the common humanity of Africans and Europeans in "political and legislative" as well as humanitarian terms. He is not under oath, however, nor was he likely to have been expecting his brief memoir to be minutely examined by historians and critics across the centuries. Rather than a series of uninflected facts, "The life" is instead a piece of political rhetoric in which the facts are carefully selected and arranged both to support its central contention and to engage the reader. What Jekyll created was a highly effective piece of persuasive writing, which ironically has been quoted from more extensively than any of Sancho's own letters and which continues to be accepted by most readers as a reasonably reliable account of his life.

Ultimately, the choice we make in reading Jekyll's "Life of Ignatius Sancho" is whether to interpret it as a literal truth or as a moral truth. In the attempt to read it as literal truth, this chapter has reached into genealogies, naval records, and newspaper reports to offer a plausible route by which the young Sancho might have traveled from Cartagena to Greenwich. It is not impossible that Sancho was born on the *Argyle* of London in 1729, taken to Cartagena, orphaned, baptized by Jesuits, brought to Cádiz in 1731 by a Spanish colonist aboard the convoy of that year, sold to Edward Legge aboard HMS *Kinsale* at Cádiz, brought from there to England, and presented to his three aunts as a Christmas gift at the end of 1731. Every element of this story fits with the account given by Jekyll in "The life" as well as with the historical record. The problem is, it is no more verifiable than Jekyll's simpler account since Sancho does not appear in any of these records, nor does he himself appear to know anything about his early life. The same issues apply to Jekyll's account of Sancho's threatened suicide, his life of dissipation, and his vanished literary works: they cannot be verified independently and Sancho himself never mentions them.

We are on more certain ground, however, when we read "The life" as a moral truth. African children with the same intellectual capabilities as European children were indisputably being born into captivity and trafficked across continents. Until just ten years before Jekyll wrote "The life," it had been quite legal for members of families at the heart of British power and politics to keep African children in bondage. Across the world, the parents of such children were indeed succumbing to disease and taking their own lives in shocking numbers. These facts were undeniable and were becoming ever more obvious to an increasingly outraged British reading public. Sancho's life story as told by Jekyll was a moral truth of enormous significance. While some details of "The life" are verifiable, it almost certainly has many omissions as well as containing much that has been altered, embellished, or invented. We can and should continue the attempt to unearth the facts and locate lost documents, but it is unlikely that we will ever fully untangle the historical from the rhetorical. We should treat Jekyll's biography with caution and end the practice of unquestioningly reproducing his account of Sancho's life without any caveats or interpretation. We should remember, however, that with all its imperfections, Jekyll's "Life of Ignatius Sancho" made a very public declaration of African humanity and rapidly became an important and influential contribution to the emerging campaign to abolish the British slave trade. It is for this reason, as much as for what it may or may not tell us about Sancho's life, that it continues to repay our attention.

Notes

1. This chapter expands on and develops some of the arguments and evidence first presented in Carey, B., "'The extraordinary Negro': Ignatius Sancho, Joseph Jekyll, and the problem of biography," *British Journal for Eighteenth-Century Studies* 26.2 (2003), 1–13.

2. The edition used here is Jekyll, J., "The life of Ignatius Sancho," *Letters of the Late Ignatius Sancho, an African* (1782), ed. V. Carretta (Peterborough, ON: Broadview Press, 2015), 49–52 (henceforth "The life"). Quotations from Sancho's letters are also from this edition.

3. Sancho, I., *Letters of the Late Ignatius Sancho, an African* (1782), ed. V. Carretta (Peterborough, ON: Broadview Press, 2015) (henceforth *Letters*), 52n1.

4. Clergy of the Church of England Database, https://theclergydatabase.org.uk.
5. Thomas, H., *The Slave Trade: History of the Atlantic Slave Trade, 1440–1870* (New York, NY: Simon & Schuster, 1997), 236–7, 242.
6. *Slave Voyages*, www.slavevoyages.org.
7. Suau, P., "St. Peter Claver," *The Catholic Encyclopedia*, Vol. 11, www.new advent.org/cathen/11763a.htm.
8. Serrano García, M., *El obispado de Cartagena de Indias en el siglo XVIII (iglesia y poder en la Cartagena colonial)*, PhD Thesis, Seville, Universidad de Sevilla, 2015, 347.
9. Snyder, T. L., *The Power to Die: Slavery and Suicide in British North America* (Chicago, IL: University of Chicago Press, 2015), 46.
10. Carey, B., *British Abolitionism and the Rhetoric of Sensibility: Writing, Sentiment, and Slavery, 1760–1807* (Basingstoke: Palgrave Macmillan, 2005), 75–84; Carey, B., *The Unnatural Trade: Slavery, Abolition, and Environmental Writing, 1650–1807* (New Haven, CT and London: Yale University Press, 2024), 182–9; Snyder, *The Power to Die*, 121–41.
11. Thomas, *The Slave Trade*, 237.
12. *The Daily Journal*, 3386 (11 November 1731).
13. Greenwich Education Services, *Ignatius Sancho: (1729–1780) Life and Times* (London 1998). Teaching Pack, section 2.4.
14. Powell, C., Chapter 4 in this volume, 74–87.
15. Kulisheck, P. J. D. J., *"The Favourite Child of the Whigs": The Life and Career of Henry Bilson Legge, 1708–1764*, PhD Thesis, Minneapolis, University of Minnesota, 1996, 13.
16. HMS *Kinsale* Muster Roll, United Kingdom National Archives, PRO ADM 36/1647.
17. HMS *Kinsale* Log, United Kingdom National Archives, PRO ADM 52/421.
18. Nichols, J., *Literary Anecdotes of the Eighteenth Century*, 9 vols. (London: self-published, 1812), Vol. IX, 682–3.
19. Clergy of the Church of England Database.
20. Powell, C., Chapter 4 in this volume, 74–87.
21. Smith, J. T. *Nollekens and His Times*, 2 vols. (London: Henry Colburn, 1828), Vol. I, 29.
22. Anon, *Fortescue; or, the Soldier's Reward* (Dublin: P. Byrne, 1789), 46–60.

Further Reading

Carey, B., "'The extraordinary Negro': Ignatius Sancho, Joseph Jekyll, and the problem of biography," *British Journal for Eighteenth-Century Studies* 26.2 (2003), 1–13.
British Abolitionism and the Rhetoric of Sensibility: Writing, Sentiment, and Slavery, 1760–1807 (Basingstoke: Palgrave Macmillan, 2005).
The Unnatural Trade: Slavery, Abolition, and Environmental Writing, 1650–1807 (New Haven, CT and London: Yale University Press, 2024).

Nichols, J., *Literary Anecdotes of the Eighteenth Century*, 9 vols. (London: self-published, 1812).

Powell, C., Chapter 4 in this volume.

Sancho, I., *Letters of the Late Ignatius Sancho, an African* (1782), ed. V. Carretta (Peterborough, ON: Broadview Press, 2015).

Smith, J. T., *Nollekens and His Times*, 2 vols. (London: Henry Colburn, 1828).

Thomas, H., *The Slave Trade: History of the Atlantic Slave Trade, 1440–1870* (New York, NY: Simon & Schuster, 1997).

CHAPTER 2

Sancho and His Family

Montaz Marché

Ignatius and Anne Sancho formed one of eighteenth-century London's most well-documented Black middling families. Anne and Ignatius married on 17 December 1758, in St. Margaret's Church in Westminster, and then had eight children, six daughters and two sons: Mary Ann, Frances Joanna (or Fanny), Ann Alice, Elizabeth Bruce (or Betsy), Johnathan William, Lydia, Catherine Margaret (or Kitty), and William Leach (or Billy). Whilst Ignatius was the Duke of Montagu's valet, Ignatius and Anne lived in homes across London, including one on Cannon Row, close to the duke's Westminster estate. Then, the family moved to the Charles Street shop in 1773, where the family would remain for the next thirty years. After Ignatius's death, Anne ran the Charles Street shop.[1] From 1782, the Charles Street shop was known as "Mrs Sancho's" in notices. Anne was listed as occupier of the Charles Street property, paying rates between 1782 and 1803. Meanwhile, William Sancho apprenticed as a bookseller with bookseller Edward Jeffery in Pall Mall from 2 March 1798.[2] After William's apprenticeship, Anne and William converted the Charles Street shop into a printer, where the third to fifth editions of *Letters of Ignatius Sancho* ... were printed. Further evidence of their partnership appears in Royal and Sun Alliance insurance records, stating that on 26 June 1807, both "Ann and William Sancho of Castle Street, Leicester Square, Booksellers" were insured, insinuating their joint business.[3] The family remained together when the printing business and home moved to Mews Gate, Leicester Fields, in 1803, when William became the printer to the Princess of Wales (Caroline of Brunswick). The family remained there until William died in 1810, after which Elizabeth Sancho lived in Tothill Fields in Westminster before moving to stay with her cousin, William Riddle Lyon, at 15 William Street, Blackfriars.[4] It is plausible that Anne remained with her last surviving daughter until she died in 1817. Elizabeth died at her cousin's residence in York Street, Blackfriars, in 1837.

After Ignatius's marriage to Anne, the family were inseparable. Moreover, the Sancho family members feature notably throughout Ignatius's published letters, *Letters of the Late Ignatius Sancho, an African* (1782). Ignatius includes at least 118 recorded mentions of his wife, Anne, across his letters and at least 45 recorded mentions of one or more of his children. He observes and records aspects of the family's everyday lives, such as his daughters' exchanges with visitors, his son William learning to walk, their visits to the country, or sharing correspondences with Anne. With the regular inclusion of this close-knit family evidenced in Ignatius's letters, family is a central theme in Ignatius's story and legacy. When collated and analyzed, the recorded mentions of each family member across the *Letters* curate a specific image of the Sancho family as an ideal eighteenth-century family, comprised of an affectionate but authoritative father and husband; a dutiful, nurturing, and genteel wife and mother; and industrious, obedient, and educated children. They closely parallel the social expectations of middling families in this period and consolidate a rare image of a racialized black middling family in eighteenth-century London. In this chapter, I examine a sample of 158 of Ignatius's published letters from the *Letters*. I contemplate the Sancho family's representations, notably of marriage, parenthood, and childhood. I consider the politics of race, gender, and class and their role in curating the Sancho family image.

Conceptually, the family is a central image and an important social ideal, particularly in the eighteenth century. The family was "the basic building block of society."[5] Furthermore, the family household was "the primary unit of social control" and a symbol of social order.[6] In this order, the man – as the husband and father – led the household as the patriarchal authority, and he would possess control over the house as a king would over a country. The stability of the family was perceived as the key to maintaining social balance and morality. Who or what constituted family in the early modern period varied. Samuel Johnson's definition of family in his dictionary attests to this, describing it as "those who descend from one common progenitor" or "a class, a tribe"; it could also relate to a household, namely all "those who live in the same household."[7] Higher-class households often include their servants as a part of the family image, with the "family in its complete form, consist[ing] of a householder, with his wife and his children, and in the higher classes with his servants."[8] Cultural changes saw family formations evolve over the early modern period. A growing emphasis upon individualism and affective relationships encouraged "individual gratification and intense loyalty amongst the elementary members of the family (husband, wife and children)."[9] The impact of this affective relationship was a pivotal shift from the late medieval period's "open lineage family," including extended family members, to a restricted patriarchal nuclear family by the seventeenth century and then to the intimate domestic nuclear family by 1800.[10] Although debates on extended kinship ties either diminished throughout the early modern period or have progressed since Stone's work, historians concede that the nuclear family, comprised of parents and their children within one household, was an important concept in the early modern period. The Sanchos, for the most part, embody a nuclear family and participate in the changing eighteenth-century family cultures.

Perceiving the family as "an agent of change rather than passively influenced by historical processes" is important.[11] In this chapter, I contemplate the role of the Sancho family as "an agent of change," adapting perceptions of the ideal eighteenth-century middling family to include the Black middling family. While the Sancho family's representations parallel what was expected of middling-class eighteenth-century families, they also present a rare public image of a racialized family of African heritage whose ideals and representations were steeped within eighteenth-century cultural values. As a family, they demonstrate the pervasive nature of class and gender ideals in eighteenth-century society while demarcating dimensions where race impacted their daily lives, social impressions, self-identity, and representations.

Class played an important role in shaping the Sanchos' representation. Ignatius's reputation as a celebrity, composer, writer, businessman, property owner, and one of the first African Briton to vote in a parliamentary election results from his ascension to a man of middling sorts. Scholars have established social criteria for a lower-middle-class man, which confirms Ignatius's middling status. Notably, lower-middling-class men often owned or operated "a single-person enterprise," such as a grocery shop. They were often "Methodist, Baptist, or Independent Anglican"; they were expected to live in the city center, have a local social circle, and have a wife to assist with the business.[12] Ignatius exhibited all these criteria: he was a well-connected married man, a practising Anglican, and a member of St. Margaret's church in Westminster. He also teased that he was "half Methodist" (*Letters* 93). As a shop owner in Westminster, Ignatius would likely have been one of the "Tradesmen in London and country: expanding between £40 and £300 p.a."[13] Ignatius imbued a middling status unto his family by extension of his own status.

However, immersion into eighteenth-century middling society required more than wealth or property. There were important social qualities that middling people had to embody. Middling men, for example, were expected to be the family patriarchs, the moral, intellectual, and emotional centers of their households.[14] Their characters were to epitomize Christian values, sentiment, and authority. Work and family were their primary responsibilities, centered around their homes as a domestic space.[15] Furthermore, an understanding of "independent manliness" emerged, "predicated upon sentimental domesticity." This understanding shifted cultural and political attitudes from emphasizing rank or property attrib-uted to elite men to manly qualities demonstrated as a "father, husband, breadwinner and householder."[16]

In the *Letters*, Ignatius is not critical or descriptive about himself as a father and a husband. Indeed, writing letters from his home and business and casting moralistic commentary on his family, business, and wider society, Ignatius positions himself as the paternal authority and center of his sentimental household as the writer of the *Letters* overall, thus epitom-izing the ideals of manhood. Yet, alongside the few explicit comments relating to his family, one can interpret his thoughts and values on family, marriage, and parenthood through his commentary on wider topics, representing his paternalistic qualities and marital experiences. Below, I explore the evidence of Ignatius's actions, observations and thoughts as a father and husband and how Ignatius embodied the ideals of eighteenth-century middling men regarding marriage and family.

The ideal eighteenth-century father was affectionate and sensitive; he offered emotional support to his children through hugs, protection, and guidance.[17] As a father, Ignatius's commentary on his wife and children is largely observational, providing brief updates to his various correspond-ents. Within these observations and actions, Ignatius demonstrates his affection for and knowledge of his kids. For example, he observes his children's personalities as they grow up. He describes Mary Ann as "a little angel," Kitty as "as troublesome as ever" and "as mischievous as a monkey" (*Letters* 91, 127, 111). He notes that Betsy talks as usual, Fanny works hard, and Billy improves in sauciness (*Letters* 256, 200). His comments about his children's personalities differ between letters, attesting to his regular obser-vation and knowledge of what his children are like. He indicates the growing relationship between him and his children, for example, how Billy has an affinity for his father: "Billy gains something every day – the rouge is to the excess fond of me" (*Letters* 154). These collated examples speak to Ignatius's emotive, personal relationship with each of his children. They are bolstered by the examples of events the family shares, such as social visits, dinners, or birthdays (*Letters* 232).

Moreover, Ignatius expresses his feelings toward his children through joy, contentment, sadness, and tears. Upon their trip to the Vauxhall Gardens, Ignatius writes, "Last night – three great girls – a boy – and a fat old fellow were as happy and pleased as a fine evening" (*Letters* 147). Ignatius communicated his emotional reactions to life events; for example, when, in 1777, Billy took steps toward his mother, Ignatius writes that "it gave me no small pleasure" (*Letters* 140). He feels his children's illness acutely; for example, "I am very low in the heart. Poor Mrs Sancho is so indifferent and Lydia, tho' on the whole better, yet weak and poorly" (*Letters* 121). Eighteenth-century fatherhood engaged with sensibilities and emotions experienced through nervous sensations and tears. Fathers felt deeply; "Their hearts stirred, and their bodies shook, and they overflowed with kisses and tears."[18] Ignatius was no exception.

Ignatius highlights his concerns about providing for the household. He consistently references his work, the fluctuating business, and providing for his family. For example, in 1776, Ignatius references his dwindling trade: "Trade is duller than ever I knew it – and money scarcer"; before this, he writes, "If we can achieve money – but we have somehow no friends and, bless God! – we deserve no enemies" (*Letters* 131). Ignatius expresses how diminished trade and a lack of wealthy patrons threaten his family's maintenance. Elsewhere, Ignatius describes how "self-felt poverty and the heart-felt cares of a large family" caused him anxiety, amongst other issues. Beyond monetary concerns, Ignatius alludes to his responsibility to pro-vide for his children when reasoning why he could not send a letter to fellow Black Briton Julius Soubise in India, stating, "I cannot afford to pay five pence for the honour of your letters . . . it will keep my girls in potatoes two days" (*Letters* 98). Ignatius prioritizes his family's provision over correspondence.

Ignatius actively participated in his children's development. Ignatius emphasizes education, having his children participate in the shop and his business affairs. In 1777, Ignatius wrote, "I had an order for Mr Henderson on Thursday night . . . I put some money to it and took Mary and Betsy with me – it was Betty's first affair, and I think she enjoyed it" (*Letters* 146). He also implies that the children have work activities that they abandon when Jacob, son of Mrs. H–, comes to visit in June 1779, writing, "whenever he calls on us, the work is flung by, and the mouths are distended with laughter" (*Letters* 217). Ignatius also desires that his children have industrious qualities. He writes that "Mary must learn some business or other" (*Letters* 131). At the very least, Ignatius acknowledges his engagement in the children's education on business.

Ignatius also communicates his thoughts on parenthood to his friends, such as Miss Leach, stating, "the errors of most children proceed in the great part from their ill cultivation of their first years – Self-love . . . bewitches parents to give too much indulgence to infantile foibles" (*Letters* 120). In the advice he offers to others, Sancho demonstrates a belief in the role of fathers as guides and fonts of knowledge and discipline. He writes to Charles Lincoln, the Black sailor and musician, to "remember young man . . . let not the levity of frothy with – not the absurdity of fools breaks in your happier principles . . ., but I meant merely fatherly advice, and I have wrote a sermon" (*Letters* 158). By using the word "fatherly," Ignatius acknowledges paternalism in his advice to a younger Black man, communicating values central to the middling man's reputation.

Ignatius uses his paternal authority and guidance to instruct Julius Soubise. He reprimands Soubise for his "foppish" behavior and seeks to refine Soubise into a gentleman. He advises Soubise to "write anything and everything . . . improve our mind with good reading, converse with men of sense . . . be humble to the rich – affable open and good-natured to your equals – compassionately kind to the poor" (*Letters* 205). Moreover, Ignatius observes changes in Soubise's behavior, stating that "the style of [his] letter indicated a mind purged from its follies" (*Letters* 204). While there may have been other external factors for Soubise's change in character, such as his marriage in India, Ignatius observes and contributes to Soubise's change over time. Overall, Ignatius centers his paternalistic advice, notably supporting "deserving young black men" as protégés, facilitating their social ascension into a middling/upper-class society.[19]

Beyond himself, Ignatius comments more frequently about Anne as a wife, partner, and mother. The last twelve years of the Sancho marriage are represented in the *Letters*; expressions of Anne and Ignatius's love, adoration, and partnership remain constant. Ignatius peppers his letters with affectionate notions of Anne as the "best of women," "the chief ingredient of my felicity," "diamond in the dirt," and "treasure of my soul" (*Letters* 237, 123, 111, 93). Anne is said to share these emotions, with Ignatius being her "barometer" and her emotions contingent upon his (*Letters* 156–7). As Ignatius wrote these comments, they may be exaggerated. Nevertheless, Ignatius conveys a reciprocal, balanced affection between husband and wife. Ignatius demonstrates that from a basis of shared affection and demarcated gender roles, Ignatius and Anne created a companionate, co-dependent marriage. Moreover, this idyllic representation of a partnership parallels the changing cultures of marriage in the eighteenth century.

Ignatius alludes to how his marriage to Anne was grounded in clearly demarcated gendered positions in the household. For example, in an adoring account of his wife, Ignatius describes Anne "as the only intrinsic nett worth, in my possession," before describing her as "a diamond in the dirt" and how he "would case her in gold" (*Letters* III). Still, Ignatius asserts that Anne, as his wife, is his possession. This strongly relates to the core value of marriage in this period: that wives were subject to their husband's authority. Moreover, the law of coverture stipulates that married couples form one legal identity under their husband upon marriage, with the very "being or legal existence of the woman . . . suspended . . . or at least is incorporated into that of the husband."[20] Significantly, Ignatius situates the patriarchal authority over Anne and the household, as was expected for a husband. More broadly, this authority is reiterated in how Ignatius exercises control of Anne's representation, the details and events known about her, as the writer of the letters and thus a primary writer of Anne's history. These various paradigms of control and authority here establish an important frame for the Sancho marriage. The marriage radiates a companionate, co-dependent model filled with love, equality, and affection. Yet one of the primary reasons for this is that the authoritative positions of Anne and Ignatius, as a wife and husband, are demarcated, gendered, and respected by the other. Ignatius was the established head of the household, the patriarchal and domestic authority over the household; this authority was likely undisputed because of his positionality as the husband, father, householder, businessman, and writer of the *Letters* and thus went without explicit statement. Anne was the domestic authority over the daily household management and the family.

As I have demonstrated thus far, Ignatius is an overarching authority of the household; he is also its primary observer concerned with its business affairs, its maintenance, and the children's moral and refined education. On the other hand, Anne is presented as a domestic authority, primarily as a housewife, managing the daily running of the house. For example, she balances household work and working in the shop. Ignatius writes on one occasion that Anne "read" two papers he gave her "though it broke in upon her work" (*Letters* 237, 123, III, 93). Ignatius also writes, "Mrs. Sancho has had a blessed week of it . . . – it was the washing-week . . . – She was forced to break sugar and attend shop" (*Letters* 156–7). She performs specific household and shop-related tasks. Married women of the early modern period worked alongside their husbands or in the same trades. Still, records typically "omit the wives working with a husband."[21] Anne also acts as a hostess to the guests, "On Sunday evening we expected him – the hearth was swept – the kettle boiled – the girls were in print – and the marks of the fold of Mrs Sancho's apron still visible" (*Letters* 159).

Moreover, Ignatius alludes to Anne's centrality in the daily household tasks when stating, during Anne's pregnancy, that the house would not be ready. Ignatius states, "We cannot remove till after Mrs Sancho is up – The house will not be ready till towards Christ- mas . . ." articulating how house management stalled without Anne's contribution (*Letters* 120). Ignatius respects Anne's control of the daily routine/household activities, "just upon the stroke of eleven – as I was following (like a good husband) Mrs. Sancho to bed" (*Letters* 117). Being "a good husband" here (even with a sense of irony) indicates that, to Ignatius, an effective marital unit operates well when the domestic rules set by wives are respected. As a housewife, Anne is shown to be dutiful and attentive to her duties, as was expected of wives in this period. This dutiful representation is also bolstered by her role as a mother, which I will expand upon momentarily. But as I stated, the primary representation of Anne is as a housewife in the home, creating the impression that the home and its daily running is a primary focus for her. Now, I do not imply that this division of labor was simple or fixed in real life or that Ignatius did not perform domestic tasks around the house. Instead, I emphasize that the representation of their marriage in the *Letters* is balanced on the basis of specifically gendered realms of authority attributed to Anne as a wife and Ignatius as a husband.

The characteristics of Anne and Ignatius's marriage described above epitomized a companionate marriage. Companionate marriage in the early modern period was premised upon "equality and friendship" and allowed partners "to exchange their views freely and openly and . . . develop and negotiate their relationships across time and space."[22] The Sanchos' marriage demonstrates friendship, equality, and free exchange (within the perimeters of conventional gender roles), magnified over time by their marriage's longevity. In reading and writing letters and their day-to-day activities, they share each other's lives as partners. For example, Ignatius highlights how his wife expresses different opinions when stating, "Mrs Sancho joins me in everything but the abuse of Mr W[ingravle]," championing her kinder nature (*Letters* 229–30). Despite Ignatius's control over the narrative, Ignatius freely expresses Anne's participation in the letter-writing and shows her disagreement with him. Thus, their relationship is presented as not entirely structured around Ignatius's authority as the husband and his right to "govern absolutely and entirely."[23] Letter-writing is presented as a joint venture on five occasions, with signatures from both Anne and Ignatius. Finally, Anne and Ignatius's marriage possessed these qualities over time. We can observe these characteristics represented throughout the twelve years of the *Letters* and take them as symbolic of the twenty years of friendship and affection they shared. Ignatius admits this when saying, "I oft assume a gaiety to illume her dear sensibility with a smile – which twenty years ago almost bewitched me; – and mark! – after twenty years enjoyment – constitutes my highest pleasure! –" (*Letters* 156–7).

Anne and Ignatius embody the eighteenth-century model of co-dependency. In this model, husbands and wives are mutually effective and order the home and children together by working together and performing their gendered household roles effectively.[24] Writers such as Defoe regarded marriage as "the great duty between the man and the wife," but believed that "the end of both [partners] should be the well-ordering their family, the good-guiding their household and children, educating, instructing and managing them with the mutual endeavour."[25] The co-dependency is epitomized in the first instance by sharing letters and the letter-writing process and respecting domestic authorities. Anne and Ignatius show partnership and support for one another. Anne, for example, attends the shop, but more specifically, she attends the shop to support her husband in his declining illness. I referenced how Mrs. Sancho "has had a blessed week of it . . . it was the washing-week . . . She was forced to break sugar and attend shop." Ignatius prefaces this observation with a remark on his health, saying, "Alas, my friend, I was never but half so bad before – both feet knocked up at once – plenty of excruciating pain" (*Letters* 153). Anne faced the challenges of attending the shop when her husband could not. This was likely important preparation for her taking over the shop after Ignatius's death.

According to Ignatius's representation, Anne is the ideal wife. Her behaviors parallel those of women who were to be "temples of modesty" with a "retiring delicacy," a gentle piety and quietness that speaks to gentility and sensible emotions.[26] They were to be polite, well-read, converse well, and engage with social leisure cultures, such as visiting tea and social events.

Equally through these same sporadic but indicative references to Anne, Ignatius represents Anne's maternal experience as a Black middling mother over twelve years. In so doing, Anne's representation as a mother is a highly exceptional representation of a Black mother. He parallels her representations with other eighteenth-century middling mothers, providing an important and rare insight into the experiences of Black mothers. Consequently, Anne's representation adds nuance to many of the known conditions of eighteenth-century Black motherhood, with Black mothers often appearing as single mothers, mistresses, concubines, or servants or their representations as immoral or being "torn away from their families."[27]

Eighteenth-century women were expected to be "prudent, affectionate" wives but also "nurturing mothers."[28] Anne would have "shouldered many of the practical burdens of providing care and training for young children."[29] Maternity was to be "natural but learned," a derivative of the woman's innate sensibility, but was believed to be "biologically determined."[30] These ideas were not unique to the eighteenth century, but the expansion of print culture afforded a greater articulation and consciousness of these ideas across texts and visual images. These qualities did not detract from their domestic authority over the household and family. The gendered division of labour made women family providers and moral authorities.

Ignatius's representation of Anne embodies women's mutually exclusive role in this period as "prudent affectionate" wives and "nurturing mothers."[31] For example, he consistently notes Anne's and her children's welfare. For example, "she [Anne] and the brats are very well, thank you" (*Letters* 84). Ignatius uses punctuation as a connector between mother and children, such as "the best of women – the girls – the boy – all well" (*Letters* 237). By extension, he presents Anne as a constant parental figure and a nurturing mother.

Anne's maternal representations take readers of the *Letters* through the experiences of pregnancy, childbirth, and child death. For example, regarding Anne's pregnancies of four children during the time of the *Letters*, the final two are most noted because of the pregnancy symptoms she experiences. Anne, like many married women in this period, was seasoned in pregnancy. Most married women would experience pregnancy at least six times in their lives.[32] In her earlier pregnancies, Ignatius described her as "well" or "round" (*Letters* 91–2). But during her pregnancy with William, Ignatius described her as "not very stout," meaning she was not strong and that she was "not so alert as I have known her," likely describing memory impairment as a pregnancy symptom. It is plausible that Ignatius highlighted this because it was unusual. Furthermore, he signifies that each pregnancy differs, even after years of experience.

One example of Anne in childbirth is Kitty's birth in 1773. Ignatius writes, "Mrs Sancho is in the straw – she has given me a fifth wench" (*Letters* 102). The term "in the straw" refers to a "lying in woman" or a woman's postpartum experience, where, if there had been a difficult birth, women (laboring women but also middling women) were given straw mattresses to sleep upon.[33] It was also used to describe the recovery period after birth. Whether Ignatius is referring to a difficult birth or afterbirth is unclear. Nevertheless, it characterizes Anne's body as recovering from delivery and beginning to reintegrate into society.[34] In the letters, Ignatius references the period before birth alongside William's birth, expressing concern for Anne's health, saying, "God grant safety and health to the mother" (*Letters* 120). This concern characterizes the physical strain of bearing eight children, and parents rationalized the dangers of childbirth, with 5–25 maternal deaths occurring per 1,000 births in London from the late eighteenth century.[35]

Eighteenth-century mothers were expected to participate actively in their children's development at every stage of life, from care and support for growth and nourishment to education and moral training. Clear expectations of maternal authority and middling child development permeated the culture surrounding children and child-rearing, setting the perimeters of social expectations for middling women. Whilst Ignatius is not overly forthcoming about Anne's daily care of the children, he does present important images of Anne as a nurturing and active mother. The most notable examples of this are moments with Billy. For example, she comforts Billy during his teething and describes when Billy takes some of his first steps toward Anne, writing, "he took a resolution at last, and walked to her [Anne] some few steps quite alone" (*Letters* 142).

A single reference characterizes the seven experiences of child loss amongst the Sanchos. Anne lost seven of her eight children before she died in 1817. However, only upon the death of Kitty in 1779 is Anne's experience of grief articulated. Ignatius describes their "recent very distressful situation" and that "for thirty nights (save two) Mrs Sancho had no cloaths off – but you know the woman" (*Letters* 211). Anne and Ignatius experience the challenges of nursing a child's lengthy illness and the grief of child loss in this observation. Overall, with child loss, the *Letters* depict the full scope of the maternal experience through Anne's representation whilst continuing to root her representation in the development and nurturing of her children.

Regarding the Sancho children, Ignatius details in small references how they grow and develop into children of middling standing. The Sancho children's characteristics, particularly those of the daughters, correlate with what was expected of middling children during this period. The early modern period saw a greater appreciation for children's immaturity, innocence, and dependence "upon adult care and protection."[36] It was believed

and more widely articulated that children needed to be socialized with
discipline and education to instill characteristics such as self-improvement,
obedience, industry, thrift, and benevolence. Possessing these characteristics would cultivate the children into upstanding citizens of their respective
social standing. Naturally, there is a disconnect between these ideal representations of men, women, and children and their lived experiences.
Indeed, these ideals may not reflect how eighteenth-century men,
women, and families behaved in real life. Still, the importance of these
ideals is rooted in their social consciousness, which permeates eighteenth-
century religious, secular, social, and theological texts. These values and
identities became internalized in a new form of patriarchy, ensuring that
gender roles were maintained.[37]

Collating some of Ignatius's references over time depicts the children's
physical development. For example, we observe William's development
from birth to his growing "heavier and stronger," to his teething, "Billy has
suffered much in getting his teeth," to his growing appetite, "Billy loves
flesh," his first steps as he "tries his feet briskly," to speech, "Billy looks
wisely by turns – and will speak for himself" (*Letters* 143). Furthermore,
while thanking his friend for currant jelly, Ignatius states that during Billy's
teething process, he had been "plagued with a cough – which I [he] hope[s]
will not turn to the whooping sort" (*Letters* 139). Whilst Ignatius strives for
an ideal representation of his family, he does not overly perfect their
images, representing their children's illness alongside his emotional
reaction.

Whilst Ignatius's concern for his children was innate the *Letters* makes us
acutely aware of the emotional turmoil the Sancho family endured during
the slow decline and eventual death of some of the Sancho children. For
example, Lydia experienced nearly a year of fluctuating illness before she
died in 1776. In June 1775, Ignatius wrote, "Lydia mends – she walks
a little – we begin to encourage hope." But two months later, Lydia is
described as "exceedingly unwell" (*Letters* 117). Anne and Ignatius experienced an emotional journey of mixed emotions, where a likely awareness of
high child mortality tempered their beliefs about their daughter's recovery.
Child mortality in this period was high. It is estimated that a quarter of
children in early modern England would die before age ten.[38] Similarly,
Kitty suffers an equally lengthy illness from August 1778 that fluctuates
between improvement and decline before her death in March 1779. In
a later letter, Kitty is said to have been "very poorly for over a past month"
(*Letters* 197). Lydia and Kitty's slow demise lasted months. Within these
months, early modern sources highlight how parents tended to "their

children with devoted care, bestowing earnest prayers and nursing their offspring day and night."[39] But this was likely an emotional experience for the whole family.

While demonstrating his children's development over time, Ignatius's comments also referenced their education, learning new skills such as music, or working with Ignatius. Ignatius describes their education, sociability, and industry when sporadically referencing his daughters' welfare. They were sociable girls who interacted with Ignatius's friends ("The girls giggle their respects . . .") alongside friends of their own ("Mary invited two or three young friends") (*Letters* 242, 232). Scholars write that "French, dancing, music, drawing . . . were the ornamental accomplishment which provided the core of the education of most girls in the middle classes . . . along with reading, writing and elementary arithmetic."[40] By some of these standards, the Sancho daughters were educated. The *Letters* indicates many skills the girls developed, including reading "the noisy rouges with the Gazette Extra," "the girls were in print," and learning artistic skills, "Fanny goes on and on well in her tambour work" (*Letters* 244, 212, 131). Crucially, the Sancho girls' education extended beyond domesticity, with Ignatius also exposing his eldest daughters' business. Whilst it was customary to "educate daughters in the knowledge of things that relate to the affairs of the household," such as spinning, needlework, food preparation, and embroidery, for middling girls, education in reading, writing, and music, for example, was a primary distinguisher of one's cultural refinement.[41] It signaled their higher social status, access, and economic position (to afford a better education) alongside their suitability for marriage and knowledge of the correct behavior as mistresses of households. Overall, Ignatius's daughters represent Black middling girls of that time whose childhoods were shaped by social and cultural expectations of being a middling woman.

Ignatius describes his children, particularly his daughters, as having an ideal childhood: energetic, nurturing, and affectionate, rooted in contemporary cultural ideas of child development, growing industrious and genteel. We do not know how far they engaged with child-centered materials, such as children's toys and books. Still, we see important cultural parallels between their childhood and an ideal middling childhood. Later records of the daughters highlight their full social integration into middling society, with Elkanah Watson observing on his visit to the Sancho shop in 1784, "one of the daughters, when we [Anne and Elkanah] entered, was sitting at the harpsichord" and singing in concert with a white gentleman. What followed was a "pleasant hour in conversation, interspersed with singing and music and yielded to the females the same respectful attention that we should extend to white ladies."[42] The Sancho daughters' education and development resulted in middling women of personality, refinement, and intelligence.

Overall, the idealistic Sancho family appears on three fronts: "Ignatius as a man of letters and feeling; an idyllic companionate marriage between Anne and Ignatius; and a firm family hierarchy."[43] Arguably, this representation is strategic, designed to propagate the Sanchos as people of middling sorts. The rationale behind the strategic representations of the Sanchos and their paralleling of eighteenth-century ideals becomes clear when considering the intentions of the writer and editors of the *Letters*. Ignatius and other third persons produced the recorded instances and representations of the Sanchos. Hence, these commentators curated our historical perception of the family. Scholarship and comments by the writers and editors reveal possible factors influencing how the *Letters* were written or constructed. First, as the letter-writer, Ignatius tempers our historical perception of the Sancho family. Notably, the public-facing dimensions of letter-writing in this period force us to question the accuracy of the family's representations. Letter-writing in this period was recognized as "rhetorical art," with a performative dynamic where the author takes on "roles" and "adapts performances with audiences in mind," either for a recipient or for the public.[44] Literary analysis of Ignatius's letters highlights how Ignatius "parrots" the stylized writing of his correspondent and friend Laurence Sterne with "sentimentalism and libertinism."[45] Thus, the representations of the Sancho family members are, in one way, exaggerated because of the performative tendencies of letter-writing.

Moreover, in his *Letters*, as the writer, subject, and spectator, Ignatius presents himself as the epitome of masculine patriarchal authority, writing at his home and business surrounded by his wife and family, fulfilling the rites of passage to manhood, obtaining a wife, a household, and a business.[46] He constructs an identity of himself that emphasizes his education, middling social position, and racial identity as an African. He likely does this to prove the Africans' capacity for refinement. To some, Ignatius possesses a sense of double consciousness, W. E. B. Du Bois' concept, where, in this case, Ignatius writes with "this sense of always looking at oneself through the eyes of others."[47] Throughout the letters, Ignatius racialized himself; for example, describing himself as "a poor African" and discussing the plight of African people, particularly the enslaved (*Letters* 120, 96–7). In this way, Ignatius demonstrates his consciousness of how Blackness and African people can be perceived as inferior. It is plausible that he uses his idealistic representations in the *Letters* to counter any possible association between him and negative stereotypes of African people whilst also recommending their abilities. Ignatius curates an idealistic representation of himself and his family throughout his letters, resulting in an exaggeration that limits our perception of each family member's character.

The editor of the *Letters*, Frances Crewe-Philips, also influences our historical perception of the Sancho family. Crewe-Philips selected the letters for publication and openly expressed her desire to show that "an untutored African may possess abilities equal to a European" (*Letters* ii). It is possible that she chose letters specifically to achieve these aims. She does demonstrate her influential hand elsewhere. Although claiming to have only published letters given to her by their recipients, Crewe-Philips undermines her selectivity by including copies of letters sent to William Stevenson and Julius Soubise, which she was not provided by the recipients, proving that the content of the *Letters* was tailored to some degree.[48] In Crewe's case, the desire to care for Sancho's family and his reputation led to the collection, editing, and publication of some of his letters. Overall, most representations within the *Letters* are shaped by others. This same condition often impacts many marginalized groups in the archives, particularly Black women. Nevertheless, the Sancho family's representation contends with two essential but opposing facts. On the one hand, the Sancho family is exceptional in its comprehensive and idealistic representation as an "ordered middle-standing family" household.[49] On the other hand, Anne and the Sancho children's representation and how they are recorded in archival materials echo those of other Black individuals in eighteenth-century Britain.

Like other Black individuals in this period, the family still had experiences of race, racism, and racialization. Arguably, there were occasions of racial labeling and stereotyping, or times when the family were conscious of their racial identity and complexion. For example, the family were racialized because of their complexion using racial labels: Ignatius is called a "jet black negro" and a "blackamoor," Ann is described as a "mulatto," and the family are described as being "all of the same sooty complexion."[50]

Commentators highlight a tendency for the daughters to be compared with other middling girls. In the Sancho daughters' case, Elkanah describes how he "yielded to the females the same respectful attention that we should have extended to white ladies."[51] Other upper-class Black girls had similar experiences. For example, Dido Elizabeth Belle was described as having the "articulation and accent of a native" (even though she was "a native") and possessing "some pieces of poetry, with a degree of elegance, which would have been admired in any English child of her years" (again despite the fact she was born in England as a second-generation migrant).[52] Young women were often compared to women of similar standing. The middling and upper-class identities were constructed around significant social and cultural rules, expectations, values, and norms. Moreover, generations of patriarchal figures in both men and women operated as "agents of control and regulation," upholding these social values amongst the upper classes.[53] However, particularly in the case of Dido Elizabeth and the Sancho daughters, race is an important dimension in why these comparisons are made. Historical commentators underscore that these Black girls were social equivalents to white girls their age. These sources imply that Black girls were not always accomplished or perceived as social equivalents.

Ignatius recalls a family trip to the Vauxhall Pleasure Gardens, writing, "Heaven and Earth – how happy how delighted were the girls ... We went by water – had a coach home – were gazed at – followed, &c. &c. But not much abused" (*Letters* 146). This quote recognizes how the Sanchos experienced public reactions to their race and, by implication, that their race was observed frequently, likely more so as a Black family in fashionable places, where Black people were more commonly servants. The statement "not much abused" implies that there were occasions when the Sanchos were abused and that this visit was a rarity compared with the common experiences of commentary and possibly harassment in London's streets. William Stevenson also recounts an occasion where someone shouted "Smoke Othello" at Ignatius, to which he "exclaimed with a thundering voice and a countenance which awed the delinquent 'Aye Sir, such Othellos you meet with but once a century .... Such Iagos as you, we meet with in every dirty passage. Proceed, Sir!'" (*Letters* 270). There are few records of these experiences of racism. It is unlikely that Ignatius would want to recall such traumas or recount them to his friends. But these occasions and the lack of commentary allude to the experiences missing from the archives, which Black people and families like the Sanchos experienced in everyday exchanges, that ultimately it is "personal knowledge that dictates how one internalises and experiences race in daily life."[54] Moreover, with a likely awareness of their racial difference, it is plausible that the rest of the family also experienced a sense of double consciousness, like Ignatius.

To conclude, the Sanchos are a rare representation of a Black family in the eighteenth century. In this way, they can be perceived as exceptional.

My broader research into Black women in eighteenth-century London has not uncovered another Black woman's family who were as well documented or publicly reputable.[55] However, in many ways, their representation in the *Letters* presents the Sancho family as social equivalents to any other middling family. Ignatius is depicted as the ideal, affectionate, but patriarchal authority, Anne as the dutiful wife and nurturing mother, and the Sancho children as well-educated, genteel, and bright children. Ignatius and his family attached a racial dimension to the ideal representations of middling families. They demonstrated how – in the middling and upper classes – class-based ideologies were prevalent across racial lines. The *Letters* also allude to a consciousness of racial difference that may have shaped how the Sancho family were presented, both in print and plausibly in real life.

This chapter examined the Sancho family as a nuclear family contemplating marriage, parenthood, and childhood representations, detailed across recorded instances in the *Letters*. It focused on Ignatius's immediate family, but this was not the extent of Sancho's family. He had extended family in his brother-in-law, John Osborne, and his wife, a sister-in-law, Mary Osborne (although she goes unremarked in the *Letters*). Elizabeth Sancho spent her last years with her cousin William Riddle Lyon and his wife, Isabella. Moreover, Sancho treated his dearest friends and their families as his own, namely Lydia Leach and John Meheux. Whilst his immediate family bolstered Ignatius's public image as a patriarchal figure, his extended family emphasized the lineage of the Sancho family, their close-knit kinship, and their expansive grasp across London. The Sancho family, both as a nuclear family and as a lineage, emphasized Black families, networks, relationships, and lived experiences within London's communities, expanding upon the different themes that enrich our perceptions of early modern Black experiences.

Notes

1. St. Margaret and St. John Evangelical rate books/Land Tax record, 1800, 1801, 1802, 1803, City of Westminster Archives.
2. Apprenticeship Books, Year: February 1796–March 1799, The National Archives, reference no. IR 1; Piece 37.
3. Royal and Sun Alliance Insurance Group records, London Metropolitan Archives, reference no. CLC/B/192/F/001/MS11936/440/804280.
4. Archives of the Royal Literary Fund, registered case no. 583 (1826); Christ Church Southwark burial records, Years 1833–1940, London Metropolitan Archives, reference no. P92/ctc/061.

5. Shoemaker, R., *Gender in English Society 1650–1850: The Emergence of Separate Spheres?* (London: Routledge, 2014), 23.

6. Cowen Orlin, L., *Private Matters and Public Culture in Post-Reformation England* (London: Cornell University Press, 1994), 3.

7. Johnson, S., *A Dictionary of the English Language: In Which the Words Are Deduced from Their Originals, and Illustrated in Their Different Significations by Examples from the Best Writers*, 2 vols. (London: W. Strahan, 1755).

8. Tadmor, N., *Family and Friends in Eighteenth-Century England: Household, Kinship and Patronage* (Cambridge: Cambridge University Press, 2001), 42–3.

9. Flint, C., *Family Fiction: Narrative and Domestic Relations in Britain, 1688–1798* (Stanford, CA: Stanford University Press, 1998), 9.

10. Hall, C. and Davidoff, L. (eds.), *Family Fortunes: Men and Women of the English Middle Class 1780–1850*, 3rd ed. (Oxon: Routledge, 2019); Barker, H. and Chalus, E. (eds.), *Gender in Eighteenth-Century England: Roles, Representations and Responsibilities* (Harlow: Routledge, 1997).

11. Bailey, J., *Parenting in England 1760–1830: Emotion, Identity and Generation* (Oxford: Oxford University Press, 2012), 4.

12. Hall and Davidoff (eds.), *Family Fortunes*, 24.

13. Joseph Massie quoted in Corfield, P., "Class by name and number in eighteenth-century England," *History* 72 (1987), 51–3. See Massie, J., *Calculations of Taxes for a Family of Each Rank, Degree or Class: For One Year* (London: Thomas Payne, 1756).

14. Harvey, K., *The Little Republic: Masculinity & Domestic Authority in Eighteenth-Century Britain* (Oxford: Oxford University Press, 2012), 9.

15. Tosh, J., *A Man's Places: Masculinity and the Middle-Class Home in Victorian England* (London: Yale University Press, 2007), 14.

16. McCormack, M., *The Independent Man: Citizenship and Gender Politics in Georgian England* (Manchester: Manchester University Press, 2005), 19.

17. Bailey, J., "'A very sensible man': Imagining fatherhood in England c. 1750–1830," *History* 95.319 (2010), 275–80.

18. Ibid., 275.

19. Le Jeune, F., "'Of a Negro, a Butler and a Grocer' – Ignatius Sancho's epistolary contribution to the abolition campaign (1766–1780)," *Etudes Anglaises* (2008), 9, https://hal.science/hal-03298913.

20. Evans, T., "Women, marriage and the family," in Barker, H. and Chalus, E. (eds.), *Women's History, Britain 1700–1850: An Introduction* (London: Taylor and Francis, 2005), 57–77, 58.

21. Erickson, A. Louise., "Married women's occupations in eighteenth-century London," *Continuity and Change* 23.2 (2008), 267–307, 272.

22. Gardner, A.-C., "Toward a companionate marriage in late modern England?: Two critical episodes in Mary Hamilton's courtship letters to John Dickenson," in Tousdale, G., Honeybone, P., Los, B., and Cowie, C. (eds.), *English Historical Linguistics: Change in Structure and Meaning, Papers from the XXth ICEHL* (Herndon, VA: John Benjamins Publishing Company, 2022), 287–308, 294.

23. Astell, M., *Reflections upon Marriage*, 3rd ed. (London: R. Wilkin, 1706), 56.

24. Bailey, J., *Unquiet Lives: Marriage and Marriage Breakdown in England, 1660–1800* (Cambridge: Cambridge University Press, 2003).

25. Defoe, D., *Conjugal Lewdness, or Matrimonial Whoredom* (London: T. Warner, 1727), 26.

26. Gregory, J., *A Father's Legacy to His Daughters* (London: A. Strahan, T. Caddell and W. Davies, 1774), 16.

27. Gerzina, G., *Black England: A Forgotten Georgian History* (Liverpool: Liverpool University Press, 2022), 81–4.

28. Bailey, J., *Parenting in England 1760–1830: Emotion, Identity and Generation* (Oxford: Oxford University Press, 2012), 3–6.

29. Shepard, A., "Provision, household management and the moral authority of wives and mothers in early modern England," in Braddick, M. J. and Withington, P. (eds.), *Popular Culture and Political Agency in Early Modern England and Ireland: Essays in Honour of John Walter* (Cambridge: Cambridge University Press, 2017), 87.

30. Perry, R., "Colonizing the breast: Sexuality and maternity in eighteenth-century England," *Journal of the History of Sexuality* 2.2 (1991), 204–34, 214.

31. Bailey, *Parenting in England 1760–1830*, 3–6.

32. Vickery, A., *The Gentleman's Daughter: Women's Lives in Georgian England* (London: Yale University Press, 1999), 17.

33. Grose, F., *A Classical Dictionary of the Vulgar Tongue* (London: S. Hooper, 1788), 47.

34. Wilson, A., "The ceremony of childbirth and its interpretation," in Fildes, V. (ed.), *Women as Mothers in Pre-industrial England: Essays in Memory of Dorothy McLaren* (London: Routledge, 2003), 68–107, 97.

35. London, I., "Deaths in childbed from the eighteenth century to 1935," *Medical History* 30.1 (1986), 13–41.

36. Pollock, L., *Forgotten Children: Parent–Child Relations 1500–1900* (Cambridge: Cambridge University Press, 1983), 55.

37. Kowaleski-Wallace, E., *Their Fathers' Daughters: Hannah More, Maria Edgeworth, and Patriarchal Complicity* (New York, NY and Oxford: Oxford University Press, 1991), 17–20.

38. E. A. Wrigley and R. S. Schofield quoted in Pollock, *Forgotten Children*, 127.

39. Newton, H., "The sick child in early modern England, 1580–1720," *Endeavour* 38.2 (2014), 122–9, 124–5.

40. Hill, B., *Eighteenth-Century Women: An Anthology* (London: Allen & Unwin, 1984), 45.

41. Watts, I., *The Improvement of the Mind* (London: Scott Webster and Gerby, 1725), 346.

42. Watson, E., *Men and Times of Revolution; or, Memoirs of Elkanah Watson* (New York, NY: Dana and Company, 1856), 233.

43. Marché, M., "'A diamond in the dirt': The experiences of Anne Sancho in eighteenth-century London," in Adi, H. (ed.), *Many Struggles: New Histories*

of African and Caribbean People in Britain (London: Pluto Press, 2022), 1–21, 6.

44. Carretta, V. (ed.), *Letters of the Late Ignatius Sancho, an African* (London: Broadview Editions, 2015), 24–7.

45. Ellis, M., "Ignatius Sancho's *Letters*: Sentimental libertinism and the politics of form," in Gould, P. and Carretta, V. (eds.), *Genius in Bondage: Literature of the Early Black Atlantic* (Lexington, KT: University of Kentucky Press, 2001), 199–217, 206.

46. Harvey, K., *The Little Republic: Masculinity & Domestic Authority in Eighteenth-Century Britain* (Oxford: Oxford University Press, 2012), 17.

47. Du Bois, W. E. B., *The Souls of Black Folks: Essays and Sketches* (Chicago, IL: A. C. McClurg & Co, 1903); Nussbaum, F. A., "Being a man: Olaudah Equiano and Ignatius Sancho," in Gould, P. and Carretta, V. (eds.), *Genius in Bondage: Literature of the Early Black Atlantic* (Lexington, KT: University of Kentucky Press, 2001), 54–71, 56.

48. Hanley, R., "Ignatius Sancho and posthumous literary celebrity 1779–1782," in Hanley, R., *Beyond Slavery and Abolition: Black British Writing c. 1770–1830* (Cambridge: Cambridge University Press, 2018), 31–50.

49. Marché, "'A diamond in the dirt,'" 6.

50. *Stamford Mercury*, Friday 29 December 1786; *Public Advertiser*, 4 June 1778.

51. Watson, *Men and Times of Revolution*, 233.

52. Beattie, J., *Elements of Moral Science* (London: T. Cadell and W. Davies, 1807), 56.

53. Tim Stretton quoted in Berry, H. and Foyster, E., "Introduction," in Berry, H. and Foyster, E. (eds.), *The Family in Early Modern England* (Cambridge: Cambridge University Press, 2007), 1–17, 10.

54. Turda, M. and Quine, M. S., *Historicising Race* (London: Bloomsbury Academic, 2018), 13.

55. This conclusion stems from my PhD research at the University of Birmingham, examining Black women's lives in eighteenth-century London, funded by the Wolfson Foundation and the Institute of Historical Research, Marché, M., *Mapping the Dark and Feminine: Black Women in Eighteenth-Century London*, PhD Thesis, Birmingham, University of Birmingham, 2025, 81–4.

Further Reading

On Sancho and Family

Carretta, V. (ed.), *Letters of the Late Ignatius Sancho, an African* (London: Broadview Editions, 2015).

Ellis, M., "Ignatius Sancho's *Letters*: Sentimental libertinism and the politics of form," in Gould, P. and Carretta, V. (eds.), *Genius in Bondage: Literature of the Early Black Atlantic* (Lexington, KT: University of Kentucky Press, 2001), 199–217.

Hanley, R., "Ignatius Sancho and posthumous literary celebrity 1779–1782," in Hanley, R., *Beyond Slavery and Abolition: Black British Writing c. 1770–1830* (Cambridge: Cambridge University Press, 2018), 31–50.

Marché, M., "'A diamond in the dirt': The experiences of Anne Sancho in eighteenth-century London," in Adi, H. (ed.), *Many Struggles: New Perspectives on African and Caribbean Lives in Britain* (London: Pluto Press, 2022), 1–21.

On Black Lives in Eighteenth-Century Britain

Adi, H., *African and Caribbean People in Britain: A History* (London: Penguin Books, 2022).

Germann, J., "'Other women were present': Seeing Black women in Georgian London," *Eighteenth-Century Studies* 54.3 (2021), 537–48.

Gerzina, G., *Black England: A Forgotten Georgian History* (Liverpool: Liverpool University Press, 2022).

On Eighteenth/Nineteenth-Century Families and Children

Berry, H. and Foyster, E. (eds.), *The Family in Early Modern England* (Cambridge: Cambridge University Press, 2007).

Hall, C. and Davidoff, L. (eds.), *Family Fortunes: Men and Women of the English Middle Class 1780–1850*, 3rd ed. (Oxon: Routledge, 2019).

Muller, A. (ed.), *Fashioning Childhood in the Eighteenth Century: Age and Identity* (London: Routledge, 2016).

Tadmor, N., *Family and Friends in Eighteenth-Century England: Household, Kinship and Patronage* (Cambridge: Cambridge University Press, 2001).

CHAPTER 3

Ignatius Sancho's London

Oliver Ayers

Ignatius Sancho is rightly considered first and foremost as a literary figure, an African "man of letters" with an additional claim to fame as one of the first documented Black Britons to vote in parliamentary elections. But what of London, the city where so much of his life took place: how did its streets and peculiar sights and smells shape his life? How, in turn, did he make his mark on the metropolis? Sancho's letters often seem to pay rather peripheral attention to the changing city. The scholarly literature, correspondingly, typically treats London in general terms, for instance by talking of "London society." This is notwithstanding work like *Black England*, which studies eighteenth-century Black London and uses Sancho to illustrate how it was possible for a Black family to become part of both Black and white communities, and *London in the Eighteenth Century*, which deploys Sancho as an entrée to the Black urban presence more broadly.[1] For the most part, it is fair to say scholarship has been dominated by literary analysis, where London plays a background role – a setting for his life, rather than a space that shaped its course.

This chapter puts geography center-stage to argue that we can indeed consider Sancho as a "Londoner." Recent mapping projects allow the recreation of a fuller spatial picture of the multiracial character of Sancho's eighteenth-century London, from the granular level of buildings and streets, to neighborhoods and regions in the city, to the capital's myriad international connections. The portrait that emerges shows that, despite the fact Sancho was distinctive and remarkable, he was no island. He lived a London life intimately connected to numerous overlapping worlds: he was a shopkeeper in a consumer-orientated city economy; a participant in the "proto-democracy" pioneered in the heart of the Westminster "court," where urban development and political citizenship were newly entangled; a figure whose social connections were enabled by physically traversing the city's spaces as well as corresponding from a distance; and a husband and father whose familial ties shed light on the depth, diversity, and geographic range of the Black urban presence. For all that made Sancho different, in many ways he was central to the period as a whole – in multiple senses of the word.

Life on Charles Street

Sancho composed most of his letters in the years after 1773 when he ran a shop on Charles Street, Westminster. This location was not coincidental. It was 250 meters away from the Montagu House in Privy Garden, Whitehall, the home of the family whom Sancho had served for decades. Duke George Montagu (the 1st Duke of Montagu of the Second Creation) provided funds for the shop, a reward for many years of service working as the duke's valet, which often involved staying in the family's property overlooking the River Thames. Privy Garden remained part of Sancho's world, being mentioned in his first letter to Jack Wingrave and on two subsequent occasions. For their part, the Montagu family continued as patrons of Sancho and, when he died, these connections continued through his son William and Lady Elizabeth Montagu after she became the Duchess of Buccleuch. These familial links were enabled by a longstanding physical proximity in Whitehall, which also predated the shop. The Westminster Rate Books for 1762 record Sancho living on Cannon Row, just 150 meters from both Charles Street and Privy Gardens. This was four years after his marriage to Anne, when the couple already had two daughters, pointing to Sancho's burgeoning independence even while remaining in service. All three of Sancho's central London abodes were therefore within an area of 0.01 square miles, emphasizing Sancho's enduring presence in the tightly focused heart of the city.

At the same time, Sancho's world was far from parochial or insular. His shop on Charles Street was located at number 19, on the southwest corner of Crown Court. It stood at the intersection of two roads that themselves were set back a short way from King Street and Parliament Street, the parallel thoroughfares that constituted the main arteries connecting Parliament, Whitehall, and the rest of the city. Contemporary drawings depict a building on three levels, visible from Parliament Street and well situated for passing trade. Many correspondents visited the shop, possibly including his two most famous associates, Laurence Sterne and David Garrick. John

Thomas Smith recollected the time he and sculptor Joseph Nollekens visited shortly before Sancho's death, detailing how "as we pushed the wicket door, a little tinkling bell, the usual appendage to such shops, announced its opening. We drank tea with Sancho and his black lady, who was seated when we entered in the corner of the shop, chopping sugar, surrounded by her little Sanchonets."[2] Several of his letters add to the flavor of day-to-day life, such as the time a fellow "bolted into the shop," having had his cart robbed outside, and relating how his son, Billy, would stay in the shop and cling around his legs (*Letters* 155–7, 161–3).

Evidence from the Westminster Historical Database provides less immediately evocative but arguably just as instructive details about life on Charles Street. Sancho was one of fifty-three rate payers living there in 1774. The rate books calculated amounts of tax payable by residents by assessing the nominal average annual rental values of each property. These sources, therefore, give an indication of the size and status of each household. The average on the street was £18.68, whereas Sancho's property was assigned a rateable value of just £12. This amount was typical for the five other shopkeepers listed on the street (in 1774 Sancho was listed as a tea dealer, while his neighbors traded in food, drink, coal, and other goods). By 1780, however, Sancho's property was assigned a rateable value of £23, above the £20.83 average for the street. Among the twenty-five people to have been recorded in both surveys, Sancho's property increased in value by the largest amount by far.[3]

By 1780, Sancho was recorded in the Poll Books as a "grocer." These labels reflected both how people described their occupation and the perception of parish officials. In Sancho's case, this generic category seemed to reflect reality: he lamented his struggles trying to procure high-quality sugar in one letter, his business card promoted the sale of his "best Trinidado" tobacco, and Smith described the shop as a chandler's. Diversification of this sort, moreover, was typical for traders trying to navigate a consumerist economy buffeted frequently by international headwinds (which, in the 1770s, stemmed from the American Revolution in particular). Sancho was, therefore, fairly typical: the average rateable value for grocers like him in 1784 across Westminster as a whole was £26, placing them fifth highest among the twenty most common occupational categories.[4]

The rate books also show the demographic diversity of life on Charles Street. Alongside fellow shopkeepers were men involved in manufacturing, construction, and agriculture. Five residents, mean-while, were categorized as rentiers/gentry (Westminster Historical Database). That lower-, middling-, and higher-status sorts lived in proximity seems unusual to modern eyes, but it was fairly typical for Westminster in this period. To be sure, late eighteenth-century London was a place of sharp divisions between rich and poor, but the Industrial Revolution had not yet fully hardened socio-economic divisions into more recognizable hierarchies of class; nor had these stratifications become so connected to specific streets and neighbor-hoods as they were later in the nineteenth century. There was much about Sancho's life that was remarkable, therefore, but his story culminating in the ownership of a shop on Charles Street has a historical logic to it. Westminster's growth was fueled by out-of-town immigration and the emergence of a modern consumer-driven urban economy, where people of different backgrounds and status commingled on the same streets. Sancho the shopkeeper sat firmly within the variety of life on 1770s Charles Street.

Yet Sancho's socio-economic world was also part of a political one. The very existence of rate books in the first place stemmed from the need to record propertied male heads of household in order to levy rates (taxes). This, in turn, conferred the right to vote in parliamentary elections. In Sancho's London, therefore, matters of political citizenship were inextricably bound up with questions of urban development. Westminster (still distinct from the older City of London, although the term "London" was often used to encapsulate both) was the largest political constituency in the country at this time. As the seat of parliament, it became a key battleground in election years. The growth of government meant this western part of London grew rapidly as a municipality; its rising population and political importance, in turn, meant the district pioneered new methods of urban governance that only became familiar in other parts of country decades later. This all occurred at a time when most Britons could not vote at all. Westminster was a pioneer of a "proto-democracy," where all adult male rate payers qualified to vote – especially noteworthy during a time of both wide-spread disenfranchisement and uncontested parliamentary seats.[5] Women, for example, were not eligible to vote until the early twentieth century, although they headed around one in ten households in Sancho's Westminster – a reminder that eighteenth-century barriers to the franchise were even more fixed on lines of gender than they were on race.

Westminster's growth posed challenges for the devolved parish-level modes of governance the city had inherited from its medieval past. In response, the city passed one of the country's first paving acts in 1762, which regularized the layouts of streets and sanitation, and eventually created street lights. This was the reason the rate book evidence exists of the Sancho property on Cannon Row in the same year, making it likely he and his family lived there before this date, possible beginning after his marriage in 1758. Rates also contributed to poor relief, a problem that grew in political salience as the century progressed. Sancho's money, therefore, directly contributed to the development and governance of his city. With this in mind, it is revealing to return to one of Sancho's own (somewhat reluctant) comments on the duties of urban citizenship. In 1779, he wrote to Daniel Braithwaite, the clerk to the Postmaster General, asking to have a post office located in his shop. Part of his reasoning cited his unsuitability for other duties in the parish offices, "for which I am utterly unqualified through infirmities – as well as complexion" (*Letters* 248). This hinted at potential discrimination, but Sancho also made reference to his weight. He invited Braithwaite to consider the comic sight of him "waddling in the van of poor thieves and prostitutes – with all the supercilious mock dignity of little office," before warning of the danger to his health that would be caused by being "summoned out at midnight in the severity of eastern winds and frosty weather" (*Letters* 248–9). Sancho's request was unsuccessful, but the letter gives a revealing glimpse into how he had to respond (and try to navigate to his best advantage) to his status as an urban citizen, a position involving responsibilities as well as conferring rights. It also demonstrates how the Montagu family's Whitehall location meant Sancho acquired independence at a very particular time and place, and emphasizes the often-overlooked reality that his national-level claim to fame one of the first documented Black Britons to vote in a parliamentary election depended on profoundly local circumstances.

In the "Court" and across the City

These links between urban life and political participation go back to the ancient world (to the origin of the word "citizen" itself), but the connections were especially direct in late eighteenth-century Westminster. This was an era when the relationship between Crown and Parliament was still being defined and occasionally contested, especially as revolutionary events overseas in America and continental Europe reverberated at home. This relationship had a physical corollary on the city's streets: politicians would often begin their day in the residences clustered around St. James's Palace (the king's official residence) before traveling the half-mile distance south to attend parliamentary business later in the day. Politics in the "court" was both formal and informal: it was conducted through debates and discussions in Parliament, but also in coffee houses and taverns, theaters, and dining rooms. Crucially, therefore, politics was conducted across (and blurred the boundaries between) private and public realms and involved women as well as men. This was, as Hannah Greig and Amanda Vickery put it, a "dense campus" of political activity and movement that spread throughout the public and private spaces of the "court" and which had day-to-day rhythms and seasonal patterns.[6]

Understanding Sancho the Londoner requires placing him at the heart of this vibrant but contested political world. Charles Street was two-thirds of the way on the one-mile journey from St. James to Parliament. Sancho's shop was visible from the main thoroughfare of Parliament Street, as well as positioned on the intersection with Crown Court for anyone seeking a short-cut. Yet Sancho did not just let the political world of the court come to him; as much as the image of him sat at the back of his shop writing letters "to the ringing of the shop-door bell" is alluring, it is rather static. Sancho was constantly moving through the city, even as his debilitating illness hampered his movements in later life. Traveling around the city, moreover, was also central to what it meant to be a "Londoner" in this period. It is estimated half of residents in the eighteenth century were born outside of the capital. Part of the process of moving through and coming to belong in the growing metropolis, therefore, involved learning the city's streets, dialects, social mores, and codes of behavior, especially where those elements differed from other parts of the country or world (*Letters* 134–5).[7]

There was breadth and depth to Sancho's knowledge of the city. Before Charles Street, he lived within and moved between several Montagu properties on the outskirts of the London area, from Blackheath in the east, to their villa in Richmond on the banks of the Thames to the west. Within the city, Sancho most likely spent time at the family's dilapidated property in Bloomsbury and a newer house in Grosvenor Square. In later life, meanwhile, Sancho's letters reveal a knowledgeable insider – in both literal and figurative senses – of a more focused social world in and around "the Court" and the "Town" of the West End. Although correspondents were often in other parts of the country or even overseas, the letters were not just a means of keeping in touch; many were connected on a more day-to-day basis and lived locally for periods of time. For example, Lydia Leach resided on Jermyn Street, Laurence Sterne rented a house on nearby Old

Bond Street (until his death in 1768), and a couple of streets away stood John James Barralet's art academy, with which Sancho's friend John Mortimer was associated. The Haymarket theater, which Sancho visited along with his children, was nearby and other theaters visited by Sancho stood to the west around Covent Garden (where John Mortimer's art academy was located) and Drury Lane. All these locations were within half a mile of each other, a walkable distance even for Sancho. Rather than merely providing a contextual background for the associations in the letters, therefore, this tight-knit urban geography played an active role fostering Sancho's social connections.

Sancho was a regular presence in the "town," a useful short-hand for the West End district centered around Piccadilly. This area developed many of its modern features in Sancho's lifetime. For example, although theaters had been located in the area for a long time, the London stage increased in popularity during the eighteenth century. There is doubt over whether Sancho acted himself, but many productions had multiracial cast members and dealt with contemporary questions of empire, citizenship, and race – albeit in ways highly distinctive to the period. The built environment was redeveloped to cater to new consumers and their leisurely pursuits, with the growth of fashionable Bond Street a prime example. Sancho did not live to see John Nash's development of Oxford Circus and Regent Street, but his London was a world where public sociability and consumerism were already interwoven. The boundaries between social, cultural, and political life were especially porous in the eighteenth-century tavern and coffee house. Sancho rarely mentioned it directly, but he was clearly au fait with these worlds too. For example, Letter II makes a reference to Ashley's punch, associated with James Ashley's Coffee House and Punch House on the northside of Ludgate Hill near St Paul's cathedral (*Letters* 78).

Sancho remained connected to the rest of London even as his health deteriorated. One of his final letters referenced the "airings" he took in open spaces to try to alleviate his symptoms. He visited Greenwich to the east, and Newington and Clapham to the south, likely traveling to the former by river and to the latter locations via carriage across Westminster Bridge. As he put it bluntly to John Spink in the penultimate letter before his death, "Walking kills me" (*Letters* 297–8). Yet through his enduring, albeit increasingly curtailed, ability to move across the city, Sancho can be read as a newly modern type of Londoner. The ability to walk the city's streets, to travel between its districts by carriage, to journey across its eastern and western hinterlands by boat, all meant Sancho was embedded within London's evolving "spaces of modernity."[8] This emerging modern city was a public space to be known, understood, enjoyed, and consumed – all of which centered on the visual journey undertaken from "spectator to spectacle."[9] Having achieved independence as the male head of his household, and as a literate figure with social connections into the elite London worlds of the aristocracy, intelligentsia, and arts, Sancho participated and contributed daily to this distinctly modern creation.

Slave-Ownership and Black London

This is not to say Sancho was an archetypal "everyman" able to cross London's evolving boundaries of class and race without comment, incident, or restriction. The *Letters* themselves contain a possible passing reference to Sancho being subjected to negative racially motivated attention. Writing to Roger Rush in 1777, Sancho described a "Vauxhall evening" with his family, almost certainly a trip to Vauxhall Pleasure Gardens just across the river. They had much enjoyed the music and company but, on the way home, were "gazed at – followed ... but not much abused" (*Letters* 148). This suggests possible racist intent, but Sancho signed off without elaborating. The only explicit account of Sancho being directly challenged on racial grounds comes from a posthumous anecdote from his friend and correspondent William Stevenson, who recorded how:

> We were walking through Spring-gardens-passage, when a small distance from before us, a young Fashionable said to his companion, loud enough to be heard, "Smoke Othello!" This did not escape my Friend Sancho; who, immediately placing himself across the path, before him, exclaimed with a thundering voice, and a countenance that awed the delinquent, "Aye, Sir, such Othellos you meet with but once in a century," clapping his hand upon his goodly round paunch. "Such Iagos as you, we meet with in every dirty passage. Proceed, Sir!" (*Letters* 147– 8)

This vivid scene mirrors the wit associated with Sancho's letters, portraying him as an urbane and assertive figure, comfortable within his racial identity and willing to stake physical claim to his place on the city's streets. This was, moreover, a period when it was not uncommon for members of the London "mob" to intimidate people perceived as socially superior and for the city's streets to be used as arenas to challenge behavior and conduct disputes. These could, on occasion, lead to larger levels of disorder, as Sancho himself described during the Gordon Riots in 1780. Where this encounter took place is also possibly instructive: Spring Gardens was a "fashionable quarter" for politicians and civil servants just off Whitehall, less than 500 meters from Sancho's house in the part of town where he was most at home.[10]

These encounters remain somewhat ambiguous, but London was undoubtedly a city where racial dividing lines could be stark. This was most obviously the case with slavery and slave-ownership. Many planters were part of London society: Stevenson detailed as much in another part of his letter, describing how Sancho was eyed "disdainfully from head to foot" by a West Indian planter to whom he had been sent by the Duke of Montagu. No mention was made of who this was, but there were plenty of enslavers to choose from. Alongside those traveling back and forth across the Atlantic were absentee landlords and thousands of others with financial stakes in slavery through investments, acquired debt, or inheritance. Recent scholarship excavating the depth and breadth of the slave-holding presence in Britain has demonstrated vividly that it was not just an overseas phenomenon, but permeated multiple aspects of domestic life.[11]

A geographic approach again helps to consider Sancho's connections to slavery. Data collected by the Centre for the Study of the Legacies of British Slavery shows over 2,500 associations with slave-ownership in London, across various categories of involvement.[12] The connections obviously adapted over time, but two broad geographic patterns stand out. The first is a cluster of ownership in the north-west corner of central London, spreading up from Whitehall, through the court around St. James to the newly emerging prosperous parts of the city around Marylebone. The second is further east in the older City of London, which was then, as now, the center of banking, insurance, and financial services. This geographic distribution, therefore, offers a powerful corollary to the point that slave-ownership permeated both politics and business.

In terms of Sancho's world, there were eleven known associated addresses within just the small 0.05 mile radius of Charles Street. Among them were banker Joseph Biddulph of Spring Gardens, who was compensated upon emancipation in the 1830s for ten estates in Jamaica. George Lodowick Wilder, a Colonial Office official, lived two blocks from Sancho on Downing Street (this street became home to the Prime Minister around 40 years before Sancho set up shop just 125 meters away). Wilder was one of 13 individuals awarded compensation as trustee of the marriage settlement of his sister-in-law for 146 enslaved individuals. Shortly to the south on Great George Street, the claimants included Alexander Grant 5th Baronet, part of a large Scottish family with multiple involvements with Caribbean slavery. Grant built a business in Jamaica before returning to London, where his enterprises including trading in drugs, sugar, naval supplies – and enslaved people. When he died in 1772, probate documents recorded property including 672 enslaved people in the Caribbean and the slave "factory" on Bunce Island off the coast of West Africa. How much Sancho knew directly about these individuals, some of whom he predeceased, is unknowable, but these micro examples illustrate a macro picture. Slave-ownership came in different forms, from the direct involvement of people like Grant, to more indirect routes like Wilder's. Some Londoners were actively involved in the trade in the time of Sancho, while others' entanglements surfaced only when they claimed compensation after emancipation in the 1830s. A comparison can be made, therefore, between the role of slavery in Sancho's letters and his local neighborhood: across both his literary and geographic worlds, this presence was not always explicit and central, but it was there nonetheless, permeating his world and shaping his place within it.

Slavery was also, of course, one of several reasons for the Black presence in Sancho's London, variously estimated at between 5,000 and 20,000 out of a total population that rose to one million by 1800. In addition to those brought back from the Caribbean, there were usually around 1,000 visitors from the North American colonies at any time, many of whom brought enslaved people to act as their servants.[13] More broadly, determining whether some Black Londoners were employed as servants, bound in service, and/or enslaved is often a murky question, hampered both by lack of evidence for payments of wages as well as by the ambiguous legal status of domestic slavery (the bequests from the Montagus to Sancho offer unusually clear evidence of his free status, yet even for him, matters are less clear-cut for his early life). What is clear is that Black people, mostly but not exclusively men, became "fashionable" and visible figures serving "downstairs" for many aristocratic eighteenth-century families. On the streets, meanwhile, the Black presence also became more visible as the century progressed. This was especially the case after US independence, when many Black Americans drawn to fight for the British for the promise of freedom ended up moving to the capital after defeat. The "alarmingly conspicuous" presence of these former soldiers, some of whom fell into destitution, coincided with more negative racialized commentary on their presence in London, including becoming the pejorative subjects of popular jokes.[14]

Although perhaps ironic to modern eyes, this hardening of racial divisions occurred in an era when the abolitionist movement gained traction: these two developments were, in fact, connected. Justice Mansfield's 1772 judgment in the well-known case of James Somerset (a Black Bostonian living in London who successfully avoided being re-enslaved) was not the definitive ruling against domestic slavery which some perceived. It did, however, energize a wider movement within which Black Londoners were involved. A newspaper account, for example, detailed how 200 of them gathered at a Westminster pub to celebrate the verdict, signaling an increasingly visible and assertive Black presence in the city's heart that takes us beyond the iconic singularity of famous figures like Equiano, Sancho, and Francis Barber (Samuel Johnson's "manservant").[15]

Pursuing this wider picture of Black London, moreover, helps expand the focus beyond slavery. Parish records of baptisms, burials, and some marriages provide the fullest, albeit incomplete, picture of this presence. Over 3,000 people of African, Caribbean, Asian, and Indigenous (used to include Native American and Aboriginal Australian people) backgrounds have been identified by the London Metropolitan Archives' Switching the Lens database from parish records, spanning a period from around 1560 to 1840.[16] The City of London and waterside parishes to the east are especially well represented. This gives a glimpse of the historical reality, but also reflects where most scholarly research has been conducted thus far. One north-western exception to the database's concentration in the east is the parish of Saint Marylebone, where 285 baptisms have been unearthed, dating back to the 1690s but predominantly from Sancho's era. Corroboration of a substantial Black presence in this corner of town comes from contemporary accounts of Black visitors regularly patronizing another pub, the Yorkshire Stingo, 800 meters from the church. It is also no coincidence that slave-ownership was prevalent in this growing and wealthy part of London. The Duke and Duchess of Buccleuch (Henry Scott and Elizabeth Montagu) were among the many aristocratic families in the district: their house in Grosvenor Square, which Sancho almost certainly visited, was just two-thirds of a mile from Saint Marylebone parish church. In Westminster, however, most parishes have not yet been systematically studied, including St. Margaret's Church where Sancho was married and where his children were baptized. The fact that Olaudah Equiano's baptism took place here provides one instant example of what was surely a much larger Black presence in the area. In any event, baptismal records are both a help and a hindrance to the effort to recover the Black presence in eighteenth-century London. Across the city, Black people show up more frequently in records in the second half of the century, partly because baptism came to be seen – largely erroneously – as a way of asserting one's free status. The increase in archival visibility thus reflected demographic changes, but also how racial categorizations became more important in a period when questions of "whiteness" and "blackness" acquired new legal and political meanings across the Atlantic.

Yet if baptismal records capture only a partial picture of Black London, genealogical approaches allow us to work backwards to earlier decades when racial signifiers were used less frequently by parish clerks. Sancho's extended family provide a case in point. Anne Sancho's family, the Osbornes, had a longstanding presence in the Whitechapel area in the east of the city. Her parents, John Osborne and Mary Clark, were married in St. Mary's church in the parish in 1732, where Ann and her siblings were also baptized.[17] The family lived on Lambert Street when Ann was born in 1733 and on Petticoat Lane when her brother John arrived in 1743. Land tax records show John Osborne Sr. owning property on nearby Buckle Street through the 1740s. None of this evidence makes reference to these individuals' racial backgrounds, making us consider how many other racially diverse family trees in the 1700s await discovery.

The Osborne and Clark families' backgrounds cannot be identified definitely (although a connection to the West Indies has been suggested), but their presence in the East End fits with other emerging evidence of Black London in the eighteenth century. In total 123 other burials and baptisms of non-white Londoners, hailing from places including St. Lucia, Antigua, Jamaica, Suriname, the Gold Coast, and the American colonies, were recorded at St. Mary's in the period between the 1660s and the 1820s. Even in this one parish, we get a snapshot of the growing international diversity of London as a heart of empire, and of the lives people were carving out for themselves in the city. Crucially, the Sancho-Osborne-Clarks show this included not just enslavement but also property ownership and the formation of families and enduring kinship networks to connect them. Even within the immediate family of a famous Black Briton, we can cut through the celebrity to glimpse the diversity of Black historical life and, crucially, explore its wide-ranging geographic dimensions.

The breadth of Ignatius Sancho's London encompassed more than its Westminster epicenter. Upon following his family after his death, the depth of the Sancho presence in the city becomes clearer. Anne spent several more years on Charles Street, where she also paid rates to the parish, before eventually moving with her son, William, to a book shop at the Mews Gate on Castle Street. The entire family, and William in particular, remained associated with the Montagu family (styled the Buccleuchs after the death of Duke George), who paid for William's apprenticeship to

Edward Jeffery, a bookseller on Pall Mall, before he went to work for the Vaccine-Pock Institute as it trialed methods for using cowpox to inoculate against smallpox in nearby Soho. The last known surviving child, Elizabeth Bruce Sancho, was recorded living on Old Tothill Street in the 1810s, before moving in with her second cousin, William Priddie Lyons, on York Street in the parish of Christ Church, Surrey (subsequently part of Southwark) shortly before the time of her death in 1837. While it has been known for some time that Black London was not divided between a presence as slaves and servants in the west and a free population of sailors and runaways in the east, Sancho's wider family further disrupts any tendency to apply neat categories to Black Londoners' lives.[18]

Conclusion: Sancho's London and Black and British History

Any consideration of Sancho the Londoner should conclude with what he said about the city. This theme has not loomed large in Sancho scholarship, not least because London often does not feature explicitly in his letters. Yet, although he was no chronicler of city life in the mold of Samuel Pepys, there are revealing references nonetheless. For example, in a letter to Francis Crewe, Sancho lamented "the town" is empty; the only ones left were "a few sharks of both sexes, who are too poor to emigrate to the camps or watering places, and so are forced to prey upon one another in town" (*Letters* 176). He made a similar point to Roger Rush, describing how the latter's forthcoming return would lift his spirits, "for, large as the town is, I cannot say I have more than one friend in it" (*Letters* 195). Other letters also connote feelings of antipathy toward, or even estrangement from, the city. To James Kisbee he complained: "Trade is duller than ever I knew it – and money scarcer; – foppery runs higher – and vanity stronger; – extravagance is the adored idol of this sweet town" (*Letters* 131). To John Spink he described in even fuller terms that:

> I am far from being sorry that you have not been in town this autumn – for London has been sickly – almost every body full of complaint – add also that the times are equally full of disease – Luxury! Folly! Disease! and Poverty! you may see daily riding in the same coach – the doors ornamented with the honours of a virtuous ancestry topped with coronets; surrounded with mantle ermined – and, alas! Corruption for the supporters. (*Letters* 245)

These comments were part of the sentimental literary conventions associated with Sancho's writing, but they can also be mapped on to real-world urban developments: the occasional "emptiness" of the city corresponded to episodic patterns where people in "the court" left and returned according the rhythms of Parliament and the aristocratic season; wars and the economic crises that accompanied them were all-too-real problems for those seeking to make their way in London's burgeoning consumer economy; and problems and pathologies associated with corruption, poverty, crime, and disease were fast becoming central to the modern urban-industrial experience. Sancho was both a literary *and* a historical figure responding (not altogether positively) to the collisions among the city's varied constituencies at a time of rapid urban growth.

It is fitting that some of Sancho's most vivid descriptions of London life in his *Letters* came a few months before his death when describing the Gordon Riots in June 1780. What became the most violent urban unrest in British history began just a few hundred meters from Charles Street when Lord Gordon, the President of the Protestant Association, led several hundred supporters in a march on Parliament to present a petition calling for the repeal of the 1778 Papists Act, which sought to give Catholics more rights. For about a week afterwards, anti-Catholic mobs burned chapels and attacked property, and several hundred people were killed in the violence. Sancho described memorably how: "the shouts of the mob – the horrid clashing of swords – and the clutter of a multitude in swiftest motion – drew me to the door – when every one in the street was employed in shutting up shop" (*Letters* 271). A map produced by the Quartermaster General, responsible for the deployment of over 10,000 troops to suppress the disturbances, recorded one of the biggest conflagrations in Sancho's immediate neighborhood. While condemning the violence, Sancho went on to describe how "Hyde Park has a grand encampment, with artillery . . . St James's Park has ditto . . . The Parks, and our West end of the town, exhibit the features of French government" (*Letters* 276). In other references, Sancho describes events further afield, including how Newgate Prison in the City of London was "partly burned, and 300 felons from thence only let loose upon the world" (*Letters* 274), and the "two fires in Holborn now burning" (*Letters* 275). Sancho was not, therefore, giving just an eyewitness account, but providing second-hand reports of events and adding his own interpretations and allusions.[19] That he did not visit all these places personally is not the point: more important is that Sancho was speaking about, and condemning the destruction of, a city he had experience and knowledge of going back decades. In other words, he was writing as a Briton, an African, *and* a Londoner, while ensconced in the heart of the city where these identities were conjoined.

Applying an urban-historical approach to Sancho, therefore, helps us better understand not only his life and letters, but also the city, nation, and wider world to which he was connected. Sancho's story takes us to the central parts – in multiple meanings of the word – of the most important forces in London's development and, by extension, of the British state and its evolving place in the world. These contests included the clash between slavery and freedom (and a variety of ambiguous states in between); the transition to modern parliamentary democracy, within which tensions were fought over on the streets as well as in oratorical debates; and the growth of an urban metropolis on the cusp of full industrialization, connected to the wider world by innumerable commercial and political ties. Considering Sancho as a Londoner – as an urban citizen – therefore provides essential context to read his letters, but it also does something more: it provides an important reminder that neither "Black History" nor "British History" makes proper sense when each is considered in isolation from the other.

Notes

The original research for this chapter was conducted for the Ignatius Sancho's London project that collated mentions of specific places mentioned by Sancho to his correspondents, demographic data about neighborhoods and genealogical records of his extended family. Funding is gratefully acknowledged from the NULab for Texts, Maps and Networks, the College of Social Sciences and Humanities and the Office of the Provost, all at Northeastern University. Special thanks are due to Libby Collard for her background research and to Jo Langston for information on the Priddie-Lyons side of the Sancho family tree. I am also grateful to the other projects that granted access to their geospatial data, including the London slave-owners' addresses collected by the Centre for the Study of the Legacies of British Slavery and the London Metropolitan Archives' Switching the Lens dataset of baptisms, marriages, and burials. Interactive maps featuring all locations referenced in this chapter can be explored at https://map pingblacklondon.org.

1. White, J., *London in the Eighteenth Century: A Great and Monstrous Thing* (London: Bodley Head, 2012); Gerzina, G., *Black England: Life before Emancipation* (London: Allison & Busby, 1999), 65.
2. Smith, J. T., *Nollekens and His Times* (London: Richard Bentley & Son, 1895), 51–3.
3. Corfield, P., Harvey, C., and Green, E. Westminster Historical Database, 1749–1820; Voters Social Structure and Electoral Behaviour. UK Data Service (2000), https://datacatalogue.ukdataservice.ac.uk/studies/study/3908? id=3908#details.

4. Harvey, C., Green, E. M., and Corfield, P. J., "Continuity, change, and specialization within metropolitan London: The economy of Westminster, 1750–1820," *The Economic History Review* 52.3 (1999), 469–93, 486.

5. Corfield, P., "Proto-democracy: Summary," London Electoral History: Steps toward Democracy (2013), www.penelopejcorfield.com/PDFs/3.4.2-Corfield Pdf34-Short-Summary-Proto-Democracy.pdf.

6. Greig, H. and Vickery, A., "The political day in London c. 1697–1834," *Past and Present* 252.1 (2021), 101–37.

7. Jarrett, S., "'A Welshman coming to London and seeing a jackanapes . . .': How jokes and slang differentiated eighteenth-century Londoners from the rest of Britain," *London Journal* 43.2 (2018), 120–36.

8. Ogborn, M., *Spaces of Modernity: London's Geographies 1680–1780* (New York, NY and London: Guilford Press, 1998).

9. Ibid., 108–9.

10. Shoemaker, R., *The London Mob: Violence and Disorder in Eighteenth-Century England* (London: Hambledon, 2004), 111; White, J., *London in the Eighteenth Century: A Great and Monstrous Thing* (London: Bodley Head, 2012), 127; "Spring Gardens," in British History Online's "Survey of London," www .british-history.ac.uk/survey-london/vol20/pt3/pp58-65.

11. Hall, C., Draper, N., McClelland, K., Donington, K., and Lang, R., *Legacies of British Slave-Ownership: Colonial Slavery and the Formation of Victorian Britain* (Cambridge: Cambridge University Press, 2016).

12. Centre for the Study of the Legacies of British Slavery, www.ucl.ac.uk/lbs.

13. White, *London in the Eighteenth Century*, 130.

14. Jarrett, "'A Welshman coming to London.'"

15. *London Packet*, 26–29 June 1772. The article did not record the name or precise location of the pub.

16. Switching the Lens Database, https://tinyurl.com/4kmsse9e.

17. Mapping Black London, https://mappingblacklondon.org/maps/#isl.

18. Ibid.; Myers, N., *Reconstructing the Black Past: Blacks in Britain, c. 1780–1830* (London: Frank Cass, 1996), 63.

19. Olaleye, B., "Locating Sancho through Westminster: A topographical reading of *The Letters of the Late Ignatius Sancho, an African*," *Çankaya University Journal of Humanities and Social Sciences* 14.1 (2020), 112–25.

Further Reading

Gerzina, G., *Black England: Life before Emancipation* (London: Allison & Busby, 1999).

White, J., *London in the Eighteenth Century: A Great and Monstrous Thing* (London: Bodley Head, 2012).

CHAPTER 4

Sancho and the Montagu Family

Crispin Powell

This chapter is my attempt, as archivist at Boughton House, to reconstruct something of the life of Charles Ignatius Sancho within the household of two Dukes of Montagu, initially as a protégé and later, after an interlude, as a servant, from boyhood and on into the last decade of his life. Attempting to do this with any servant in an eighteenth-century setting is tricky because much depends on the survival of the archives, documents such as stewards' accounts and memoranda, also letters generated by the running of that particular establishment and those kept for the personal remembrance of the family. Sancho is no exception, and the many gaps in the Montagu archives leave us with a succession of mysteries and speculations which I outline here. As archives are discovered, no doubt more evidence of his career will emerge. Sadly, the gaps are such that I cannot even be sure of his exact term of employment with the Montagus.

Sancho's published *Letters* of 1782 are naturally an important source for his relationship to the Montagu family, but they do not begin until 1769, and references to his employers seem confined to the first few years. By his own admission, his connection to the family stretched back to his boyhood, under John 2nd Duke of Montagu (1690–1749), who held that title between 1709 and 1749. We do know that Sancho seems to have left service with the Montagu family in 1773 or 1774. He spent most of his life with them.

The 2nd Duke's house steward's accounts kept by Andrew Marchant and his successor Josiah Allen at Montagu House are the best surviving sources for glimpses into the lives of the Montagus, their servants, and friends who might have come into contact with Sancho.[1] Montagu House Whitehall was the principal London residence of the family from 1735. However, Sancho's own connection with them begins at Blackheath, the location of a suburban villa used by the duchess as a retreat, to the southeast of the city.

In the "biography" written by Joseph Jekyll (1754–1837), that preceded the Sancho's published *Letters*, he tells the story of the boy Sancho's encounter with the 2nd Duke on Blackheath and the impromptu "education" he received in his house on the edge of the park after the duke and duchess recognized Sancho's natural precocity (*Letters* 49). The tale of Sancho's early years with three ladies of the Earl of Dartmouth's family nearby is supported a little by the fact that the 2nd Duke paid a ground rent to the Earl of Dartmouth for the stables he kept there.[2] Estimating his birth year at 1729, I would expect evidence of Sancho in the Montagu household during the mid to late 1730s, but discovered nothing certain in the accounts.

In 1735, Thomas Shaw received payment for shoes "for the black boy," and there are several bills from between July and November 1739 for transportation of a "Black boy" along the Thames, between Greenwich and Montagu House at Whitehall.[3] A reference to teaching another "Black boy" in 1734 seems to relate to a man or boy called July Green, rather than Sancho.[4] These are isolated rather than routine payments, so they must have had specific causes. It's tempting to wonder whether the transportation costs could have been for taking Sancho to see the duke and duchess when they were at Montagu House.

There is a more certain reference to Sancho in a "water taxi" in 1749, dated a day before the Royal Fireworks Display, which the duke had organized in Green Park as Master General of the Board of Ordnance.[5] A bill from a George Smith provides probably the earliest explicit reference to Sancho in the duke's household.[6] Smith was a Thames waterman, and on 26 April 1749 a bill records that Smith had "carried and waited upon Sancho a black."

Perhaps Sancho was rowed up the Thames to that event, which was watched by the king and the duke's ever-eclectic group of friends, including the archaeologist William Stukeley (1687–1765) and the botanist Henry Baker (1698–1774).

Some evidence has recently emerged that Sancho was older than first thought. A copy of his first published letter (*Letters* 1) in the National Records of Scotland identifies a man known as "Mr. G" as "Mr. Griffiths."[7] Sancho tells us he was an "old acquaintance" whom he had known since he "was young." He was probably Edward Griffith, the household upholsterer, who was born in 1707 and had served in that capacity since 1752.[8] Before that year, he had undertaken freelance cabinet-making commissions back to at least 1746.[9]

Sancho's "first" Duke John was an attractive but forceful personality, often viewed as eccentric by his contemporaries. He was passionately interested in history, science, and the world beyond Europe; overall, he was insatiably curious, with the power and wealth to indulge himself. Holding an overriding regard for humanity, he sought out and cultivated friends and contacts from across the world at every opportunity. I have the impression that Duke John had an almost Buddhist respect for all kinds of life, and in an age of cruelty to animals, he abhorred their mistreatment. He planted many miles of trees, excavated local archaeological sites, joined the Egyptian Society, grew cacti and electrified potted myrtle trees; he kept a decrepit lion and cosseted monkeys; he owned a canoe and a copy of the Koran; he even had a Chinese-style teahouse for his Whitehall riverside terrace as well as a Chinese-style boat to sail on the Thames outside Montagu House.

The 2nd Duke had a wide reputation for being benevolent. Horace Walpole (1717–97) remembered,

> You have seen the death of the Duke of Montagu in all the papers. His loss will be extremely felt. He paid no less than £2,700 a year in private pensions, which ought to be known, to balance the immense history of his plans, of which he was perpetually obtaining new, and making the utmost of all. He had quartered in the Great Wardrobe (his court post supplying furnishings to the royal palaces) no less than thirty nominal tailors and arras workers . . . this employment is to be dropped . . .[10]

Walpole added, "In short, with some foibles, he was a most amiable man and one of the most feeling I ever knew." Sancho, indeed, needed only a chance of proximity or circumstance to be "adopted" by such an individual as Duke John, with his philosophy, interests, and reputation.

Sadly, for Sancho, the 2nd Duke died relatively young of a "violent fever" at Montagu House, Whitehall, on 5 July 1749. It had been an unexpected illness, and Duke John's unsettled bills or vouchers for the previous few months had stacked up for his executors to deal with. This was the reason why George Smith's bill survived. Other bills found along with his are more mysterious. The next in the pile is from the duke's butler, James Montagu, "for going to Smithfield to receive a black boy and for carrying him and his box to Woolwich" on 8 March 1749.[11] If Sancho was born around 1729, he would have been in his early twenties by 1749 and may well have been considered as a "boy" in James Montagu's eyes. Then we have "cotton hose" and gloves paid simply for "the black."[12] Around the same time, James Cockburn submitted an expense for "coach hire and for a Dinner at Pontac's for the black gentleman," who was also treated to two bottles of claret.[13] Pontack's, to give it its correct spelling, was a fashionable French restaurant in London, and Cockburn was Captain of the Cadets at the Royal Military Academy of Woolwich. The 2nd Duke had founded the academy in his role as Master General of the Board of Ordnance in 1741. The anonymity of the "boy" and the "gentleman" suggest the individual referenced might be new to the household. But it is possible that they might not even be one and the same person. It would not have been atypical of the duke to have tried to introduce a new Black cadet to the Academy – but who was this young Black man, and why did Cockburn take him to Woolwich? Perhaps for some impromptu lessons there? If it was Sancho, maybe this offers another example beyond the access to Duke John's library in regard to Jekyll's tale of Sancho's "education."

As butler to the Montagus, James Montagu would not have been surprised at his orders to collect a black "boy." Over a period of twenty years, Duke John had cultivated a string of friendships with people of other ethnicities, amongst whom were the free Jamaican poet, musician, and scholar Francis Williams (c. 1690–c. 1770); Ayuba Suleiman Diallo (1701–73), a Senegalese prince who had been kidnapped, enslaved, and then eventually freed; and Tomochichi (c. 1644–1741), an indigenous Creek leader, who had traveled to London in 1734. The 2nd Duke had also sought out Black protégés, some of whom had entered his household as servants. Sancho's predecessors and colleagues in the household included Charles Manwell, July Green, George Joseph, Caesar Montagu, William Montagu Rio, and Miss Julie Green. Some of the servants had, like Sancho, joined the household as children and were educated by the 2nd Duke, as he was a steadfast advocate of the power of education and believed everyone to be capable of achievement if they were taught. He was keen all his servants should be literate. Francis Williams was famously one among the group of non-white or poor white people who became subjects in the 2nd Duke's "experiments" to prove that all could attain prominence if given opportunity. The duke had an enduring interest in human psychology and became celebrated for creating hoaxes or scenarios to prove some of his views, most notoriously causing "the Bottle Conjuror riot" in the cause of proving mass public credulity. The "Conjuror" was meant to be a contortionist who would, before a theater audience, squeeze himself into a quart bottle, something physically impossible. The theater had a full house for the performance, all with the belief that this would take place.

One of Sancho's Black contemporaries in the Montagu household, Caesar Montagu, was educated in a village school close to Boughton, the duke's country residence in Northamptonshire.[14] He eventually married a white lady and died as a carpenter in Manchester in 1796. He was survived by his sons, whom he had named after the two Montagu dukes. William Montagu Rio, another Black Montagu servant, died in 1754 in Bristol, having had his medical bills paid by the family.[15] It was thought fitting to have servants bear the same surname as their employers. Then there was Charles Manwell, who had been painted in the portrait with Duchess Mary, and who died a footman in 1735, as well as July Green, who might have been related to Miss Julie Green, perhaps father and daughter or brother and sister. During the mid 1730s, the schoolmaster George Crockley taught July Green in London.[16] Miss Julie was taught music by the king's trumpeter Joseph Abington in the 1740s.[17] Both Julie and July Green died at dates unknown but around the time of Sancho's arrival in the household. Consequently, at least during his early years with the Montagus, Sancho did not live in isolation, but rather amongst a small group of fellow Black servants.

Sadly, however, I found little trace to corroborate stories of Sancho's boyhood tutoring by the 2nd Duke and his duchess in the houses' surviving archives. Although there are several anonymous references to "black boys," it is difficult to definitively assert Sancho's presence amongst his several Black contemporaries.

Sancho was to find a favored place in the widowed duchess's household after 1749. In an annotated copy of John Nichols's *Biographical Anecdotes of William Hogarth* (1781), the artist's 1742 painting *Taste in High Life* is discussed. The picture satirizes a fashionable group, including a Black pageboy and a pet monkey, which is examining a bill of fare including ducks' tongues, fricassee of snails, and rabbits' ears. The young man at the center of the illustration is identifiable as the dandy Lord Portmore and the younger lady as the celebrated courtesan Kitty Fisher. According to Nichols, "her familiarity with the black boy alludes to a similar weakness in a noble duchess"; a manuscript note identifies the reference as to the Duchess of Montagu; "who educated two brats of the same colour. One of them afterwards robbed her, and the other was guilty of some offence equally unpardonable."[18] These startling references are probably to Sancho and William Montagu Rio, both of whom are mentioned in the duchess's will. Rio was still in enough favor with the family at the time for the duchess's daughter Mary to pay his doctor's bills.[19]

The pageboy in the Hogarth was traditionally identified as Sancho, but Nichols does not name him. Hogarth was well known to the late 2nd Duke, who had been painted at least twice by him. Both the duke and the duchess are portrayed, with their family and a Black pageboy serving tea, in a wonderful "conversation piece," now displayed at the Yale Center for British Art. The pageboy seems to have almost disappeared, after being cut from the edge of the canvas when the painting was cropped in the early nineteenth century.

Black servants of the Montagus were portrayed in several paintings. In about 1720, Enoch Seeman painted Duchess Mary with her servant Charles Manwell, depicted in a working livery instead of fancy or exotic dress, and engaging us directly rather than gazing up adoringly at his mistress (*Mary Duchess of Montagu with a Black Page Boy*, attributed to Enoch Seeman). Records exist for additional pictures: the young trumpeter Julie Green was captured in pastel, probably by the younger Duchess Mary, who was a talented artist of that medium.[20] Sadly, that portrait has vanished. Intriguingly, there is also a reference to another image of a "black boy," who was also depicted on paper at Boughton, but again that work is also lost.[21] Consequently, Thomas Gainsborough's 1768 portrait of Sancho should not be seen as an isolated example of the Montagus' investments in visual representations of Black people in England.

Other, friendlier, voices than Nichols's give me the impression that after the death of her husband the 2nd Duke in 1749, the duchess was a poor creature, sunk in a grief-stricken depression, isolating herself and waiting to join him. What is certainly true is that she did remember her Black servants in her will. Rather touchingly, she specified that "my desire is to [lye] just as I die till I am troublesome and I think Mrs Reason would take care of me in that but if she can't I hope someone else will."[22] This charity is also reflected in a codicil from May 1750 that lists her legacies: Mrs. Reason was given £50 per annum for life, "for her use only"; Daniel received £30 per annum for life; "Urea" also received £30 per annum for life; and Ignatius Sancho was provided with £30 per annum for the rest of his life.[23] Urea, who was probably William Montagu Rio, had also received an annuity from Duke John. Like Sancho and Rio, Daniel may also have been a Black servant of the Montagus. The duchess finally died in May 1751, and was buried in the ducal vault at Warkton church, close to Boughton. All three, Sancho, Daniel, and William Montagu Rio, were presumably amongst the mourners at Warkton.

The annuity from the duchess might have allowed Sancho to establish himself in London as a man of independent means. It is easy to find annuity payments to him in the Montagu household accounts, disbursed in half-yearly installments in May and November throughout this period.[24] The first £15 came on 29 November 1752 – worth almost £2,000 by today's standards. There is no evidence in the archives of a wage paid on top of this annuity, but I assume that, like the other servants in the Montagus' employ, he would have received one. Annuities were often based on one's annual salary, but only Sancho's annuity can be traced.

In his "biography" of Sancho, Joseph Jekyll (1754–1837) suggests that Sancho was extravagant after receiving the annuity and subsequently that he ran out of money and was taken in again by the Montagu household (*Letters* 50). This was now headed by the 2nd Duke's daughter Mary Countess of Cardigan (1711–75) and her husband George (1712–90), the earl, who was a neighbor of her father's, living at Deene in Northamptonshire. They were later re-created Duke and Duchess of Montagu. Reading Duke George's letters gives one the impression of a warm, charming, and witty man. He had a happy marriage to a rather formidable wife, Mary Montagu. In March 1756, Sancho was witness to a bond for Lord Cardigan.[25] Witnesses tended to be someone at hand, like solicitors, clerks, and servants. Sancho was occasionally witness to such bonds up to 1769. This signature in 1756 marks the earliest reference in the archive to Sancho's employment as a servant.

Sadly, no household accounts recording wages seem to have survived, so we are left only with haphazard clues like the bonds and a selection of odd references in Duke George's private accounts for Sancho's second, pro-longed period of service. The private accounts begin in 1753, but make no mention of Sancho for that decade. In 1760 there are two payments: £9.9s for a "suit of clothes" for Sancho in May; and then in November, payment of £40 to John Shaw, Sancho, and a Mr. Ford for mourning expenses.[26] Shaw received a £30 salary in 1775; the highest pay of the Montagu servants apart from William Dixon, who received £50 as the House Steward, so we have some evidence of Sancho's high ranking within the household.

All the evidence points to Sancho being employed as Duke George's valet de chambre, his personal servant, and it was in this capacity he was paid for purchasing "installation clothes" in 1762.[27] These were presumably the robes as a baron of the duke's son Lord Monthermer (1735–70), when he got his own peerage. Certainly, years later, in other correspondence, Lord Ailesbury told his nephew that Sancho would remember where these robes were as his brother's "valet."[28]

Sancho's first specific mention of the Montagus in his published letters is a reference to Duke George in a letter dated October 1769 (*Letters* 83–4). It was written from Richmond, the duke's suburban villa and retreat on the edge of the metropolis, to Sancho's friend James Kisbee, who had traveled to Dalkeith, Scotland for birthday celebrations. Dalkeith House was the main Scottish residence of the duke's daughter and son-in-law, the Duke and Duchess of Buccleuch. Kisbee was a fellow servant of Montagu House, the main family residence in Whitehall, and is the only certain recipient of Sancho's *Letters* whom we know to have been a fellow member of the household. He was a footman who rose to be House Steward after Sancho's death and would have died a wealthy man in 1820, had it not been for grasping relatives. Kisbee hailed from a long-established family of Northamptonshire tenants and had come to London in 1757 as a junior servant.[29] His brother was a gamekeeper. In the letter to Kisbee, Sancho relays "the good Duke of Montagu's" charity over the death of "poor Pat," promising an apprenticeship for Pat's son if he didn't want to continue in service and sending his widow a £20 note (*Letters* 84).

In a letter dated 21 April 1770, again from Richmond, but written to one of the Montagus' friends, Edward Young, Esq., Sancho discusses the untimely death of Lord Monthermer, Duke George's only son and heir; "I bless God, their Graces continue in good health, though as yet they have not seen anybody," he wrote, ". . . Time will, I hope, bring them comforts" (*Letters* 87). The young man was only thirty-five when he died on 11 April 1770. In addition to their son John Lord Monthermer, Duke George and his wife Mary had three daughters, but tragically two of the daughters also died young, leaving only Lady Elizabeth (1743–1827) or Betty, who married Henry 3rd Duke of Buccleuch (1746–1812), for love, in May 1767. Only when her brother died in 1770 did Duchess Elizabeth become her father's heiress. Duke Henry already had vast estates of his own in the Borders of Scotland, with his principal seat at Dalkeith House near Edinburgh.

The family tried to recover by taking an expedition to Scotland in the summer of 1770 and, in another letter to Kisbee on 16 July, Sancho writes from Dalkeith about having been on a "Highland excursion" (*Letters* 90). He lists some of the places they went, including Dumbarton, Loch Lomond, and Inveraray, then ends the letter with a charming reference to a baby granddaughter; "Lady Mary grows a little angel, the Duchess gets pretty round, they all eat, drink and seem pure merry and we are all out of mourning this day" (*Letters* 91). They probably also went via Blair Castle.[30]

The duke's private account book records the family in Scotland from 2 June to 16 August 1770.[31] At the end of August, Sancho learnt from someone that the Duke of Montagu had been to Tunbridge Wells, so the duke had evidently traveled south without him. Sancho may have made a surprise discovery when out shopping as valet for the duke in Inveraray, for John Jamieson (1759–1838), a Scottish antiquary, records that "a Duke of Montague" found manuscripts there from the monastery of Iona being used as snuff paper.[32] In that September, Sancho, still at Dalkeith, again refers to a "week in the Highlands" (*Letters* 93).

Elizabeth Buccleuch would have known Sancho since her childhood in the house of her grandfather, John 2nd Duke of Montagu. Sancho may have been the sole Black member of Duke George and Duchess Mary's household, in contrast to that of the latter's father, the 2nd Duke. Duke George's possible Black servants included "Jenny," mentioned when the duchess died in 1775,[33] who looked after the menagerie at Richmond, and Julie Green, Duke John's young trumpeter, who may have lived on as a kind of pensioner. In neither instance can we be sure.

As valet to Duke George, Sancho had his own room in the family's private villa at Richmond, as well as in the Round Tower of Windsor Castle, where Duke George had his apartment as constable of the castle. The contents of both rooms are recorded in inventories, at Richmond in 1766 and 1772, at Windsor in 1763.[34] As an important courtier and a great friend of George III, the duke was often at Windsor, and it seems likely that Sancho would have met the king. The royal family were not unknown visitors for tea and would sometimes come to the villa at Richmond by boat. The villa was newly built, overlooking the Thames, with fine gardens up the side of the hill, which the duchess tended assiduously.

Sancho would have also traveled with Duke George as his valet. As the duchess had problems with her eyes, and often felt in poor health, they were frequently at Bath or at some other spa; Tunbridge, Buxton, Harrogate, and Clifton Hotwells near Bristol all received visits during Sancho's time within the household. In the winter of 1767, we see Sancho as Duke George's valet in Bath from 10 December to 24 January 1768.[35] During this period, on 12 December, Sancho witnessed another of the Duke's bonds.[36] I was excited to find mention of Sancho in one of the duke's letters, written on this trip, telling his daughter Duchess Elizabeth about the furore surrounding the ticketed funeral of Lord Buchan (1710–67). "All this you may imagine has made a great noise in such a place as this" he wrote, "Sancho says, he hears, that the family were all <u>weild</u>."[37] So far, this is the only explicit mention of Sancho in all Duke George's letters that I have found. The duke took every opportunity to try to be witty with his daughter and always underlines words such as "wild" which he wants to pronounce in a Scottish accent.

Between 28 April and 25 May 1768, the duke and duchess were in Bath again, where Gainsborough painted the duke, and they returned for a consecutive winter when Gainsborough painted the duchess.[38] Sancho's own portrait by the great artist was painted during the same stay, according to an inscription on the back of the painting, on 29 November 1768. Duke George records payments to the artist for the portraits of the duke and duchess, but I found no payment for Sancho's own.[39] Importantly, in the portrait Sancho does not appear to be wearing Montagu livery, which was green, red, and yellow. His coat looks black or dark navy, and his bright-red waist coat has shiny gold trim – more in keeping with the style of a gentleman, rather than what a servant would wear. The Bath trip of the winter of 1768 was made in the company of the Montagus' daughter Elizabeth and her new Scottish husband Henry, 3rd Duke of Buccleuch. The intervening summer had seen the duke and duchess decamp to Scotland via Deene, the duke's country house, and their destination would have been Dalkeith, their daughter's new home.

Sancho's 16 July letter to James Kisbee implies that he didn't travel to Dalkeith with the Montagus until 1770 (*Letters* 89–90). Perhaps because he was away in Bath over two winters, Sancho missed that summer trip to Scotland of 1768, possibly to stay with his own family. Sancho's wife had given birth to their first son, and fifth child, Jonathan William, on 21 March. Sancho certainly appears to have been at the villa in Richmond at the same time as the duke when he wrote to Kisbee on 20 October 1769, a few days after which the duke departed for Adderbury in Oxfordshire to stay with the Buccleuchs (*Letters* 83–4). Over Sancho's years of service there were trips into Norfolk and Suffolk in 1760, to Worcester in July 1763, one to Lord Nugent's (1709–88) seat Gosfield in Essex in 1764, and one into the West Country in 1766.

Like his father-in-law, Duke George was charitable in his private accounts, and in 1761 he paid the christening fee for Sancho's daughter Frances Joanna (1761–1815),[40] and then in 1767 he purchased copies of Sancho's published music.[41] The household accounts describe his purchase as for "an entertainment for the servants" at Montagu House on 24 April.

Duke George's daughter, the Duchess of Buccleuch, was similarly generous, and she paid the apprenticeship fee for Sancho's son, William Sancho (1775–1810),[42] in 1791; "Billy" was to be taught by a bookbinder and thus began another association with the Montagus and Buccleuchs that lasted as long as the one enjoyed by his father. William Sancho acted as Duchess Elizabeth's bookbinder, book and print seller, and on occasions as her librarian in his adult life. The duchess's letters to her steward at

Montagu House clearly convey a warmth and indulgence that was presumably founded on her fondness for William Sancho's father, Ignatius, whom she would have known since her girlhood.

Toward the close of 1773, Sancho left his service employment with the Montagus/Buccleuchs, possibly because of an increasing disability from gout. In November, he wrote from Charles Street, not far from Montagu House, to a "Mrs. H———" for advice on setting up a shop (*Letters* 102–3). "Mrs. H———" could have been Elizabeth Higgarson Margaret Hughes, or Sarah Howman, all of whom were servants at Montagu House. In February 1774, the duke paid Sancho £20, presumably to help him establish his grocery business.[43] I found no written evidence anyone from Montagu House bought groceries from him, but the new steward, Thomas Pilliner, kept things anonymous and merely recorded "grocer" beside the amounts in his account book.[44]

John Masterton, Sancho's successor as valet, appears in the duke's private accounts in May 1774, when he received "point ruffles" and a waistcoat, so this perhaps marks Sancho's final departure for his grocer's shop.[45] The duke seems to have become frustrated by his new personal servant. In 1777, the duke walked from the Richmond villa to his "neighbour Cam," probably the poet and gardener Robert Owen Cambridge (n. d.) at Twickenham, but got caught in the rain coming back over the river. Returning with wet legs and feet, the duke evidently angered "little Masterton," "who had to unpack for shoes and stockings." The duke told his daughter he had more reason to be angry with Masterton, as he knew the duke was out in the rain, and "I had not given him any orders," he added sarcastically, but, "in short he grows more agreeable every day and I more absurd, I believe."[46] Masterton received an annual salary of £30, the same as Sancho, and stayed until October 1780,[47] when he may have been dismissed.

Sancho himself died in December 1780, but his passing goes unrecorded within the Montagu and Buccleuch archives. In July 1780, the Duke of Buccleuch gave Sancho £20, presumably to ease his final months.[48] Both Ignatius's son, William Sancho, and his daughter Elizabeth were supported by the Montagu family after their father's death. Elizabeth received an annuity of £40 under Duchess Elizabeth's will, and on William Sancho's death in 1810, his mother received £20.[49] It was an association that had lasted three generations of the Montagu family and two of the Sanchos'. Reading Duchess Elizabeth's letters about Sancho's son William from the early nineteenth century, I think the two shared as much equilibrium and warmth as could be had between a bookseller and a duchess.[50] But William

Sancho's relationship with the Buccleuch family remains a further tale to tell elsewhere.

Sancho's published *Letters* remain in the present 10th Duke of Buccleuch's library at Bowhill, and this chapter charts the evidence of him that I have been able to find so far in the Montagu archives. The physical settings of his life as a servant have mostly disappeared – Montagu House Whitehall and the villas at Blackheath and Richmond are all gone. The gardens and ancillary buildings at Richmond, however, remain as a public park, together with a tea pavilion, the predecessor of which Sancho would have known. Dalkeith House is still owned by the Duke of Buccleuch. The Northamptonshire country houses remain in splendid occupation by descendants, the Duke of Buccleuch at Boughton and Mr. and Mrs. Robert Brudenell at Deene.

The Sanchos are actively remembered in both houses, both of which are open to the public, in the literature and during the guided tours, but, as we have seen, much remains tantalizingly elusive. The Buccleuch Living Heritage Trust hopes to facilitate a Collaborative Doctoral Award to try to chart the lives of the Sanchos and the other Black members of the households they knew.

Notes

1. Montagu archive, Boughton House: House stewards' account books: Andrew Marchant, Josiah Allen, 1721–46, and Thomas Webster 1768–71.
2. Montagu archive, Boughton House: House stewards' accounts: Andrew Marchant, no. 34, box 108.
3. Ibid.: Andrew Marchant, nos. 23 and 31, boxes 107–8.
4. Ibid.: Andrew Marchant, no. 21, box 34.
5. Montagu archive, Boughton House: 2nd Duke's executors' vouchers, box 30.
6. Ibid.: 2nd Duke's executors' vouchers, box 30.
7. National Records of Scotland GD24/1/553, ff. 339–40.
8. Monumental inscription, St. Mary's churchyard Paddington.
9. Montagu of Beaulieu archive, Beaulieu; Cardigan receipts.
10. Lewis, W. S. and South, R. A. (eds.), *Horace Walpole's Correspondence* (New Haven, CT and London: Yale University Press, 1961), Vol. II, 400.
11. Montagu archive, Boughton House: 2nd Duke's executors' vouchers, box 30.
12. Ibid.: 2nd Duke's executors' vouchers, box 30.
13. Ibid.: 2nd Duke's executors' vouchers, box 30.
14. Ibid.: estate vouchers.
15. Ibid.: trust accounts, box 26.
16. Montagu archive, Boughton House: House stewards' accounts: Andrew Marchant, no. 21, box 34.

17. Ibid.: House stewards' accounts: Andrew Marchant, no. 34, box 108 and Thomas Allen, no. 1, box 85.
18. Nichols, J., *Biographical Anecdotes of William Hogarth with a Catalogue of His Works* (London, 1781), 158.
19. Montagu archive, Boughton House, trust accounts, box 26.
20. Montagu archive, Boughton House: Inventory of Montagu House Whitehall 1746, box 10.
21. Ibid.: Inventory of Boughton House 1801, box 13.
22. Ibid.: Copy will of Mary Duchess of Montagu 1749, MR box C.
23. Ibid.: Copy codicil of Mary Duchess of Montagu 1750, MR box C.
24. Ibid.: Chief steward William Folkes's accounts, box 26.
25. Ibid.: Bond, Earl of Cardigan to Robert Brudenell 1756, box U21.
26. Ibid.: George Duke of Montagu's private accounts, box 95.
27. Ibid.: George Duke of Montagu's private accounts, box 95.
28. Joan Wake archive Northamptonshire Record Office: Letter transcript, Lord Ailesbury to James Brudenell 1780.
29. Montagu archive, Boughton House: Barnwell estate letters, box 47.
30. Home archive, The Hirsel: Letter Duke of Buccleuch, 1788.
31. Montagu archive, Boughton House: George Duke of Montagu's private accounts, box 95.
32. Jamieson, J., *Historical Account of the Ancient Culdees of Iona* (Edinburgh: J. Ballantyne & Co., 1811), 315.
33. Ibid.: List of annual wages left under Duchess Mary's will, 1775, box W.
34. Ibid.: Richmond inventories 1766 and 1772, box 27, and Round Tower apartment Windsor inventory 1763, box 8.
35. Ibid.: George Duke of Montagu's private accounts, box 95.
36. Ibid.: Bond, Duke of Montagu to Rebecca Stanley 1767, box U21.
37. Home archive: The Hirsel: Letter Duke of Montagu to Elizabeth Duchess of Buccleuch 1767.
38. Montagu archive, Boughton House: George Duke of Montagu's private accounts, box 95.
39. Ibid.: George Duke of Montagu's private accounts, box 95.
40. Ibid.: George Duke of Montagu's private accounts, box 95.
41. Ibid.: House steward's accounts, Thomas Webster, box UII.
42. Ibid.: John Reynolds's accounts, box 29.
43. Montagu archive, Boughton House: George Duke of Montagu's private accounts, box 95.
44. Ibid.: House stewards' accounts Thomas Pilliner, box 14.
45. Ibid.: George Duke of Montagu's private accounts, box 95.
46. Home archive: The Hirsel: Letter Duke of Montagu to Elizabeth Duchess of Buccleuch 1777.
47. Montagu archive, Boughton House: House stewards' accounts Thomas Pilliner, box 14.
48. Buccleuch archive, National Records of Scotland: GD224/1092/1.

49. Montagu archive, Boughton House: Will of Elizabeth Duchess of Buccleuch 1819–28, MR box V.
50. Ibid.: House steward John Parker's "in" letters, 1809–12, box W.

Sources

Buccleuch Archive, Montagu papers at Boughton House:

1. House stewards' account books: Andrew Marchant, Josiah Allen, 1721–46, and Thomas Webster, 1768–71
2. Letters to John Parker, house steward, 1809–1812 (for William Sancho)
3. Vouchers for John 2nd Duke of Montagu's executors' accounts, 1749–53
4. John 2nd Duke of Montagu's trust account books, 1749–71
5. Will of Mary Duchess of Montagu, 1749/50
6. George Duke of Montagu's private accounts, 1753–76
7. George Duke of Montagu's bonds, 1762–7
8. Inventories of Montagu villa, Richmond, c. 1766 and 1772
9. Inventory of George Duke of Montagu's apartment in the Round Tower at Windsor Castle, 1763

George Duke of Montagu's letters to his daughter Elizabeth, Box 192, Home archive at The Hirsel.

Letter, 1780, Earl of Ailesbury to his brother George, in Joan Wake archive at the Northamptonshire Record Office.

Further Reading on the Montagu and Buccleuch Families

Falk, B., *The Way of the Montagues: A Gallery of Family Portraits* (London: Hutchinson & Co., 1947).

Fraser, W., *The Scotts of Buccleuch*, 2 vols. (Edinburgh: self-published, 1878).

Murdoch, T. (ed.), *Boughton House: The English Versailles* (London: Faber & Faber/Christies, 1992).

Scott, J. M. D. (ed.), *Boughton: The House, Its People and Its Collections* (Bicester: Bellendaine Books and Buccleuch Living Heritage Trust, 2022).

Bowhill: The House, Its People and Its Paintings (Bicester: Bellendaine Books and Buccleuch Living Heritage Trust, 2018).

Wake, J., *The Brudenells of Deene* (London: Cassell & Co., 1953).

CHAPTER 5

Sancho's Networks of Subscribers

Lawrence Evalyn

At the beginning of the first edition of Sancho's *Letters* (1782), after the two-page preface by Frances Crewe (1759–1834), and before the twelve-page biography by Joseph Jekyll (1754–1837), we are presented with forty-one pages of subscribers' names. Who are these people, and what is their relationship to the book that follows? This chapter is an examination of these forty-one pages, exploring those two questions for their insights into Sancho's literary and social position. Sancho's *Letters* eventually became a major piece of "evidence" in the discourse around the abolition of slavery.[1] As the book was read and cited, Sancho's intellect and sensibility were used as "proof" of the humanity of Black people in general. The preface to Sancho's *Letters* invites this racialized and politicized framing, stating that the editor's motive for publication is "the desire of shewing that an untutored African may possess abilities equal to an European" (*Letters* ii). We might naturally assume, therefore, that abolitionist activists will make up most of the names listed as subscribers. However, a closer examination shows that the list is more strongly shaped by a sentimental literary milieu and the social ties of the book's editor. In keeping with Hanley's reminder that "[a]ny reading of Sancho's *Letters* must be influenced by the knowledge that they were posthumously published to support the author's family,"[2] this chapter also examines the social relationships underlying the publication of Sancho's *Letters*.

Publishing "by Subscription"

Before we go farther into the particular details of Sancho's subscribers, it is useful to orient ourselves to the practice of eighteenth-century subscription publishing more broadly. The term "subscription" in the eighteenth century did not imply, as it does today, a product delivered in installments over time. Rather, to subscribe was to write ("scribe") one's name beneath ("sub") a particular document. Petitions, charities, and collectively funded projects of all kinds might invite their supporters to subscribe to a publicly visible list. Following this model, when a book was published by subscription, this means that individual book-buyers (subscribers) agreed in advance to buy it, adding their names to a list often published in the book. In contemporary terms, subscribers could be equated to the backers who pledge money in an online crowdfunding campaign.

Raising a subscription meant contacting potential subscribers and securing their promise to purchase the book. It was a labor-intensive and sometimes socially awkward process, whether the author drew on their own social circles or went door-to-door soliciting strangers. Since many authors failed to complete the books for which they collected subscriptions, subscription-collectors were often seen as mildly respectable scammers.[3] Most books were not published by subscription, and it was sometimes seen as faintly embarrassing to have to rely on subscriptions to publish, since doing so implied that the book could not gain investment from a traditional publisher. In other cases, however, subscription publishing was associated with high-prestige works that turned to subscriptions because they were so expensive to produce, such as collections of prints or translations of Classical poetry.

Subscription publishing was one strategy to address a core truth: printing a book is expensive, and it was an even bigger financial risk in the eighteenth century than in today's world of computer typesetting and print-on-demand. Book production was still in what is referred to as the "hand-press period" (roughly 1450 to 1800), meaning that printing presses were not yet automated. Particularly time-consuming was the typesetting process, in which metal letters (the "type") were individually placed ("set") into a frame that would hold them while ink and paper were applied. Once the type had been set, the most cost-effective path was to print as many copies as possible before the frame was disassembled to make the next item. If a print run was too small and a book sold out quickly, printing a new edition meant the major expense of re-setting all the type. However, if a print run was too large, unsold books meant a waste of expensive materials. Paper was still made of linen or cotton and much more costly than the wood pulp which became the norm 100 years later. Printing a book, therefore, required estimating the size of the potential audience and taking a calculated risk.

Different publishing approaches distributed the risk and reward in different ways. Most commonly, an author would sell the copyright of their book to a publisher, who would pay for all the costs of printing the book and then sell copies to booksellers, who would in turn sell them to readers. The roles of publisher, printer, and bookseller often overlapped in the eighteenth century, so there were many variations within this model. The key distinction was that with non-subscription publishing, the author was paid once only, before the book was released. Eighteenth-century publishing did not typically involve our current system of royalties, in which an author is paid a small fraction of the price of each book sold. In other words, the author was safe from the risk of unsold books, but also cut off from the reward of extra earnings when a book sold well. At the other extreme, a book could be "printed for the author" – essentially self-published, with the author keeping all the money from sales – but this required substantial financial resources up front. Subscription publishing, therefore, bridged some of the gaps between traditional publishing and self-publishing. If 500 buyers committed to making a purchase, the author could print 1,000 copies with some assurance that they wouldn't be bankrupted. And if those buyers provided some payment in advance, the author had the cash to buy paper and hire printers. As a result, the author could maintain the high reward of controlling their book's revenue, while reducing their risk.

Subscription publishing could be attractive for authors who couldn't convince a publisher to buy their manuscript, as might have been the case with politically contentious material. It could also be attractive for authors who *did* think they had a successful book and wanted to fully capitalize on it. The question naturally arises: which situation applied for Sancho's *Letters*? I would suggest it was the latter: the book was partly presented as a fund-raiser for Sancho's widow and young children, an aim that would be best accomplished if surplus profits did not go to a publisher. Indeed, after the first edition quickly sold out, Anne Sancho collected an additional fee from the booksellers who produced the second edition (*Letters* 20), and in 1803 William Sancho published the fifth edition of his father's *Letters* for his fledgling book business, still able to profit from Ignatius Sancho's legacy twenty years later.[4] Moreover, the number and quality of Sancho's subscribers – who will serve as the primary focus of the rest of this chapter – suggest that a mainstream audience was already expected for the book.

Sancho's Subscribers

Sancho did not undertake the gathering of subscriptions on his own behalf. He may have planned to publish a letter collection and may have made some preparations before his death for a book, perhaps collecting or preserving some letters to be given to an editor.[5] However, the bulk of the organizational work was undertaken after Sancho's death, led by Frances Crewe. As a frequent correspondent of Sancho's, Crewe wrote to and visited the members of Sancho's social networks, both to request letters and to gather subscribers, between Sancho's death on 14 December 1780 and the book's publication in 1782.

In 1782, Sancho's *Letters* was one of at least forty-two books published in Britain with a subscriber list; of these, I have been able to examine thirty-five, which can contextualize Sancho in the year's book production. With 1,181 individuals listed, this list reflects a tremendous feat of networking, placing it within the upper echelon of the year's books with subscribers in terms of length. More specifically, the list for Sancho's *Letters* is the third-longest of 1782, as seen in Figure 5.1. Only 4 books exceed 1,000 names, and the average subscriber-list length is closer to 450.

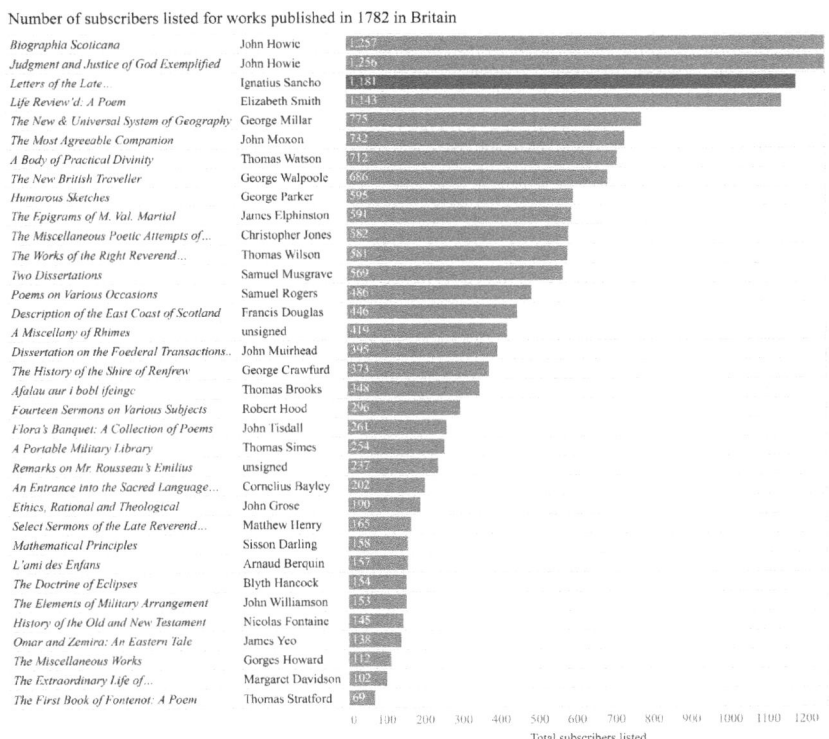

Number of subscribers listed for works published in 1782 in Britain

Biographia Scoticana	John Howie	1,257
Judgment and Justice of God Exemplified	John Howie	1,256
Letters of the Late...	Ignatius Sancho	1,181
Life Review'd: A Poem	Elizabeth Smith	1,143
The New & Universal System of Geography	George Millar	775
The Most Agreeable Companion	John Moxon	732
A Body of Practical Divinity	Thomas Watson	712
The New British Traveller	George Walpoole	686
Humorous Sketches	George Parker	595
The Epigrams of M. Val. Martial	James Elphinston	591
The Miscellaneous Poetic Attempts of...	Christopher Jones	582
The Works of the Right Reverend...	Thomas Wilson	581
Two Dissertations	Samuel Musgrave	569
Poems on Various Occasions	Samuel Rogers	486
Description of the East Coast of Scotland	Francis Douglas	446
A Miscellany of Rhimes	unsigned	419
Dissertation on the Foederal Transactions...	John Muirhead	395
The History of the Shire of Renfrew	George Crawfurd	373
Afalau aur i bobl ifeingc	Thomas Brooks	348
Fourteen Sermons on Various Subjects	Robert Hood	296
Flora's Banquet: A Collection of Poems	John Tisdall	261
A Portable Military Library	Thomas Simes	254
Remarks on Mr. Rousseau's Emilius	unsigned	237
An Entrance into the Sacred Language...	Cornelius Bayley	202
Ethics, Rational and Theological	John Grose	190
Select Sermons of the Late Reverend...	Matthew Henry	165
Mathematical Principles	Sisson Darling	158
L'ami des Enfans	Arnaud Berquin	157
The Doctrine of Eclipses	Blyth Hancock	154
The Elements of Military Arrangement	John Williamson	153
History of the Old and New Testament	Nicolas Fontaine	145
Omar and Zemira: An Eastern Tale	James Yeo	138
The Miscellaneous Works	Gorges Howard	112
The Extraordinary Life of...	Margaret Davidson	102
The First Book of Fontenoi: A Poem	Thomas Stratford	69

0   100   200   300   400   500   600   700   800   900   1000   1100   1200
Total subscribers listed

Figure 5.1   Subscriber counts for thirty-five works published in Britain in 1782 known to have subscriber lists, including Sancho's *Letters*.

The list for Sancho's *Letters* likely made an impression for its length not only because of the number of names, but also due to the number of pages they took up. Figure 5.2 illustrates this distinction.

Among Sancho's 1782 peers, Howie and Smith both use two columns to list their subscribers and tightly compress the lines of text, taking up less than fifteen pages. Two of the next longest lists in terms of names – Watson's 712 names and Walpoole's 686 – are compressed even further into 3 columns, resulting in only 4 pages each. By contrast, Sancho's subscriber list appears as a single column, with the same size of type as the rest of the book. With so many names, the result is a list nearly *twice* as long as the next-longest subscriber list by pages. In Sancho's *Letters*, the subscriber list functions not simply as the expected record of names, but

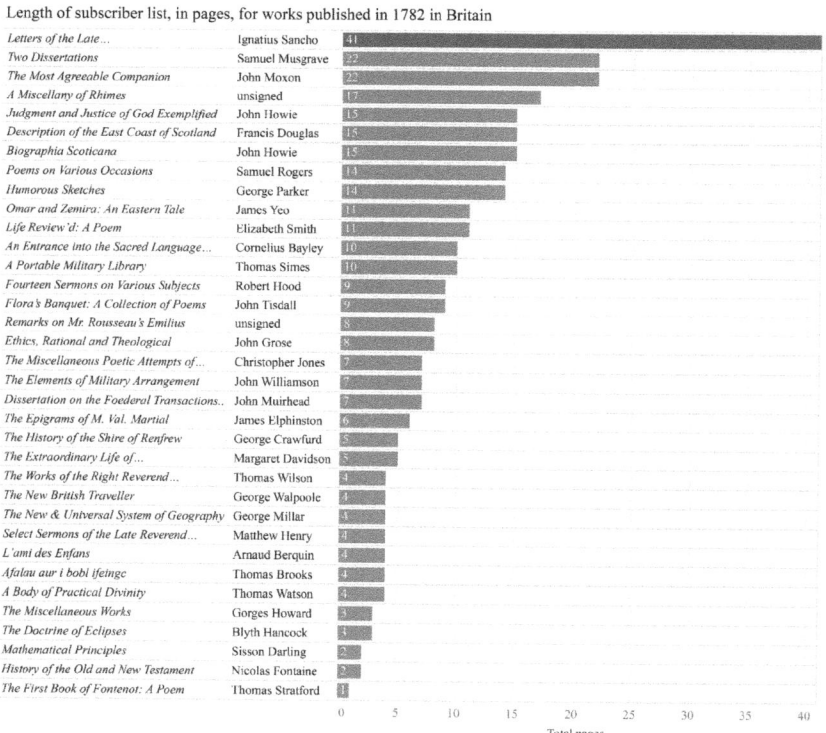

Figure 5.2   Page counts for thirty-five works published in Britain in 1782 known to have subscriber lists, including Sancho's *Letters*.

also as a bold insistence, placed at the front of the volume, of the importance and number of the people who contributed to it financially.

Figures 5.1 and 5.2 contextualize Sancho's subscription list by his year of publication. Sancho is also frequently compared to two other Black Britons who published by subscription in the eighteenth century, Olaudah Equiano (1745–97) and Ottobah Cugoano (1757–91). Equiano was kidnapped from Africa and then enslaved. Though he operated as a slave trader for several years after he was manumitted, he eventually became an ardent abolitionist and published his autobiography, *The Interesting Narrative of the Life of Olaudah Equiano, or Gustavus Vassa, the African*, in 1789. Equiano's *Interesting Narrative* was published by subscription, and was a sufficient financial success that he printed a total of nine editions during his lifetime. In the following comparisons, I will address only his first edition, though later editions added new subscribers. Cugoano, also formerly enslaved, was also a political activist; he worked as a house servant for two artists, Richard (1742–1821) and Maria Cosway (1760–1838) in London. His major publication, *Thoughts and Sentiments on the Evil and Wicked Traffic of the Slavery and Commerce of the Human Species*, appeared in three forms, of which only one was published with a subscriber list. In 1787, he published a 148-page version of *Thoughts and Sentiments* as well as a 4-page pamphlet that was a summary of the longer version. In 1788, a French translation was published in Paris. In 1791, he published a shorter, revised, version with a slightly different title, *Thoughts and Sentiments on the Evil of Slavery; Or, the Nature of Servitude as Admitted by the Law of God, Compared to the Modern Slavery of the Africans*. This 54-page work concludes with a list of subscribers. It also requests financial contributions for a school and suggests that if the book sells well, it might be followed by another full edition of *Thoughts and Sentiments*, though no such edition follows. Although Sancho's *Letters* are often compared to Equiano's *Interesting Narrative* and Cugoano's *Thoughts and Sentiments* in terms of abolitionist content, the three works substantially differ in their subscriber lists. Most obvious is the relative scale of those lists: for Sancho's *Letters*, as mentioned, 1,181 names are listed across 41 pages; Cugoano in 1791 lists only 165 (across 6 pages), and Equiano's first edition in 1789 lists 311 (across 9 pages), increasing to 895 (across 17 pages) in 1794 for the ninth edition.

Sheer numbers are not the only way for a subscriber list to be exceptional. Key to the organizational logic of Sancho's subscriber list is an emphasis on his subscribers' social ranks. Subscription lists could be organized in a variety of ways: alphabetically, by location, even by the order in which names were received. In Sancho's list, names are grouped by first letter of the last name, so that the list itself begins with the 'A' names, but within each letter they are not alphabetized. Instead, each letter section begins with the subscriber of the highest rank, and the list proceeds carefully in order of social hierarchy. The titles accompanying his subscribers' names therefore allow for a numerical comparison of the broad social categories from which his subscribers are drawn (Figure 5.3). In the simplified classification used here, "Aristocratic" titles include any named rank of baronet and above; "Esq." is as listed; "professional" titles include religious titles like "Reverend," scholarly post-nominals like "M.A.," and military titles like "captain." "No title" indicates a name listed only with the honorific of "Mr.," "Mrs.," or "Miss." Sancho's subscriber list is often admired for the great range of social backgrounds represented, so the following section will consider those broad categories in more detail.

To begin with the most "elevated" titles: 169 of the subscribers to Sancho's *Letters* appear with a title identifying them as a member of the aristocracy or gentry. Equiano's later subscription list is often highlighted for the illustriousness of its names, since he specifically targeted public figures as supporters.[6] Although Sancho did not gain the interest of the Prince of Wales or Duke of York (both of whom subscribed to Equiano's book), in terms of sheer quantity, Sancho's titled subscribers outnumber those of Equiano's first edition – indeed, Sancho lists more aristocrats than many books (including Cugoano's) have subscribers in total. Proportionally, too, Sancho's list demonstrates a striking aristocratic involvement: aristocratic titles make up 14.3% of his list, compared with 13.2% of Equiano's first edition and only 2.4% of Cugoano's. A further 193 names on Sancho's list are followed by the honorific "esquire," which could be used professionally by barristers and as a courtesy title for those with minor connections to the nobility, such as the eldest son of a knight or the eldest son of the younger son of a peer. At 16.3% of the names, "esquires" form the largest group of titles (other than "no title").

Another substantial number of subscribers are listed with non-hereditary titles such as degrees or military ranks. Eighty-two subscribers or 7% have religious titles, primarily "Rev." for "Reverend." Two of Sancho's subscribers with religious affiliations are in fact bishops: "Right Rev. Lord Bishop of Chester" and "Right Rev. Lord Bishop of Rochester." Some of Sancho's religiously titled subscribers specify that they are also a "Dr." or hold a D.D. (Doctor of Divinity) or M.A. degree (Master of Arts). Less common are military titles: Sancho's subscribers include eight captains, two admirals, two lieutenants, and one each of major, colonel, major general, and general, for a total of sixteen military or 1.4%. A further

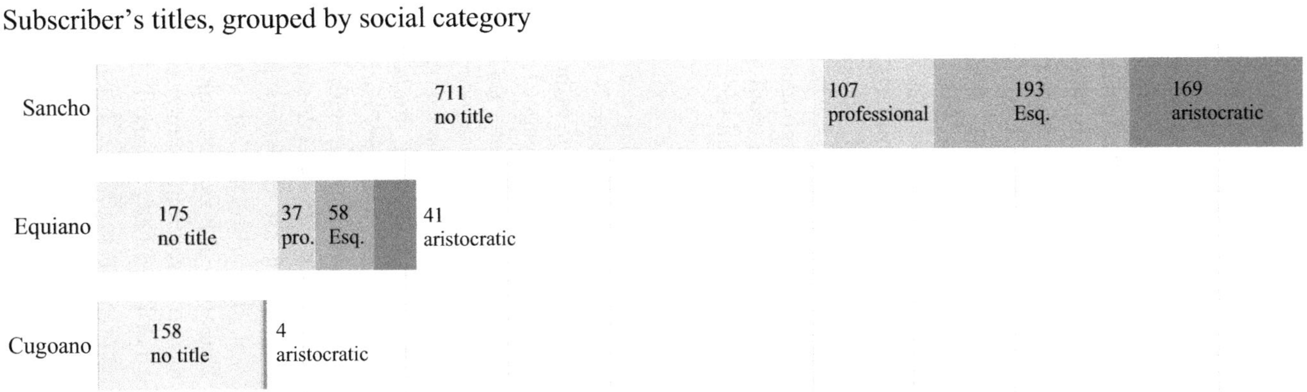

Subscriber's titles, grouped by social category

Sancho

711
no title

107
professional

193
Esq.

169
aristocratic

Equiano

175
no title

37
pro.

58
Esq.

41
aristocratic

Cugoano

158
no title

4
aristocratic

Figure 5.3 Subscribers to Sancho's *Letters* (1782), Equiano's *Interesting Narrative* (1789), and Cugoano's *Thoughts and Sentiments* (1791), categorized on the basis of their listed titles or post-nominals.

nine subscribers have scholarly degrees without religious affiliations: six "Dr." and three "M.D.," or 0.8%. Together, these "professional" titles consist of 107 names, or 9% of the list.

The majority of Sancho's subscribers, however, list only the non-honorific title of "Mr.," "Mrs.," or "Miss": 711 or 60% fall in this category. Because Sancho's list does not include clarifying details like occupations or addresses, it is harder to confidently identify the persons behind these names. There is only one "Earl of Ashburnham" at a time, for example, but there could be many people known as "Mr. Green." It is not impossible, however, to surmise that Sancho's "Mr. Green" might have been the same person who subscribed to Cugoano as "Mr. Green, Wood-street, Cheapside," potentially William Green, a Black Briton who joined Cugoano in abolitionist activism in 1786. Similarly, "Mr. R. Rush" could be Roger Rush, a clerk and a servant of Sir Charles Bunbury, and "Mr. Kisbee" is likely James Kisbee, a servant in the Montagus' household, both of whom were among Sancho's correspondents. The many "ordin-ary" names among Sancho's subscribers are often seen as evidence of his ability to make social bridges between the full spectrum of society's social ranks.

Most noteworthy in Sancho's list is the high proportion of female subscribers. Sancho's subscriber list includes 329 women, indicated by gendered titles like "Countess," "Lady," "Miss," and "Mrs." At 28% of the list, this is a much higher percentage of women than the 12% who subscribed to Equiano and the 4% for Cugoano. It is more similar to the proportions seen on works written by women, such as the 25% of Anne Francis's *Poetical Translation of the Song of Solomon* (1781) and 22% of *The Poetical Works of Janet Little, the Scotch Milkmaid* (1792). On Sancho's list, many women subscribed alongside their husbands, such as "Lord Grantham" with "Lady Grantham," and the "Earl of Spencer" with the "Countess of Spencer." Some women appear with other relatives, such as "Lady Abdy" and "Mrs. Abdy" or "Dowager Viscountess Midleton" and "Viscountess Midleton." Women are especially prominent among the aristocratic subscribers: of the aristocrats on Sancho's list, 50% are women. By contrast, Equiano's aristocratic subscribers are only 19% women, and Cugoano has no aristocratic women subscribing alone, only the couple "Right Hon. Lord and Lady Barnard" listed together on one line. Of the "title-less" names (that is, "Mr.," "Miss," and "Mrs."), 35% of Sancho's are female, contrasted with 17% for Equiano and 4% for Cugoano. At the time, women could not hold the title of esquire, or any of the professional titles. The large number of female names on Sancho's list might reflect Francis Crewe's own social network. Crewe was generally an involved and selective editor of Sancho, and it is possible that she might have had more personal connections to, for example, the Duchess of Gloucester (who subscribed) than to the Duke of Gloucester (who didn't).

Interpreting Subscribers' Relationships

The relationship of a subscriber to a book is not obvious or simple. An illustration of some of the practical and social dimensions of subscribing to a book can be seen in a letter written to Sancho by Laurence Sterne (1713–68). Sterne was the author of the widely beloved novel *The Life and Opinions of Tristram Shandy, Gentleman* (1759–67). Sterne writes:

> I was very sorry, my good Sancho, that I was not at home to return my compliments by you for the great courtesy of the Duke of M[onta]g's family to me, in honouring my list of subscribers with their names – for which I bear them all thanks. – But you have something to add, Sancho, to what I owe your good will also on this account, and that is to send me the subscription money, which I find a necessity of dun[n]ing my best friends for before I leave town [. . .] and so, good Sancho dun the Duke of M[ontagu] the Duchess of M[ontagu] and Lord M[onthermer] for their subscriptions, and lay the sin, and money with it too, at my door – I wish so good a family every blessing they merit, along with my humblest compliments. You know, Sancho, that I am your friend and well-wisher, L. Sterne.[7]

Sterne writes after having missed a visit from Sancho. If Sterne had been home, he says, he would have had Sancho convey Sterne's thanks to Sancho's patrons, the Montagus, who had agreed to subscribe to *Tristram Shandy*. First published in installments from 1759 to 1767, the novel was reprinted several times; the 1768 reprint about which Sterne is writing here was the first to which the Montagus subscribed. At the time of the letter, Sterne has received authorization to include their names but had not received their promised funds.

Though Sterne makes light of the crassness of "dunning" (pestering) his friends for money, he is also resolutely doing so. In 1767, Sancho still worked as a valet to George Montagu (1712–90), who had been created Duke of Montagu (second creation) the previous year. His wife, Mary (1711/12–75), Duchess of Montagu, was the daughter of John Montagu (1690–1749), the 2nd Duke of Montagu (first creation), Sancho's first patron in the Montagu family. As Crispin Powell explains in Chapter 4 of this volume, George Brudenell, the Earl of Cardigan, took his wife's last name and inherited the Montagu estates in 1749 when John Montagu died, but George was not given the title until 1766, just before this letter. The Lord Monthermer (1735–70) that Sterne refers to was George and Mary's son. In other words, Sterne is asking Sancho to submit Sterne's request to his employer's entire family. Their names bring honor to Sterne's subscribers list through their elevated titles, and their finances do a concrete service to him as an author. The same tension between social ties and money underlies Sancho's subscriber list.

In general, one straightforward reason to subscribe to a book would be the desire to read it, though this may have motivated a surprisingly small number of subscribers. (Indeed, many may not even have completed their purchase of the book.) Instead, subscribers might have added their names under various forms of social pressure. Those who are public figures might have felt the demand of patronage; those who wished to gain public standing might have wished to place their names alongside the already illustrious. Personal acquaintances might have felt obligated to show kindness to a friend's personal project, or consider their subscription a charitable donation. In the case of a book like Sancho's, which has political as well as artistic implications, those with strong views might have found themselves using the subscriber list as a place to show their alignment. None of these motivations would be spelled out alongside the name, but tracing the underlying personal connections could suggest one or another. In the following sections, I will consider how some of Sancho's subscribers might have been motivated by issues of patronage and clout, friendship and philanthropy, as well as abolitionist politics.

Patronage and Clout

For many of the aristocratic names on the list, a key motivation to subscribe might have been to discharge the duties of patronage. For example, the most prolific patrons in 1782 were the Earl and Countess of Carlisle, who subscribed to at least five books in 1782, including Sancho's. This earl was the Fifth Earl of Carlisle, Frederick Howard (1748–1825). After a somewhat dissipated, aristocratic youth (in which he published some poetry), he married Lady Margaret Caroline Leveson-Gower (1753–1824), whose politically powerful father connected him to the cabinet. In 1780, Carlisle was made Lord Lieutenant of Ireland, a position of colonial power sometimes informally called viceroy. The earl and countess were likely approached by many aspiring authors, and may have considered it part of their obligations as political figureheads to publicly support literary works.

Since aristocrats might subscribe to uphold their social status, others might follow suit in order to join their company. An illuminating example can be found in one of the books published by subscription in the same year as Sancho's: James Yeo's *Omar and Zemira: An Eastern Tale* (1782), which garnered 138 names for its subscriber list, roughly a tenth of Sancho's. After the tale, Yeo (1752–1825) presents his list of names with the same formalities as Sancho's, grouped by letter and listed only as a title and last name, sorted by rank. This list is followed by an essay titled "To the Reader," which expresses many of the stock sentiments with which an author might frame their work in the period. Yeo's essay is particularly illustrative of the cliches of authorial modesty:

> When Mr. Yeo looks on the long list of respectable names which ornament and do honour to the tale of OMAR and ZEMIRA, and especially the names of Admiral RODDAM and Mrs. RODDAM, for whose singular bounty and benevolence towards him, he feels it impossible to express himself sufficiently grateful, he should be overcome with shame and confusion, were he not persuaded that the principal part of them subscribed from motives of a much HIGHER NATURE than the expectation of entertainment or information; and as such he ceases to be uneasy in suspecting they will be in the least disappointed; for he is assured that their philanthropy has solely induced them to promote the present publication, and HIS HAPPINESS.[8]

The relationship of subscriber to book is here presented as one where the book is subordinate: subscriptions "ornament" the book, and the names themselves "do honour" to its contents. The author is in a position of ostentatious humility. As a point of comparison, Equiano's preface to the first edition of his *Interesting Narrative* begins with "Permit me with the greatest deference and respect, to lay at your feet the following genuine Narrative," and later comments "I am sensible I ought to entreat your pardon for addressing to you a work, so wholly devoid of literary merit" (pp. iii–iv). Yeo's praise of his patrons and subscribers carries the same intensity as Equiano's preface, which was addressed to "the Lords Spiritual and Temporal, and the Commons of the Parliament of Great Britain," as though the Roddams would inspire the same immediate recognition of their status. Indeed, just as Equiano placed the names "His Royal Highness the Prince of Wales" and "His Royal Highness the Duke of York" at the top of the list of subscribers, before the "A" section, so too does Yeo place "Admiral RODDAM" and "Mrs. RODDAM" physically above all other subscribers' names on the page. Both books illustrate the literary conventions of praise and flattery by which an author addresses their subscribers.

Yeo obviously singles out the Roddams in his rhetoric, but some level of flattery would accrue to all subscribers. When these kinds of notes of gratitude are published, the entire list is thanked as one group, a rhetorical move which turns the list into evidence of the respectability and importance of every individual subscriber. We can imagine quite ordinary people eagerly hunting in these lists for their own names and for the names of important members of their community. For those who wish to rise in the world, or even just those who wish to rise in their own esteem, belonging to the same list – and receiving the same thanks – as a figure of established importance may allow them to gain some transitive glamor and clout.

Friendship and Philanthropy

The example of Yeo's humbler subscription list also highlights a potential motivation for subscription that is more personal than those of patronage or status: friendship. Yeo's emphasis on his subscribers' benevolence directs its attention away from the crasser matters of money that Sterne's letter to Sancho had to bring up so apologetically. Here, money is implied only through the implication that their "bounty" and "philanthropy" were necessary in order to bring the book itself into being. Yeo suggests that the aim of his subscribers' philanthropy is simply to promote his personal happiness; in Sancho's case, the call of philanthropy was much stronger, since the book was explicitly presented as a means of additional financial support for Sancho's surviving family. As discussed by Montaz Marché in Chapter 2 in this volume, his widow had some income from assuming ownership of his store, but the immediate influx of subscription money would have been a welcome buffer during a time of grief and change while raising four children between the ages of four and twenty-one. Many of Sancho's subscribers might have been motivated by philanthropy or friendship, especially those who knew him personally. For example, many names in Sancho's subscribers list can be recognized as correspondents or friends, including "Mrs. Cocksedge," "Mr. G. Cumberland," "Miss L. Leach," "Mr. J. Meheux," "William Norford, M.D.," "John Spink, Esq.," "Rev. Mr. Stevenson," "Mr. William Stevenson," and "Mr. Wingrave." As a further example of how subscriptions reflect personal connections, many of these names are found in familial groupings: the Stevensons are followed by "Mr. S. E. Stevenson" and "Miss Stevenson," and Spink is followed by "Mrs. Spink" and "Miss Spink."

Similarly, Thomas Lord appears to be on the subscriber list because of these ties of personal friendship. On 24 July 1781, he wrote to Sir Martin Holkes and described the solicitation he received for his subscription: "Miss Crew[e] lately dind [*sic*] here, she patronizes Ignatius Sancho's family, a widow, & three children, one a cripple, Mr. Holkes answered for one of them, Miss Crew[e] hath received already near one hundred pounds by subscription for his Letters, knowing Sancho I threw in my mise."[9] Sancho's case is presented as one which might appeal to anyone's pity ("a widow, & three children, one a cripple" – though Lord has the wrong count of children), but Lord's own motivation for throwing in his "mise" (his monetary support) is the personal one of "knowing Sancho." The "Mr. Lord" on Sancho's subscriber list is surely this Thomas Lord. Intriguingly, however, no "Mr. Holkes" or "Sir Martin Holkes" appears on the list, despite the evidence that they knew Crewe was collecting subscriptions, and felt warmly enough toward Sancho to provide some direct support. Holkes may have "answered for" one of Sancho's children by providing a job or an apprenticeship, a greater commitment than purchasing a book, and may have considered his charitable duties fully discharged by doing so. As such, the Holkes' absence indicates that the book was just one part of a broader network of patronage and financial support.[10]

The association of Sancho's book with philanthropy may also have contributed to its large number of female subscribers. The late eighteenth century saw a rise in charitable fund-raising as an acceptable reason for women to engage publicly with stereotypically masculine business activities while maintaining a genteel feminine reputation. For example, the prominent social reformer Hannah More (1745–1833) raised subscriptions for charitable works and moral publications, building a public persona that traded on stereotypes of feminine domesticity.[11] In the early nineteenth century, female philanthropists (including More) became particularly associated with abolitionism. Poetry about slavery became a common theme by which early nineteenth-century white women writers expressed proto-feminist politics; the suffering of enslaved persons was seen as a "natural" subject to inspire women's sympathy.[12] By 1832, there were nearly twice as many women's anti-slavery groups as men's, with at least seventy-three active groups between 1825 and 1833.[13] Crewe might have experienced the beginnings of these changing social mores in the 1780s as she visited and wrote to her and the Sanchos' acquaintances, organized advertisements and biographers, and managed the business of publication.

Abolitionist Politics

In addition to the philanthropic aim of supporting this particular Black British family, a subscriber could have been motivated by a broader sentiment against slavery. Equiano's later cultivation of abolitionist literary celebrity certainly invited subscribers to see their book purchases as a moral and political statement. As scholars have suggested, "by investing financially in Equiano through the purchase of his book, readers could also perform their own 'humanity,' proclaiming to the world their emotional and moral sensitivity and their commitment to freedom and equality."[14] And after publication, Sancho's *Letters* were often discussed and circulated in abolitionist debates. But prior to the book's publication, and before the 1787 establishment of the first anti-slavery society (the Society for the Mitigation and Gradual Abolition of Slavery throughout the British Dominions), how large a role did abolitionist campaigning play?

One member of Sancho's subscriber list who is easily linked to abolitionist activism is the "Right Rev. Lord Bishop of Chester," Beilby Porteus. Porteus delivered a well-known abolitionist sermon the year after the publication of Sancho's *Letters*: his 1783 *Anniversary Sermon of the Society for the Propagation of the Gospel in Foreign Parts* criticized the Church of England's complicity with slavery. The "Right Honourable Charles James Fox" (1749–1806), too, would become a prominent abolitionist.

Also notable, however, is the number of abolitionists who do *not* appear on Sancho's list, in part because this "burgeoning" movement (as it is often described during this time) had not yet burgeoned enough to include the figures with which it would later become most prominently associated. Thomas Clarkson (1760–1846), for example, who did not subscribe, wrote about Sancho's *Letters* four years later in *An Essay on the Slavery and Commerce of the Human Species* (1786). William Wilberforce (1759–1833), similarly, does not appear on Sancho's list, and did not begin his anti-slavery activism until 1787. Clarkson did subscribe to Equiano's book in 1789, as did the abolitionist playwright Thomas Bellamy (1745–1800) and the aforementioned Hannah More, though not William Wilberforce. None subscribed to Cugoano's book in 1791.

The intermittent appearance of abolitionists on Sancho's subscription list might indicate that, in 1782, a book by "an African" was not yet fully politicized as a statement about slavery itself. Even an active abolitionist might not have considered subscribing to Sancho's book an obligation of his political activism: the abolitionist lawyer Granville Sharp does not appear on Sancho's list, even though he began advocating against slavery in 1767, and did subscribe to Equiano's book in 1789. In fact, some subscribers might have been on the "other" side (as it were) of slavery activism. Here, "Sir Charles Bunbury, Bart." on Sancho's list is the most striking example.

Sir Thomas Charles Bunbury (1740–1821), the sixth baronet – more commonly known as simply Charles Bunbury – is best known for his horse racing. Unlike some other subscribers, Bunbury did not have a literary reputation to motivate his connection to the book. Instead, he had prior ties to Sancho: the Bunburys were neighbors twice over, with their London house near the Montagus in Privy Gardens in Westminster and their country house near Sancho's in-laws the Osbornes in Bury. Bunbury was also connected to Sancho's correspondents Frances Crewe and Margaret Cocksedge, the latter of whom he would eventually marry.[15] In August 1775, Sancho wrote to Bunbury's steward, Charles Browne, to give a letter of reference for an unnamed Black servant.[16] This steward might be one of the two "Mr. Browns" (without the e) on Sancho's subscriber list, or, if he had undergone a change of career, he could be "Rev. Charles Browne."

At the same time that he had a seemingly close relationship with the Sanchos, Bunbury also owned estates in Grenada and Dominica, worked by enslaved laborers. He appears to have been a largely absentee landlord, but in the same year that he subscribed to Sancho's letters, Bunbury subscribed his name to a very different list: he was one of 265 West Indian estate-owners who urged the king to send military reinforcements to reclaim property captured by the United States during the ongoing American Revolutionary War.[17] Much of this "property" would consist not only of the physical plantations, but also of the enslaved workers. After 1784, Bunbury's political interests changed, and he eventually supported the abolition of slavery. Nevertheless, he never divested from slavery, and at his death in 1821, he still held estates in Grenada. Overall, then, Bunbury's name on Sancho's list of subscribers seems to reflect how patronage of a Black author could be treated as a separate matter from the political status of slavery as an institution.

Conclusion

I have argued, in part, that Sancho's subscriber list shows him as much more closely tied to the sentimental literary milieu of Sterne than to the soon-to-emerge abolitionist movement. In many ways, however, the 1,181 names on Sancho's subscriber list represent 1,181 different relationships to the man and his words. The stock rhetorical conventions around subscriptions emphasize that subscribers lend importance to a work as well as demonstrate generosity. The actual practice of collecting subscriptions might turn more on the conversion of social capital into monetary capital, as personal relationships are exploited, and favors are called in. Sancho's subscriber list is an unusual one, both for its length and for the number of women's names on it. The list captures a particular moment in Britain's history of nation, race relations, and slavery, and also captures the deeply personal and individual network of relationships by which Sancho's family was supported after his untimely death. Like the letters themselves, the proudly displayed subscribers' names offer slim but exciting documentary traces of the full complexity of Sancho's life.

Notes

1. Rezek, J., "The print Atlantic: Phillis Wheatley, Ignatius Sancho, and the cultural significance of the book," in Langer Cohen, L. and Stein, J. A. (eds.), *Early African American Print Culture* (Philadelphia, PA: University of Pennsylvania Press, 2012), 19–39.
2. Hanley, R., *Beyond Slavery and Abolition: Black British Writing, c. 1770–1830* (Cambridge: Cambridge University Press, 2018), 50.
3. Lockwood, T., "Subscription-hunters and their prey," *Studies in the Literary Imagination* 34 (2001), 123–4.
4. Moffatt, K., "A search for firm evidence: Uncovering Ann Sancho, bookseller," The Women's Print History Project, 25 June 2020, https://womensprinthistoryproject.com/blog/post/20.
5. Carey, B., "'The hellish means of killing and kidnapping': Ignatius Sancho and the campaign against the 'abominable traffic for slaves,'" in Carey, B., Ellis, M., and Salih, S. (eds.), *Discourses of Slave Abolition: Britain and Its Colonies, 1760–1838* (London: Palgrave Macmillan, 2004), 81–95.
6. Hanley, R., "Olaudah Equiano, celebrity abolitionist," in Hanley, R., *Beyond Slavery and Abolition: Black British Writing, c. 1770–1830* (Cambridge: Cambridge University Press, 2018), 51–75.
7. "Letter LXXXVI. To Ignatius Sancho," *Letters of the Late Rev. Mr. Laurence Sterne, To His Most Intimate Friends*, Vol. III (London: T. Becket, 1775), 32–3.
8. Yeo, J., *Omar and Zemira: An Eastern Tale*, 2 vols. (London: H. Goldney, 1782), Vol. I, 170–1.
9. Hanley, *Beyond Slavery and Abolition*, 37.
10. Ibid., 38
11. Elliott, D. W., *The Angel out of the House: Philanthropy and Gender in Nineteenth-Century England* (Charlottesville, VA: University of Virginia Press, 2002).

12. Koretsky, D. P., "Chained to life and misery," in Koretsky, D. P., *Death Rights: Romantic Suicide, Race, and the Bounds of Liberalism* (New York, NY: State University of New York Press, 2021), 47–72.

13. Midgley, C., *Women against Slavery: The British Campaigns, 1780–1870* (London: Routledge, 1992), 45.

14. Hanley, *Beyond Slavery and Abolition*, 64.

15. Barker-Benfield, G. J., "'To produce remorse in every enlightened reader.' Frances Crewe's publication of Sancho's *Letters*," in Barker-Benfield, G. J., *Ignatius Sancho and the British Abolitionist Movement, 1729–1786: Manhood, Race and Sensibility* (Cham: Palgrave Macmillan, 2023), 195–230.

16. Carey, "'The hellish means,'" 87.

17. "The humble address and petition of the planters and merchants whose names are hereunto subscribed, on behalf of themselves, and others interested in the British West India Islands," *Whitehall Evening Post*, 3 January 1782.

Further Reading

Carey, B., "'The extraordinary Negro': Ignatius Sancho, Joseph Jekyll and the problem of biography," *The British Journal for Eighteenth-Century Studies* 26.1 (2008), 1–14.

Ehrlich, J., "Subscription publishing and the eighteenth-century origins of Indian print culture," *Book History* 27.1 (2024), 32–50.

Mattes, M. A., "Penman's Devil: The chirographic and typographic urgency of race in the *Letters of the Late Ignatius Sancho, an African*," *Early American Literature* 48.3 (2013), 577–612.

New, M. and Gerard, W. B. (eds.), *The Florida Edition of the Works of Laurence Sterne*, Vol. IX: *The Miscellaneous Writings and Sterne's Subscribers, an Identification List* (Miami, FL: University Press of Florida, 2014).

Olaleye, B., "Locating Sancho through Westminster: A topographical reading of *The Letters of the Late Ignatius Sancho, an African*," *Çankaya University Journal of Humanities and Social Sciences* 14.1 (2020), 112–25.

Pink, E. E., "Frances Burney's *Camilla*: 'To print my grand work . . . by subscription,'" *Eighteenth-Century Studies* 40.1 (2006), 51–68.

Raven, J., *Publishing Business in Eighteenth-Century England* (Woodbridge: Boydell Press, 2014).

CHAPTER 6

Sancho's Correspondents

Vincent Carretta

Writing in 1815, thirty-five years after Ignatius Sancho's death, his friend and correspondent William Stevenson remarked, "[Sancho] had seen more of human life, in all its varieties, from the Prince to the Beggar; and no one . . . ever made a better use than he did, of the knowledge resulting from his observations" (*Letters* 358).[1] The accuracy of Stevenson's description is attested by the economic, geographic, political, and social range of the more than 1,200 subscribers to Sancho's *Letters*. Sancho's correspondents spanned the British Empire, from India to the Caribbean and North America. One of the earliest reviewers of Sancho's *Letters* remarked that "Sancho may be styled – what is very uncommon for men of his complexion, *A man of letters*. His commerce with the Muses was supported amid the trivial and momentary interruptions of a shop" (*Letters* 347). The posthumous publication in 1775 of the *Letters* of Laurence Sterne (1713–68) established Sancho's public persona as *a man of letters* because many of the reviews of Sterne's *Letters* reprinted their correspondence. The posthumous publication of Sancho's own *Letters* in 1782 revealed him to also be *a lettered man*.

Eighteenth-century reviewers appreciated letter writers as performers whose correspondents are their immediate audiences. Authors choose roles and adapt performances for their readers because only the words and forms of their letters connect the physically separated correspondents. Sancho's interest in the theater suited him for playing the roles demanded of a writer who at appropriate times assumes the official voice of a representative of the Montagu family announcing the death of its heir, or of the humble supplicant acknowledging Daniel Braithwaite's rejection of his petition to allow him to open a post office; the voice of the sober, older sage advising the young Frances Crewe, the enterprising Jack Wingrave, the promising John Meheux, or the irresponsible Julius Soubise; the flirtatious married voice addressing the unmarried Margaret Cocksedge; the voice of the loving and affectionate father relating the joys and sorrows of family life;

the playful voice swapping literary jokes and Shandean imitations with Meheux and William Stevenson; the serious reportorial voice describing to John Spink the anti-Roman Catholic Gordon Riots in London in 1780; or the stoical voice in his later letters facing approaching death.

At the center of a Venn diagram of Sancho's social networks would be his relationship with the dukes of Montagu. Through his noble employers, Sancho gained his initial access to "commerce with the Muses," as well as to "life, in all its varieties." According to Sancho's first biographer, Joseph Jekyll, the 2nd Duke of Montagu introduced Sancho to literacy. Hardly any of what Jekyll says about Sancho's life before 1773, however, has been corroborated by other sources. In a letter to Sterne, Sancho writes, "a little Reading and writing, I got by unwearied application" (*Letters* 311). Irrespective of whether Sancho owed his education to the duke or was an autodidact, his "commerce with the Muses" grew exponentially when the duke's widow hired him as her butler. Sancho's access to Montagu's library enabled him to inform Sterne, "my chief pleasure has been books" (*Letters* 311). As the duchess's butler, Sancho hired and supervised her approximately twenty other servants. He oversaw the home's maintenance and provisions, which brought him into contact with various kinds of tradespeople. And he greeted and accommodated his employer's guests.

Although Sancho may have remained in the Montagu household after the duchess died in 1751, Jekyll claims that following her death, Sancho squandered the legacy she left him on gambling, women, and the theater, spending his last shilling to see David Garrick play Richard III. According to Jekyll, "a defective and incorrigible articulation" frustrated Sancho's own theatrical ambitions (*Letters* 50). The reviewer of Sancho's *Letters* in the September 1782 issue of *The Gentleman's Magazine* wishes "that honest Sancho had not followed [Sterne] in his blanks or dashes" (*Letters* 344). If Sancho did have a speech impediment, and if it was a stutter, or stammer, his "blanks or dashes" – which conservative grammarians deemed unorthodox – may not simply imitate Sterne's punctuation but might also reflect Sancho's own cadence.

Sancho initiated his correspondence with Sterne on 21 July 1766 (Frances Crewe, the editor of Sancho's *Letters*, inexplicably misdates this letter "July 1776"). He imitated the distinctive writing style of the clergyman author of the extremely popular multi-volume comic novel *The Life and Opinions of Tristram Shandy, Gentleman* (London, 1759–67). Apologizing to Sterne "for the Liberty of this address – *unknowing* and *unknown*" from "one of those people whom the illiberal and vulgar call a Nee-gur," Sancho entreated him to address "the distresses of my poor moorish [*sic*] brethren" (*Letters* 311). Sterne responded that he wanted to include "a tender tale of the sorrows of a friendless poor negro-girl" in the next installment of *Tristram Shandy*, which he did (*Letters* 312). By 30 June 1767, Sancho is Sterne's "good friend" (*Letters* 315) and "honest friend Sancho" (*Letters* 316). In the course of the year-long correspondence, Sterne asks "my good Sancho" on 16 May 1767, to "dun" (*Letters* 314) the Duke and Duchess of Montagu, as well as their son, for their subscriptions to his *A Sentimental Journey through France and Italy* (1768). The duke and duchess, as well as several of their Scottish relatives, also subscribed both to Sterne's posthumously published *Sermons* in 1769 and to Sancho's *Letters* in 1782.

Sancho was clearly well placed to lobby the Montagu family on Sterne's behalf. Sancho was employed by George Brudenell, whom George III made the Duke of Montagu of the second creation in November 1766. The new duke was the son-in-law of the late 2nd Duke and Duchess of Montagu. Sancho had been the new duke's valet since at least January 1761, when Montagu paid the christening fee for Sancho's daughter Frances (Fanny) Joanna (1761–1815). As Montagu's valet, the preeminent servant in an aristocratic household, Sancho normally attended the duke at his dozens of residences in England and Scotland, as well as in public. Montagu was appointed to the Privy Council in 1776. His position as governor and captain of Windsor Castle since 1752, as well as his appointment in 1776 as governor of the Prince of Wales and the Duke of York, gave Sancho access to the royal family. Montagu was a member of the Royal Society since 1749, and of the Society for the Encouragement of Arts, Manufactures, and Commerce since the 1760s. These societies' members, who ranged from aristocrats to artisans, included several of Sancho's correspondents, as well as other people he mentions in his letters. Sancho's public duties as Montagu's valet familiarized him with the spectrum of society, from shopkeepers to the royal family – "human life, in all its varieties" (*Letters* 358).

Sancho's 21 April 1770, letter to Edward Young, Esq., written in response to Young's expression of condolences to Montagu over the recent death of his heir, demonstrates that Sancho also acted as the spokesperson for the Montagu family (*Letters* 87). Sancho's correspondent may have been the Edward Young, Esq. whose house was in Palace-yard, Westminster[2] or perhaps the Edward Younge, Esq. who was "waggoner to his Majesty."[3]

Most of Sancho's earliest surviving correspondence is with fellow servants of the Montagu households and aristocrats. For example, the recipient of Sancho's 20 October 1769 and 16 July 1770, letters was James Kisbee, or Kisby, probably the Mr. Kisbee listed among the subscribers to *Letters* (*Letters* 64). One of Kisbee's duties in the Montagu household was as its confectioner, a maker of fruit preserves. At the time of the first letter, Sancho remained at the Montagu villa in Richmond while Kisbee accompanied Elizabeth, the daughter of the Duke and Duchess of Montagu, to Dalkeith House, the ancestral home in Scotland of the Buccleuch family. By the second letter, Sancho and Kisbee have traded places. Sancho writes to Kisbee in Richmond from Dalkeith, where he has been sent to accompany Elizabeth back to England (*Letters* 89). The Mr. Simon to whom Sancho writes from Dalkeith on 15 September 1770, may have a been a servant in Sir (Thomas) Charles Bunbury's household, and the Mrs. H to whom Sancho writes from Richmond on 22 December 1771 may have been the Mrs. Howard mentioned in the Montagu account records (*Letters* 94).

One of Sancho's correspondents whose identity can most fully be reconstructed was employed by the Duke of Montagu's aristocratic peers, the Duke and Duchess of Queensberry. The duke's cousin, a captain in the Royal Navy, brought an enslaved child from the Caribbean island of St. Kitts to England in 1764, and gave the approximately ten-year-old boy as a "gift" to the sixty-four-year-old duchess. Though the child's fellow servants referred to him as "the young Othello," the duchess named him Julius Soubise (1754?–98). The boy quickly gained her favor, and she manumitted him.

Sancho was one of many observers who expressed concern that the duchess encouraged Soubise to conduct himself above his station. The duchess's patronage enabled young Soubise to become an amateur violinist, composer, singer, sonneteer, and actor. The duchess's generosity quickly led to accusations of a scandalous relationship between the elderly aristocrat and her much younger servant. William Austin depicted the alleged relationship in an untitled caricature print in 1773. Sancho's avuncular letters to Soubise, which began before October 1772, were unsuccessful attempts to guide his young protégé to avoid repeating the mistakes of Sancho's own youth. On 8 November 1772, Sancho wrote to John Meheux, another young protégé: "When you see S[oubise], note his behaviour – he writes me word that he intends a thorough and speedy reformation; – I rather doubt him, but should be glad to know if you perceive any marks of it. –" (*Letters* 100–2).

Ignoring Sancho's advice, Soubise ran up large debts. The duchess enabled Soubise to relocate to India, where he might repair his fortunes by teaching fencing and riding. She was also helping him avoid prosecution for rape. *The Morning Post* reported on 22 July 1777 that one of the duchess's house-maids claimed that Soubise had sexually assaulted her about two months earlier. The duchess was rumored to have tried to bribe the maid into dropping the charges. Whatever the truth behind the accusations, Soubise departed for India on 15 July 1777. The duchess died two days later. Soubise reached Madras, India, on 9 February 1778, and moved to the English settlement at Calcutta (modern-day Kolkata) in early 1780. He never returned to England.

Sancho maintained his correspondence with Soubise after his protégé left England. On 29 November 1778, Sancho encouraged Soubise to reform, reminding him of the debts he owed to creditors, who included Sancho's Black brother-in-law, John Osborne (another of Sancho's correspondents), as well as Sancho himself. Sancho admonished Soubise to study the Bible, and keep better company than he had in London, in order to be able to "return some years hence into England – with credit and reputation" (*Letters* 205). He also encouraged Soubise to befriend another of his Black correspondents, Charles Lincoln, a musician who had sailed to India on the same ship as Soubise. Writing on 14 February 1778, to John (Jack) Hanmer Wingrave, a young white protégé in India, Sancho is far more hardheaded about the likelihood of Soubise's reformation:

> If he should chance to fall in your way, do not fail to give the rattlepate what wholesome advice you can; but remember, I do strictly caution you against lending him money upon any account, for he has every thing but – principle; he will never pay you; I am sorry to say so much of one whom I have had a friendship for, but it is needful; serve him, if you can – but do not trust him. (*Letters* 75)

But, as pessimistic as Sancho was about the probability of Soubise's improvement, he never lost interest in his protégé. In a subsequent letter to Jack Wingrave, Sancho wistfully writes,

> That poor wretched young man I once warned you of is I find (from under his own hand) now resident at Calcutta: – 'tis not in the power of friendship to serve a man who will in no one instance care for himself: – so I wish you not to know him – but whatever particulars you can collaterally glean of him, I shall esteem it a favour if you would transmit them to [me]. (*Letters* 283)

By the end of 1780, Soubise had opened a manège, or riding academy, as well as a fencing school, in Calcutta.[4] Despite the promising start of Soubise's enterprise, however, it soon failed, the first of many cycles of business successes and failures. Soubise's apparent success after 1790 ended abruptly when he died on 25 August 1798, from injuries he suffered while training a horse.

When Sancho became too overweight to continue as Montagu's valet, the duke helped him establish a grocery shop in early 1774 at 19 Charles Street, next to his new residence at 20 Charles Street in Westminster. Sancho's diminished physical mobility may explain why so many of his surviving letters are to friends in the greater London area. *The Gentleman's Magazine* correctly predicted in 1776 that the publication of Sancho's correspondence with Sterne would increase business at his Westminster shop (*Letters* 333). Sancho's letter to Sterne also increased his influence. The letter revealed the breadth of Sancho's own reading, his opposition to slavery, and his involvement with publishing. Many of his subsequent letters include recommendations of specific authors and books to his male and female correspondents, as well as advice to prospective authors.

Publication of Sancho's letter to Sterne raised interest in Sancho's correspondence in general. On 20 April 1779, Edmund Rack (1735?–87), a Quaker, wrote to Sancho from Bath. Rack, who had published *Mentor's Letters, Addressed to Youth* (1777), sought Sancho's permission to include "two letters of thy writing, the one to a gentleman in the East Indies [presumably either Julius Soubise or Jack Wingrave], the other to my friend Jabez Fisher from Philadelphia ... in a collection of *Letters of Friendship*" (*Letters* 335). Jabez Maud Fisher (1750–79), another Quaker, had moved from Philadelphia to England in 1775. Sancho thanked Fisher on 27 January 1778, for having sent him books "upon the unchristian and most diabolical usage of my brother Negroes" (*Letters* 165). Phillis Wheatley's *Poems on Various Subjects, Religious and Moral* (1773) was one of those books. Fisher had visited "the celebrated Poetess Miss Phillis Wheatly [*sic*]" in Boston on 20 September 1773. She "had but just returned from England – where she had been much caress'd." She showed Fisher the manuscript "of her Poetry which is shortly to appear in Print," as well as "a Number of her Letters sensible."[5] Sancho deemed Wheatley a "Genius in bondage" (*Letters* 165, 166). Although Sancho gave Rack permission to include his correspondence, Rack's proposed *Letters of Friendship* apparently never appeared. Rack's *Essays, Letters and Poems* (1781) does not include any Sancho letters.

Several of Sancho's London correspondents were in the book trade. John Wingrave (1729–1807), a Freeman of the Dyers' Company, was primarily a bookbinder who also sold books at his shop at 10 Red Lion Court, Fleet Street, in the parish of St. Dunstan-in-the-West. He married his second wife, Mary Newman, in St. Dunstan-in-the-West on 14 February 1773. John and Mary Wingrave both subscribed to Sancho's *Letters*. Sancho also corresponded with Mary Wingrave. John Wingrave wrote and published in 1767 *A Narrative of the Many Cruelties Inflicted by Elizabeth Brownrigg upon the Body of Mary Clifford, Deceased; and for which the Said Elizabeth Received Sentence of Death, on Saturday the 12th of September 1767. Together with An account of the Sufferings of Mary Mitchell and Mary Jones*. Wingrave had been involved in the case as one of the constables in the ward of Farringdon Without.

Wingrave was a nexus between Sancho and another subset of his correspondents who were also publishers. Sancho sought Wingrave's aid on 12 March 1778 in getting his letter, signed "Africanus," to William Parker (d. 1784), editor of *The General Advertiser*. He published it the next day. Parker published another letter by Sancho, also signed "Africanus," on 29 April 1778. Parker printed *The General Advertiser* from 1778 to 1781, renaming it *Parker's General Advertiser* when he bought it in August 1781. He remained its publisher until his death on 7 May 1784. Parker also printed *Owen's Chronicle* (1778–c. 1783), *The Morning Intelligencer* (1778–84), and *The London Intelligencer* (1777–83).

Sancho tells Wingrave that he prefers "Mr. Parker's paper for many reasons" to *The Morning Post* (*Letters* 167). The editor of *The Morning Post*, Reverend Henry Bate (1745–1824), refused to publish the letter Sancho submitted to him in June 1777, signed "I S." Bate clearly appreciated the significance of his correspondent's public persona, which he apparently appropriated for his own partisan political ends. On 28 August 1778 and 29 December 1779, Bate published letters signed, respectively, "Africanus" and "Sancho" that express antisemitic and jingoistic pro-government sentiments unlike any found in Ignatius Sancho's own surviving public or private correspondence. Bate's known corruption – the government subsidized *The Morning Post* – was the subject of several satiric engravings.

The "many reasons" Sancho had for preferring Parker's newspaper over Bate's probably included Bate's personality. He was called the "Fighting Parson" because of his irascible nature. Samuel Johnson spoke to James Boswell about Bate on 12 June 1784: "Sir, I will not allow this man to have merit. No, Sir; what he has is rather the contrary; I will, indeed, allow him courage, and on this account we so far give him credit, We have more respect for a man who robs boldly on the highway, than for a fellow who jumps out of a ditch, and knocks you down behind your back."[6]

Sancho would also have been repulsed by Bate's theatrical representation of racism and xenophobia. Given Sancho's love of plays and his friendship with Garrick, he must have known that Garrick was forced to withdraw Bate's two-act comic opera *The Blackamoor Wash'd White* from production when it was hissed off the Drury Lane stage after only three performances in 1776. One can imagine Sancho's reaction to the lament that closes the first act: "O that I should ever live to see the day when White Englishmen must give place to foreign Blacks" (*Letters* 169). Bate added the surname Dudley in 1784 to comply with his uncle's will. Repeatedly accused of corruption, Bate Dudley continuously sought ecclesiastical preferment and social advancement. The Prince of Wales made him a baronet in 1812 and gave him a stall in Ely Cathedral in 1817.

Sancho found a more compatible newspaper correspondent in Henry Sampson Woodfall (1739–1805), the publisher and editor of *The Public Advertiser* from 1758 to 1793. Woodfall, a political moderate with a reputation for incorruptibility, considered his rival publisher Bate "beneath every thing but contempt."[7] Woodfall gained notoriety in 1770 when he and others were prosecuted in June for seditious libel. Woodfall had published Junius's "Letter to the King" in December 1769, one of a series of letters by the pseudonymous Junius that *The Public Advertiser* printed that year. The verdict that the accused were responsible only for having disseminated the "Letter" was received as equivalent to an acquittal. A series of further encounters with the law during the 1770s led Woodfall to later brag "that he had been *fined* by the House of Lords; *confined* by the court of the king's bench, and indicted at the Old Baily."[8] Woodfall published Sancho's letter, signed "Ignatius Sancho," on 13 May 1778 (*Letters* 174).

John (Jack) Hanmer Wingrave (1757–97), the son of John Wingrave and his first wife, Jane, was apprenticed to the bookseller Nathaniel Conant from 1772 to 1775. Rather than joining his father's business, however, he sought his fortune in India as a soldier serving the East India Company. He was promoted to lieutenant on 30 June 1783. Jack was stationed in Calcutta (Kolkata) throughout the course of his correspondence with Sancho. Sancho recommended numerous books to him. He also counseled him to avoid racial prejudice. Sancho's letters reveal that Jack left in England a brother Joseph, "Joe," and Francis Charles, "Frank," a half-brother by John Wingrave's second wife, Mary. Jack also had a married sister, Mrs. Elizabeth Collingwood, whose husband, "Mr. Collingwood," subscribed to Sancho's *Letters*. Jack Wingrave died in India in 1797.

John Ireland (d. 1808) and his wife, Mary, were other correspondents involved in the book trade. Ireland was a watchmaker who also sold prints and books from his shop at 21 Maiden Lane. Ireland's shop was probably the Maiden Lane address where the fourteen members of the Shandean Society met during the late 1760s. Sancho acquired discounted theater tickets at Ireland's shop from the celebrated actor John Henderson (1747–85), who lodged with the Irelands whenever he stayed in London before his marriage on 13 January 1779. In December 1779, Sancho encouraged Ireland "to meet a young unfledged genius of the first water" – probably George Cumberland – no doubt to help him get published (*Letters* 336). Ireland's Maiden Lane address is one of the three listed in Sancho's appeal in *The Public Advertiser* for charitable contributions to support Isaac de Groote (1694?–1779), the indigent great-grandson of the renowned Dutch jurist, theologian, and historian Hugo Grotius (1583–1645). The other addresses are de Groote's and Sancho's. Ireland was a member of a society of artists, art collectors, and amateurs that for years met at the Three Feathers Public-House, in Leicester Fields. Ireland's edition of William Hogarth's prints, *Hogarth Illustrated*,[9] was the first to mention that Sancho was said to have been the model for the Black boy in Hogarth's satirical *Taste in High Life*.

John Meheux (1751–1839), another subscriber, was a young amateur writer and artist when he became Sancho's correspondent and protégé. Meheux was born to John and Anne Meheux on 26 March 1751, and baptized at St. Mary, Woolwich, on 6 April 1751. His correspondence with Sancho reveals that Sancho helped him submit to publishers his designs for prints to be engraved or etched by others (*Letters* 149). Meheux provided the design for the print *Robin Hood & Clorinda* that William Blake engraved and published in 1783.

Sancho's relationship with Meheux is exemplified by Sancho's comments on 7 August 1777 (this letter was misdated 1768 in the *Letters*) about an exchange of letters between the pseudonymous "Linco" and "Pro Bono Publico" in the 13 and 20 June 1777 issues of *The Morning Chronicle* (*Letters* 79). Pro Bono had encouraged the prime minister, Lord North, to "make your name dear to succeeding generations . . . by reducing the number of *Blacks* among us, and, as far as possible, extirpating their disgraceful growth in a fair and beauteous land" (*The Morning Chronicle*, 3 June 1777). Pro Bono advocated castrating Black men to avoid their fathering children with white women. In his reply, Linco suggests that jealousy may motivate Pro Bono, noting that white men conversely seem to find Black women sexually attractive. Linco ends by quoting Sterne's anti-racist sentiments in his published letter to Sancho, though he omits Sancho's name, referring to him only as "one of the colour."[10] Pro Bono assumes in his counterattack that Linco is also Black. Sancho's comment that "I went to the coffeehouse to examine the file, and was greatly pleased upon the second reading of your work" reveals that Meheux was "Linco," and may imply that Sancho had read Meheux's letter in manuscript (*Letters* 79). Sancho encourages his protégé Meheux on 25 August 1777, to exercise his "talents" to "write me a bitter Philippick against the misusers of Jack-asses – it shall honor a column in the Morning Post" (*Letters* 145).

The obituary published after Meheux's death on 4 November 1839 says, "In his 90th year, John Meheux, esq. of Hans Place, formerly many years Secretary to Board of Control. He has bequeathed 5000£. to Indigent Blind School, 200£. to Deaf and Dumb Institution, and 100£. each to St George's Hospital, Westminster Lying-in Hospital, and Society of Arts, all duty free."[11] Meheux was also a governor of, as well as a subscriber to, the British Institution for Promoting the Fine Arts in the United Kingdom. And he was a subscriber to the Naval Gallery of Greenwich Hospital. Meheux financially supported Sancho's daughter Elizabeth during her impoverished old age.

Sancho's other London correspondents included local authorities, tradespeople, and relatives. The recipient of Sancho's 17 December 1779 petition to have a post office located in his grocery shop was Daniel Braithwaite (1731–1817), clerk to the Postmaster General, and eventually comptroller of the Foreign Post-Office (*Letters* 249). Although Sancho acknowledges on 30 December 1779 Braithwaite's rejection of his request, Braithwaite later helped Sancho publish a pamphlet written anonymously by a friend, *A Reply to an Appeal from the Protestant Association to the People of Great Britain* (1780). Sancho's 1 March 1780 letter to John Wingrave indicates that Wingrave also played a role in the publication of the pamphlet, which was probably authored by John Field Highmore, another young Sancho protégé. Braithwaite and Highmore subscribed to Sancho's *Letters*. Sancho's relationships with Meheux and Highmore make him the only known eighteenth-century Black patron of aspiring white artists and authors.

Two of Sancho's younger women correspondents were sisters in the millinery trade: Miss Leach and Miss Lydia Leach. Both subscribed to his *Letters*. The younger Miss Lydia Leach was the namesake of Sancho's daughter Lydia (3 July 1771–April 1776); the older Miss Leach was the godmother of his son William (Billy) Leach Osborne Sancho (20 October 1775–c. 1814). The Broadview edition of Sancho's *Letters* identifies Lydia Leach as the recipient of all the letters addressed to Miss L, but, except for the one dated 26 July 1775, most were more likely addressed to Lydia Leach's older sister. The Leach family home was in

Tunbridge, Kent, about thirty miles south-east of central London. The town was later renamed Tonbridge to distinguish it from nearby Tunbridge Wells, a popular upscale resort in the later eighteenth century. Lydia Leach opened her own millinery shop on Bond Street in the upmarket Mayfair section of London, after withdrawing from partnership in a similar establishment at a less fashionable Butcher-row address in London.[12] Sancho may have met the Leach sisters through their proximity to his brother-in-law, John Osborn, who also lived on Bond Street. Osborn and the Leach sisters certainly knew each other through their shared roles as godparents of Sancho's children.

John Osborn(e) or Osbourne (1743–90), the brother of Sancho's wife, Ann(e), was another of Sancho's Black correspondents. John and Ann(e)'s parents, John Osborn(e) (Osbourne) and Mary Clarke, married in the Church of St. Mary, Whitechapel, London, on 5 November 1732. Their three children were all christened in the same church: Ann(e) on 26 September 1733; Mary on 28 September 1735; and John on 4 December 1743. Like Sancho, John Osborne suffered from the gout. He was the godfather of Ann(e) and Ignatius Sancho's youngest child, William (Billy) Leach Osborne Sancho (born 20 October 1775; baptized 5 November 1775; buried 3 May 1810). In 1778, Sancho's brother-in-law relocated from his Bond Street address in London to Fornham All Saints, two miles north-north-west of Bury St. Edmunds in the county of Suffolk. There he sold provisions to the seven regiments of troops and cavalry stationed since March 1778 at Culford Heath camp, Cavenham. The military camp was established in response to the announcement in February 1778 of France's alliance with the rebellious American colonists in their war for independence. Although the camp broke up in late August 1778, John Osborne remained in Fornham All Saints. He had become a successful liquor merchant there by the time he died.[13] John Osborne also subscribed to Sancho's *Letters*.

John Osborn was one of the nexuses between Sancho's London and Bury St. Edmunds-area networks of correspondents. Bury was about eighty miles north-north-east from Sancho's Westminster shop. The center of Sancho's constellation of correspondents in and around Bury was the household of Sir (Thomas) Charles Bunbury, 6th Baronet (1740–1821). Bunbury was a Member of Parliament and represented Suffolk in the House of Commons (1761–84, 1790–1812). Bunbury subscribed to Sancho's *Letters*. Sancho probably knew Bunbury's servants from the time he worked for the Montagu family. Bunbury, like the duke, had a house in Privy Gardens, a wealthy residential area of Westminster bordering Whitehall Street, a block north-east of Sancho's Charles Street address. Bunbury's country estate and primary home was Barton Hall, or House, at Great Barton, about three miles north-west of Bury St. Edmunds in the county of Suffolk, between Mildenhall and Bury. Nearby was the Culford Heath military camp at Cavenham, where Osborn sold his goods.

Bunbury married Sarah Lennox in 1762, but she separated from him in 1769, admitting that William Gordon was the father of her daughter. Sir Charles received a Sentence of Divorce on the grounds of adultery from the Consistory Court of the Bishop of London on 17 June 1769. Parliament passed a private bill on 14 May 1776, dissolving the marriage, thus enabling both parties to remarry. Sarah married George Napier in 1781. The Napiers also subscribed to Sancho's *Letters*.

Bunbury's valet, Roger Rush, exchanged letters with Sancho. In the divorce proceedings of 1776 recorded in the *Journals of the House of Lords*, Rush is named as the "Servant to Sir *Charles Bunbury* [who] had lived with him Thirteen Years," and who testified on his behalf "that in February 1769 Lady *Sarah* eloped from *Great Barton*: That he has never seen her since, and believes that Sir *Charles Bunbury* has never seen her since that Time, he generally attending him, and must have known it, if Sir *Charles* had seen her."[14] Roger Rush had earlier given the same testimony in the Consistory Court. Roger Rush's position as Clerk of the Course at the Newmarket horse races was undoubtedly due to the influence of Bunbury, who was Steward of the Jockey Club. Roger Rush is probably the "R. Rush" who subscribed to Sancho's *Letters*. Rush's son John ("Johnny") corresponded with Sancho while serving as a surgeon with the British army in New York during the American Revolution. He was probably the "John Rush" listed as a subscriber. The subscriber "Mr. Richard Rush," likely either another son, or a brother, was also a medical man.

Charles Browne (1733/4–1809) was Bunbury's steward at Barton. He may have been one of the Browns who subscribed to Sancho's *Letters*. Like Roger Rush, Browne testified on Bunbury's behalf in the Consistory Court and in the House of Lords. The recipient of at least the first of Sancho's four letters addressed to Browne, in which Sancho refers to him as "my dear child," was perhaps Bunbury's steward's son, with the same name, rather than his father (*Letters* 97).

Sancho tried to use his Bury network to help another correspondent, a young multi-talented African-born protégé, Charles Lincoln. Sancho told Bunbury's valet, Roger Rush, in July 1775 that Lincoln "wishes we would enquire for a place for him – he longs to be in England; – he is an honest soul, and I should feel true pleasure in serving him; – pray remember he wants a place. −" (*Letters* 111). On 12 August 1775, Sancho recommended Lincoln to Bunbury's steward, Charles Browne:

> If I knew a better man than yourself − you wou'd not have had this application − which is in behalf of a merry − chirping − white tooth'd − clean − tight − and light little fellow; − with a woolly pate − and face as dark as your humble; − Guiney-born, and French-bred − the sulky gloom of Africa dispelled by Gallic vivacity − and that softened again with English sedateness − a rare fellow! − rides well − and can look upon a couple of horses − dresses hair in the present taste − shaves light − and understands something of the arrangement of a table and sideboard; − his present master will authenticate him a decent character − he leaves him at his own (Blacky's) request. . . . As I believe you associate chiefly with good-hearted folks − it is possible your interest may be of service to him. − I like the rogue's looks, or a similarity of colour should not have induced me to recommend him. (*Letters* 114−15)

On 26 November 1776, Sancho told William Stevenson that Lincoln hoped to begin a new career: "my friend Lincoln is in town, & intends trying his fortune amongst us − as teacher of Murder & neck-breaking − alias − fencing & Riding" (*Letters* 318). By 1777, Lincoln was a musician in a military band and bound for India on an East India Company ship. Sancho brought Lincoln to Jack Wingrave's attention on 14 February 1778: "There is in the same ship [as Soubise], belonging to the Captain's band of music, one C[harles] L[incol]n, whom I think you have seen in Privy Gardens: he is honest, trusty, good-natured, and civil; if you see him, take notice of him, and I will regard it as a kindness to me" (*Letters* 75). When Sancho writes to Lincoln for the last time, on 25 October 1780, Lincoln is serving in the militia.

The Bury network to which Sancho tried to connect Charles Lincoln extended beyond Bunbury's servants. The familiarity with which Sancho refers to Mrs. Margaret Cocksedge (1744?−1822) and Frances Crewe (or Crew) suggests that they were members of Bunbury's social circle, though not his equals. Both women subscribed to Sancho's *Letters*. In a 27 August 1777 letter to John Rush, Sancho refers to his future editor as "the little Syren Miss C[rewe]" (*Letters* 147). On 5 March 1782, Frances Crewe married John Phillips, later a surgeon in the household of the Prince of Wales, the future King George IV. "John Phillips, Esq." is listed among the subscribers to Sancho's *Letters*.

Mrs. Cocksedge may have been the paid companion or governess of the younger Miss Crewe. The honorific *Mrs.* meant that Margaret Cocksedge was either a widow or an unmarried woman no longer considered young.

Sancho's flirtatious comments on Cocksedge's looks indicate that she was quite attractive. On 14 August 1775 (apparently a misdating by Crewe of the trip she took with Cocksedge in 1777), he tells her, "I imagine I see you rise out of the waves another Venus – and could wish myself Neptune, to have the honor of escorting you to land" (*Letters* 115–16). Sancho addresses her as "MA CHERE AMIE" on 25 August 1779 (*Letters* 223). And on 9 September 1780, he asks Frances Crewe, "how does my good, my half-adored Mrs. C – ?" (*Letters* 290).

Margaret Cocksedge's relationship with Sancho and his family was so intimate that she gave him a portrait of herself painted by the fashionable artist Daniel Gardner. Sancho tells her on 31 July 1775 that her picture is now "the best ornament of my chimney piece" (*Letters* 112). Mrs. Cocksedge was the godmother of Sancho's daughter Katherine (Kitty) Margaret Sancho, who was born in October 1773 and died in March 1779. As was customary, the child's middle name was her godmother's given name.

Margaret Cocksedge married Sir (Thomas) Charles Bunbury on 21 November 1805. The former Mrs. Cocksedge was probably a poor relation of the prominent and wealthy Cocksedge family in Bury: James Oakes had dinner with Sir Charles and Lady Bunbury at the home of (Thomas?) Cocksedge on 25 November 1806. Both Oakes and Thomas Cocksedge subscribed to Sancho's *Letters*.

William Stevenson (1750–1821), originally trained as a drawing master, was living in Bury St. Edmunds while he corresponded with Sancho. Having studied under Sir Joshua Reynolds, Stevenson was a professional painter of miniatures in Bury from 1774 to 1782. He exhibited at the Royal Academy in 1777 and 1778. In 1782, he moved to Norwich, where he opened a drawing academy. He eventually became a printer, bookseller, and banker there. Stevenson and John Crouse began co-publishing *The Norfolk Chronicle* in 1785. They also co-published dozens of books on numerous subjects. Stevenson, a Fellow of the Society of Antiquaries, frequently contributed to *The Gentleman's Magazine*, edited by John Nichols, as well as to Nichols' multi-volume *Literary Anecdotes of the Eighteenth Century*. Nichols published the first three editions of Sancho's *Letters*. Elizabeth Sancho sent Stevenson the Gainsborough portrait of her father in 1819 out of gratitude for Stevenson's providing her with an annuity of five guineas during her impoverished old age.

Sancho also corresponded and traded goods with Stevenson's father, the Reverend Seth Ellis Stevenson (1723?–93), an Anglican minister. His obituary says that he died on 17 July 1793, "[a]t Retford, co[unty]

Nottingham, in his 70th year ... M.A. formerly of Peter-house, Cambridge, rector of Waddingworth, co[unty] Lincoln, 39 years, and of Tuswell, co[unty] Nottingham, 32. He was also 45 years master of the royal grammar school in East Retford ..."[15]

Sancho's correspondent John Spink (1729–94) was a draper, a maker and seller of cloth, in Buttermarket, Bury. He became a banker in partnership with John Scotchmer from about 1770 to 1775, when Scotchmer retired, leaving the bank in Spinks's hands. During the period of his friendship with Sancho, Spink was also Receiver General for the Eastern Division of the County, County Treasurer, founder of the Bury Sunday Schools, and, in 1771, elected Common Councilman of Bury Corporation. Spink married Margaret Gough in March 1778. Sancho frequently mentions Mrs. Spink in his correspondence with her husband. Spink was a wealthy and generous man, leaving at his death hundreds of pounds to religious and medical charities, as well as to individuals. Spink, his wife, and his sister, Ann, all subscribed to Sancho's *Letters*.

Sancho's last excursion from London, a few months before his death, was to Bury St. Edmunds to see his friends, relatives, and correspondents in the area. He also met and consulted a new correspondent there, Dr. William Norford (1715–93), a local physician and surgeon. Norford had published *An Essay on the General Method of Treating Cancerous Tumors* (1753) and *A Letter to Dr. Shapin in Answer to His Appeal to the Public Concerning His Medical Treatment of Mr. Ralling, Apothecary, of Bury St. Edmunds in Suffolk* (1764). He published *Concisae et Practicae Observationes de Intermittentibus Febribus Curandis* (*Concise and Practical Observations on the Curing of Intermittent Fever*) in Bury St. Edmunds in 1780, shortly before meeting Sancho. On 13 October 1780, Sancho thanks Norford for having so "much benefited my health" (*Letters* 291), and on 1 November 1780, Sancho informs John Spink that Norford was "my preserver" (*Letters* 295). Norford subscribed to Sancho's *Letters*.

Sancho wrote his last surviving letter on 7 December 1780, from London to John Spink in Bury, one week before Sancho's death. Sancho tells Spink that "Sir John E[llio]t, physician extraordinary, and ordinary to his Majesty" met with him, a consultation made possible only because of Sancho's abiding relationship with the Montagu family (*Letters* 299).

Sancho occasionally chooses to embrace his African identity fully, to enable himself rhetorically to judge the corruption of England from a seemingly more innocent point of view. For example, in a letter to John Spink dated 6 June 1780, describing the destruction of property and loss of lives during the Gordon Riots, Sancho says, "I am not sorry

I was born in Afric" (*Letters* 272). Sancho elsewhere embraces a dual identity as a Black in Britain. When Sancho criticizes British imperialism and slavery in India, Africa, and the West Indies in a 1778 letter to Jack Wingrave, he rhetorically positions himself as simply "a resident," or outsider, judging the sins of "your country" (*Letters* 188). Sancho's stance of objectivity enables him in the same letter to criticize the complicity of some Africans as well in the slave trade, though the objective voice is effectively replaced at the end of the passage by his emotional response to the subject. Sancho tells Soubise on 11 October 1772, "Happy, happy lad! what a fortune is thine! – Look round upon the miserable fate of almost all of our unfortunate colour – superadded to ignorance, – see slavery, and the contempt of those very wretches who roll in affluence from our labours superadded to this woeful catalogue – hear the ill-bred and heart-racking abuse of the foolish vulgar"(*Letters* 98). Sancho expresses a double consciousness of Soubise's personal luck and the general misfortune of Blacks, a term used during the eighteenth century to refer to all dark-skinned people, including Asians. Sancho and Soubise knew that Black Britons were arguably the freest people of their color in the world following a June 1772 decision by Lord Mansfield, Lord Chief Justice of the King's Bench, that enslaved people brought to England could not legally be forced to return to the colonies.

Several of Sancho's strongest responses to slavery, as well as accounts of his own experiences of racial prejudice, are heard indirectly, through the voices of his correspondents Stevenson and Meheux. Sancho's references to his young friend Meheux's newspaper articles show that Sancho was certainly aware of the nastiest variety of racial discrimination being discussed in print, and that he recognized the role his correspondence with Sterne played in that discussion. Meheux invokes the example of Sancho's obvious humanity in his argument against a published call for the castration of Blacks who had fathered children with white women. Stevenson tells us that although he had "often witnessed [Sancho's] patient forebearance, when the passing vulgar have given vent to their prejudices against his ebon complexion, his African features, and his corpulent person," Sancho also demonstrated "his manly resentment" in the face of such prejudice. Insulted by a young white "fashionable" man in the street shouting, "Smoke Othello!" Sancho, "immediately placing himself across the path, before him, exclaimed with a thundering voice, and a countenance which awed the delinquent, 'Aye, Sir, such Othellos you meet with but once in a century,' clapping his hand upon his goodly round paunch. 'Such Iagos as you, we meet with in every dirty passage. Proceed, Sir!'" (*Letters* 359).

Sancho frequently exploits being a Black man in a white land to position himself rhetorically as an outsider, in order to convey a stance of disinterest rather than uninterest in national affairs. Sancho asserts in his 4 May 1778 letter to Jack Wingrave, "I say nothing of politics – I hate such subjects" (*Letters* 171). On 7 September 1779, he writes to Roger Rush, immediately after a very circumstantial account of recent military events and their likely political consequences, "[f]or my part, it's nothing to me – as I am only a lodger – and hardly that" (*Letters* 231). Despite such statements, however, Sancho was no apolitical "lodger." Unlike the great majority of his countrymen, as a male householder in Westminster, Sancho was an enfranchised citizen eligible to elect Members of Parliament. He proudly tells John Spink on 9 September 1780 that he has given his "hearty vote" to candidates opposed to the ruling administration, and that he hopes Sir Charles Bunbury "meets with no opposition" to his bid for reelection (*Letters* 289). A disinterested stance allows Sancho to claim an objective rather than partisan perspective, as someone reliably concerned for the good of the country and not just for the interest of a narrow political faction.

The contents and style of Ignatius Sancho's writings demonstrate that he was truly *a man of letters* in every sense of the phrase. The demographic, geographic, and social diversity of Sancho's correspondents ultimately substantiates the observation he made to Margaret Cocksedge on 31 July 1775: "I have lived with the great – and been favoured by beauty" (*Letters* 112).

Notes

1. William Stevenson to John Nichols, 14 September 1815, in John Nichols, ed., *Literary Anecdotes of the Eighteenth Century*, 9 vols. (London, 1815), 8: 682–83.
2. *Public Advertiser*, 17 June 1772.
3. *Whitehall Evening Post*, 26–8 July 1785.
4. *Hickey's Bengal Gazette*, 4–11 November 1780.
5. Fisher, J. M., *A Quaker's Tour of the Colonial Northeast and Canada: The 1773 Travel Journals of Jabez Maud Fisher of Philadelphia*, ed. Campisi, J. and Starna, W. A. (Philadelphia, PA: American Philosophical Society Press, 2014), 65.
6. Boswell, J., *Life of Johnson*, ed. Rogers, P. (Oxford: Oxford University Press, 1989), 1295.
7. Woodfall, H. S., British Library, Additional Manuscript 36593, folio 128.
8. Nichols, J (ed.), *Literary Anecdotes of the Eighteenth Century*, 9 vols. (London: self-published, 1815), Vol. i, 301.
9. Ireland, J., *Hogarth Illustrated*, 3 vols. (London: self-published, 1791–8).

10. *The Morning Chronicle*, 13 June 1777.
11. *The Gentleman's Magazine* (December 1839), 662.
12. *Independent Chronicle*, 7–9 May 1770; *Daily Advertiser*, 30 November 1772.
13. *Bury and Norwich Post*, 19 January 1791.
14. *Journals of the House of Lords*, 673.
15. *The Gentleman's Magazine*, issue 2 (1793), 768.

Further Reading

Carey, B., "Ignatius Sancho: A bibliography," https://brycchancarey.com/sancho/biblio.htm.

Social Contexts

CHAPTER 7

Ignatius Sancho, Sentiment, and "African Sensibility"

Markman Ellis

Describing his own epistolary practice in 1779, Sancho suggested his letters were "the warm ebullitions of African sensibility" (*Letters* 225). The claim he makes here to "African sensibility" holds a complex tension that this chapter seeks to elucidate: what does it mean to be both a man of sensibility and an African? As the chapter will show, Sancho's letters have an accomplished, but complicated, relation to ideas of both sentiment and sensibility, terms he uses frequently. Sancho writes about the importance of feeling and emotion, and he often expresses his own strong emotions, such as love, benevolence, and anger. Sancho deploys sentiment and sensibility in his criticism of the slave trade and the treatment of African people and uses it to explore the hypocrisy of the supposedly civilized and Christian people who sustain and support slavery. Sancho is a sentimental writer.

Both sentiment and sensibility were keywords in the Enlightenment discussion of thought and feeling in the science of man. This is the context for Sancho's claim to "African sensibility." When the philosopher Henry Home, Lord Kames (1696–1782), defined sentiment in *Elements of Criticism* (published in 1762), he located it within a philosophical framework: "Every thought prompted by passion, is termed a sentiment."[1] By passion, Kames meant something like emotion or feeling, so a sentiment was a form of cognition motivated by emotion rather than deliberation or reasoning (or, even more remotely, by a sense impression such as sight, sound, or touch). Adam Smith (1723–90), in his *Theory of Moral Sentiments* (1759), also proposed that a sentiment was a thought that stemmed from a passion or feeling, rather than from reason or sense. Sentiment for Smith was proximate to opinion, and central to the production of approbation and sympathy. As an essay in *The Universal Magazine* declared in April 1778, "The character of delicacy of sentiment [...] is certainly a great refinement on humanity [and] adds greatly to the happiness of mankind, by diffusing an universal benevolence. It teaches men to feel for others as for themselves; it disposes us to rejoice with the happy, and by partaking to increase their pleasure."[2] Sancho uses sentiment in this sympathetic sense when he talks about feelings generated by or reflecting his Christian faith. In a letter to his friend John Meheux (1751–1839) in August 1777, reflecting on the blessings of his life, Sancho explains how his "heart and affections" pour forth "the grateful sentiments of his enraptured soul" (*Letters* 141). Sancho uses the adjectival form "sentimental" to describe, in a witty sense, the appealing "sentimental ladies" that he imagines Meheux encountered at a fashionable spa town; or again, after having read Voltaire's *Tragedy of Semiramis* (1749), Sancho complained to Meheux that he has "found nothing of the striking kind of sentimental novelty—which I expected from its great author—the language is good in most places – but never rises above the common pitch" (*Letters* 133).

In one of the first appearances of his name in print, in the *Gentleman's Magazine* in 1776, Sancho was praised for the "sensibility" and "delicacy" of his opinions (*Letters* 333–4).[3] The term "sensibility" referred to an individual's capacity for emotional sensitivity and refinement. It was often used to describe the ability to experience and express strong emotions, notably in response to beauty or art, but also for political causes involving victims of distress. *The Monthly Magazine* argued in 1796 that "Sensibility is that peculiar structure, or habitude of mind, which disposes a man to be easily moved, and powerfully affected, by surrounding objects and passing events."[4] Sensibility was seen as a positive quality, and those who were thought to possess it were often admired for their emotional depth and sensitivity; equally, those with an excess of sensibility might feel pain or pleasure too intensely. As Sancho said, "They who have least sensibility are best off for this world," advising his friend Miss Leach "May you know no pains but of sensibility!" (*Letters* 117). Sensibility as a concept, and as a mode of expression, was grounded in forms of sociability, communication, and fellow feeling that were ineluctably human.

That Sancho is a sentimental writer matters politically, as well as aesthetically. To express sentiments, and to possess sensibility, was both to feel and to think humanly. The third edition of the *Encyclopaedia Britannica*, published in 1797, defined "Sensibility" as "a nice and delicate perception of pleasure or pain, beauty or deformity. It is very nearly allied to taste; and, as far as it is natural, seems to depend upon the organization of the nervous system."[5] As a definition, that seems like a conventional, if rather bloodless, account derived from the Scottish enlightenment philosophers, for whom this encyclopaedia was a major project. However, the unknown writer added further that sensibility is capable "of cultivation, and is experienced in a much higher degree in civilized than in savage nations, and amongst persons liberally educated than among boors and illiterate mechanics" (mechanic: a person engaged in a manual occupation or trade; a labourer). The encyclopaedist argued that sensibility, in short, was an attribute of enlightened people in civilized and polite society, and as such, not of people who were either savage (in the state of nature) or uneducated. Some eighteenth-century philosophers argued that Africans, such as Sancho, remained savage, even when living in a civilized society. Edward Long (1734–1813), for example, in *The History of Jamaica* (1774) argued that Africans lived in a savage state of nature even when brought into the civilized domains of the slave plantations: they "remain," he said, "in the same rude situation in which they were found two thousand years ago."[6]

In the period when Sancho was writing his letters, many Enlightenment *philosophes* explicitly denied that Africans possessed the intellectual capacity for the higher arts and sciences, including David Hume, Thomas Jefferson, James Monboddo, Edward Long, and Lord Kames. These men denied Africans and enslaved people – sometimes considered together – the same status as humans that they themselves enjoyed. In his essay "Of National Characters," first published in 1753, Hume (1711–76) argued that

> I am apt to suspect the negroes, and in general all the other species of men (for there are four or five different kinds) to be naturally inferior to the whites. There never was a civilized nation of any other complexion than white, nor even any individual eminent either in action or speculation. No ingenious manufactures amongst them, no arts, no sciences.

In case his point was unclear, he continued: "Not to mention our colonies, there are Negroe slaves dispersed all over Europe, of which none ever discovered any symptom of ingenuity; tho' low people, without education, will start up amongst us, and distinguish themselves in every profession."[7] Kames, who spoke so eloquently about the universality of sentiment, nonetheless argued in his *Sketches of the History of Man* (1774) that "The colour of the Negroes [...] affords a strong presumption of their being a different species from the Whites," concluding that this "presumption was supported by inferiority of understanding in the former."[8] Enlightenment philosophy's culture of interdiction denied the possibility of African arts and letters, and denigrated the evidence of African sensibility when it was found. As this chapter argues, Sancho's *Letters* give evidence that rational Enlightenment debate about equality of human feeling and intellectual capacity encouraged the development

of ideas about race that rationalized why some other humans were
excluded from those conditions of equality.

Sancho's Epistolary Sentiments

Sancho's *Letters* give repeated evidence of sensibility and sentiment as both
terms of value in themselves, as well as part of his epistolary practice. He
writes about the importance of feeling and emotion, and often expresses his
own strong emotions, such as love, grief, and anger. The *Letters* are a record
of his sentiments, and testify to his sensibility. His extended criticism of the
slave trade, the treatment of African people, and the slave system is built on
sentimental arguments. He writes about the suffering of slaves and appeals
to the emotions of his readers to help end slavery and the slave trade. In this
way, sensibility is a mode of argument for Sancho, as well as a style of
writing especially accessible to the playful reach of irony and satire.
Sentiment is sincerely and strongly felt, but it is also something of a joke,
embarrassing and revealing all at the same time. This ambidextrous quality
is what makes sentiment and sensibility an ideal mode of address and topic
of conversation for Sancho.

The primary quality that contemporaries admired about the sentimental
was its ability to muster sympathetic feeling for objects worthy of compas-
sion. For Sancho, this focused on the treatment of enslaved Africans in
British sugar colonies in the Caribbean. This forms the subject of Sancho's
first letter to Laurence Sterne (1713–68), the ground zero of Sancho's
epistolary sentimentalism, written in 1766, but dated for no known reason
in the *Letters* as July 1776. It is a good example of "sentimental rhetoric," as
Brycchan Carey calls it.[9] Sancho begins by putting his addressee at ease, by
establishing his own subject position as a grateful subaltern, "one of those
people whom the vulgar and illiberal call '*Negurs*'"; his status as
a sentimentalist, "Philanthropy I adore"; and his admiration for Sterne's
writing, especially that element of amiable generosity, both in *Tristram
Shandy* but also in Sterne's *Sermons*, "Your Sermons have touch'd me to the
heart" (*Letters* 128). He focuses on Sterne's tenth sermon, quotes selectively
from it, and launches his request:

> In your tenth discourse, page seventy-eight, in the second volume—is this
> very affecting passage—"Consider how great a part of our species—in all
> ages down to this—have been trod under the feet of cruel and capricious
> tyrants, who would neither hear their cries, nor pity their distresses.—
> Consider slavery—what it is—how bitter a draught—and how many
> millions are made to drink it!" (*Letters* 128)

Sancho interprets his quotation from Sterne's sermon as an address to the enslaved African population in the Caribbean. This is a notable observation, as arguments like this were, in the 1760s, little known outside some Quaker publications.

Sancho continues his sentimental address, after a genuflection to Sarah Scott's treatment of a benevolent slave ameliorationist in her novel *Sir George Ellison* (1766):

> Of all my favourite authors, not one has drawn a tear in favour of my miserable black brethren—excepting yourself, and the humane author of Sir George Ellison.—I think you will forgive me;—I am sure you will applaud me for beseeching you to give one half hour's attention to slavery, as it is at this day practised in our West Indies.—That subject, handled in your striking manner, would ease the yoke (perhaps) of many—but if only of one—Gracious God!—what a feast to a benevolent heart!—and, sure I am, you are an epicurean in acts of charity.—You, who are universally read, and as universally admired—you could not fail—Dear Sir, think in me you behold the uplifted hands of thousands of my brother Moors.—Grief (you pathetically observe) is eloquent;—figure to yourself their attitudes;—hear their supplicating addresses!—alas!—you cannot refuse.—Humanity must comply. (*Letters* 128)

His argument is a sentimental one, it might be said, as it makes explicit appeal to the tropes of sentimentalism: benevolent hearts, pathetic eloquence, and common humanity. It also reinforces the "supplicating addresses" of the enslaved Africans, with their grateful uplifted hands rather than insurrectionary violence. Sancho's sentimental rhetoric promises passive obedience. All these elements make this a characteristically sentimental argument. In Carey's analysis, it depends on ideas of "common feeling and mutual sympathy" bringing about the emotional subversion of reason.[10]

Further letters continue Sancho's sentimental arguments against slavery and colonial exploitation. The first letter of the second volume, dated 1778, is addressed to Jack Wingrave (1757–92), a young man of twenty-one years, the son of a bookseller John Wingrave (1729–1807). Jack had been apprenticed to a bookseller but instead of joining the trade, he sought his fortune as a soldier in the army of the East India Company. During Sancho's correspondence with him, he was stationed in Calcutta. Sancho writes to him about the disparity between colonial ambition and practice, in response to unsympathetic and racist language he detected in Jack's letters home to his father (excerpted at the end of the letter). As with his letter to Sterne, Sancho begins in an arguably ironic mode, describing himself as a grateful and patriotic British citizen: "I am sorry to observe that the practice of your country (which as a resident I love—and for its freedom—and for the many blessings I enjoy in it—shall ever have my warmest wishes—prayers—and blessings)" (*Letters* 188). He then continues with his main thesis about the hypocrisy of British global endeavor, which claims a Christian and civilizing purpose, but whose conduct reveals it to be driven by profit and exploitation: "I say it is with reluctance, that I must observe your country's conduct has been uniformly wicked in the East—West-Indies—and even on the coast of Guinea.—The grand object of English navigators—indeed of all christian navigators—is money—money—money—for which I do not pretend to blame them—" (*Letters* 188). Sancho argues that desire for gain, for money, has corrupted the English colonial actors in the Caribbean, in South and South-East Asia, and in Africa. Money corrupts. But Sancho does not stop there. Rather, he goes on to develop a counter-argument that relies on the Enlightenment doctrine of commerce, which sees it as a force for good that improves trust and sociability between commercial actors, even in cross-cultural encounters. As Silvia Sebastiani argues, commerce is "the distinctive characteristic of advanced societies and the main vector of human sociability," leading to "a general improvement of private and social life, by strengthening the principle of sympathy."[11] Commerce and civility go hand in hand, agrees Sancho:

> Commerce was meant by the goodness of the Deity to diffuse the various goods of the earth into every part—to unite mankind in the blessed chains of brotherly love—society—and mutual dependence:—the enlightened Christian should diffuse the riches of the Gospel of peace—with the commodities of his respective land—Commerce attended with strict honesty—and with Religion for its companion—would be a blessing to every shore it touched at. (*Letters* 188)

Sancho's argument embeds itself in the discourse and rhetoric of the Enlightenment argument about commerce. Advancing this does not mean Sancho excuses the British colonists. Although commerce ought to be the occasion for trust and mutual exchange, and ought to bring civilization to the places it touches, Sancho argues it has brought nothing but misery to Africa:

> In Africa, the poor wretched natives—blessed with the most fertile and luxuriant soil—are rendered so much the more miserable for what Providence meant as a blessing:—the Christians' abominable traffic for slaves—and the horrid cruelty and treachery of the petty Kings—encouraged

by their Christian customers—who carry them strong liquors—to enflame
their national madness—and powder—and bad fire-arms—to furnish them
with the hellish means of killing and kidnapping. (*Letters* 188)

Sancho concludes by arguing that the Christian slave traders corrupt
African commerce, by their horrid cruelty, their use of strong liquors,
their subversion of petty coastal kingdoms, and the disruptive effect of
European weapons. In Sancho's historical geography, African commerce
ought to be improving, but is instead immiserating and corrupting. He
then breaks off, reflecting his embittered mood:

> But enough—it is a subject that sours my blood—and I am sure will not
> please the friendly bent of your social affections.—I mentioned these only to
> guard my friend against being too hasty in condemning the knavery
> of a people who bad as they may be—possibly—were made worse—by
> their Christian visitors.—Make human nature thy study—wherever thou
> residest—whatever the religion—or the complexion—study their hearts.—
> Simplicity, kindness, and charity be thy guide—with these even Savages will
> respect you—and God will bless you! (*Letters* 188)

In response to the catastrophe wrought in Africa by the European commerce in slaves, Sancho can only recommend study of human nature
(hearts, not complexion, nation, or religion). Hearts, he argues, are shared
in common by all humankind, even by "savages." Sancho offers this advice
to Jack Wingrave as a guide to improve the young man's conduct in
colonial India, by recognizing the common humanity of the indigenous
population of India, whom Jack has referred to as "Savages."

Sancho's philosophical defense of commerce and the science of man
reminds us that Sancho himself is also a rational Enlightenment thinker,
well versed in recent political theory and the science of man. That is
reinforced later in the letter, where, in a postscript addendum, Sancho
gives Jack an improving reading list of Enlightenment theory, including
William Robertson's *History of Charles the Fifth* (1769); Oliver
Goldsmith's histories of Greece, Rome, and England; sermons by the
controversial religious theorist David Williams; the genteel philosophy of
Addison and Steele in the essay tradition (*Spectator, Tatler, Guardian*);
and finally, poetry by Young, Milton, and Thomson. Reading these
thinkers, he claimed, had "mended my heart—they improved my vener-
ation for the Diety—and increased my love to my neighbours" (*Letters*,
1778, 189–90). A little later, in a letter addressed to his fellow servant
James Kisbee, Sancho recommended Robertson's *History of Charles the
Fifth* again, as part of a serious educational strategy: "I recommend to you

to make extracts upon the passages which strike you most—it will be of infinite use to you" (*Letters* 194).

Sancho's letter to Wingrave develops a complex and sophisticated discussion of race and commerce that he uses to develop sentimental arguments about the immorality and unchristian nature of slavery. This was not his first articulation of a moral and sentimental construction of slavery. Writing to his fellow African servant Julius Soubise in 1772, Sancho expounded on the abuses of slavery: "Look round upon the miserable fate of almost all of our unfortunate colour—superadded to ignorance,—see slavery, and the contempt of those very wretches who roll in affluence from our labours superadded to this woeful catalogue—hear the ill-bred and heart-racking abuse of the foolish vulgar" (*Letters* 98). To Jabez Fisher, in 1778, Sancho writes giving thanks for a gift of anti-slavery publications from Philadelphia, where he notes "the unchristian and most diabolical usage of my brother Negroes—the illegality—the horrid wickedness of the traffic—the cruel carnage and depopulation of the human species" (*Letters* 165). In 1779, he read and praised Granville Sharp's "strictures upon Slavery," which he thought "of consequence to every one of humane feelings" (*Letters* 219–20).[12]

This kind of sentimental letter, the mode of sentimental political rhetoric it deploys, and the reading list of improving works are emblematic of Sancho's interest in and command of Enlightenment philosophy. But although a letter like that to Jack Wingrave (*Letters* 187–91) is an excellent demonstration of his sensibility, it is not wholly typical of his writing. Usually, Sancho is a different kind of sentimentalist, one that revels in a witty and garrulous turn to his writing. In this mode, he constructs himself as a benevolent, self-ironizing character, an object of sentimental curiosity and introspection, at home with his family, his business, and his network of friends. The third letter in Volume II, to Margaret Cocksedge (1744?–1822), is a good example of this equally characteristic witty senti-mentalism, using gentle raillery to effect a good-humored teasing of inno-cent follies. His letter begins by describing a dream Sancho had about his addressee, but then slips, by a series of eccentric associations and the liberal use of dashes, from the tea-table to discussion of drinking chocolate, to an account of a sociable dinner with some acquaintances, and on to some more sociable notes about mutual friends. The mode is gossipy, invoking friendship, sociability, and benevolence in an ironic and witty mode. The addressee, Margaret Cocksedge, was one of Sancho's close friends, a woman of comparatively humble origins who may been employed as a governess for Frances Crewe. Sancho ends with self-deprecating irony,

addressing himself "to every one who delighteth in Blackamoor greetings.—
We have no news but old lies—scoured and turned like misers coats which
serve very well. We gape and swallow—wonder and look wise—[like]
conjurers over a news-paper, and blockheads at home" (*Letters* 193).

In this instance, Sancho's letter-writing followed Alexander Pope's
advice when he defended letters of friendship, in a letter to an unknown
correspondent dated 5 December 1712, as "thoughts just warm from
the brain, without any polishing or dress, the very dishabille of the
understanding."[13] Sancho's combination of conversational casualness and
description of mundane events seems to reinforce the letter-writing theorist George Seymour's view, in his *The Instructive Letter-Writer* (1763), that
"A fine letter does not consist in saying fine things, but expressing ordinary
ones in an uncommon manner. It is the *proprie communia dicere*, the art of
giving grace and elegance to familiar occurrences that constitutes the merit
of this kind of writing."[14] Sancho's easy familiarity with his addressee,
his enthusiasm for gossip and the mundane details of everyday life, allows
him to adopt a sentimental domestic sociability in his letters. The
addressee, and the reader of the printed letters, are invited into the ebb
and flow of Sancho's family and business as much as his life and opinions.
This familiarity extends to his friends, as when he affectionately refers to
Meheux as "Snoodlepoop!" and urges him to write longer and more often
(*Letters* 192).

Here and elsewhere, sentiment and sensibility are a mode of argument
for Sancho, but they also provide a compositional method for the epistolary form, and a style of writing. Sancho is able to spin a letter of sentimental domesticity out of gossamer-thin material, exploiting his knowledge of
literature and philosophy to generate allusions and his ready wit to turn
simple quotidian events into amusing anecdotes, both aerated by punning
and wordplay. Sentiment and emotion are sincerely and strongly felt, but
are also a bit of a joke, embarrassing and revealing at the same time. This
fluid and ambidextrous quality is what makes the combination of sentiment and sensibility an ideal mode of address and topic of conversation for
Sancho.

Sancho and the Dashing Style

As is immediately clear to any reader who opens his book, a very distinctive
feature of Sancho's writing is his use of the dash. As confirmed by the
autograph letters to William Stevenson (1750–1821) now in the British
Library, Sancho habitually used the dash in his correspondence (*Letters*

331).¹⁵ Sancho's handwriting indicates he was a compulsive dasher, reflecting the action of a hand moving at speed over the paper—what Mark Mattes has called a "chirographic urgency."¹⁶ What makes Sancho's dash distinctive is that it is preserved in his printed letters. While the dash is common in autograph or handwritten letters, when it came to publication, it was conventional for punctuation to be regularized and made more orthodox, as one of the processes of textual transformation undertaken in the press-house by the compositor and proofreader. The preservation in print of Sancho's dash demonstrated his allegiance to Sterne and the sentimental style. Although the *Letters* went to press posthumously, a punctuational precedent had been established by the publication of Sancho's own letters in Sterne's *Letters of the Late Rev. Mr. Laurence Sterne* in 1775, edited by his daughter Lydia de Medalle.¹⁷ Sancho's letter to Sterne was subsequently reprinted in many newspapers and periodicals (*Letters* 333–4). Sancho's dash, in short, was already a characteristic feature of his printed writing, one that was immediately legible to his readers as a sentimental trope, with its own distinctive cultural politics. As the *New Annual Register* said in 1783, "The letters are a kind of imitation of Sterne's manner, interspersed with long strokes, or dashes" (*Letters* 346). Dashes made the correspondence Sternean and also sentimental.

In the first letter of Volume II, written to Jack Wingrave in Calcutta, Sancho writes:

> I never see your poor Father—but his eyes betray his feelings—for the hopeful youth in India—a tear of joy dancing upon the lids—is a plaudit not to be equalled this side death!—See the effects of right-doing, my worthy friend—continue in the tract of rectitude—and despise poor paltry Europeans—titled—Nabobs.—Read your Bible—as day follows night, God's blessing follows virtue—honour—and riches bring up the rear— and the end is peace.—Courage, my boy—I have done preaching.—Old folks love to seem wise—and if you are silly enough to correspond with grey hairs—take the consequence.—I have had the pleasure of reading most of your letters, through the kindness of your father.—Youth is naturally prone to vanity—such is the weakness of Human Nature, that pride has a fortress in the best of hearts—I know no person that possesses a better than Johnny W——e—but although flattery is poison to youth, yet truth obliges me to confess that your correspondence betrays no symptom of vanity—but teems with truths of an honest affection—which merits praise—and commands esteem. (*Letters* 187)

Sancho writes to Jack imploring him to act responsibly in India, in such a way that will make his father proud not only of the money he has gained, but also that his behavior has been moral. The dash is doing a lot of work in the grammar of the paragraph: many sentences seem to be constructed from phrase-fragments placed in proximity to cognate ideas, generating a sentence that is a little like thinking. Elsewhere Sancho's dashes seem to suggest the hesitations, changes of direction, and asides characteristic of conversational speech: addressing Stevenson in 1780, Sancho described his letter as "a kind of medley, a heterogeneous, ill-spelt, heteroclite, (worse) excentric sort of a—a—; in short, it is a true Negroe calibash—of ill-sorted, undigested chaotic matter" (*Letters* 256). Here the hesitation almost resembles a rhetorical stammer, breaking off the subject, it is fully revealed.

Historians of punctuation argue that the dash derived from the ellipsis, the three dots that indicate omitted material (. . .). They argue that the morphology of the ellipsis transformed from ellipsis to dash in the early modern period. In eighteenth-century print culture, the dash is formed in at least four forms, distinguished by their length. The hyphen is the shortest dash, usually used to "hyphenate" or connect two words together as a compound, or to join two syllables of a word at the end of a line. The compositor has used the hyphen in this way on nearly every page of Sancho's *Letters*. There are also dashes of two lengths: the "en dash" is slightly longer than a hyphen, the same width as an "n" letter (not used by Sancho's compositor); and the "em dash," the characteristic dash of both Sancho and Sterne, the same width as a letter "m." The "two-em dash," comprising a double em dash, is used to indicate omission of the substance of a name, as an ellipsis (Mr. W———e for John Wingrave).

Using the em dash in this way was a comparatively recent development in the history of punctuation. Historians of punctuation point to a period in the late eighteenth century when the dash suddenly rose in significance. The dominant account—for example, that in Malcolm Parkes's *Pause and Effect* (1992)—explains this in relation to the elocutionary movement in British rhetorical culture.[18] The dash in this mode is used to indicate different kinds of pause in writing that is recording or emulating speech or oratory. Sterne scholars, such as Roger Moss, similarly argue that his use of the dash has this sort of rhetorical effect, in that the dash indicates hiatus, and is associated with Sterne's conversational style and mimetic use of language.[19] Moss quotes Ian Watt's suggestion, made in his edition of *Tristram Shandy* in 1959, that the dash is often used for "a non-logical junction between one level of discourse and another."[20] Although Sancho's dashes are similar to Sterne's, his use of the dash is more writerly than conversational, indicating a delight in non-logical combination.

In Sancho's case, the dash is used in a more expansive mode than simply to indicate elocutionary fluency. Joseph Robertson (1726–1802), in his 1785 *Essay on Punctuation*, was the first to include the dash on the list of the primary marks of punctuation. Robertson defined the dash, or ellipsis as he called it, as a point that is used when "some letters in a word or some words in a verse are omitted." He added, "The dash is frequently used by rhapsodists instead of the regular points."[21] Sterne and Sancho are rhapsodists, a rhapsodist being defined as a user of enthusiastic or effusive language. In an earlier part of his *Essay*, Robertson says: "The dash is frequently used by hasty and incoherent writers, in a very capricious and arbitrary manner, instead of the regular point. The proper use of it is where the sentence breaks off abruptly; where the sense is suspended; where a significant pause is required; or where there is an unexpected turn in the sentiment."[22] Robertson gives an example, which he explores through some examples in Pope's writing, that expands the idea of the dash to include those cases "Where there is an unexpected turn in the sentiment; or a sort of epigrammatic point."[23] One of Robertson's followers, David Steel (fl. 1785), clarified the argument about sentimental rhapsodists, who "substitute a dash (—) in many places where points would have as full an effect." In Steel's view, rhapsodists have abandoned full and proper pointing (punctuation), in a "needless substitution" that has produced "obscurity." Steel's target is explicitly Sterne, but Sancho would not escape the same censure:

> for I know no other author, whose works have been so terribly be-dashed, or who has been generally considered more unintelligible. The abolition of these sometimes unnecessary marks, I hope, will bring Sterne down to the common scale of reason; his faint and masterly touches will, I trust, be not less felt when deprived of such needless trapping.[24]

The only justification for Sterne's "be-dashed" prose, he later observes, is its power to generate feeling and sentiment: he observes that "Sterne has paid less attention to grammar than to the exciting of our feelings; and of those he appears such a perfect master, that we lose, in the rapidity of reading, all idea of vicious syntax."[25]

Robertson and Steel, writing after the publication of Sterne and Sancho, retrospectively criticize Sterne's sentimental mode of punctuation as an improper affectation, but also admit its force, in the way it develops feeling and sentiments rhapsodically. Sancho writes in the mode of the sentimental rhapsody, an effusive language pointed by dashes that creates sympathetic feeling between reader and author—although that doesn't adequately cover the full range of effects of his dashing style. Embedded in the idea of a rhapsodist is the suggestion of enthusiasm, which indicates that there is a politics to the rhapsodic dashing style: it is associated with modernity and the erosion of established hierarchies. Sancho's adoption of the dash identifies him with these reformist and radical forces, and also with the high-culture literary associations of Sterne and his followers. These high-cultural associations were felicitous in the familiar letters of the literary scene, but were contradicted by Sancho's status as an African without formal education, and in trade. Unsurprisingly, some critics were hostile to Sancho's dashing style. *The Gentleman's Magazine* declared the letters were "little more than commonplace effusions, such as many other Negroes, we suppose, could, with the same advantages, have written" (*Letters* 344). The reviewer especially objected to Sancho's dashes: "we wish that honest Ignatius had not followed him [Sterne] in his blanks and dashes" (*Letters* 344). But others recognized the force it afforded his writing. The critic of the *New Annual Register* for the year 1782 commented that Sancho's *Letters* were "a kind of imitation of Sterne's manner, interspersed with long strokes, or dashes," before concluding that "They display an excellent heart, and will be entertaining to a great number of readers" (*Letters* 346).

Sensibility and Race in Sancho's Letters

Sancho was aware that his writing style was both distinctive and unorthodox. He doesn't describe himself as a Shandean, as the critics did, and the punctuation theorists might have done. But he did have a self-identity as a writer of "African sensibility." His writing is littered with ironically racialized self-deprecations of this nature, that counterpose his African identity, his complexion, and his philosophical sentimentalism. He refers to one of his letters as "the simple effusions of a poor Negro's heart" (*Letters* 208); and elsewhere indicates the ideological conflict conventionally established between his race and his sentiments: "tell him he has the prayers—not of a raving mad whig—nor fawning deceitful tory—but of a coal-black, jolly African, who wishes health and peace to every religion and country throughout the ample range of God's creation!" (*Letters* 262). Sancho's irony is precarious, but confident. His references to himself as a Blackamoor operate in the same self-deprecatory mode (*Letters* 193, 206, 237, 287). The question of African sensibility becomes in this way more of a challenge to British intellectual culture than an accommodation.

In its reception, critics often drew a connection between the *Letters* and the politics of race in the debate on slavery. Frances Crewe's preface had provoked this response when she argued that the *Letters* addressed the philosophical problem of racial interdiction through her claim that they demonstrated that an "untutored African may possess abilities equal to an European" (*Letters* 47). Ralph Griffiths (1720–1803), in *The Monthly Review*, observed in December 1783 that the project to publish Sancho's *Letters* was addressed to "half-informed philosophers, and superficial investigators of human nature," especially to contest the view that Africans "are inferior to any white nation in mental abilities" (*Letters* 347). *The Critical Review* echoed this sentiment in January 1784: "The original motive for introducing his name to the world, was the desire of evincing, that an untutored African may possess abilities equal to those of an European, and it must be acknowledged that [. . .] the Letters before us afford full and indubitable testimony" (*Letters* 348).

The philosophers, however, rallied. The slave-owner Thomas Jefferson (1743–1826), in his *Notes on Virginia* (1787), reiterated Hume's and Edward Long's thoughts on African arts and culture. Jefferson sees Sancho's sentimental letters allied more to the heart (feeling) than the head (reason). "They breathe the purest effusion of friendship and general philanthropy, and shew how great a degree of the latter may be compounded with strong religious zeal." Jefferson sees the sentimental as a compound of feeling and style—and he is especially hostile to this latter element in Sancho: "He is often happy in the turn of his compliments, and his stile is easy and familiar, except when he offers a Shandean fabrication of words." Jefferson's analysis of Sancho's debt to Sterne is not unsophisticated: he compliments Sancho's style as "easy and familiar," keywords from the critical discourse on familiar letters. Jefferson identifies the "Shandean fabrication of words" as something more than a stylistic quirk of punctuation, offering as well a new way of thinking. Sancho's "imagination," he says, "is wild and extravagant, escapes incessantly from every restraint of reason and taste, and, in the course of its vagaries, leaves a tract of thought as incoherent and eccentric, as is the course of a meteor through the sky." Jefferson figures Sancho's thinking as escaping from the restraint of reason—like a fugitive from slavery's chains—but also from taste. Sancho's writing is likened to a vagary: a departure from the ordered, regular, or usual course of conduct, decorum, or propriety: a frolic of a freakish nature (*OED*). Sancho's tract (or track?) of thought Jefferson finds incoherent and eccentric, like the course of a meteor through the sky, he says. (A meteor follows a predictable and predetermined path, although, as a metaphor, the meteor or shooting star connotes the unpredictable appearance of a brief streak of light that leaves a short-lived luminous trail in the night sky.) Jefferson concludes: "His subjects should often have led him to a process of sober reasoning: yet we find him always substituting sentiment for demonstration." Jefferson accordingly determined that Sancho was in "the first place among those of his own colour who have presented themselves for public judgement, yet when we compare him with the writers of the race among whom he lived, and particularly with the epistolary class, in which he has taken his own stand, we are compelled to enroll him at the bottom of the column."[26] Although Jefferson's metaphor of the ornamented memorial column is somewhat obscure, he assessed Sancho as the best Black writer he had encountered in Britain or America, but nonetheless, the worst of writers.

As abolitionist argument was amplified in the 1780s, writers increasingly saw Phillis Wheatley Peters (c. 1753–84) and Sancho as evidence that refuted claims of African intellectual incapacity (although, as the Abolitionist movement developed in the late 1780s, the more explicitly campaigning texts of Ottabah Cugoano and Olaudah Equiano came to play a more important role). Thomas Clarkson (1760–1846) argued that Wheatley Peters and Sancho had provided "proof of their abilities" as Africans;[27] while Peter Peckard (1718–97) noted that Sancho's *Letters* "breathe the purest and most genuine spirit of universal Benevolence," with "an enthusiastic zeal for the undoubted rights of man, and for the interests of true Religion"; concluding that Sancho is a "rational and moral writer."[28] As Peckard's rhetoric makes clear, he reads Sancho's achievement within the Enlightenment discourse on African arts and letters. William Dickson (1751–1823) concurred that Sancho's *Letters*, along with the work of Wheatley Peters and Francis Williams, were "specimens of *African literature*," and compelling evidence that Africans were "*held and reputed* to be rational, moral agents."[29]

Sancho's *Letters* became something of a scandal in the debate on slavery conducted in the Whig newspaper *The Morning Chronicle* in 1788. In February, a writer identified as "Civis" wrote a letter "On the Slavery of the Blacks" in which he followed Edward Long's argument, namely that "the inferiority of the Blacks will entitle us to make them Slaves." He quoted Hume on the "natural inferiority" of "the Negroes," ending with the example of the Jamaican talked of as "a man of parts" that Hume determined was only "like a parrot, who speaks a few words plainly."[30] Hume was referring to Francis Williams, who had been discussed at greater length in Edward Long's *History of Jamaica*.[31] But Civis, in 1788, supposed that Sancho was the man Hume referred to, and, addressing Sancho's *Letters*, concluded "there does not appear to me any mark of genius, any taste, any correctness of thought or expression through the whole book."[32] A few months later, the same writer wrote that Sancho's writings do not prove African capacity for "abstract reasoning": "it would not prove equality more, than a pig having been taught to fetch a card, letters, &c, would show it not to be a pig, but some other animal."[33] To the anonymous Civis, Sancho's sentimental writing, whether considered as form or content, did not prove his humanity.

"African sensibility," as Sancho discerned, was an idea aimed at the center of the intellectual debate on slavery in the late eighteenth century. Demonstrating, displaying, testifying to African sensibility was a calculated riposte both to the Enlightenment *philosophes* and their discourse of separate races, and to the slave-holding plantation owners of the Caribbean. However, Sancho's deployment of sentiment and sensibility in his *Letters* is not merely tactical. He is not adopting the sentimental as a style or mode of address because he finds it felicitous on a particular occasion: rather, the evidence of the *Letters* suggests that this is the way he thinks and writes; and this is the way he chose to be represented in print culture. Writing in this way reflects his garrulous and infectious gift for friendship, his innate benevolence and kindness, and his enthusiasm for domestic happiness. That he was able to maintain these elements of his self in the face of the systemic racism of British society is remarkable.

Notes

1. Kames, H., Lord Home, *Elements of Criticism*, 2 vols. (Indianapolis, IN: Liberty Fund, 2012), Vol. i, 311.
2. "On delicacy of sentiment," *The Universal Magazine* 62 (April 1778), 172–4.
3. *Gentleman's Magazine* 46.1 (January 1776), 46.
4. "Question: Ought sensibility to be cherished or repressed?" *The Monthly Magazine* 2.10 (October 1796), 706.
5. "Sensibility," *Encyclopaedia Britannica*, 3rd ed. (Edinburgh: A. Bell and C. Macfarquhar, 1797).
6. Long, E., *The History of Jamaica*, 3 vols. (London: T. Lowndes, 1774), Vol. ii, 352–3.
7. Hume, D., *Essays: Moral, Political, and Literary*, ed. Miller, E. E. (Indianapolis, IN: Liberty Classics, 1987), 208.
8. Kames, H., Lord Home, *Sketches of the History of Man*, ed. Harris, J., 3 vols. (Indianapolis, IN: Liberty Fund, 2012), Vol. 1, 41–2 (from the 3rd ed., 1778).

9. Carey, B., *British Abolitionism and the Rhetoric of Sensibility: Writing, Sentiment, and Slavery, 1760–1807* (New York, NY: Palgrave MacMillan, 2005), 38.

10. Ibid., 42. Carey has "emotional subversion of the intellect."

11. Sebastiani, S., "Beyond ancient virtues: Civil society and passions in the Scottish Enlightenment," *History of Political Thought* 32.5 (2011), 821–40, 829.

12. Sharp, G., *The Just Limitation of Slavery* (London: B. White, and E. and C. Dilly, 1776).

13. Pope, A., *Mr. Pope's Literary Correspondence for Thirty Years* (London: E. Curll, 1735), 38.

14. Seymour, G., *The Instructive Letter-Writer, and Entertaining Companion* (London: G. Kearsley, 1763), 8.

15. British Library Add MS 89077.

16. Mattes, M., "Penman's Devil: The chirographic and typographic urgency of race in the *Letters of the Late Ignatius Sancho, an African*," *Early American Literature* 48.3 (2013), 577–612, 577.

17. Sterne, L., *Letters of the late Rev. Mr. Laurence Sterne, To his most intimate Friends. [. . .] Written by himself. And Published by his Daughter, Mrs. Medalle*, 4 vols. (London: T. Becket, 1775), Vol. iii, 22–6, 31–3.

18. Parkes, M., *Pause and Effect: An Introduction to the History of Punctuation in the West* (Aldershot: Scolar, 1992), 90–2.

19. Moss, R. B., "Sterne's punctuation," *Eighteenth-Century Studies* 15.2 (1981), 179–200, 197.

20. Watt, I., "Introduction," in Sterne, L., *Tristram Shandy*, Riverside ed. (Boston, MA: Houghton Mifflin, 1959), xliv–xlv.

21. Robertson, J., *An Essay on Punctuation* (London: J. Walter, 1785), 146.

22. Ibid., 129.

23. Ibid., 132.

24. Steel, D., *Elements of Punctuation* (London: self-published, 1786), 58.

25. Ibid., 77.

26. Jefferson, T., *Notes on the State of Virginia* (London: J. Stockdale, 1787), 234–5.

27. Clarkson, T., *An Essay on the Slavery and Commerce of the Human Species, Particularly the African* (London: J. Phillips, 1786), 175.

28. Peckard, P., *Am I Not a Man? And a Brother? With All Humility Addressed to the British Legislature* (Cambridge: J. Archdeacon, 1788), 19.

29. Dickson, W., *Letters on slavery. [. . .] To which are added, [. . .] accounts of some negroes eminent for their virtues and abilities* (London: J. Phillips, 1789), 77.

30. *The Morning Chronicle*, 5 February 1788.

31. Long, *History of Jamaica*, Vol. ii, 475–85.

32. *The Morning Chronicle*, 5 February 1788.

33. *The Morning Chronicle*, 19 August 1788.

Further Reading

Carey, B., *British Abolitionism and the Rhetoric of Sensibility: Writing, Sentiment, and Slavery, 1760–1807* (New York, NY: Palgrave MacMillan, 2005).

Ellis, M., "Ignatius Sancho's *Letters*: Sentimental libertinism and the politics of form," in Carretta, V. and Gould, P. (eds.), *Genius in Bondage: Literature of the Early Black Atlantic* (Lexington, KT: University Press of Kentucky, 2001), 44–68.

  The Politics of Sensibility: Race, Gender, and Commerce in the Sentimental Novel (Cambridge: Cambridge University Press, 1996).

Hammerschmidt, S., "Character, cultural agency and abolition: Ignatius Sancho's published letters," *Journal for Eighteenth-Century Studies* 31 (2008), 259–73.

Huang, K., "Blackness and lines of beauty in the eighteenth-century anglophone Atlantic world," *African and Black Diaspora: An International Journal* 12.3 (2019), 271–86.

Mattes, M., "Penman's Devil: The chirographic and typographic urgency of race in the *Letters of the Late Ignatius Sancho, an African*," *Early American Literature* 48.3 (2013), 577–612.

Rezek, J., "The print Atlantic: Phillis Wheatley, Ignatius Sancho, and the cultural significance of the book," in Cohen, L. L. and Stein, J. A. (eds.), *Early African American Print Culture* (Philadelphia, PA: University of Pennsylvania Press, 2012), 19–39.

Sandhu, S., "Ignatius Sancho and Laurence Sterne," *Research in African Literatures* 29.4 (1998) 88–105.

CHAPTER 8

Abolition and Sancho

Sören Hammerschmidt

On 21 July 1766, Charles Ignatius Sancho, then valet to the Duke of Montagu, wrote his now famous letter to Laurence Sterne, celebrity clergyman and author. In this letter, Sancho proposed that Sterne use his writing as a platform to promote anti-slavery sentiments. "That subject, handled in your striking manner, would ease the yoke (perhaps) of many," he asserts and adds: "Dear Sir, think in me you behold the uplifted hands of thousands of my brother Moors" (*Letters* 128). Invoking a crowd of hands raised in supplication as much as praise, he asks that Sterne employ his own hand in putting pen to paper and thereby lend a hand to support early arguments in favor of amelioration (though not the wholesale abolition) of slavery. Almost exactly six years later – in a letter to the son of a fellow high-ranking servant, Charles Browne, on 18 July 1772 – Sancho imagined another, similar scene of white benevolence and Black gratitude: "I thank you for your kindness to my poor black brethren – I flatter myself you will find them not ungrateful . . . I have observed a dog will love those who use him kindly – and surely, if so, negroes – in their state of ignorance and bondage will not act less generously, if I may judge them by myself" (*Letters* 96). As in his letter to Sterne, Sancho establishes a feedback loop in which his sentimental appeal to a white correspondent's sympathetic feelings will encourage that correspondent's benevolence towards Black subjects in bondage and under duress, which elicits those Black subjects' gratitude in response to white benevolence, which in turn motivates Sancho's praise of his correspondent's sympathetic feelings and ameliorative benevolence. At the center of this feedback loop stands Sancho, who, "judging from himself," both initiates the circulation of benevolent, sympathetic senti-ment and at the same time guaranties its effectiveness in ameliorating the material conditions of transatlantic chattel slavery, the prevalence of racist vitriol and violence, and the physical and emotional well-being of Black people in Britain and its colonies.

Three core strategies emerge from these two excerpts that together characterize Sancho's anti-slavery and "anti-race" work, that is, his work to critique and oppose slavery as a practice and an institution as well as his work to reject and undermine the validity of emerging concepts of "race" and to oppose their effects in the world. First among these strategies is his frequent use of racializing, often stereotyping imagery in what initially may look like a straightforward and unironic manner to characterize himself and his "black brethren" to correspondents – so apparently unironic, in fact, that this strategy has historically earned Sancho the reputation of acculturation to racist tropes and attitudes.[1] Closer inspection reveals, however, that Sancho's use of such imagery offers him occasions to satirize and critique the metaphorical mapping of moral character onto skin color instead. Second is a metaphorical or metonymical yoking of animal figures and tropes to the depiction of the persons and lives of Black people in ways that seem to further support the charge of Sancho's assimilation to a racist society. As I hope to show in this chapter, however, Sancho in fact holds up a mirror to his correspondents as well as to the concept of "race" in general as he deploys animal figures and racist tropes in his personal letters to undermine the efficacy of animal metaphors to subjugate humans and non-humans alike within a slaving society. In reflecting at them racist language current in their society, Sancho demands of his correspondents a re-examination of their racial attitudes; in the same step he reminds readers that racial discourse is intensely metaphorical and that acts of violence visited against humans as well as non-human animals are part and parcel of the same subjugating and denigrating forces active across circum-Atlantic societies. By overloading representations of himself and of other Black people in his letters with references to skin color and with (often racist) animal metaphors, he pointed out that categories such as civilization, "race," and species were cultural constructs designed to establish power relationships and modes of exploitation rather than representing scientific languages descriptive of biological or social facts. To that end, Sancho drew on the global reach of his correspondence to show that the metaphors of "the grateful dog" and "the grateful slave" actually formed part of a sentimental rhetoric that propped up anthropocentric and white-supremacist perspectives in support of a slaving society.[2]

Finally, there are the hands that abound in Sancho's letters and perform crucial work not only in composing and transmitting communications between friends, acquaintances, and allies, but also in forming and cementing social connections, swaying minds and hearts, and effecting social change. At the same time, his hands are the most visible and most visceral encapsulation of Sancho's jeopardy as a Black man living in a society that practices race-based chattel slavery, a symbol of Black people's dehumanizing reduction to and exclusive valuation as bodies performing labor. Under such circumstances, Sancho's letters offer him opportunities not only to turn his Blackness against the semiotics of race that would dehumanize him for being Black by declaring him inscrutable, unintelligible, and lacking in moral and mental coherence, but also to redeem his unruly, recalcitrant hand from the threat of appropriation by turning it against the social and cultural structures that would dispossess him of his own labor (and of himself). Through under-handed gestures, couched in the rhetoric of first-hand experience, Sancho crafts powerful arguments that induce correspondents like Sterne to lend a hand in the service of social justice and human rights. In contending with overdetermined connections between his "hand" (appendage as well as handwriting, both constitutive of character), the economics of slavery, and the semiotics of race, Sancho deploys his personal letters to demonstrate that he, too, has access to forms of agency and ownership through the manual work of writing himself.

Sancho and Slavery

Giving Sancho's stance toward slavery a definition and a proper name is in some ways a vexed issue, because he wrote about slavery decades before British opposition to that institution coalesced and became codified in the shape of the Society for Effecting the Abolition of the Slave Trade in 1787.[3] Thus, Sancho was certainly not an Abolitionist in the sense of belonging to a social or political movement that would have been recognizable as such to his contemporaries. However, it is undeniable that Sancho took a firmly anti-slavery stance and repeatedly expressed in his correspondence with friends in Britain and abroad his conviction that slavery, "as it is at this day practiced in our West Indies" (*Letters* 128), was an affront to Christian morality and an abomination of civilizational principles because of the violence and corruption it fomented among enslaved and enslavers alike.[4] In this, Sancho's views and stance agreed with that of later Abolitionist writers and activists; his letters thus offer one of "the first published challenges to slavery and the slave trade by a person of African descent. They are as direct as almost any made during the century by black or white writers and are especially noteworthy because they were made before sustained opposition to the African slave trade began in the late 1780s" (*Letters* 32).

While Sancho's views on slavery as a practice were therefore certainly aligned with the principles of Abolitionist movements later in the century, his position on slavery as an institution and his view of what should be done about it are more difficult to pin down. As exemplified in his letter to Sterne, Sancho's pronunciations on slavery often focus on current practices and tend toward an ameliorative stance of sentimental reform to improve the lives of the victims and the morals of the perpetrators of slavery. However, there are moments above all in letters to Julius Soubise, Jabez Fisher, and Jack Wingrave (*Letters* 98, 165, 188) when his condemnation of slavery and especially of the transatlantic slave trade seems to suggest that he sees violence and corruption as inhering indelibly in these institutions, which therefore require abolition rather than mere amelioration, though he never explicitly takes that stance. The same is true of the animal-rights position Sancho assumes in several of his letters, a stance that links animal and human rights as part of a principled, moral, and sentimental rejection of violence based in an extension of empathy to all sentient creatures. It is this assertion of a pan-species right to freedom from violence, exploitation, and abjection (combined with his recognition that racializing taxonomies are fundamentally metaphorical) that allows Sancho to resist emergent notions of inherent racial characteristics and hierarchies and at the same time leads him to concentrate his critique on current practices rather than systemic ills.

Did He Really Just Say That? Race, Racism, and Metaphor

Sancho's letters often assume a jovial, joyous, joking tone, one that appears in equal parts breathless and contemplative, meandering and prone to tangents according to topical associations of the moment, yet loaded with stern pronouncements and thoughtful instruction. A quirky sense of humor abounds in his letters, especially to close friends John Meheux and William Stevenson, but even in moments of apparent frivolity, he often pursues a serious agenda. His efforts to expose contemporary conceptions of race to laughter and scrutiny thus seek to undercut the efficacy of racializing metaphors and thereby counter the social, economic, and political expropriations that such metaphors facilitate. To prepare the ground for such a critique, Sancho suffuses his letters with what, at first glance, appear to be factually grounded, literal descriptions of his appearance, usually by referring to his skin color, bodily features, and putative geographic origins. In a letter dated 14 February 1778, for example, Sancho assures Jack Wingrave, a friend's son who had gone to make his fortune in

India, that "it gratifies a better principle than vanity – to know that you remember your dark-faced friend at such a distance" (*Letters* 73); on 23 July of the same year, he sends his family's "best respects . . . to every one who delighteth in Blackamoor greetings" (*Letters* 193) to their friend Margaret Cocksedge; and in a letter of 17 January 1780, he enjoins the Norwich bookseller and banker William Stevenson to assure a mutual friend of "the prayers . . . of a coal-black, jolly African" (*Letters* 262). Occasionally, Sancho describes the appearance or group identities of others instead and then aligns himself with them, as when he thanks Jack Wingrave "for the *whole* and every *part* of thy *conduct*, in regard to my two sable brethren" (*Letters* 258 [emphasis original]) in a letter of 5 January 1780; or when he deplores "the unchristian and most diabolical usage of my brother Negroes" in a letter of 27 January 1778, to the Philadelphia Quaker Jabez Fisher (*Letters* 165). Sancho's famous first letter to Sterne mentioned at the start of this chapter uses both direct and indirect self-depictions when he identifies himself as "one of those people whom the vulgar and illiberal call '*Negurs*,'" praises Sterne for having "drawn a tear in favour of my miserable black brethren," and invites him to imagine "the uplifted hands of thousands of my brother Moors" in supplication for more anti-slavery writing from Sterne's hand (*Letters* 128).

Passages like these occur in almost all of Sancho's letters, and they all have in common the demand they make of Sancho's correspondents to create or recall a mental image of Sancho himself. In other words, Sancho makes use of one of the most important functions of familiar letters as they were theorized in eighteenth-century Britain – that of making absent friends present, as Samuel Richardson had put it to Sarah Wescomb in a letter of 27 August 1746[5] – to confront his correspondents over and over again with his appearance irrespective of whether they had met him in person before or not. It may in fact be a measure of the success of Sancho's strategy to recall as often as possible the color of his skin to his close friends and correspondents that those who had been in personal or epistolary communication with him during his lifetime also tended to remember him for salient personal qualities rather than his skin color or other bodily conformations of "race" after death. His letters thus served Sancho in inoculating his correspondents against societal racist preoccupations with skin color as a marker of mental and moral characteristics: the more they were used to "seeing" him in the fullness of his person and appearance, the less that appearance became remarkable to them as a separable marker of inherent racialized difference and colonial commodifiability. Sancho's foregrounding of "race" – above all defined via skin color and external appearance – through invocations of his face and figure throughout his correspondence thus allowed him to tackle racist language, images, and attitudes literally head-on.

One of the most powerful ways in which Sancho confronts racist language is to ridicule metaphorical uses of the color black that seek to yoke markers of "race" to morality. In a letter to fellow servant Roger Rush from May 1779, for example, Sancho relates that "The gout seized me yesterday morning – the second attempt – I looked rather black all day" (*Letters* 216). On first glance an indulgence in a rather groan-worthy pun, this passage effectively undercuts the metaphorical efficacy of the word "black" within racially charged contexts by overloading it, especially when one considers it in conjunction with Sancho's request that Rush relay to a "Mrs. H—" the message that "there is a Devil that has not forgot her civilities to him – and would be glad to hear she was well and happy" (*Letters* 215–16). Sancho's short-circuiting of racist metaphor thus requires a multi-step practice of pushing it into self-satire. The color black, initially linked to Sancho's appearance in the narrow sense of his skin color, is first extended to appearance as the register of unhappiness and of feeling ill. After that, it comes to be aligned with immorality, irreligion, and general evil within a Christian world view until readers realize that Sancho's joke comes at the expense of precisely the kinds of metaphorical associations they are meant to support and thereby in a manner forestalls them.

A similar set of connections informs Sancho's pun in a letter of 26 November 1776, to Stevenson: "So – my cramp epistle fell into the hands of thy good and rev. father – *tant pis* [so much the worse] – why he must think me blacker than I am" (*Letters* 205). Sancho's play on his physical appearance always has a point, and that point is aimed squarely at the metaphorical mapping of moral character onto skin color within the racially charged environment of a slaving society. In retrospect, then, even apparently innocuous, non-metaphorical references to appearance are revealed to be overlaid and overdetermined by racializing metaphors and thus become grounds for ridicule and pointed critiques of metaphorical investments in skin color and bodily features. This is Sancho's most frequently deployed form of anti-race work: to repeatedly, persistently remind his correspondents – close friends, social contacts, and business associates alike – that they are exchanging familiar letters (a genre that implies close personal connections and open, honest, and unreserved communication) with a Black man and his Black wife and children; that their correspondence therefore implies the meaninglessness of skin color when it comes to social and personal connections, to the expression of wit and emotion in the exchange of familiar letters, and to friendships or intellectual debates or business dealings; and that the racializing language and racist metaphors he employs are therefore just as ridiculous as the puns to which he bends them in his letters.

We Are All Jack-asses! Trans-species Solidarity

Sancho also takes aim at another type of figurative language – often a mix of metaphors, similes, and analogical arguments – that is potentially much starker in its effects and in its stakes, especially to twenty-first-century ears: the alignment of racialized bodies with, or their replacement by, non-human animals. In a teasing letter of 5 October 1779, Sancho gently chides one of his closest friends, John Meheux, for complaining about Sancho's tardiness in writing, and then gives Meheux the following mock advice:

> such beings . . . as the one I am now scribbling to – should make elections of wide different beings – than Blackamoors for their friends: – the reason is obvious – from Othello to Sancho the big – we are either foolish – or mulish – all – all without a single exception. – Tell me, I pray you – and tell me truly – was there any Blackamoors in the Ark. (*Letters* 235)

Sancho's strategy of confronting his correspondent with his skin color and appearance is immediately recognizable, but there is also something new here: the use of an animal typology to describe his putative laziness or stubbornness joined with a reference to a common history of human and non-human animals that took a central position in eighteenth-century debates about race. Noah's Ark was crucial to debates between the orthodox monogenetic view of race – the idea that all humans were descended from Adam via Noah, whose progeny repopulated the post-diluvian world while diversifying into the "races" observable in modern times – and the heretic polygenetic view – that radically, innately different races had been created in various locations across the globe. In monogenetic accounts, "race" appeared only in the post-diluvian world, whereas polygenetic accounts generally assumed a localized flood that did not involve non-white races in the building of an ark.[6] Sancho's teasing question does not necessarily place him in either camp (though other passages in Sancho's letters show that he subscribed to the orthodox monogenetic view), but his jab at debates over the origins and history of race also shows that Sancho is eminently aware of the fundamentally metaphorical nature of race. Sancho's question regarding the presence or absence of Black people in Noah's Ark is not gratuitous or merely a joke, but instead indicates his fluency in the debates about race at a moment when old notions were being revised and new conceptions were being floated. In linking the question of race to cross-species alignments, Sancho's letter to Meheux takes aim at the figurative languages and typologies that enable the taxonomizing of both human and non-human animals to underwrite structures of exploitation and violence.

Sancho thus frequently voices his critiques of racializing language in conjunction with an early form of animal-rights discourse, one that primarily focuses on and rejects cruelty.[7] In a letter to Meheux of 25 August 1777, which he actually entitles "Jack-asses," Sancho draws the following tableau as it plays out in front of his shop and residence:

> My gall has been plentifully stirred – by the barbarity of a set of gentry, who *every morning* offend my feelings – in their cruel parade through Charles Street to and from market … – A tall lazy villain was bestriding his poor beast [a donkey] (although loaded with two panniers of potatoes at the same time) and another of his companions, was good-naturedly employed in whipping the poor sinking animal – that the gentleman-rider might enjoy the two-fold pleasure of blasphemy and cruelty – this is a too common evil – and, for the honor of rationality, calls loudly for redress. (*Letters* 144–5 [emphasis original])

Sancho encourages Meheux to write a satirical exposé for the papers, employing the half-joking but often suddenly serious manner characteristic of their close friendship:

> as I am convinced we feel instinctively the injuries of our *fellow creatures*, I do insist upon your exercising your talents in behalf of the honest sufferers. – I ever had a kind of sympathetic (call it what you please) for that animal – *and do I not love you?* Before Sterne had wrote them into respect, I had a friendship for them – and many a civil greeting have I given them at casual meetings. (*Letters* 145 [emphasis original])

After noting that Jesus rode upon a donkey "in his day of worldly triumph," Sancho strikes a more somber note for a while:

> I am convinced that the general inhumanity proceeds – first, from the cursed false principle of common education – and, secondly, from a total indifference (if not disbelief) of the Christian faith; – a heart and mind impressed with a firm belief of the Christian tenets, must of course exercise itself in a constant uniform general philanthropy – such a being carries his heaven in his breast – and such be thou! therefore write me a bitter Philippick against the misusers of Jack-asses – it shall honor a column in the Morning Post – and I will bray – bray my thanks to you – thou shalt

figure away the champion of poor friendly asses here – and hereafter shalt not be ashamed in the great day of retribution. (*Letters* 145)

As elsewhere in his correspondence, Sancho's jokes and puns pursue serious goals here, too. There is, first, the unmistakable association in Sancho's letter of the violence visited upon the donkey with the violence of slavery as well as an alignment of Sancho's language condemning animal cruelty with the language of sentimental anti-slavery discourse. His argument for the humane treatment of animals that is based on Christian tenets mirrors closely similar arguments forwarded against slavery from a monogenetic perspective: since Black Africans and white Europeans have a common ancestor in Noah, a correct understanding of the Bible as propagating universal philanthropy requires Britons to treat those they have enslaved as human (though not necessarily as equals) and either free them from chattel slavery or at least ameliorate the conditions of their existence. Sancho's conviction that "we feel instinctively the injuries of our *fellow creatures*" thus establishes his human/animal-rights argument in two related, parallel registers – on the grounds of spiritual and secular oppositions to violence and cruelty – and merges them through the language of sentiment into a joint demand for philanthropy toward "fellow creatures" of all species.

It is precisely at this point, where early anti-slavery and human- as well as animal-rights discourses strengthen each other, that Sancho's relationships with his correspondents and the identities he creates for himself and his friends are at their most metaphorical. Affectionately, jokingly calling Meheux an ass is one thing, but it also implies that Meheux is a victim in the violent tableau that Sancho has just described and thereby turns him into one of those ill-treated "fellow creatures" for whom he should be concerned and whose cause he should champion in public. Moreover, when Sancho picks up that same metaphorical transference again at the end of the passage and turns himself into a donkey, he comes close to creating (decades before the original "Am I not a Man and a Brother?") a parodical version of the famous abolitionist appeal for solidarity: "Am I Not a Donkey and a Brother?" But there is of course that edge to parody again, especially when Sancho wields it. For if we concur that "a constant uniform general philanthropy" also extends to donkeys and to other non-human animals; and that all humans are related to each other in a network of biblical genealogies; then we are indeed all donkeys, and what concerns donkeys concerns us. Moreover, if we are in fact all connected via a common animality – if violence against one living form is matter of concern to all living forms – then the languages of race and of species as well as the taxonomies of natural philosophy that rank human and non-human animals alike in hierarchies of ability and value are only sets of metaphors that organize the world according to the needs of their users rather than disinterestedly describing an objectively present world.

To illustrate this complex set of arguments in further detail, we turn back to the letter Sancho wrote to Charles Browne, the son of a fellow servant, on 18 July 1772, with which this chapter began. In that letter, Sancho also thanks Browne for his

> kindness to my poor black brethren – I flatter myself you will find them not ungrateful – they act commonly from their feelings: – I have observed a dog will love those who use him kindly – and surely, if so, negroes – in their state of ignorance and bondage will not act less generously, if I may judge them by myself – I should suppose kindness would do any thing with them; – my soul melts at kindness – but the contrary – I own with shame – makes me almost a savage. (*Letters* 96–7)

At first sight, this passage is stunning, even stunningly racist, in its apparent assertion that "negroes in their state of ignorance and bondage" will be as grateful as dogs if treated well. But if we assume that Sancho's letter to Browne is underwritten by the same ideal of a universal trans-species philanthropy we found in the letter on "Jack-asses" to Meheux, we can see that Sancho foregrounds the "black people are like dogs" metaphor precisely as a metaphor to highlight that all discourses surrounding civilization, race, and species in his letter are also founded on and deploy metaphors to stake their claims to empirical, objective truth. Sancho shows, for example, that the tropes of the grateful dog and the grateful slave are sentimental metaphors that are of great instrumental value to their users because they reaffirm, respectively, anthropocentric perspectives ("a dog will love those who use him kindly") and the interests of a slaving society ("kindness would do any thing with them").[8] Sancho's objection to violence against human as well as non-human animals and his ideal of solidarity between them obtain here as much as in his letter about donkeys. In this letter about dogs and slaves, however, Sancho's main point is that the transferability of metaphors and other figures of speech does not automatically entail equality among the subjects of such transfers: "kindness" makes both dogs and slaves pliable and receptive to the commands of those who claim to own them. In this way, the letter also questions and destabilizes the figure of speech according to which unkindness would in fact make him "a savage" by showing it up as yet another racializing colonial trope that maps emotions and actions undesirable in a metropolitan, polite subject onto bodies and subjects undesirable in a settler-colonial landscape. In this manner, Sancho points out to his correspondents that taxonomies and languages which appear to describe the objective attributes of civilizations, "races," and species are really tools to make the world in the image of specific sets of hierarchies, power relations, and socio-economic distinctions.

Sancho's Hands

Yet Sancho was also supremely conscious of the fact that the world being (re)made in the interest of European slaving societies actually consisted of human and non-human individuals whose lives were being shaped, uprooted, and destroyed as their labor, their agency, and their bodies were taken from them. In *The Second Treatise of Government* (1689), John Locke had proposed that subjectivity, as a measure of self-ownership, arose from the accumulation of property through (manual) labor:

> every Man [sic] has a *Property* in his own *Person*. This no Body has any Right to but himself. The *Labour* of his Body, and the *Work* of his Hands, we may say, are properly his ... he hath mixed his *Labour* with, and joyned to it something that is his own, and thereby makes it his *Property*. For this *Labour* being the unquestionable Property of the Labourer, no man but he can have a right to what that is once joyned to. (Locke, *Second Treatise* 111–2 [emphasis original])

Enslavement thus "solved" the conundrum of how to expropriate a person's "unquestionable Property" in themselves and their labor while simultaneously retaining ideals of individuality, freedom, and self-actualization through accumulation of property by stripping some people of the right to be a person and therefore of the ability to own the fruit of their labor and their bodies. Hence the "fatal flaw," according to James Baldwin's formulation, in British and other colonial settlers as well as in their metropolitan counterparts: "The people who settled the country had a fatal flaw. They could recognize a man when they saw one." The ability to recognize when someone is "a man" also implies the facility to define when they are "*not* a man," "For if he wasn't a man, no crime had been committed" in enslaving, robbing, dehumanizing, and commodifying them.[9] In Baldwin's account, Locke's hands thus remain invisible in part because the notion of instantly, inherently recognizable subjectivity requires the elision of the manual, physical labor that supports and makes possible its ideals of individual liberty, self-ownership, and self-actualization. The other reason is, of course, that colonial settlers and metropolitan traders and consumers had found a way to use other people's (or rather, other not-people's) hands to underwrite their own personhoods, and that is where it becomes complicated for Sancho. As a man who owns and accumulates property in London through the labor of his own hands (selling colonial products derived from enslaved labor, among other things), he is very much "a man" in Locke's and Baldwin's senses, and in the eyes of his colonial and metropolitan contemporaries. Yet as a Black man living in a slaving society that was increasingly defining both person-hood and enslaveability with reference to racialized bodily features,[10] the hands that accumulate property and selfhood through labor, the hands that write his letters, are always potentially also the means by which he will be robbed of his property and of himself. Sancho's hands, in other words, are always a potential liability.

Given Sancho's propensity to lean into problematic cultural features as a way to ridicule and dismantle them, it will therefore not come as a surprise that hands abound in Sancho's letters, most often as an expression of social connection – to "shake hands with" an old friend or new acquaintance (*Letters* 128) – or as an indicator of authenticity and authority in the transmission of news or services "by the hands of a friend" (*Letters* 200), "received . . . from the hands of a gentleman" (*Letters* 285), or sent "under my hand" (*Letters* 78). That last example also carries that all-important eighteenth-century meaning of "hand" as someone's writing both in the physical sense of ink traced on paper and in the social sense of a writer's personality and character embodied by the shape of their writing. The writing hand thus communicates (or fails to communicate) the meanings that would otherwise be expressed verbally and somatically between friends in close physical and social proximity, but adds a personal dimension, an opportunity to read a correspondent's character in the form of characters on the page: the written hand. Sancho's letters thus also elaborate on and profit from the eighteenth-century common-place that the written epistolary text embodies an immediate material trace of the writer's hand as well as an immediate textual presence of the writer's mind, thereby supplementing a presence in lieu of the person's physical absence. Sending a letter written "under my hand" and delivering it "by the hands of a friend" to ensure that it come "safe to hand" (*Letters* 204) is the next-best thing to actually "shak[ing] hands with" the intended recipient.

But let's return for a moment to Sancho's letter to Sterne, because there is a disparity here in the economy of hands:

I think you will forgive me; – I am sure you will applaud me for beseeching you to give one half hour's attention to slavery, as it is at this day practised in our West Indies. – That subject, handled in your striking manner, would ease the yoke (perhaps) of many – but if only of one – Gracious God! – what a feast to a benevolent heart! – and, sure I am, you are an epicurean in acts of charity. – You, who are universally read, and as universally admired – you could not fail – Dear Sir, think in me you behold the uplifted hands of thousands of my brother Moors. – Grief (you pathetically observe) is eloquent; – figure to yourself their attitudes; – hear their supplicating addresses! – alas! – you cannot refuse. – Humanity must comply. (*Letters* 128)

Whereas Sterne's hand is that of a craftsman or artist with a "striking manner," Sancho's hand is elided in the very act of writing the letter, leaving only its own mediated traces on paper to be deciphered by the letter's recipient. It also falls to that recipient's hand to express his approbation (his applause) of Sancho's request, thus reserving to Sterne any ultimate judgment of the merit of Sancho's request. At the same time, the letter turns Sancho into a cipher, into a stand-in for a mass of faceless, nameless "uplifted" hands caught in a static tableau of supplication, waiting for Sterne to extend his hand, to "comply" and exert his hand in translating their gestured request into action against white supremacy and enslavement. In fact, readers of the posthumous *Letters of the Late Ignatius Sancho, an African* (1782) encountered in the frontispiece portrait a visual encapsulation of the elision that Sancho's hand underwent in the transition from socially proximate conversation to spatially distant correspondent, from close social connection to distant humanitarian appeal. As in the Gainsborough portrait on which the engraving was based, one of Sancho's hands is hidden in the bosom of his servant's livery – a stock gentleman's pose that also (maybe unwittingly) registers the potential costs to Sancho in his bid to attain greater socio-political visibility through writing as the portrayal of Sancho elides his labor as valet, grocer, writer, and composer alike.[11] In his attempts to exert influence and become an agent for abolition, or at least for amelioration, Sancho appears forced to choose between being a recognizable but passive individual, to whom readers can assign a face and a name, or a nameless, faceless mass-subject, whose actions, however attenuated or supplemented, alter the fabric of word and world around it.

Sancho's own elision of his hands throughout his letters (an elision visualized for spectators and readers in oil portrait and engraved frontispiece) is therefore not so surprising after all. As the limb most immediately implicated in Locke's theory of property, the hand and its labor are necessary to an individual's constitution of themselves as subject and proprietor, including as proprietor of themselves. Yet, in a slaving society, that same digit turns into the most prominent signifier and cause of an individual's enslavement: the hand that through labor generates property and profit also represents the continued threat of abduction and expropriation (including in themselves) for individuals like Sancho while they are living in a slaving society. In such a context, increased visibility of a Black hand can be a liability as much as it might offer the potential for increased agency. This sense of the liability of a visible Black hand and the threat it represents for the successful, productive, self-sustaining deployment of manual labor in the service of Black selfhood, ownership, and social agency repeatedly, doubly returns in Sancho's descriptions of a body attacked by gout. "I have had a week's gout in my hand," he writes to Meheux on 3 September 1777, in a passage that locates threats to his physical well-being as well as to his ability to maintain social activity through writing in a hand both recalcitrant and excessively noticeable, sense-able, visible: "I find it painful to write much, and learn that two hands are as necessary in writing as eating" (*Letters* 149). Over and over, Sancho records the disruptions of a hand that fails to write legibly enough to support his self-inscriptions; ceases to provide the labor by which Sancho might extend himself into socio-political spaces ("I have as yet but very little use of my hand" [*Letters* 211]); and overwrites the promises of self-ownership through writing with the excessive sensitivity and visibility of a limb that refuses work: "my hand aches so, I can scrawl no longer" (*Letters* 212). On the one hand, the recalcitrant hand that refuses Sancho's commands, exertions, and desires functions as a symptom of the restrictions and threats visited upon a Black man working and writing himself into a racist slaving society yet rendered both invisible and excessively exposed (to looks, to declarations, to violence). On the other hand, that same recalcitrant hand also offers Sancho an opportunity to dramatize those restrictions and threats by embodying them as external forces that perpetually intervene in his (writing) life and to thereby turn them into the butt of yet another joke, into the target of disarming and debilitating laughter that defuses the power of those restrictions and threats, at least for the time it takes to write or read a letter.

Sancho's Face

In staging himself in this way within his letters, Sancho was confronting a deep history of linking Black bodies with illegibility, unintelligibility, and a lack of moral and intellectual clarity or coherence. Beginning in the sixteenth century, "inkface" on English stages had become the preferred way to perform the racialization of character and personality in the service of growing investments in transatlantic chattel slavery. Inscribing racial character on the bodies of actors, the theater invited audiences to participate in the formulation and deciphering of an economy of "race" that aligned "Blackamoor" figures with ink and writing to ultimately highlight their deficiencies in terms of morality, literacy (reading as well as writing), and intellect.[12] By the second half of the eighteenth century, the figure had calcified further and was beginning to postulate an essential separation and inherent incommensurability between the "inkiness" of Black bodies on the one hand and the capacity to master ink-based technologies (reading, writing, printing) on the other hand. Sancho's frequent invocations of the "Blackamoor" figure as a stand-in for himself and members of his family (*Letters* 193, 206, 235, 237, 287) thus locate him firmly within the purported gap between Black subject and epistolary object, an ideologically motivated gap (much like the gap between human and non-human animals that was being redefined and widened in the interest of anthropocentric exploitation during the period) designed to reinscribe Black subjects as exploitable and consumable objects. In vulnerably positioning himself within that gap, Sancho aims to undermine pronouncements on Black people's deficiencies of literacy, intellect, and humanity by playfully and painfully subverting late-century commonplaces about the illegibility of Black faces and Black character.[13]

To do so, he stages breakdowns of communication and comprehension in several of his own letters, before turning around and charging several of his correspondents with similar, supposedly inherent, deficits in legibility, literacy, and aptitude for letter-writing. "I hate fine hands," Sancho declares in a letter of 11 March 1779, and demands that his friend Stevenson write both legibly and plainly, rejecting elaborate forms that present obstacles to reading, communication, and understanding (*Letters* 212). Half a year later, on 17 October 1779, Sancho playfully chastises Meheux for relaxing his form, style, and sense too much: "You know nothing of figures – you write a wretched hand – thou hast a nonsensical style" (*Letters* 238). And on 7 August 1775, he mock-scolds family friend Lydia Leach: "I never can excuse intolerable scrawls – and I do tell you that for writing conversable letters you are wholly unfit – no talent – no nature – no style – stiff – formal – and unintelligible" (*Letters* 112). In performing his body as occasionally resistant to productive (manual) labor, in combination with postulations of orthographic and stylistic deficits in several of his correspondents, Sancho aims to undermine emerging orthodoxies about Black illiteracy, immorality, excessive or insufficient emotionality, and intellectual deficiency that together were coming to signal the essential separation of Black from British subjectivity as well as their fundamental incommensurability and mutual incomprehensibility.

Sancho stages his most condensed performance of this strategy in the "ink blot letter." Writing to Meheux on 3 September 1777, Sancho interrupts his news of friends and social visits mid-sentence:

> I hope confound the ink! what a blot! Now don't you dare suppose I was in fault – no, Sir, the pen was diabled – the paper worse, there was concatenation of ill-sorted chances – all – all – coincided to contribute to that fatal blot – which has so disarranged my ideas – that I must perforce finish before I had half disburthened my head and heart: – but is N[ancy] a good girl? – And how does my honest George do? (*Letters* 149)

Sancho first blames his writing implements' low quality, then demonic possession and fate, to explain the excess of ink and shortage of writing before declaring a breakdown of sociable communication, sympathetic communion, and clarity of thought, only to launch back into conversation about friends and family. The scene of the ink blot, then, is not at all about an actual disruption of epistolary communication, but dramatizes and satirizes the charge that too much ink, like skin that is too dark, precludes legibility. The ink blot is Sancho's appropriation and simultaneous send-up of inkface on theater stages and of other performances and pronouncements that would exclude Black faces and Black people from sociable exchanges, from British social bodies, and in the final instance from participation in the polity, the nation, and humanity. The ink blot thus functions as a metonym for how Sancho consciously, strategically, and explicitly "blackens" the white pages and social networks of his correspondence: it marks the locus of Sancho's resistance to discourses of racialized slavery that would mark him out as perpetual potential victim of abduction, abuse, and abjection. In staging a body that refuses to cooperate with the demands of manual labor, Sancho dramatizes his rejection of the identification of Black hands with forced labor as well as his conscious, laborious efforts to overcome his body's refusals in the voluntary service of friendship and social connections beyond/against emergent discourses of racial difference. And Sancho's hand does, of course, persist and act and alter the world around him, despite and against the threat that his self-determination and self-advocacy might be circumscribed or erased through appropriation of (parts of) his body. In writing letters – that is, in sending handwritten documents that present recipients with traces of his body and of his character in an effort to emulate immediacy – Sancho seeks to expose eighteenth-century semiotics of race to laughter and scrutiny as a means of undercutting the efficacy of racializing metaphors and countering the expropriations that such metaphors facilitate.

Posthumous, Post-script

It was only posthumously that Sancho entered formal abolitionist discourse, and he did so to his own detriment. Whereas in life his manuscript letters (and his published exchange with Sterne) had been instruments to undermine reigning and developing conceptions of "race" in general and of Blackness in particular, in death his collected correspondence was repackaged (and at times edited) to critique the institution of slavery and its underlying racist tenets while simultaneously upholding, even reinforcing, the sentimental racialization of British and colonial populations.[14] Sancho's disruptive, unsettling anti-racist and anti-slavery stances remained accessible in the individual letters collected in the posthumous, printed *Letters* and were, as far as we can tell, edited relatively lightly by eighteenth-century standards.[15] Yet, like earlier reductionist depictions of Sancho in particular and of Black people in general, especially in sentimental poetry and in reviews of Sterne's published correspondence, the publication's framing in the preface and biography highlighted themes, epistolary modes, and Sanchean voices that facilitated his subsumption under emerging sentimental abolitionist discourses.[16] To be sure, those same prefatory materials refrained from actively or explicitly discouraging readers from paying too close attention to the counter-conventional elements (dashes, tangents, joviality) in Sancho's correspondence; reviewers like Ralph Griffiths in *The Monthly Review* took care of that (*Letters* 20–1). Instead, the editorial material primed readers to look for the sentimental modes of "man of letters," patriotic Briton, and "grateful slave" or to construct them out of the available epistolary material where they could not find them ready-made, as modeled by several of the reviews, and at the same time de-emphasized or remained entirely silent about the many other Sanchean modes and voices that would discomfit his easy, unproblematic insertion into sentimental abolitionist schematics. Sancho's posthumous framers (editor, biographer, and bookseller) thus guided readers toward a partial view of the letter-writer that suited precisely those metropolitan sentimentalist conceptions of race that Sancho sought to disrupt as they were beginning to coalesce into abolitionist and ameliorating positions around him.

Sancho's own position was more fluid and therefore maybe also more expansive, shifting across those positions while eschewing easy categorizations and above all rejecting the sentimental mode of burgeoning abolitionist movements. Sancho's perspectives on the violence and exploitations of his anthropocentric, slaving society were harsher and harder than later narratives of "grateful slaves" and "benevolent masters" were comfortable portraying, at the same time that his transformative uses of racializing metaphors and animal figures carved from their very absurdity a joyful, jovial form of critique. Whether abolition or amelioration was Sancho's ultimate goal remains unclear and may not have been clear to Sancho himself, or that ultimate goal may have changed – shifted back and forth – between the various options. What crystalizes out of his letters with absolute clarity, though, is Sancho's strong, principled, and categorical rejection of violence against human as well as non-human animals, a violence that for him extended to the curtailment of the freedom of individual movement, of personal agency, and of the benefits of (manual) labor. Writing himself into his correspondents' lives in a form and manner of his own choosing represented one important way to assert his own freedom from such violence.

Notes

1. Edwards, P., "Black writers of the eighteenth and nineteenth centuries," in Dabydeen, D. (ed.), *The Black Presence in English Literature* (Manchester: Manchester University Press, 1985), 50–67; Sandiford, K., *Measuring the Moment: Strategies of Protest in Eighteenth-Century Afro-English Writing* (New York, NY: Associated University Press, 1988), 79; Walvin, J., *Black and White: The Negro in English Society, 1550–1945* (London: Allen Lane, 1973), 61.
2. Chow, J., "*Oroonoko*'s interspecies imaginary: Race, gender, and animality," *Studies in Eighteenth-Century Culture* 53 (2024), 101–17.
3. Brown, C. L., *Moral Capital: Foundations of British Abolitionism* (Chapel Hill, NC: University of North Carolina Press, 2012), 1–30.
4. Carey, B., *British Abolitionism and the Rhetoric of Sensibility: Writing, Sentiment, and Slavery, 1760–1807* (London: Palgrave Macmillan, 2005), 57–63; Carey, B., "'The hellish means of killing and kidnapping': Ignatius Sancho and the campaign against the 'abominable traffic for slaves,'" in Carey, B., Ellis, M., and Salih, S. (eds.), *Discourses of Slavery and Abolition: Britain and Its Colonies, 1760–1838* (London: Palgrave Macmillan, 2004), 81–95.
5. Richardson, S., *Correspondence with Sarah Wescomb, Frances Grainger and Laetitia Pilkington*, ed. J. A. Dussinger (Cambridge: Cambridge University Press, 2014), 6–7.

6. Kidd, C., *The Forging of Races: Race and Scripture in the Protestant Atlantic World, 1600–2000* (Cambridge: Cambridge University Press, 2006), 54–120.

7. Fielder, B., "Black dogs, bloodhounds, and best friends: African Americans and dogs in nineteenth-century abolitionist literature," in Ohrem, D. (ed.), *American Beasts: Perspectives on Animals, Animality and U.S. Culture, 1776–1920* (Berlin: Neofelis Verlag, 2017), 153–74; Johnson, L., *Race Matters, Animal Matters: Fugitive Humanism in African America, 1840–1930* (New York, NY: Routledge, 2017).

8. Boulukos, G., *The Grateful Slave: The Emergence of Race in Eighteenth-Century British and American Culture* (Cambridge: Cambridge University Press, 2008), 1–32, 173–7.

9. Baldwin, J., "The white problem," in Baldwin, J., *James Baldwin: The Cross of Redemption: Uncollected Writings*, ed. Kenan, R. (New York NY: Pantheon Books, 2010), 75.

10. Hogarth, R. A., *Medicalizing Blackness: Making Racial Difference in the Atlantic World, 1780–1840* (Chapel Hill, NC: University of North Carolina Press, 2017); Nussbaum, F. A., *The Limits of the Human: Fictions of Anomaly, Race, and Gender in the Long Eighteenth Century* (Cambridge: Cambridge University Press, 2003); Wheeler, R., *The Complexion of Race: Categories of Difference in Eighteenth-Century British Culture* (Philadelphia, PA: University of Pennsylvania Press, 2010).

11. Meyer, A., "Re-dressing classical statuary: The eighteenth-century 'hand-in-waistcoat' portrait," *The Art Bulletin* 77.1 (1995), 45–63.

12. Grier, M., *Inkface: Othello and White Authority in the Era of Atlantic Slavery* (Charlottesville, VA: University of Virginia Press, 2023), 1–26.

13. Makonnen, A., "'Our Blackamoor or Negro Othello': Rejecting the affective power of Blackness," *European Romantic Review* 29.3 (2018), 347–55.

14. Hammerschmidt, S., "Character, cultural agency, and abolition: Ignatius Sancho's published letters," *Journal for Eighteenth-Century Studies* 31.2 (2008), 259–73; Rezek, J., "The print Atlantic: Phillis Wheatley, Ignatius Sancho, and the cultural significance of the book," in Cohen, L. L. and Stein, J. A. (eds.), *Early African American Print Culture* (Philadelphia, PA: University of Pennsylvania Press, 2015), 19–39.

15. Mattes, A. M., "Penman's Devil: The chirographic and typographic urgency of race in the *Letters of the Late Ignatius Sancho, an African*," *Early American Literature* 48.3 (2013), 577–612.

16. Hanley, R., *Beyond Slavery and Abolition: Black British Writing, c. 1770–1830* (Cambridge: Cambridge University Press, 2018), 31–50.

Further Reading

Doody, M. A., "Shandyism, or, the novel in its assy shape: African Apuleius, *The Golden Ass*, and prose fiction," *Eighteenth-Century Fiction* 12.2–3 (2000), 435–57.

Festa, L., *Fiction without Humanity: Person, Animal, Thing in Early Enlightenment Literature and Culture* (Philadelphia, PA: University of Pennsylvania Press, 2019).

Gikandi, S., *Maps of Englishness: Writing Identity in the Culture of Colonialism* (New York, NY: Columbia University Press, 1996).

Slavery and the Culture of Taste (Princeton, NJ: Princeton University Press, 2011).

Menely, T., "Acts of sympathy: Abolitionist poetry and transatlantic identification," in Ahern, S. (ed.), *Affect and Abolition in the Anglo-Atlantic, 1770–1830* (Farnham: Ashgate Publishing, 2013), 45–67.

Rezek, J., "The racialization of print," *American Literary History* 32.3 (2020), 417–45.

Sandhu, S., "Ignatius Sancho: An African man of letters," in King, R. (ed.), *Ignatius Sancho: An African Man of Letters* (London: National Portrait Gallery, 1997), 45–73.

"Ignatius Sancho and Laurence Sterne," *Research in African Literatures* 29.4 (1998), 88–105.

CHAPTER 9

Sancho's Pluralistic Afterlife

David Mark Diamond

Ignatius Sancho doesn't believe in Hell. In a letter dated 25 August 1777, addressed to frequent correspondent Jack Meheux, Sancho praises an unidentified pamphlet on the "improbability of eternal damnation" (*Letters* 146). He agrees with the pamphleteer because the idea of Hell is "derogatory to the fullness, glory, and benefit of the blessed expiation of the Son of the Most High God – who died for the sins of all – all – Jew, Turk, Infidel, and Heretic; – fair – sallow – brown – tawney – black – and you – and I – and every son and daughter of Adam" (*Letters* 146). Sancho's argument for the expansive reach of Christ's intercession reverses a line from *The Book of Common Prayer*, where the phrase "Jews, Turks, Infidels, and Heretics" comprehends all of Christianity's theological others. The series in this case supports a democratizing claim, broadening salvation across religious and ethno-racial divisions. Sancho combines cultural and corporeal variety, appending to his list of the beneficiaries of Christ's redemptive sacrifice a gradient of complexions, from "fair" to "black," from "you" (the young white Englishman, Meheux) to "I" (the Black Briton, Sancho). His understanding of salvation is pluralistic in the sense that it incorporates disparate identities without denying their difference and without prescribing the content of their beliefs.

This chapter examines the theological content and political ramifications of Sancho's imaginings of the afterlife. The idea of Hell as a place is anathema to Sancho, but the figurative language of demonism furnishes him with a way to describe the evils of chattel slavery, religious bigotry, and British colonialism. Sancho spends a good deal more time in his letters calling into being the conditions of Heaven, which he imagines both as the scene of eternal reward for suffering in this life and as the world transformed through the unification of the finite and the infinite. As he describes Heaven, Sancho projects himself and his readers into an ideal religious collective that includes American Quakers, enslaved West Africans, Roman Catholics, Hindus, and Muslim clerics, as well as fellow

Anglican Protestants. The theological, cultural, and racial diversity of this polity demonstrates that Sancho's fantasy of eternal reward is calibrated to the same pluralistic doctrine of salvation conveyed through his rejection of eternal punishment.

Attending to Sancho's notion of the afterlife reveals the distinctiveness of his religious thought among Black anti-slavery intellectuals. His prominent contemporaries Phillis Wheatley Peters, Quobna Ottobah Cugoano, and Olaudah Equiano were all affiliated with Calvinist Methodism, an evangelical Protestant tradition that sorts believers into predestined types of the elect and the reprobate.[1] Black Calvinists demonstrate, often through careful explication of scriptural passages, that the division between the saved and the damned does not map neatly onto racial difference – that blackness need not function as a marker of inherent spiritual depravity nor whiteness as a sign of spiritual purity. In doing so, they extend a high-stakes form of Christian belonging to people of African descent. Sancho's writings, meanwhile, show his commitment to Anglican Protestantism, a more theologically liberal form that prioritizes individual moral agency. Salvation depends on the exercise of religious virtue. The way Sancho defines that virtue allows him to extend religious belonging further than the Black Calvinists, beyond his co-religionists and even beyond the category of the Christian. It is an explicitly nondenominational quality, evident in the lives and practices of a range of religious cultures.

The afterlife is remote, by definition, but Sancho's accounts of Heaven and Hell convey religious politics that he applies to more proximate scenes of affiliation and conflict. The same pluralism on display in his descriptions of the hereafter informs his account of anti-Catholic violence in London during the Gordon Riots of 1780, as well as his critique of British colonialism in the circum-Atlantic world and India. Sancho's figurative references to Hell, meanwhile, suggest that enslavers and Protestant chauvinists share a demonic character. The political upshot of Sancho's religious pluralism resolves into clarity when we compare it to the nominal pluralism of what is known as "world-religions" discourse.[2] Such pluralism can be a language of universalism and, thus, a rhetorical strategy of Christian empire. World-religions discourse, which originated in academia in the nineteenth century and then broke "out into the open" of liberal political theory in the twentieth, had the counterintuitive effect of strengthening European dominance.[3] Although ostensibly pluralistic, accommodating up to twelve "major" traditions, world-religions discourse relies on a "universal principle that guarantees the unity of the world, or the world as totality," and that "ultimately comes to prevail as a direct extension of European Christianity, or Europe as (erstwhile) Christendom."[4]

We might describe Sancho's idea of the "world as totality" as part of the imaginative pre-history of this discourse because there, too, a variety of traditions and people are held fast by a universal principle that is insistently, if not always overtly, Christian. Yet access to eternal reward does not, for Sancho, depend on adherence to a specifically Anglican-Protestant orthodoxy or even on the profession of Christianity. I propose that logics of mixture and mingling in these passages enable Sancho to enlarge divine love and salvation without universalizing belief. For him, salvific virtue holds a multiracial and trans-denominational community together without erasing distinctions of individual, racial, or religious identity. He, thus, attempts to pull apart pluralized belief from Euro-Christian imperialism.

Mingling in Heaven

Preparing the ground for his depiction of racial, national, and religious amalgamation, Sancho first describes the mixing of ideas in paradise. In a 1774 letter to Mrs. H., who might be Mrs. Howard, the housekeeper for the Duke and Duchess of Montagu, Sancho expresses a longing for the uninterrupted happiness of the afterlife. The specific mechanism of this happiness is the solvent property of redemption. "There," in Heaven, "may you and I – and all we love (or care for) meet the follies – the parties – distinctions – feuds of ambition – enthusiasms – lust – and anger of this miserable motley world, all totally forgot – every idea lost and absorbed in the blissful mansions of redeeming love" (*Letters* 104). A homogeneous solution replaces the motley world as "distinctions" created by political sectionalism and antisocial passions dissolve along with the very discreteness of ideas. Sancho describes this phenomenon as a kind of forgetting. The comprehensive sweep of his gesture – "all totally . . . every" – and his reference to "enthusiasms" are evidence that Sancho includes theological controversies among the distinctions "lost and absorbed" in God's redemptive love.

The social conditions of Heaven, while perhaps enabled by this process of mixture, reflect a different logic of combination: not mixing, but mingling. The difference between these processes elucidates the distinction between universalism and pluralism. Writing, again, to Jack Meheux in July 1777, Sancho imagines the convergence of the immanent world and the Celestial City to form a pluralistic utopia:

> May you, dear M[eheux], and all I love – yea the whole race of Adam, join
> with my unworthy, weak self, in the stupendous – astonishing – soul-cheering
> Hallelujahs! – where Charity may be swallowed up in Love – Hope in Bliss –
> and Faith in glorious Certainty! – We will mix, my boy, with all countries,
> colours, faiths – see the countless multitudes of the first world – the myriads
> descended from the Ark – the Patriarchs – Sages – Prophets – and Heroes! My
> head turns round at the vast idea! we will mingle with them, and try to untwist
> the vast chain of blessed Providence – which puzzles and baffles human
> understanding. (*Letters* 140)

As in the letter to Mrs. H., Sancho here figures salvation as a "swallowing
up." Religious dispositions requisite to navigating the fallen world (like
charity, hope, and faith) are consumed by superlative versions of themselves (love, bliss, and certainty). Here, too, the subsumed quantities are
abstractions rather than individual persons or communities of belief. Ideas
and constituencies associate through different mechanisms in these letters.
Intellectual mixture universalizes ideas, working through a kind of metabolism to produce a homogenized compound. Social affiliation, by contrast,
creates a collective of articulated yet discrete parts – a pluralistic collective.
The verb "mingle" denotes combination without fundamental loss of
identity. Sancho appears to expand the boundaries of Christian Heaven
while preserving individuality and, thus, heterogeneity. The "whole race of
Adam" joins in an ahistorical, intercultural chorus of "hallelujahs," their
voices harmonized but distinguishable. That Sancho and Meheux can
expect to "see" the antediluvian "myriads" implies, moreover, that the
two friends will maintain continuous consciousness through the eschaton
and that biblical figures from various epochs of sacred history will maintain
their individuated characters when they gather.

Dramatic epistemological rewards attend this mode of affiliation.
Together, Sancho, Meheux, and the gathered church of the Kingdom of
Heaven will "untwist the vast chain of blessed Providence." Given the
context, it seems likely that Sancho refers not only to God's plan –
"providence" defined as the divine direction, beyond human comprehension, of personal and cosmic histories – but also to the great chain of being.
The latter scheme arranges all creatures vertically, into strata that reflect
their relative proximity to divinity. Combined with polygenesis, the theory
that God made the different races of humankind through separate acts of
creation, this rigidly hierarchized view of the universe often served as an
authorization of slave-holding culture or the civilizing ambition of empire.
Thus, the collaborative labor of untwisting the latter chain does more than
produce crystalline truths ("glorious certainty"); it also suggests the

flattening of gnarled, prejudicial structures into the linear, horizontal shape of infinity. Though it "baffles human understanding" in the present, the "vast idea" of an inclusive multitude complements Sancho's overarching vision of futurity. In Sancho's representation, the Kingdom of Heaven welcomes non-Christian as well as non-white and non-European people, both before and after the inhabitants of Heaven and Earth merge into one polity.

If the letter to Mrs. H. imagines the end of sectarianism, the dissolution of "parties" opposed through intellectual, political, and religious conflict, the letter to Meheux hints at the pluralistic collective that takes shape under those conditions. How is this collective formed? The passages I've discussed to this point suggest that salvation is unconditional, that anyone may join. However, in a letter to Philadelphia Quaker Jabez Fisher – the same letter in which he famously praises Phillis Wheatley as a "Genius in bondage" (*Letters* 166) – Sancho acknowledges a criterion for election. He thanks Fisher for sending him, among other titles, an anti-slavery tract by Anthony Benezet, another Quaker. Then, Sancho uses religious language figuratively, equating slavery with hell:

> Full heartily and most cordially do I thank thee – good Mr. F, for your kindness in sending the books – that upon the unchristian and most diabolical usage of my brother Negroes – the illegality – the horrid wickedness of the traffic – the cruel carnage and depopulation of the human species – is painted in such strong colours – that I should think would (if duly attended to) flash conviction – and produce remorse in every enlightened and candid reader. The perusal affected me more than I can express; – indeed I felt a double or mixt sensation – for while my heart was torn for the sufferings – which, aught I know – some of my nearest kin might have undergone – my bosom, at the same time, glowed with gratitude – and praise toward the humane – the Christian – the friendly and learned Author of that most valuable book. (*Letters* 165)

Sancho does not explicitly consign enslavers to a site of punishment hereafter – we've seen that he rejects this concept – but he describes their violence against enslaved black people as "diabolical." As he disentangles the "mixt sensations" elicited by Benezet's book, sympathetic identification with the suffering of enslaved people of African descent and "gratitude" for the "humane – the Christian" arguments of the author, Sancho creates a dichotomy between the figurative hell of slavery and the salvific virtue of abolitionism.

An unspoken imperative to justify his inclusion of Quakers in the category of "Christian" precipitates a bolder claim: that the "virtue" that qualifies us for admission to Heaven cuts across theological differences. He writes,

> Blest be your sect! – and Heaven's peace be ever upon them! – I, who, thank God! Am no bigot – but honour virtue – and the practice of the great moral duties – equally in the turban – or the lawn-sleeves – who think Heaven big enough for all the race of man – and hope to see and mix amongst the whole family of Adam in bliss hereafter – I with these notions (which, perhaps, some may style absurd) look upon the friendly Author – as a being far superior to any great name upon your continent. (*Letters* 165)

Because they put at least three religions – Anglican-Protestantism, Islam, and the Society of Friends – on equal footing with respect to worldly esteem ("honour") and eternal reward ("bliss hereafter"), Sancho's "notions" about religious virtue are, indeed, "absurd" in the ironically appropriated language of Protestant chauvinism. Sancho's religious moralism is pluralistic because it extends salvation across religious and cultural borders and does so independently of processes of conversion or assimilation. True religion comes down to a question of acting rightly rather than holding – or professing – the right beliefs.

As the paragraph moves from an invocation of infernal agents to a re-articulation of Sancho's pluralistic doctrine of salvation, one regime of race-making comes into contact with another. Epidermal race, the identification of skin color with essential difference, casts a shadow over the first part of the letter. When Sancho asserts the humanity of unfree people of African descent, he counters the discourse of anti-blackness without invoking it directly. That discourse and the institution it rationalizes are sinful – "unchristian" and "horrid wickedness" extreme enough to create Hell on Earth. Religious race, an essentializing strategy in which differences of faith become fundamental and absolute, relies on a network of cultural rather than somatic signs. When Sancho declares that he would recognize salvific virtue in the garb of the Muslim as well as that of the Anglican cleric, he disrupts this racial semiotics by dislocating the cultural signifier of dress from the spiritual value that attaches to it.

Hell on Earth

So far, I have presented Sancho's afterlife and the theory of salvation that undergirds it as evidence of the author's pluralism, his conviction that different creeds and identities should coexist. We recall, however, that religious historians describe pluralism as an intellectual framework that purports to respect the diversity of global religions at the same time that it renews the "logic of European hegemony" by insinuating the universality of Christianity.[5] While Sancho does identify a universal principle that structures globality, he defines it in a way that holds the abstract good of pluralism apart from its regulatory function. This becomes clear when Sancho lowers his gaze from the afterlife to the immanent world and distinguishes "true Christianity" from the errancy of religious intolerance and Christian imperialism.

Consider the way Sancho describes proper religious morality in another letter to Meheux, this one composed in praise of the novelist and Anglican clergyman Laurence Sterne, as well as his fictional proxy, Parson Yorick:

> You have read and admired Sterne's Sermons – which chiefly inculcate practical duties, and paint brotherly love – and the true Christian charities in such beauteous glowing colours – that one cannot help wishing to feed the hungry – cloathe the naked, &c. &c. – I would to God, my friend, that the great lights of the church would exercise their oratorical powers upon Yorick's plan; – the heart and passions once listed under the banners of blest philanthropy – would naturally ascend to the redeeming God – flaming with grateful rapture. – Now I have observed among the modern Saints – who profess to pray without ceasing – that they are so fully taken up with pious meditations – and so wholly absorbed in the love of God – that they have little if any room for the love of man. (*Letters* 137)

The extent to which the concentration of moral authority in Sterne's sermons narrows the horizon of possibility for belief depends on definitional work that Sancho relegates to *et ceteras*: "feed the hungry – cloathe the naked," and so on. This refusal of specificity enables Sancho to coopt the legitimacy of Anglican orthodoxy without impressing its self-image onto the variegated bodies and beliefs that comprise the polity of the Kingdom of Heaven. Moreover, in this passage and elsewhere in his *Letters*, Sancho re-channels the disciplinary force of pluralism toward the regulation of a specifically Anglican-Protestant excess. These "modern saints" are too "absorbed" in prayerful contemplation (or its appearance) to practice the cardinal virtue of *caritas*, or charity. Though focused on concrete philanthropic acts and, therefore, on the temporal realm, true believers actually enjoy a stronger connection to the deity. Properly mediated through objects of charity, rather than conveyed directly through "pious meditations," their love of God intensifies into "rapture." Meanwhile, Sancho's call for reform travels through the optative formulation of prayer: "I would to God," he writes, that religious instruction

matched his understanding of salvific passion, with Anglican clergy applying their homiletic prowess to Sterne's sermons.

Sancho's critique of errant Anglican Protestantism converges with pluralistic politics in his first-hand account of the anti-Catholic Gordon Riots.
In 1778, Parliament passed the Relieving Act, which loosened some legal
restrictions on English Roman Catholics. The riots were a response to
a petition against the act brought by Lord George Gordon, president of the
Protestant Society, two years later on 2 June 1780. Sancho describes the
riots, often called the worst in English history, in a series of letters to John
Spink and John "Jack" Wingrave the younger. To Wingrave, who was then
in Bombay (now Mumbai) serving as an officer in the British East India
Company, Sancho writes: "we are (but do not be frightened) all, at least
two thirds of us, run mad – through too much religion; – our religion has
swallowed up our charity – and the fell demon Persecution is become the
sacred idol of the once free, enlightened, generous Britons" (*Letters* 283–4).
Accusations of fanaticism, of running mad with religious sentiment, frequently hurled at Anglican Protestantism's self-created antitheses in this
commentary ricochet back at those of its adherents who would overlay the
precincts of the Church and the borders of the state.

At first glance, Sancho's lament of "too much religion" seems to convey
support for the political doctrine of secularism, according to which religion
should be privatized, removed from civic life. Thus uncurbed, the passage
appears to argue, "religion" contravenes social passions, swallowing them
up in an image reversal of the metabolism of ideas in Heaven. But the
feeling, charity, consumed by fanaticism is itself a religious virtue, syn-
onymous with the "blest philanthropy" that Sancho valorizes in his comments on Sterne's sermons. Together with the broader arguments of the
letters, the recurrence of the term helps to square Sancho's topical commentary with his evident religious devotion. It reminds us that Sancho is
here, as in his rejection of incessant meditative prayer, engaged with the
problem of distinguishing true from false Christianity.

The specific referent for "religion" in the key phrase cited above, and the
target of Sancho's criticism, is Anglican chauvinism. Sancho does not
recognize the "two thirds of us" who reify pastoral difference through
political violence as authentically Christian. He sees them, instead, as
idolaters who worship the "demon Persecution" in place of God. This
language recalls his denunciation of the "unchristian and most diabolical
usage" of enslaved Black people in the letter to Jabez Fisher. The echoed
invocations of demonism suggest continuity between the religious virtue of
abolitionism and what appears here as a vanishing tradition of liberal

Anglican Protestantism, as well as between the infernal characters of enslavers and intolerant Protestants. Confronted by anti-Catholic violence, Sancho laments the diminution of a faith proper to "the once free, enlightened, generous Britons." That faith is explicitly grounded in the teachings of an Anglican clergyman and author, Sterne, but it is also defined against the bigotry of fellow Anglican Protestants. Sancho emphasizes the rioters' religious errancy as well as their political and moral shortcomings. They aren't merely hypocritical Christians; they are pagans adulating a "fell demon."

While the letter to Wingrave elucidates the error of the rioters' sectarianism, another letter on the Gordon Riots offers an alternative form of relation to the religious other: conversion. In the postscript to his letter to John Spink dated 6 June 1780, Sancho openly avows tolerationist politics: "I am forced to own, that I am for universal toleration. Let us convert by our example, and conquer by our meekness and brotherly love!" (*Letters* 272). Sancho's call to convert Catholics appears contrary to the pluralistic ideal he develops through his imaginings of Heaven, where people of all faiths "mingle" in a heterogeneous assembly. Yet Sancho coordinates his idea of conversion with his liberal policy position, "universal toleration." His use of the first-person plural imperative "let us" and active verbs "convert" and "conquer" belies the passivity of conversion. Sancho calls neither for proselytizing, nor for legislating adherence to Church of England doctrine. Rather, he enjoins moral modeling, and specifically the performance of "meekness" and "brotherly love." That Sancho rejects forceful conversion is clear, but it's less certain whether the other who would observe and profit from "our example" in this scenario converts in the sense of changing their religious affiliation or whether they undergo a change in moral character by adopting the practical, social values that Sancho identifies with authentic piety. The latter interpretation seems possible, if not inevitable, when viewed by the light of Sancho's discussion of pluralized religious virtue in the letter to Fisher. It may be that Sancho has in mind conversion to salvific virtue, which, as we've seen, manifests itself in people from a variety of theological traditions – and does so without their renouncing their original religious commitments.

A similar ambiguity allows Sancho to challenge British imperialism when he takes a more global view of religious difference. Writing to Wingrave in 1778, he outlines a vision of Euro-Christian influence as God intended it. Sancho describes a model based on complementarity, both in terms of the movement of goods within a global economy and in terms of the relationship between economics and religion. Commerce between cultures, Sancho claims,

> was meant by the goodness of the Deity to diffuse the various goods of the earth into every part – to unite mankind in the blessed chains of brotherly love – society – and mutual dependence: – the enlightened Christian should diffuse the riches of the Gospel of peace – with the commodities of his respective land – Commerce attended with strict honesty – and with Religion for its companion – would be a blessing to every shore it touched at. (*Letters* 188)

God's plan for transcultural intercourse, as Sancho explains it, contrasts starkly with the wickedness enacted by Euro-Christians, and by the British in particular. Against the depredations of the East India Company, Sancho juxtaposes the "mutual dependence" created by a global economy. Against the fetters of slavery, he sets the "blessed chains" of fraternal affection. What holds the world together in Sancho's counterfactual is a system of reciprocal exchange, in which participants "diffuse" the goods or "commodities of [their] respective lands" throughout the globe.

Among the commodities of Christendom are "the riches of the Gospel of peace." Sancho apparently endorses evangelism, proposing that an "Enlightened Christian" would spread the figurative wealth of the gospel along with the raw material or agricultural products typically labeled "commodities." He does not elaborate, however, on the mechanism of Christianity's global diffusion, shifting instead to the axiomatic pronouncement that "Commerce attended with strict honesty – and with Religion for its companion – would be a blessing to every shore it touched at." What does it mean for religion to be the "companion" of commerce? The loose synonymy between attendance and companionship implies that "Religion," like the apparently secular value of "honesty," would serve as a guiding principle for commercial activities. If so, then the "enlightened" Christian of Sancho's counterfactual "diffuse[s]" Christianity in much the same way that the Protestant ideally converts the English Catholic: passively, by performing moral duties that model Anglican character to the other. Sancho's conviction in the value of Christian teachings, the "riches of the Gospel of Peace," never becomes a warrant for Christian planetary dominion.

Indeed, Sancho critiques British imperialism through another allusion to Hell. He chastises Wingrave for his prejudiced description of "the treachery and chicanery of the Natives" of Bombay, countering that Britons are corrupting "a simple, harmless people," teaching them to be deceptive by deceiving them (*Letters* 187). Whatever "knavish" and "diabolical arts" the Indians practice, Sancho argues, they learned from their "teachers," nominally "Christian" colonizers (*Letters* 187–8). The recurrence of the word "diabolical," which we encountered in the letter to Fisher, lends moral intensity to Sancho's argument. It also draws the broader imperial project within his metaphorical Hell and, therefore, links the criticisms of colonialism, slavery, and religious violence scattered throughout his correspondence. Sancho's specific focus on the infernal character of the British empire becomes explicit in the subsequent paragraph, in which Sancho asserts that "your country's conduct has been uniformly wicked in the East – West Indies – and even on the coast of Guinea" (*Letters* 188). Through the comprehensiveness of his accusation, Sancho departs from the tendency of eighteenth-century anti-slavery writing to juxtapose the horrors of Atlantic slavery to the supposedly ethical practices of British colonialism in India.[6] Sancho sees not contrast but instead parallelism when he examines Britain's conduct in the West Indies, East Indies, and West Africa. When he subsequently turns his attention to "the Christians' abominable traffic for slaves," Sancho singles out the way slave traders introduce indigenous sovereigns, the "petty Kings" of the "Guinea Coast," to "Hellish means of killing and kidnapping," a dynamic that mirrors the one in which British colonizers instruct Indians in "diabolical arts" (*Letters* 188). In this way, Sancho suggests the global sweep of Britain's corrupting influence on native populations.

By the end of this long paragraph on the harms of and alternatives to British imperialism, as he leaves generalization and returns to particularized advice, Sancho de-emphasizes religious difference. He urges Wingrave to "Make human nature thy study – wherever thou residest – whatever the religion – or the complexion – study their hearts. – Simplicity, kindness, and charity be thy guide – with these even Savages will respect you – and God will bless you!" (*Letters* 188). Religion joins place and race on a list of external variables that Wingrave may disregard in favor of the deeper knowledge of "human nature." Sancho implies that Wingrave's analysis of people's essential characters will affirm the efficacy of the rule of conduct he lays down in the next sentence. The lesson: act with "simplicity, kindness, and charity," and the Englishman will garner the "respect" of "Savages" as well as God's blessing. Although they are compatible with Christian moralism or even, in the case of charity, enshrined as a cardinal virtue, these qualities are also universally legible and valued, according to Sancho.

His advice here is of a piece with his description of pluralized religious virtue in the letter to Jabez Fisher, although this time the relationship is reversed. Addressing Fisher, Sancho claims that he would honor salvific character in the outward dress of different theological traditions. Writing to Wingrave, Sancho asserts that far-flung theological–racial Others – "even Savages" – will recognize and respect the Englishman's virtue. In both cases, and in a reversal of the effect of "world-religions discourse" as Masuzawa describes it, universalism enables pluralism. Because virtuous character is legible everywhere, "wherever you reside" and "whatever the religion," the European Christian enjoys worldly success and providential favor without converting the indigenous populations they encounter. For these peoples, including the Indians about whom Wingrave complains, already espouse the secular faith of morality.

That Sancho does not advocate for the conversion of non-Christian people is surprising given the ideological temper of early Black critique. The example of Cugoano, hailed as the most radical Black abolitionist of the eighteenth century, shows that even strident calls for abolition and emancipation are amenable to empire. In *Thoughts and Sentiments on the Evil of Slavery* (1787), Cugoano proposes a one-for-one substitution of Christian imperialism for chattel slavery. One reason to abolish slavery, he contends, is that it prohibits the fulfillment of Britain's responsibility to inculcate Christianity around the world. Cugoano writes that it is the duty of "all Christian men" to "diffuse knowledge and instruction to all the heathen nations wherever they can," and the "horrible traffic of slavery" impedes that civilizing mission.[7] His remark is compatible with Sancho's claim that enlightened Christians ought to "diffuse" the Gospel of Peace with other, literal commodities.

The results of this diffusion vary widely in their texts, however. Where Sancho chooses a formulation that ties salvation to peace and foresees the vague "blessing" of commerce united with religion, Cugoano imagines Africans as willing subjects of a reformed British government. If slavery were abolished and replaced with "the righteous laws of Christianity, equity, justice and humanity," then

> multitudes of nations would flock to the standard of truth, and instead of revolting away, they would count it their greatest happiness to be under the protection and jurisdiction of a righteous government. And in that respect, *in the multitude of the people is the King's honour; but in the want of people, is the destruction of the Prince.*
> We would wish to have the grandeur and fame of the British empire to extend far and wide; and the glory and honor of God to be promoted by it,

and the interest of Christianity set forth among all the nations wherever its influence and power can extend.[8]

Coordinated with abolition, evangelism both motivates and enables British territorial expansion. Cugoano applies Proverbs 14:28 as a rationale for imperial ambition: a growing population of subjects redounds to the "honour" of a sovereign, while a diminished population is tantamount to their "destruction." He then expresses his "wish" for overlapping British and Christian empires, endorsing Britain's use of "influence and power" to promote "the interest of Christianity among all nations."

Sancho deviates from such anti-slavery imperialism – not only through his breathless imaginings of a world to come, but also through his engagement with the realities of life in Britain and its colonies. He omits the language that Cugoano uses, terms, like "instruction" and "jurisdiction," that denote the will to convert and the power to do justice. Irrespective of whether this omission is strategic or incidental, I think it is important because it marks the limits, for Sancho, of Christian universalism. Christianity can be a universalizing force in a moral and social sense where it informs commerce, binding the elements of a global "society" to each other by "blessed chains of brotherly love." But Sancho tacitly rejects the idea of Christianity as the principle of political organization for the "world as totality." I make this point not to vindicate Sancho at Cugoano's expense. Both of them make their contributions to Black liberation from within rather than fully outside of the dominant ideologies in Britain. Christian imperialism enables Cugoano's impassioned challenge to unfreedom by providing an alternative to the slave economy. Sancho cannot escape, but redirects, a religious discourse of othering that bifurcates the world into true and errant forms of belief.

Like Cugoano's anti-slavery argument, Sancho's pluralistic fantasies of Heaven and his social commentaries affirm the importance of thinking beyond the binary between "complicity and resistance" that tends to structure evaluations of early Black writing.[9] Debates over the "supposed radicalism of black texts" preclude "more nuanced understandings of how black writers come to terms with their circumstances."[10] Sancho's *Letters* demand such nuance from modern readers, as they combine direct criticism (what might pass for "resistance" in the argot of contemporary scholarship) with more subtle ways of engaging with hegemonic cultural formations (what might be construed as complicity).

Sancho does, on occasion, strike an overtly adversarial pose, as when he uses the figurative language of Hell and damnation to condemn racial slavery in the West Indies, rapacious colonialism in India, and Protestant bigotry in England itself. But his reflections on religion also bespeak subtler modes of critique. One of those forms we might call strategic elision. Sancho leaves out a full enumeration of the duties required by the Anglican-Protestant moralism to which he subscribes, thereby leaving open possibilities for beliefs and practices that might otherwise be fore-closed. He acknowledges the salutary effects of spreading the gospel around the world, yet he does not describe the mechanisms of its diffusion, nor endorse a program of conversion, nor equate evangelism to colonial jurisdiction. We might call the second form of response exhibited by Sancho's letters inflection. Sancho constructs Heaven in ways that unsettle the conditions handed down to him as reality. He does so thematically, by envisioning a multiracial, pluralistic society, but also grammatically. Sancho conjugates the Anglican faith that he learns from Sterne, alter-nately, in the optative mood and the future tense: "I would to God that"; "May you . . . and I . . . and all we love"; "we will" (*Letters* 137, 104, 140).

We might think of Sancho as inaugurating a grammar of early Black critique, a way of writing beyond the ideological and material constraints of the present. The hereafter that Sancho imagines is remote, deferred to the end of his life or the end of the world, yet it ties his writing to the more proximate future of Black Atlantic intellectualism. Within a decade of the publication of his letters, Black anti-slavery writers would adopt similar speculative modes and subjunctive moods to imagine alternatives to the status quo. We've seen an example of how Cugoano routes reformist prescriptions through conditional logic. Equiano "commemorates the end of the slave trade" almost two decades before it happens, in a gesture that may be classified as an expression of faith, or knowledge without certainty.[11] David George and Boston King narrate fictions of Black sovereignty that, in turn, animate the Nova Scotia and Sierra Leone resettlement projects.[12] The ultra-radical orator and pamphleteer Robert Wedderburn prophesies racial and class liberation as part of his apocalyptic vision.[13] Along with these writers, Sancho exemplifies faith as conviction that a more just future is inevitable.

Notes

1. Hanley, R., *Beyond Slavery and Abolition: Black British Writing c. 1770 to 1830* (Cambridge: Cambridge University Press, 2019), 99–119; May, C., "Phillis Wheatley and the charge toward progressive Black theologies," in May, C., *Evangelism and Resistance in the Black Atlantic, 1760–1835* (Athens, GA: University

of Georgia Press, 2010), 49–63; Stewart, D. D., "Cugoano and the hermeneutics of Black Calvinism," *ELH* 88.3 (2021), 629–59.

2. Masuzawa, T., *The Invention of World Religions: Or, How European Universalism Was Preserved in the Language of Pluralism* (Chicago, IL: University of Chicago Press, 2005).
3. Ibid., xiv.
4. Ibid., xiv.
5. Ibid., xiv.
6. Kohn, M. and O'Neill, D. I., "A tale of two Indias: Burke and Mill on empire and slavery in the West Indies and America," *Political Theory* 34 (2006), 192–228; Nussbaum, F. A., "Between 'Oriental' and 'Black so called,' 1688–1788," in Carey, D. and Festa, L. (eds.), *The Postcolonial Enlightenment: Eighteenth-Century Colonialism and Postcolonial Theory* (Oxford: Oxford University Press, 2009), 137–66.
7. Cugoano, O., *Thoughts and Sentiments on the Evil and Wicked Traffic of the Slavery and Commerce of the Human Species* (London: n.p., 1787), 143.
8. Ibid., 143.
9. Wheelock, S. M., *Barbaric Culture and Black Critique: Black Antislavery Writers, Religion, and the Slaveholding Atlantic* (Charlottesville, VA: University of Virginia Press, 2015), 21.
10. Ibid., 21.
11. Hartman, S., "How Saidiya Hartman changed the study of Black life," interview by Rodriques, E., *The Nation*, 3 November 2022, https://www.thenation.com/article/society/saidiya-hartman-interview.
12. George, D., "An account of the life of Mr. David George, from Sierra Leone in Africa," in *The Baptist Annual Register, For 1790, 1791, 1792 and Part of 1793* (London: n.p., 1793); King, B., "Memoirs of the life of Boston King, a Black preacher," *The Methodist Magazine for March, 1798* (London, 1798).
13. Wedderburn, R., *The Horrors of Slavery and Other Writings*, ed. McCalman (Princeton, NJ: Markus Wiener, 1991).

Further Reading

Cohen, A. L., *The Global Indies: British Imperial Culture and the Reshaping of the World, 1756–1815* (New Haven, CT and London: Yale University Press, 2021).

Conway, A. and Alvarez, D. (eds.), *Imagining Religious Toleration: A Literary History of an Idea, 1600–1830* (Toronto: University of Toronto Press, 2019).

Haywood, I. and Seed, J. (eds.), *The Gordon Riots: Politics, Culture and Insurrection in Late Eighteenth-Century Britain* (Cambridge: Cambridge University Press, 2012).

Levecq, C., *Black Cosmopolitans: Race, Religion, and Republicanism in an Age of Revolution* (Charlottesville, VA: University of Virginia Press, 2019).

Nwankwo, I. K., *Black Cosmopolitanism: Racial Consciousness and Transnational Identity in the Nineteenth-Century Americas* (Philadelphia, PA: University of Pennsylvania Press, 2005).

Reeves, J. B., "Antislavery literature and the decline of Hell," *Eighteenth-Century Studies* 53 (2020), 571–87.

Sandiford, K. A., *Measuring the Moment: Strategies of Protest in Eighteenth-Century Afro-English Writing* (Selinsgrove, PA: Susquehanna University Press, 1988).

Sterne, L., *The Sermons of Laurence Sterne. The Florida Edition of the Works of Laurence Sterne*, Vols. IV and V, ed. New, M. (Miami, FL: University of Florida Press (1996).

Wheelock, S. M., *Barbaric Culture and Black Critique: Black Antislavery Writers, Religion, and the Slaveholding Atlantic* (Charlottesville, VA: University of Virginia Press, 2015).

CHAPTER 10

Sancho's Humor

Amit S. Yahav

Ignatius Sancho's letters are sentimental, friendly, topical, and erudite. They are also funny. In this chapter, I outline how Sancho's humor engages eighteenth-century comedy in its various approaches, and how it deploys these cultural forms to comment on thorny issues of belonging. Sancho wields jokes in abundance yet with precision, demonstrating facility with the different functions laughter could serve, humor's myriad representational forms, and the tastes for comedy among his contemporaries. He deploys humor to interrogate the fragile lines demarcating insiders from outsiders and to draw attention to the varying scales on which such differentiations are effected – the group of intimate friends and family, the circle of urbane literati, those who belong in a nation, and those acknowledged as partaking in humanity. And such searching humor, in turn, invites readers to consider how collectivities secure their boundaries, or, conversely, how they may open up to persons whose membership cannot be taken for granted.

In an influential early eighteenth-century essay, Anthony Ashley Cooper, Third Earl of Shaftesbury, reclaims laughter for the social good after Thomas Hobbes has castigated it as vainglory – a false estimation of one's power over others. Ridicule, Shaftesbury explains, is a test of truth, and crucial for healthy social engagement. If practiced benevolently as "a sort of amicable collision," jokes can sharpen reasoning, make it fun, and cultivate congenial sociability ("Sensus communis" 31). Shaftesbury titles his 1709 essay "Sensus communis, an essay on the freedom of wit and humour in a letter to a friend," signaling a constitutive relation between comedy, liberty, and community; wit and humor express freedom and function as tools to construct commonsense. But, in presenting his argument in the form of a "letter to a friend," Shaftesbury's title also suggests that wit and humor are most comfortably engaged among those who hold mutual affinities. In an especially telling moment in the essay, Shaftesbury explains: "For you are to remember, my friend, that I am writing to you in defence only of the liberty of the club, and of that sort of freedom which is taken among gentlemen and friends who know one another perfectly well" ("Sensus communis" 36). Concerned with securing freedom for sociable humor, Shaftesbury reveals that comedy is a privilege of insiders.

Shaftesbury's approach to humor itself became a kind of commonsense in eighteenth-century Britain, fostering an association of Britishness with congenial comedy that is acutely aware of its social efficacies. The following discussion demonstrates how Sancho's jokes contribute to this culture. Sancho's humor displays his proficiency in Britain's foundational institutions – its Christian beliefs, its political and economic priorities, its celebrated authors, and its preferred modes of comedy. Sancho uses puns to underscore the comic potentials of the English language, jokes both with and about mainstay values of home, hearth, love, and tears, and makes fun with popular literature by William Shakespeare and Laurence Sterne. But Sancho does not only underscore his affinities with British national culture; he also constantly interrogates divisions within his community and calls on his readers to attend to the lines that separate insiders from outsiders. He uses farce to create internal tiers of closeness within his group of affiliates, parody to forge pathways for bonding with strangers, and satire to criticize his society while also promoting recognition of commonalities. Moreover, Sancho often declares his differences from a white and affluent ruling class that depends for its daily practices and self-conception on wealth generated by imperialism and on racial and economic hierarchies. Within such a classist and racist context, Sancho's joking with his mostly white and economically comfortable correspondents destabilizes his readers' perceptions of belonging.

The *Oxford English Dictionary* cites several definitions for the word "humor," carrying both physical and mental valences: the physiological fluids and corresponding temperaments it denoted in ancient and medieval medicine; the moisture of the earth and the air or sap of trees the word signified through early modernity; temporary mood or permanent dispositions; a whim or a preference; and, finally, "[t]he ability of a person to appreciate or express what is funny or comical; a sense of what is amusing or ludicrous."[1] Popular eighteenth-century literature combines a number of these meanings to propose comedy as medicine for physical pain, mental suffering, and a depressive disposition; collections of comic poems, stories, and epigrams such as *Laugh and be Fat: or an Antidote against Melancholy* (1741), *Splenetick Pills* (1750), and *The Cure for the Spleen: Or, Kill Care and Laugh* (1769) advertise their therapeutic ambitions in their titles. Such understanding of humor as palliative partook in a broader privileging of a cultivated positivity. Joseph Addison, in one of his popular *Spectator* essays, identifies cheerfulness as a commendable habit, and casts it as a duty that distinguishes good Christians from heathens and atheists. "Chearfulness keeps up a kind of Day-light in the Mind, and fills it with a steady and perpetual Serenity," Addison writes; "An inward Chearfulness is an implicit Praise and Thanksgiving to Providence under all its Dispensations," he adds.[2]

Sancho's letters participate in this culture of cheerfulness, often reporting on his own illnesses and responding to his correspondents' aches through jokes, thus promoting a genial disposition in himself and in those close to him. In one letter, he recommends the discipline of joyfulness to his friend John Meheux: "few can rise superior to pain . . . yet certain I am, the more you can be master of yourself (I mean as to cheerfulness, if not gaiety of mind) the better it will of course be with you" (*Letters* 137). Pain abounds in Sancho's correspondence – Sancho's debilitating gout, Ann Sancho's rheumatism and her burdens during pregnancy, and Meheux's recurring headaches. Sancho never seems to hide or ignore these hardships; instead, he wraps bad news in jokes, raising smiles while conveying troubling information.

But Sancho's comedy also indicates a key difference between "Splenetic Pills" one might swallow – material medicine to alleviate physical or mental suffering – and "Splenetic Pills" one reads – discursive attempts to elicit good cheer. For one could ingest pills without ever thinking about anyone else, while the curative capacities of laughter, he suggests, inhere in sociable exchange. When Sancho jokes about headaches, rheumatism, or gout, he recasts solipsistic pain into pleasing interpersonal artifacts. Unlike Addison, who situates cheerfulness within the individual and his relation to providence, Sancho prompts his readers to recognize that comedy relies on relations among people. As Sancho worries about Meheux's headaches in another letter, he follows with a buoyant absurdity about friendship: "I am uneasy about your health – I do not like your silence . . . it is a folly to like people and call them friends, except they are blest with health and riches" (*Letters* 81). Sancho also uses witty euphemism to turn Mr. and Mrs. Sancho's suffering into pleasing music: "my better self has been but poorly for some time – she groans with the rheumatism – and I grunt with the gout – a pretty concert" (*Letters* 108). And he reveals that deliberate merriment in response to hardships guides his domestic haven: "Dame Sancho would be better if she cared less. – I am her barometer – if a sigh escape me, it is answered by a tear in her eye; – I oft assume a gaiety to illume her dear sensibility with a smile – which twenty years ago almost bewitched me; – and *mark!* – after twenty years enjoyment – constitutes my highest pleasure!" (*Letters* 156). When moralizing about cheerfulness, Sancho underscores interpersonal exchange – Ignatius "assumes gaiety" to raise a smile on Ann's face, and Ann's smile, in turn, gives Ignatius his "highest pleasure."

Sancho does not only point out a necessary social dimension to good humor; he also uses comedy to interrogate the making of communities in their dynamic and various scales of affiliation. Often Sancho's jokes demarcate a tight-knit group of family and friends who share confidence of understanding among themselves that the correspondence both relies on and promotes. In a letter to Meheux, for example, Sancho emphasizes the comforts one may count on with old friends as these contrast with the discomfort of being among strangers. Comically narrating a distressful stagecoach ride he recently endured, Sancho writes: "The stage contained five good souls and one huge mass of flesh: – they, God bless them – thought I took up too much room – and I thought there was too little – we looked at each other, like folks dissatisfied with their company – and so jolted on in sullen silence for the first half hour" (*Letters* 222). The ride is crowded, rough, and strained with estrangement; representing it to Meheux, Sancho composes a set of contrasts – "five" opposed to "one," "souls" to "flesh," "they" to "I," and "too much" to "too little," – whose comic effect confirms William Hazlitt's observation that "The essence of laughter is the incongruous, the disconnecting one idea from another, or the jostling of one feeling against another" ("Lecture Introductory on Wit and Humor" 7). But the comedy of Sancho's narrative relies not only on highlighting incompatibilities among the anecdote's characters, but also on emphasizing the differences between the impersonal social context of the stagecoach and the intimacy he shares with his correspondent. Sancho alternates between his account of the ride and details of his enjoyment with Meheux's younger brother earlier that day: "for my part, quoth I to myself, I have enjoyed true pleasure all day . . . the animated flow of soul in I[ohn] M[eheux] the little, but elegant, treat high-seasoned with welcome" (*Letters* 222). And he continues:

> Contention flew in at the coach-windows, and took possession of both the females: – "Madam, if you persist in drawing up the glass, we shall faint with heat" – "Oh dear! Very sorry to offend your delicacy; but I shall be suffocated with dust – and my cloaths. –" . . . I chewed the cud of sweet remembrance, and with a heart and mind in pretty easy plight, gained the castle of peace and innocence about nine o'clock. (*Letters* 222)

Inside the carriage six strangers endure sullen silence, first, and then, high-pitched contention, while through Sancho's letter two friends can laugh at such distress by interlacing the unpleasant situation with recollections of the people they both cherish. Surely, the vantage from which Sancho retroactively recounts the ride – a home more spacious than a carriage – helps to relieve the discomfort of a crowded stagecoach while it lasts. But Sancho emphasizes how remembered intimacy doesn't require a tranquil setting and can be conjured in the midst of suffering; he arrives at "the castle of peace and innocence" late in the evening after already gaining "a heart and mind in pretty easy plight" by "chew[ing] the cud of sweet remembrance."

Much of the comedy of Sancho's correspondence concentrates in his letters to John Meheux and William Stevenson – two young men with whom Sancho shares humor in the sense of merriment, as well as in the sense of mood, dispositions, and preferences. The jokes in Sancho's letters to Stevenson and Meheux rely on and reinforce a range of affinities – of gendered attitudes, of literary loves, of habitual actions – indicating a special camaraderie among these three. Their friendship also becomes apparent through a distinctive comic style that sets Sancho's letters to Meheux and to Stevenson apart from those he writes to other principal correspondents such as Jack Wingrave or Lydia Leach. A shared comic writing style, and not just shared interests or a common social milieu, constitutes the three as a cohesive unit – a textually close-knit trio that readers of the bounded print volume would group together despite knowing very little or even nothing of Sancho, Stevenson, or Meheux beyond what can be gleaned from the letters at hand. More specifically, Sancho uses farcical elements and Shandean parody to draw the lines of his stylistic inner circle with Meheux and Stevenson. How Sancho, Meheux, or Stevenson really felt about one another we can never know; but readers of the book of Sancho's letters will almost certainly imagine them as an intimate community, without needing (or having access to) much evidence beyond epistolary moments that radiate familiarity through these distinctive and recurring comic modes.

Farce was a popular but loose comic form in the eighteenth century, identifiable through ridiculous extravagance and gaudy and wild elements. Take, for instance, Sancho's representation of a different trip by stagecoach in another letter to Meheux. Sancho shares this ride with his wife, one of their children, and Stevenson; but while the discomforts of the carriage occur among intimates rather than among strangers, Sancho's recounting of it estranges one intimate – Ann Sancho – as it piles vulgarities of bodily volume, odors, noises, and fluids that service the bond among himself, Meheux, and Stevenson. Mr. and Mrs. Sancho along with one of their children and Mr. Stevenson are harassed by passers-by as they sit in the stagecoach; then a bawdy scene ensues:

> how that the fat woman waxed wrath with her plump master, for his being serene – and how that he caught choler at her friction, tonguewise – how he ventured his head out of the coach door, and swore liberally – whilst his [arse] in direct line with poor S[tevenso]n's nose–entertained him with *sound* and sweetest of exhalations, – I shall say nothing of being two hours almost on our journey – neither do I remark that S[tevenso]n turned sick before we left G[reenwhich], nor that the child p[issed] upon his legs: – in short it was near nine before we got to Charles Street. (*Letters* 228)

Sancho confesses to great pressure and to its literal relief through releasing excess bodily wind, which he stages in the anecdote as farting right onto Stevenson's nose. He, thus, turns the scene into comic relief, and conveys confidence in intimacy both with the friend who partakes in person in the situation (Stevenson) and with the friend who comes to participate through reading the anecdote (Meheux). But Sancho's narration also flags "the fat woman" as instigator of "wrath," without indicating any relaxation she might have attained – inside the scene or through its telling. And while we don't know whether Stevenson partook in the laughter enabled by the farcical narrative, his rendering in the anecdote makes him more of an intimate by virtue of his being individualized with a name while Ann is typified as a nameless "woman." Sancho's transformation of factual distress into farcical comedy, then, indicates how narrational style might internally divide a circle of intimates; the smaller group of men are drawn together in homosocial jokes that relegate women to partial outsiderism.

Sancho's correspondence with Meheux and Stevenson also uses a set of literary techniques associated with Laurence Sterne's *Tristram Shandy*. This set of techniques includes profuse, sometimes bawdy, punning, jocular sentimentality constituted by literalist associations, sympathetic yet ridiculous situations, animal tropes, and hyperbolic punctuation of dashes and exclamation marks. There has been much discussion of Sancho's Shandean style both in early commentary on his published letters and in recent studies. Eighteenth-century reviewers complained that Sancho's writing is derivative; "Among other imitations of Sterne, who seems to have been his idol, we wish that honest Ignatius had not followed him in his blanks or dashes" (*Letters* 344), one condescending commentator opines. More recently, scholars have argued that Sancho appropriates Sterne innovatively, rather than simply copying his style. Sukhdev S. Sandhu explains that Sancho uses Shandeanism to challenge his readers to slow down; Markman Ellis demonstrates how Sancho's adaptation of Sterne troubles the boundaries between high and low culture; John Salliant maintains that Sancho's Shandean style traffics in erotic sentiments; and Charles Michael Pawluk reveals how Sancho's enthusiasm for Sterne engages political violence.[3] Sancho does indeed deploy Sterne's influence for all these purposes; he also uses Sterne's distinctive techniques to construct and maintain a shared textual stylistics that demarcates his comradery with Meheux and Stevenson.

In a letter to Stevenson, Sancho establishes Sterne's writing as a preference that he and Stevenson share. He crowns Stevenson as having "catched the mantle" of "poor Yorick" (*Letters* 155) – a character in Sterne's *Tristram Shandy* and *Sentimental Journey* and a pen name Sterne published under. Stevenson's letter, Sancho enthuses, "unbended the brow of care – and suspended, for some hours, disagreeable thoughts" (*Letters* 155); and Sancho continues: "but surely – half the wit – half the good sense – of this present age – were interred in Sterne's grave ... Your invocation has mounted me, Merry Andrew like, upon stilts. – I ape you as monkeys ape men, by walking upon two" (*Letters* 155–6). Sancho here not only directly states that Stevenson's imitation of Sterne gave him pleasure, but also evidences his improved mood through his response's own Shandean parody. Casting himself as monkey on stilts set off by dashes, Sancho comically appropriates Sterne's signature tropes and punctuation. In the next paragraph he flags a mutual delight in puns, along with shared familiarity with the gossip of London's literary circles: "Samuel Foote, Esq. [a celebrity comic actor, dramatist, and theater manager in London] is dead – a leg was buried some years since – and now the whole *foote* follows. – I think you love a pun" (*Letters* 157). And he concludes with another literal wordplay and more dashes and exclamation marks: "and ever while you live – never omit – no – not that – what? – what! – dates! Dates! – am not I a grocer? – Pun the second" (*Letters* 157). Different kinds of dates concern grocers and epistolary writers, but the two collapse in Sancho's writing, and the linguistic observation of their fusion affords the kind of comic pleasure that Sancho's contemporaries would identify as Shandean and that within the volume of Sancho's published correspondence remains distinctive to his letters to Stevenson and Meheux.

Sancho participated in a wave of Shandean writing that proliferated after Sterne's death in 1768 and that contributed to Sterne's transition from celebrity for the moment to an enduring mainstay of English literature. Eighteenth-century literary fans often used parodic imitation not for ridicule, but rather to express enthusiasm and to enshrine an author as treasured public property – "comic appropriation as a mode of celebration," David Francis Taylor explains, serving "to reinforce the ideological robustness of a 'national' literary culture."[4] Thus, in addition to offering a path for intimates further to cultivate their exclusive bonds, the adoption of Shandean style enables Sancho, Stevenson, and Meheux to contribute to Sterne's inclusion in a consolidating English literary canon. And a canon, in turn, enables strangers to share literary loves – bonding through familiarity with certain authors, texts, characters, tropes, and writing styles rather than through direct personal acquaintance.

In one especially interesting instance, Sancho uses parodic appropriation of Shakespeare to approach a local government official, Daniel Braithwaite, clerk to the Postmaster General. Now a shop owner and thus citizen of London, Sancho has been called to serve as a night watchman, a job "for which I am utterly unqualified through infirmities – as well as complexion" (*Letters* 249), he explains; instead, Sancho asks Braithwaite for permission to host a post office in his grocery store. He then invites Braithwaite to imagine a hypothetical scene of Sancho on policing duties, fashioning himself as an especially fat and extraordinarily black Falstaff, who, like Shakespeare's character, becomes an object of laughter by resembling the criminals whom it is his duty to apprehend: "Figure to yourself, my dear Sir, a man of convexity of belly exceeding Falstaff – and a black face into the bargain – waddling in the van of poor thieves and penniless prostitutes – with all the supercilious mock dignity of little office – what a banquet for wicked jest and wanton wit" (*Letters* 249). The reference to Falstaff serves to inform Braithwaite of Sancho's large dimensions and his disposition for comedy; it also invokes a mid eighteenth-century taste for congenial humor that, as Stuart Tave puts it, features "amiable oddities and foibles whom one would choose as companions in real life."[5] Falstaff's canonical fortunes changed through the century, turning from vicious rogue in the estimation of seventeenth- and early eighteenth-century reviewers to loveable, albeit flawed, figure in the assessments of the late eighteenth-century public, as Tave demonstrates. But Sancho here does not only participate in the rebranding of Falstaff as an exemplary "amiable humorist," in Tave's terms; he also, importantly, grants the status of "amiable humorist" to the black man who can, in his rendering, embody this national literary mainstay. If Falstaff can change from rogue to friend, then why not also from white to black?

I am suggesting that Sancho's fashioning of himself as a black Falstaff functions doubly – first, in the street scene that he renders for Braithwaite to imagine; and, second, in the canon-making scene that his letter consti-tutes, and through which Sancho participates in the rebranding of Falstaff into an icon of amiable humor. The first function serves to entertain and inform Braithwaite; the second serves to position Sancho as an agent within British culture, who both participates in shaping national taste and invites strangers to bond with him through this activity. But, in his capacity as agent of canon-making, Sancho doesn't simply fall in line with hegemonic trajectories; rather, he pushes the boundaries of inclusivity. For Sancho grants the status of amiable humorist not only to Shakespeare's odd rogue, but also to the black man who can, in Sancho's rendering, inhabit and perform this national literary mainstay. Sancho begins his letter to Braithwaite by stating his confidence that his addressee is "no respecter of country or color" (*Letters* 248); by inviting Braithwaite to imagine a black Falstaff with him, as unlikely as it may be, Sancho constructs a version of the English canon whereby not only his interlocutor, but also their con-textual culture, could be "no respecter of country or color."

Sancho's vignette, however, is counterfactual; Falstaff, to my best know-ledge, was never played by a black actor on an eighteenth-century London stage, and the eighteenth-century project of English literary canon-making was very much "a respector of color" – as Sancho often reminds his correspondents. In another letter to Meheux, Sancho invokes Shakespeare's *Othello* and the Biblical story of Noah – the two references most often implicated in eighteenth-century debates on blackness and African origins – to apologize for his deficiencies. Sancho writes:

> such beings I say as the one I am now scribbling to – should make elections of wide different beings – than Blackamoors for their friends; – the reason is obvious – from Othello to Sancho the big – we are either foolish – or mulish – all – all – without a single exception. – Tell me, I pray you – and tell me truly – was there any Blackamoors in the Ark. (*Letters* 235)

Sancho's contemporaries debated Othello's tragic flaw and whether black-ness originates in biblical sin – in Noah's curse of his son Ham. Sancho's allusion to these discussions certainly mocks their pretentions to serious examination of either humanity or literature by aligning the faults they consider with instances of mundane omissions. But the reference also underscores the diminishing representation of blackness within the English canon – "foolish – or mulish – all – all – without a single excep-tion," he stresses.

As British national identity consolidated in the eighteenth century, many individuals and groups contended for inclusion, usually against vigorous, sometimes violent, opposition. Sancho engages these wider social conflicts through several invocations of Shylock, Shakespeare's notorious Jewish character. Like Falstaff's critical fortunes, Shylock's also changed during this period; but in the latter's case the trajectory moved from farcical clown to vengeful tragic villain. Sancho's Shylock, however, in the brief epistolary contexts in which he appears, cannot but be genial, thus reversing the direction of mainstream approaches to Shakespeare's Jew. In one letter, Sancho quotes Shakespeare's *Merchant of Venice* to harangue Meheux; bantering his friend for a "wretched hand," a "nonsensical style," and "a poor cowardly heart," Sancho culminates his attack thus: "thou art a silly fellow – incumbered with three abominable inmates; – to wit – Conscience – Honesty – and Good-nature – I hate thee (as the Jew says) because thou art a Christian" (*Letters* 238). Sancho's Shylock here must be amiably parodic; for just as Sancho's ridicule cannot mean that Meheux is a menacing coward, it cannot suggest that Sancho is a fierce hater of Meheux or of Christians. Moreover, the two other references to Jews in the published volumes of Sancho's correspondence indicate a tolerant perspective. One letter puts Jew, gentleman, and Methodist in parallel syntactic constructions to jokingly communicate improbable conversions of Sancho and two other acquaintances: "S – is turned Jew, and is to be circumcised next Passover. W – is turned fine gentleman – and left off work – and I your humble friend, I am for my sins turned Methodist" (*Letters* 84). Another letter recommends to Meheux a pamphlet on "the improbability of eternal Damnation," explaining that it confirms Sancho's own opinion about "the Son of the Most High God – who died for the sins of all – all – Jew, Turk, Infidel, and Heretic; – fair – sallow – brown – tawny – black – and you – and I – and every son and daughter of Adam" (*Letters* 146).

Sancho's parody of Shylock as a misguided friend participates in debates about Jewish identity and its belonging in the British nation. Michael Ragussis observes that the Acts of Union framing England's eighteenth century on both its ends and the Jewish Naturalization Act in its middle occasioned "a crisis of acculturation and assimilation" that played out vigorously on the Georgian stage, especially through popular comic representations of ethnic characters.[6] Jews were usually caricatured, but varying concurrent portrayals generated possibilities for recognizing affinities between Jewish and English characters and for accommodating Jewish belonging in the British nation. Sancho's references to Shylock promote inclusion for at least two different identities in at least two different ways. First, recasting the popular antisemitic stereotype into the status of jovial oddity, Sancho puts the Jew on par with other amiable humorists embraced by the emerging British literary canon. Second, by casting himself in the role of such a recaster, Sancho participates as an insider in the British debate about Jews – he is among those who can extend membership to others.

Yet Sancho's brief sketches of himself as Falstaff and Shylock claim membership in the British nation for people whom many of his contemporaries did not recognize as persons. For if Sancho advocates for inclusion by virtue of British national culture's preference for congenial comedy, he also makes obvious the humanity of such characters as Falstaff, Shylock, and himself – a status that his contemporaries debated, especially when it came to Africans. Conflicts about the representation of Jews in eighteenth-century Britain were often ugly, violent, and fatal; but these tensions revolved around belonging to the British nation, whereas in the case of Africans the debate focused on inclusion in humanity. The most sympathetic reviewers of Sancho's posthumously published letters repeatedly argued that his writing showcases a heart and mind that cannot but evidence the humanity of Africans. His correspondence with Laurence Sterne was first introduced to the public "to shew that the writer, though black, as Othello, has a heart as humanized as any of the fairest about St. James's" (*Letters* 333). And advocates for the abolition of the slave trade and of slavery in England repeatedly argued that to claim property in African persons constitutes a crime against humanity as defined by scripture and by English law. By transposing the question of African belonging to the scale of the nation, Sancho pronounces the debate about their humanity moot because the human status of national subjects is already presumed. In Sancho's correspondence, both Jews and Africans make claims to Britishness, with their personhood taken for granted.

Thus far my discussion has focused on jokes in Sancho's correspondence that evidence boldness but, for the most part, communicate good cheer rather than criticism. Sometimes, however, Sancho's humor directly expresses censure and as such it becomes satirical. Like many other comic modes and figures in the eighteenth century, satire also underwent transformation through the period, evolving from a predominantly acerbic tone, delivering strong negative judgments, to a more benevolent approach designed for thought-provoking entertainment. I want now to turn to Sancho's satire so as to demonstrate how this more overtly critical comedy can be used to challenge, through congenital familiarity, the presumed demarcations of belonging.

In a satirical letter to Meheux, Sancho nests ridicule within references to the identities, knowledge, and interests he shares with his objects of censure. In its overall design, the letter moves from a mock lament of humanity's failings, to jocular complaints about Meheux's neglect, to ridicule of Meheux's fashion choices pitched through biblical allusions, to cryptic references to Meheux's printed exchange with a racist interlocutor over the status of Africans in England, and finally to invocations of Sancho's and Meheux's common penchant for writing presented with deflationary wit. Each of these parts combines critique and assertions of comradery; as a composite whole, the letter delivers a satire of Meheux, of London's fashionable literati, and of humankind more generally, while also emphasizing Sancho's and Meheux's belonging within all of these groups. Sancho begins by declaring that "Man is an absurd animal" (*Letters* 78), only soon to declaim "Truth, fair Truth I give thee to the wind!" (*Letters* 78), thus positioning himself among the community of absurdities. He continues to catalog ridiculousness by chiding Meheux for prioritizing fashion over health:

> the best recipe for your aching head (if not the only thing which will relieve you) is cutting off your hair – I know it is not the *ton*; but when ease and health stand on the right – ornament and fashion on the left – it is by no means the Ass between two loads of hay – why not ask counsel about it? (*Letters* 78)

But Meheux's misguided fashion choices also expose him to grimmer fates: "Absalom had saved his life, but for his hair" (*Letters* 79), Sancho reminds with a biblical allusion to the story of rebellion against King David, which ended with Absalom's death after his hair became caught in a tree. Here foolishness appears not only in Meheux's preferred hairstyle, but also in Sancho's yoking the trivialities of unfortunate fashions with more consequential tragedies such as a prince's fatal insurrection. And, soon after attacking Meheux's coiffure, Sancho acknowledges that his friend's headache may also have been occasioned by a more profound cause. As Vincent Carretta explains in the editorial notes, Meheux participated in a public exchange on the pages of *The Morning Chronicle* in which he sharply replied to racist remarks about "the number of Blacks among us" and ways for "extirpating their disgraceful growth in a fair and beauteous land."[7] In the familiarity of Sancho's letter to Meheux, the specific content of Meheux's public endeavors is omitted; instead, Sancho lets his friend know that he went to a coffeehouse to read the statement and found in it blended "the Gentleman and the Scholar" (*Letters* 79), which then leads him to establish affinities between Meheux, Pope, and Spenser on grounds of their writing genius as well as their chronic migraines. "Pope had the head-ach vilely – Spenser, I have heard, suffered much for it – in short, it is the ail of true geniuses. – They applied a thick wreath of laurel round their brows – do you the same" (*Letters* 79). Yet, if Sancho places Meheux in the milieu of celebrated English authors, this is not only to compliment his interlocutor, but also to underscore another commonality between them – Sancho shares with Meheux a penchant for compulsive writing. "I pity your head, for this confounded scrawl of mine is enough to give the head ach to the strongest brain in the kingdom – so remember I quit the pen unwillingly, having not said half what I meant" (*Letters* 79), he concludes.

The relation between satire on hair and racism that remains implicit in this letter to Meheux becomes more direct in a piece Sancho writes a decade later for the newspaper *The General Advertiser*. In this epistle written, to begin with, for print publication, Sancho similarly combines censure with a shifting point of view that promotes both critical distance and belonging. He targets the silliness of idle gentlemen and ladies, the senselessness of the war between England and its colonies, and the grotesque brutality of England's treatment of Africans, while all along underscoring the insider status of the satirist. Sancho begins by addressing his public letter to "FRIEND EDITOR" and declaring that he aims to engage "this present crisis of national jeopardy" and "to serve my king and country" (*Letters* 266). He proposes to conscript hairdressers to the military in response to a recent parliamentary complaint about the "scarcity of men" (*Letters* 267) at the frontlines; for hairdressers, he explains, "are happily half-trained already for the service of their country – by being – *Powder proof* " – a pun that evokes the eighteenth-century fashion of powdering hair, combats' reliance on gunpowder, and the possibility of conscripting Londoners of African descent – for hairdressing was a profession associated with free black persons in London. This scheme, Sancho continues, will also encourage modish Londoners to "prodigious saving in the great momentous article of time" (*Letters* 267) by inducing them to spend less of it on their hairstyles and to manage it by themselves. "[T]he ladies, by once more getting the management of their heads into their own hands, might possibly regain their native reason and oeconomy – and the gentlemen might be induced by mere necessity to comb and care for their own heads – those (I mean) who have heads to care for" (*Letters* 267). Promoting independence on grounds of both reasonableness and economy, Sancho adds a jab here by attributing "native reason" to all ladies but not to all gentlemen. And, in a final twist of interlaced belonging and difference, Sancho signs this letter "AFRICANUS," declaring that its triple critique is issued from the position of a writer who holds more than one allegiance; he identifies as eager "to serve my king and country," while also professing his affiliations with other regions of the world. Candice McCall details three meanings conveyed by "Africanus," ironically resonating with one another and with Sancho's satirical proposal as a whole: the Roman General Scipius Africanus, who conquered North Africa and defeated Hannibal; Sancho's natal belonging; and the common European custom of naming enslaved persons for famous Romans.[8] With these connotations raised by his signature, Sancho seals his plea to his fellow citizens to reconsider their priorities for themselves as much as their attitudes toward others – the colonists they fight, the Africans they enslave, and the marginalized Londoners they exploit.

Sancho subtly deviates from the commonsense of middle-class white British men and women throughout his letters, boldly albeit amiably challenging his society's demarcations of belonging. Whether critical or convivial, Sancho's humor navigates social conflicts with nuance and sophistication to compose a pluralistic and tolerant textual Englishness for himself to inhabit together with his readers. By Joseph Addison's precept, which I quoted earlier in this chapter, "Chearfulness keeps up a kind of Day-light in the Mind, and fills it with a steady and perpetual Serenity"; but Sancho's humor demonstrates that sometimes such happy enlightenment conveys not just "implicit Praise and Thanksgiving," as Addison has it, but also the urgent imperative to reconsider how Shaftesbury's proverbial club secures its boundaries, and what opportunities it affords for those it deems foreign. Such troubling of the lines that separate insiders from outsiders constitutes the profundity of Sancho's humor.

Notes

1. "Humor," *Oxford English Dictionary*.
2. Spectator 381, Saturday 17 May 1712.
3. Sandhu, S. S., "Ignatius Sancho and Laurence Sterne," *Research in African Literatures* special issue The African Diaspora and Its Origins 29.4 (1998), 88–105; Ellis, M., "Ignatius Sancho's letters: Sentimental libertinism and the politics of form," in Carretta, V. and Gould, P. (eds.), *Genius in Bondage: Literature of the Early Black Atlantic* (Lexington, KY: University Press of

Kentucky, (2001), 199–217; Saillant, J., "The invisible man of indecency: Profanity and the *Letters of the Late Ignatius Sancho, an African* (1782)," *Journal of Eighteenth-Century Studies* 43.2 (2020), 221–38; Pawluk, C. M., "'Almost a savage': The rhetoric of comic violence in Ignatius Sancho's *Letters*," *Eighteenth-Century Studies* 55.1 (2021), 1–19.
4. Taylor, D. F., "The practice of parody," in Bullard, P. (ed.), *The Oxford Handbook of Eighteenth-Century Satire* (Oxford: Oxford University Press, 2019), 353–68, 358.
5. Tave, S., *The Amiable Humorist: A Study in the Comic Theory and Criticism of the Eighteenth and Early Nineteenth Centuries* (Chicago, IL: University of Chicago Press, 1960), 138.
6. Ragussis, M., *Theatrical Nation: Jews and Other Outlandish Englishmen in Georgian Britain* (Philadelphia, PA: University of Pennsylvania Press, 2012), 6.
7. Carretta, V. (ed.), *Letters of Ignatius Sancho, an African* (Peterborough, Ontario: Broadview Press, 2015), 80, note 12.
8. McCall, C., "'Counsellor' among many: Ignatius Sancho's 'Africanus' persona and the construction of public voice," in Stone Stanton, K. and Chappell, J. A. (eds.), *Transatlantic Literature of the Long Eighteenth Century* (Newcastle upon Tyne: Cambridge Scholars Publishing, 2011), 65–76, 70.

Further Reading

Anderson, E. H., "*The Merchant of Venice* and memorial debt," in Anderson, E. H., *Shakespeare and the Legacy of Loss* (Ann Arbor, MI: University of Michigan Press, 2018), 111–37.
Bullard, P., "Describing eighteenth-century British satire," in Bullard, P. (ed.), *The Oxford Handbook of Eighteenth-Century Satire* (Oxford: Oxford University Press, 2019), 1–19.
Carey, B., *British Abolitionism and the Letters of Sensibility* (London: Palgrave Macmillan, 2005).
Clarkson, T., *The History of the Rise, Progress and Accomplishment of the Abolition of the African Slave-Trade by the British Parliament*, 2 vols. (London: Longman, Hurst, Rees, and Orme, 1808).
Eagleton, T., *Humor* (New Haven, CT and London: Yale University Press, 2021).
Festa, L., "Satire to sentiment: Mixing modes in the later eighteenth-century British novel," in Bullard, P. (ed.), *The Oxford Handbook of Eighteenth-Century Satire* (Oxford: Oxford University Press, 2019), 645–60.
Giamario, P. T., *Laughter as Politics: Critical Theory in an Age of Hilarity* (Edinburgh: Edinburgh University Press, 2022).
Hanley, R., *Beyond Slavery and Abolition: Black British Writing, c. 1770–1830* (Cambridge: Cambridge University Press, 2018).
Hughes, L., *A Century of English Farce* (Princeton, NJ: Princeton University Press, 1956).

Mallipeddi, R., *Spectacular Suffering: Witnessing Slavery in the Eighteenth-Century British Atlantic* (Charlottesville, VA: University of Virginia Press, 2016).

Marshall, A., *The Practice of Satire in England* (Baltimore, MD: Johns Hopkins University Press, 2013).

Taylor, D. F., *The Politics of Parody: A Literary History of Caricature, 1760–1830* (New Haven, CT and London: Yale University Press, 2018).

PART III

Performance, Visual Culture, and the Afterlives

CHAPTER 11

A Social Pursuit
Music in the Life of Ignatius Sancho

Devin Leigh

In August 1784, a traveler and diarist from the United States named Elkanah Watson was lounging in a London library when he stumbled upon the *Letters of the Late Ignatius Sancho*. He was so moved by the work that he decided to visit Sancho's home and grocery at Nos. 19 and 20 Charles Street in Westminster. Sancho had been dead for nearly four years by this time, but Watson hoped to have a conversation with his widow, Ann, who was mentioned frequently in the letters, and to set foot in the place where Sancho had first drafted the correspondence that now fired his imagination. Like so many visitors before him, Watson opened the shop's wicker door to the chiming of its bell. After browsing the shelves for a while as a pretense, he introduced himself to Ann and revealed his true intentions. Obliging him, Ann shared memories of her husband and let Watson see some manuscript copies of his letters. But the encounter did not end there. After talking, Ann ushered Watson into the store's intimate back parlor, where one of Sancho and Ann's daughters – either Mary Ann, Frances, or Elizabeth – was seated at the family's harpsichord in concert with a friend. As Watson later recalled in his memoirs, he lingered at the Sanchos' residence and there enjoyed "a pleasant hour in conversation, interspersed with singing and music."[1]

This brief anecdote from Watson's published memoirs captures the foundational role of music in Ignatius Sancho's world. Just like Watson, readers coming to Sancho for the first time are generally drawn in by his letters, only to discover later that music was one of the centers of his life. Sancho was known in his own time, and is still largely known today, for a 2-volume collection of 160 letters that he wrote between 1766 and 1780, and that were collected by his friend Francis Crewe and published two years after his death. These were the letters that had inspired Watson to make his unannounced visit to Charles Street. And yet, Sancho also holds the distinction of being the first published Black composer in Britain currently known to historians. Over thirteen years, from 1767 to 1779, he wrote and published at least one book of vocal music and four books of instrumental music. These books contain eighty-six original songs and dances in popular social genres of the day, mostly minuets, cotillions (also written as cotillons), and country dances. And so, whether Watson realized this or not, he had connected with Sancho's memory as much in singing and playing with his family as he did in reading and discussing his letters. Music was one of Sancho's enduring passions. He had almost certainly encouraged his daughters to learn the harpsichord and had accompanied them on countless nights in that same parlor. To further oblige their guest, perhaps it was some of Sancho's own domestic music, set for the harpsichord, that the family played that day.[2]

Crucially, and unlike almost all of his letters, Sancho apparently oversaw or was involved in the publication of his music. His music books were all inscribed or dedicated by him, the first three were printed "For the Author," he signed his actual name on the last two, and he stocked at least one of them at his grocery store. Arguably, it was Sancho's compositions, and not his correspondence, that he most wanted to be remembered by.

That Sancho's music has been studied so little compared with his epistles is hard to explain. In the early-modern period, people in Western society viewed both a musical and a literary education as outward signs of a person's cultural superiority and class status. Most people among the gentry and nobility in the eighteenth century received training in the epistolary and musical arts during their youth. And yet, the sources we have inherited are largely one-sided. Contemporaries saw it as remarkable that Sancho, a Black man writing just before the beginnings of the formal movement to abolish the transatlantic slave trade, had mastered the epistolary arts. They debated in print about whether or not his correspondence proved that peoples of African descent were, in fact, the equals of whites. By comparison, they saw his music work as unnoteworthy. There are only a handful of surviving contemporary references – Watson's memoirs being one of them – that acknowledge that Sancho composed, played, or was even interested in music. For instance, his only known obituaries make no mention of his music; his only contemporary biographer seems to be unfamiliar with his work in music; no reviews of his music, and just one advertisement for one of his volumes, have yet been found; and the only music scholar from the period who seems to have referenced him writes that he knows nothing particular about his work in music.[3] And this trend even applies to Sancho himself. Despite the fact that music was clearly central to his life, he rarely mentions it in his surviving correspondence.

His letters contain only a few passing references to his musical compositions and practices.

Scholarship on Sancho has come a long way toward overcoming these archival silences. For nearly two centuries after Sancho's death, writers had mostly perpetuated this silence. As late as 1897, when a short biography about Sancho was commissioned for the first edition of the *Dictionary of National Biography*, the author, like all those who had preceded him, made no reference to music in Sancho's life.[4] This began to change after 1945, when the British Library started to purchase Sancho's books of music that featured his actual name on the title page. A BBC radio broadcast in 1958, called "African composers in eighteenth-century London," re-introduced Sancho as a composer of works of music.[5] Starting in the late 1970s, a series of scholarly texts began to set the foundation for the study of Sancho's music, which continues today.[6] Thanks to this thorough and pioneering scholarship, those interested in learning about Sancho's music today have the benefit of over two generations of rigorous and detailed research on the topic. To this, they can add a handful of references in contemporary primary sources, Sancho's five extant books of music themselves – all of which are now accessible online or in print – and educational recordings and performances of his songs and dance pieces by such groups as the Raritan Players and the Early Dance Circle, and such projects as Rutgers University's Antiracism and the Arts in Eighteenth-Century London.[7] These sources, taken together, make it possible to explore the role of music in Sancho's life.

Unfortunately, too many readers still presume Sancho's letters to be the single representation of his identity, and they view his relationship with music as something incidental: a surprising, albeit pleasant, afterthought. As this chapter will show, music was central to who Sancho was as a person. It was an integral component of his multifaceted identity as a free Black man and anti-slavery advocate; a patriotic British subject; a gentleman scholar and man of letters; a father and husband; a person with an illness; an orphan; a devoted Christian; a friend and correspondent; and a proprietor and small business owner. No one aspect of Sancho's identity can be understood apart from his work in music. For Sancho, music was a stable presence throughout his life; it was a passion he carried with him from his earliest years, at least as far as we can tell, up until the moment of his passing. It was at the heart of his personal relationships, complementing, sustaining, and nourishing them. It was around music, more than anything else, that Sancho built a life in England that was at once joyful, dignified, and audacious. By choosing to compose social dance music for, with, and in the company of others, Sancho honored his conviction that music was a social pursuit. Through both its production and its consumption, Sancho's music was a practice meant to be shared.

Music in Sancho's Life

Since he was only about two years old when he arrived in England, Sancho's relationship with music might have started during his residence with the Greenwich sisters. In his own words, Sancho described these years as a time of "ignorance" and credited his education to his residence with the Montagus (*Letters* 311–12). Notwithstanding, the Greenwich sisters were socialites. Sancho would have been, at the very least, an unwilling consumer of their music. He would have learned a great deal about the musical tastes of London's elite class by observing them and their friends both at home and at social events. After he had run away to the Montagu household, Sancho found that books were his "chief pleasure," and we can presume that he started to study music more formally. This would have included studying scores in the family's private collections at their personal libraries, taking lessons from a private music tutor, performing in the family's bands at private events, and possibly continuing his observations of elite musical culture. A copy of the third volume of Ambrose Philips's *Collection of Old Ballads* in the FitzWilliam Museum has the word "Sancho" engraved on the cover and may be an example of a surviving music book he studied in his youth.[8]

We do not know for sure which instruments Sancho might have played, but his compositions suggest that he was a multi-instrumentalist, with knowledge of the violin, mandolin, flute, French horn, harpsichord, and perhaps also the piano. The Montagus had an interest in sponsoring the education of young persons of African descent. For example, in the 1740s, they paid to give their Black servant, Julie Green, violin lessons from the London-based music master Joseph Abington.[9] Generally, the Montagus might have encouraged Sancho's learning of music as part of a broader Enlightenment education in the arts and sciences, and they may have paid the cost of publishing his first books. His first three volumes were written and published in the latter part of his time with the Montagus, between 1767 and 1770, and each was dedicated to relations of the family. Sancho seems to have written the first, *Minuets Cotillons*, to honor the marriage of his patron's daughter at Montagu House in Whitehall in 1767. Elizabeth enjoyed minuets and country dances.[10] The book was likely a wedding gift and, while researchers have not yet found any record of Sancho's music being played, it is possible that his dances were first performed at her wedding reception.

Despite the formative role played by the Montagus, it would be a mistake to presume that Sancho learned about music only through his relationship to his employers. Although Sancho would have attended balls, assemblies, and concerts throughout the city and country while in the service of his patrons, he might also have attended soirées on his own and with friends in London and its surroundings. For example, by the 1780s, there were around 10,000 Blacks resident year-round in greater London. Many of them had been enslaved like Sancho from either Africa or the Americas to serve in the homes of white Britons. By Sancho's day, they had established their own network of private, social clubs held in public houses around London.[11] Here, on a semi-regular basis, the Black community could gather together at night – free from the gaze and without the harassment of whites – to talk and laugh; share food and drinks; and play, dance, and sing. It is likely Sancho attended these parties. Even though almost all of his surviving correspondence is addressed to his white friends, it is apparent that he was no stranger to London's Black community. He counted at least two Black musicians among his personal friends. The first of these was Julius Soubise, who sang, played the violin, and pursued work as a fencing and riding instructor in British East India.[12] The second was Charles Lincoln, who performed at the Privy Gardens in Westminster and sailed aboard an East India Company vessel as a member of the captain's music band. And yet, Sancho's most important relationship within the city's Black community was to his wife Ann and her family. It is not clear how the two met, but perhaps it was during a night of socializing at a London club.

Crucially, Sancho was not only a producer of music, but a consumer of music as well. His interest in consuming music was not a singular one but, rather, a piece of his broader engagement with popular, British artistic and performance culture. This fact is perhaps best demonstrated in a letter to his friend William Stevenson on 11 March 1779. Here Sancho mentions the then-famous German-born composer George Frideric Handel, one of only two composers he cites explicitly in his letters, by including him as his music representative on a list of national luminaries, alongside the poet Alexander Pope, the painter William Hogarth, the statesman William Pitt the Elder, and the actor David Garrick (*Letters* 211–12). Sancho's letters also reveal that he was familiar with the music venues near his residence on Charles Street, including the Privy Gardens and Vauxhall Gardens, and that he sought out live performances to attend with his family. In August of 1777, Sancho brought his children to a "fine evening" of "good songs" and "good music" at Vauxhall on the southern bank of the Thames (*Letters* 147–8). Vauxhall was at the time the home venue of François Hippolyte Barthélemon, a renowned French composer and violinist who was then active in London. The following January, he and Ann expressed their interest in attending the opera *Cymon* as it was being restaged for the Theatre Royal in Drury Lane (*Letters* 209). In another letter, Sancho re-gifted a ticket to a benefit concert for the Lock Hospital which had been organized by the Italian composer and music instructor Felice Giardini, one of the preeminent violinists in London. According to Sancho, the ticket had been a present from Giardini himself, a connection suggested by the fact that Giardini's and Sancho's portraits by the artist Thomas Gainsborough are strikingly similar (*Letters* 170).[13] Aside from special occasions like these, Sancho and his family could have appreciated music in more regular settings, such as during their weekly church services at St. Margaret's in Westminster.

Even if Sancho's musical publications were underwritten by the Montagu family, Sancho undoubtedly produced them on his own initiative and for his own reasons. Likely one of the most important of these reasons was to oppose racism in Great Britain and support the cause of anti-slavery in the British Empire.[14] The key to understanding this aspect of Sancho's music is the fact that his first three music books – *Minuets*

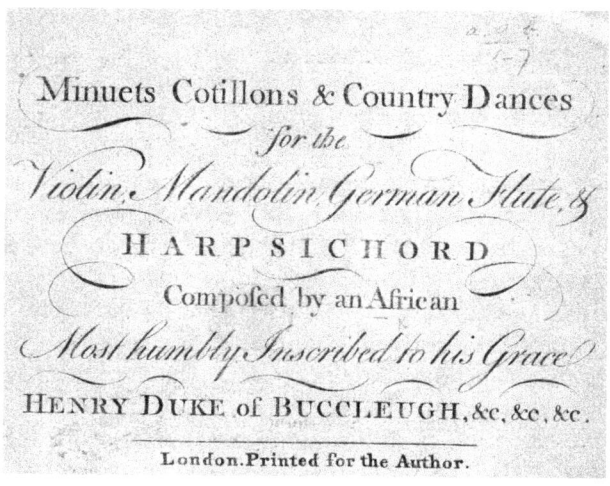

Figure 11.1   Title page to *Minuets Cotillons & Country Dances*, 1767.
© British Library Board, shelfmark a.9.b. (1.).

Cotillons (Figure 11.1), *A Collection of New Songs*, and *Minuets &c. &c.* – do not feature his actual name. Instead, the books are labeled as having been written only by "an African." That this choice to identify as "an African" was Sancho's own is supported by the fact that he also identified himself that way frequently in his letters. Sancho signed at least two letters that he submitted to newspapers in the late 1770s as "Africanus," and he referred to himself as "African" in several letters included in his published correspondence. In one of them, he even implies that he had been born in Africa (*Letters* 272). Most importantly, the publication of his first music book as "an African" in 1767 came just one year after he wrote his 1766 letter to Sterne, in which he had also proudly embraced an "African" identity (*Minuets Cotillons*). This 1766 letter, which implored Sterne to use his platform as a renowned author to criticize racial slavery, suggests that Sancho believed in the powers of art to affect political and social change.[15] His identification as "an African" in 1767 may thus be seen as an extension of this 1766 letter, an effort to embody the anti-slavery work that he had just requested of Sterne. The year after Sterne's correspondence was published, in 1776, Sancho began printing his own name on the cover of his books (*Cotillions &c.* and *Twelve Country Dances*). He could do that without compromising his message, as his race was now common knowledge.

Seeing as Sancho's music does not explicitly address issues of race or slavery, it is worth taking a moment to look closely at how it supports the cause of anti-slavery. First, the decision to identify as "an African" should not be understated. Because Sancho had not lived in Africa since the age of two, if he had ever lived there at all, the identification had nothing to do with either his musical influences or his music's content. Rather, it was about claiming a space for people of African descent within English and, more broadly, European society, culture, and history. By juxtaposing an "African" identify with popular British dance music, and titles and lyrics that honored aspects of British social culture, Sancho was saying that there was nothing incompatible between Blackness and Britishness. He was declaring the right of Black people who lived in Great Britain to claim a Black British identity. On this topic, it is worth noting that Sancho was the first person of African descent whom we know of to identify as "African" on the title page of his own printed work in the eighteenth century. Nonetheless, his example was followed up by Black authors who succeeded him, foremost among them Olaudah Equiano, who identified as "The African" on the title page of his *Interesting Narrative*. Second, although Sancho did not publish compositions that condemned slavery explicitly, scholars have argued that he drew attention to the cause in indirect ways. For example, the title of one dance piece, "Mungo's Delight," alluded to a character in *The Padlock*, a 1768 comedic opera written by Charles Dibdin and Isaac Bickerstaff (*Twelve Country Dances* 12). The character in question was an enslaved Black man who was routinely abused by his "master." As with Sancho, he found relief and pleasure in music. Even more subtle is that a piece entitled "The Feathers" might have been a reference to the anti-slavery passage that Sterne had assured Sancho he would add to *Tristram Shandy* (*Cotillions &c.* 4–5).[16] The passage featured the story of a persecuted, "friendless poor negro-girl" who embodied mercy by shooing away flies with "a bunch of white feathers."

Certainly the most intriguing of Sancho's pieces when it comes to his views about anti-slavery and anti-racism is "The Runaway" (*Cotillions &c.* 42–3, Figure 11.2). "The Runaway" was a common name for a tune in the eighteenth century, and Sancho was probably referencing a contemporary theatrical production of the same name by Hannah Cowley.[17] That being said, the song almost certainly would have carried a double meaning for London's Black community. Enslaved Blacks had been running away from their "masters" in England since at least the late seventeenth century; and yet, in Sancho's time, Black runaways such as Jonathan Strong and James Somerset attracted national attention when their cases were taken up by an emerging group of anti-slavery activists and covered in the press. This topic would have been especially close to Sancho's heart. After all, according to his biographer, he had been a runaway himself when he fled the Greenwich sisters to find "protection" with the Montagus in 1749. Just four years before Sancho published "The Runaway," Lord Chief Justice Mansfield had ruled in favor of Somerset, declaring that enslavers had no legal authority to forcibly deport the people they claimed to own back to the colonies. At the time this verdict was announced, Sancho and his family were living in a house on Cannon Row in Westminster. According to a story in the *Public Advertiser*, about 200 prominent Black couples organized a ball at a public house in Westminster to celebrate the result.[18] We may never be able to say with certainty whether or not Sancho attended this event, but we can draw two other conclusions with confidence. First, Sancho and Ann almost certainly would have known about it; and, second, Black Londoners who saw and heard Sancho's "The Runaway" four years later may have connected it with their memory of Somerset.

That being said, Sancho did not produce music only to promote the causes of anti-slavery and Black inclusion in British society. Although it may seem obvious, he also produced music as a means to support his

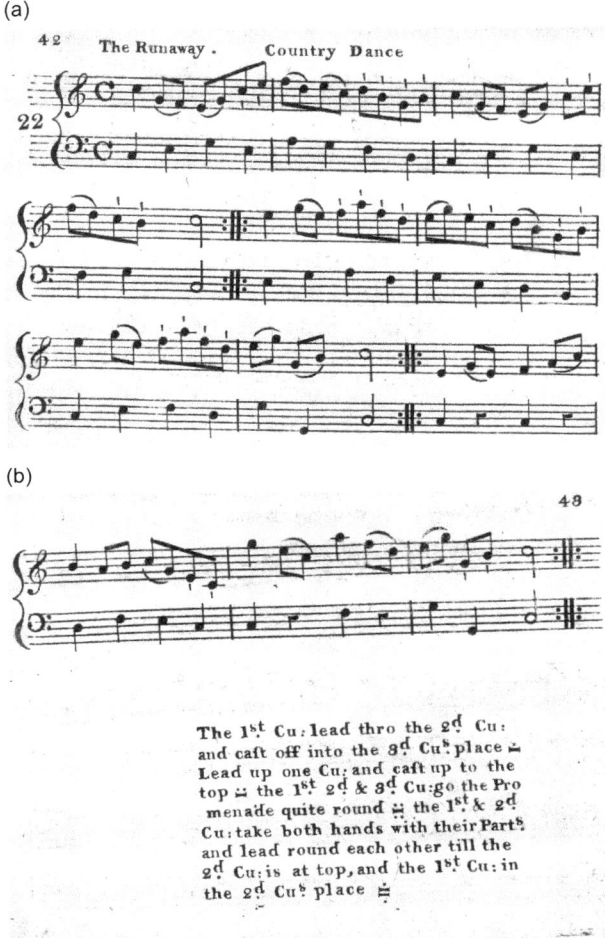

Figure 11.2 (a) and (b) "The Runaway" from *Cotillions &c.*, 1776.
© Houghton Library, Harvard University, TS 552.15.14.21.

family. His biographer claimed he had considered acting as a way to escape poverty in his twenties, and it seems likely that he also worked professionally as a musician from time to time in the 1750s and 1760s. No documentation has been found showing that he was ever paid to play music, yet it is clear that he recognized music's commercial value and leaned on it for income whenever possible. For example, while only one record has been found documenting the purchase of Sancho's music, that record shows that he was selling his work from the moment he began publishing it. In 1767, an entry from the Boughton family account books shows that the Duke of Montagu paid 5s for Sancho's first book of minuets dedicated to his son-in-law (*Minuets Cotillons*).[19] From the title pages of his books, we know that Sancho sold his first two volumes of minuets at Richard Duke's music shop at Great Turnstile in Holburn (*Minuets Cotillons* and *Minuets &c. &c.*). The two books he wrote in the late 1770s were printed by the Thompson family, at No. 75 St. Paul's Church Yard, and appear to have been sold for 2s and 6d, respectively (*Cotillions &c.* and *Twelve Country Dances*). An advertisement for his *Cotillions* volume in the year 1776 – the only one of Sancho's books that researchers have yet found an advertisement for – says that it can be purchased at his shop.[20] Also intriguing is that the advertisement concludes by announcing two instruments for sale: "an exceeding fine old Violin to be sold, lowest Price 15 Guineas; and a one-ton'd Mandolin, by Donatus Filano, of Naples" (Figure 11.3). Why these instruments were sold and whether they were Sancho's own is not clear. What is clear is that Sancho's home and grocery functioned as a site of his ties to London's broader music community and his work as a composer.

(a)

(b)

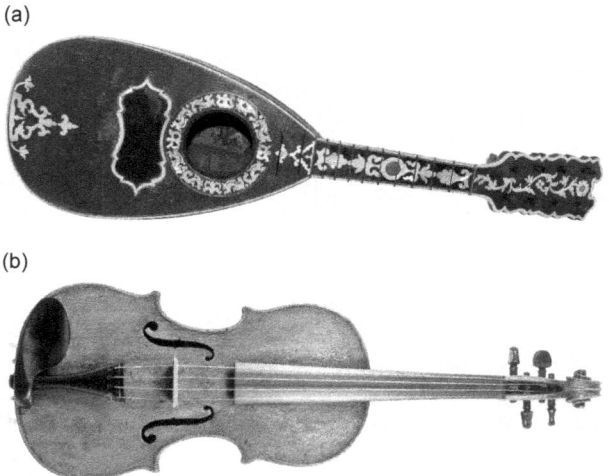

Figure 11.3   (a) Contemporary mandolin by Donatus Filano.
Courtesy of the National Park Service, Longfellow House-Washington's Headquarters
National Historic Site, Catalog # LONG 35728.
(b) Fine violin.
Courtesy of Corilon Violins, München Germany, www.corilon.com, Inventory No. 4093.

Notwithstanding the evidence above, Sancho did not compose music only to make money or a political statement. Rather, for Sancho, music was also a way to practice friendship and cope with challenges. In March 1779, for instance, Sancho and Ann responded to the untimely passing of their six-year-old daughter Kitty by calling their friends to "be merry" together at the home of Ann's brother John Osborne (*Letters* 211–12). A recent flare-up of Sancho's gout may have prevented him from playing music on this occasion, as he wrote only days earlier that "I have as yet but very little use of my hand," yet he would have been able to sing along with his friends as they played and found a much-needed solace in their company. Elsewhere, Sancho characterizes his home as a "castle of peace and innocence," a place where he could escape the gazes of strangers and commotion of life in the metropolis (*Letters* 222). At least three sources written after Sancho's death show that music resided at the heart of this sanctuary. His biographer claimed that music was "discussed, published, and dedicated" "amid the trivial and momentary interruptions" of his shop; an editor of an epistle that lamented his death said that he was "conversant with music in its happiest branches," and that he "spontaneously produced, at moments of recreation, the most cheerful compositions for inspiring mirth and good humour in the dance"; and then there was Watson, who, as we recall, had dropped in on Sancho's home to find a concert under way in the back parlor (*Letters* xii, 277–80). Clearly, music was more to Sancho than a personal avocation, a means of profit, or a vehicle for communicating his political opinions. First and foremost, it was a sociable practice and a communal experience.

For Sancho, music was a collaborative art that was designed to be shared with friends. He affected a playful, humble, and self-deprecating tone in his extant letters and presented his music with those same qualities. In a letter to an unidentified correspondent named "Mrs. H–," he asks forgiveness for troubling her husband with his "musical nonsense," claiming that "I wish it better for my own sake – bad as it is, I know he will not despise it, because he has more good-nature" (*Letters* 217). Elsewhere, he describes his work as "a book of *Cogniscenti dilitanti divertimenti*," an Italian phrase that means "Amusement for the knowing dilettantes" (*Letters* 239–41). At least two letters reveal that he even included his friends in his artistic process. When one of his closest friends, John Meheux, sent him a poem he had drafted to a women he admired, Sancho promised that he would set it to music, replying "I have critically examined thy song – some parts I like well – as it is a maidenhead it should be gently treated . . . I will certainly attempt giving it a tune – such as I can – the first leisure – but it must undergo some little pruning when we meet" (*Letters* 153–5). About six weeks later, Sancho asked if one of his other friends, Mrs. Margaret Cocksedge, could help him arrange dance steps for one of his pieces. In a transitioning passage, he implores her: "the little dance (which I like because I made it) – I humbly beg you will make Jack play – and amongst you contrive a figure . . ." (*Letters* 159–61). Equally suggestive is the fact that Sancho describes the lyrics to one of his songs as "The Words by a young Lady."[21]

In a more subtle way, Sancho's letters reveal that he thought about music as a component of everyday life and an essential part of the material world. Throughout his correspondence, he is quick to amuse his readers with rhetoric that evokes aurality. After the Gordon Riots broke out in the summer of 1780, he quipped in his description that "the ballad-singers" had been "exhausting their musical talents – with the downfall of Popery, S[andwic]h, and N[ort]h . . ." (*Letters* 270–4). Writing to his friend Mrs. Leach in the summer of 1775, he used musical language to make light of Ann and his health, exclaiming "she groans with rheumatism – and I grunt with the gout – a pretty concert!" (*Letters* 108–9). In a letter to Miss Crewe, he finds meaning in expressions of music in nature: ". . . the blackbirds and thrushes suspend their songs . . ." and ". . . the cuckoo sings – on every tree – the joys of married life" (*Letters* 172–3). Again writing to Meheux, he describes his friend's mood as being embodied by the sounds of the hearth, writing that it is "as melancholy – as a tea kettle when it sings (as the maids call it) over a dead fire" (*Letters* 153–5). In a different letter, he compares his friend's attitude to an instrument that must be maintained. "As you have found out that your spirits govern your head," he advises, "you will of course contrive every method of keeping your instrument in tune" (*Letters* 138–40). To mention a final example, in a letter to Mr. Stevenson, Sancho invokes a Spanish dance for couples, writing that "your worship has a book to castrate – and a Fandango to dance – with a *Tol de le rol, de le lol*" (*Letters* 260–2). Passages like these speak to the many ways in which aurality suffused Sancho's everyday thoughts.

One last reason that Sancho wrote and published his music was to honor both his adopted homeland and all the people who had supported him throughout his life. A great deal of attention has been directed toward a few letters in which Sancho condemns the conduct of British subjects overseas in the West Indies, West Africa, and India as barbaric and unchristian. However, no one could read the entirety of Sancho's correspondence and come away believing anything other than that he loved British society and culture. It has already been noted that he dedicated his first three volumes to the Montagus. His fourth and fifth music books were dedicated to the Princess Royal, Charlotte Augusta Matilda, and the eldest daughter of the prime minister, Lord North, respectively (*Cotillions &c.* and *Twelve Country Dances*). Moreover, Sancho used both his lyrics and titles to dignify his family, friends, patrons, and inspirations, and to showcase expressions of polite, English high society. Hamilton has done some comprehensive work on Sancho's titles and has identified many of his references.[22] For example, pieces like "La Loge de Richmont" and "Dalkeith Palace" were named for residences of his employer in London and Scotland; pieces like "Fornham Johnny" and "Mariannes Reel" referred to his brother-in-law John and his daughter Mary Ann; while pieces like "The Merry Wives of Westminster" playfully combined a reference to Shakespeare and parliamentary politics (*Minuets Cotillons* 8–9, 12–13, *Minuets &c. &c.* 15, and *Cotillions &c.* 19–21). In his *Collection of New Songs*, the only one of Sancho's volumes that contains vocal music instead of dance pieces, Sancho used for his lyrics lines from Shakespeare's *Measure for Measure* and two odes written by Garrick, with whom he was reportedly acquainted (2–7). The titles of the dance pieces in Sancho's *Cotillions* volume from 1776 include various references to the life and works of Sterne, whose correspondence with Sancho from 1766 was published the year before and had enhanced Sancho's reputation.

The Music of Ignatius Sancho

When it comes to interpreting Sancho's notation itself, the best and most recent work has been done by Rebecca Cypess.[23] Cypess argues that Sancho's music must be analyzed within the context of the genres in which he wrote, mostly instrumental social dance music. Throughout the eighteenth century, music in this genre was expected to conform to a set of standard conventions. For example, because the music was meant to be danced to, compositions required regular phrase lengths and predictable melodies and harmonies. In addition, dance pieces tended to be written in what Cypess describes as "thin" rather than "thick notation." This means that composers kept the notation undetailed, unspecified, and skeletal on purpose in order to maximize its utility and marketability. For example, by not specifying the instrumentation of an individual piece, a composer made that piece accessible to players of multiple instruments. A treble line with unspecified instrumentation might be played by any of the instruments that operated in the treble range. Moreover, by limiting the amount of ornamentation and the number of articulations – markers that indicated how notes connected to one another – a composer could maximize their musicians' opportunities for improvisation. As long as musicians adhered to the time signature and any dynamic markings that conveyed either tone or tempo (especially important in the performance of dance pieces), they could personalize the music by elaborating on its "thin notation." They could add slurs, staccato or legato articulation, and trills at their discretion; they could play the music softer or louder where they felt compelled; or they could embellish the melody by adding grace notes, a second treble line, or a bass line if one had not been included. In these ways and more, staff notation for social dance music was simplistic by design.

That being said, Cypess argues that readers can hear Sancho's authorial voice in his notation by directing their attention to the specific moments where he breaks from these conventions. These are moments in which Sancho directed musicians to perform his dance pieces in a specific way, a way he viewed as being essential to the composition's character but not obvious, given the genre's conventions. For example, Cypess analyzes two minuets: the eleventh dance composition from Sancho's 1770 *Minuets* volume and the dance piece that begins his 1776 *Cotillions* volume (*Minuets &c. &c.* 9 and *Cotillions &c.* 1). The notation for these dance compositions is uncharacteristically detailed. It includes affective indications, such as "Dolce" for sweet and "Plaintive" for sorrow; slurred articulations and harmonic progressions; and dynamic markings, like "piano" or "crescendo." These details work together to communicate the piece's intended tone: a doleful or longing style that contrasts sharply with the spirited and joyous nature of most minuets. Here Cypess argues that Sancho is adapting to music the sentimental literary style, a style well known for its emotional sensibility and its attentiveness to one's surroundings and the concerns of others. In another example, Cypess suggests that Sancho's contrast between slurred and staccato notes in "The Runaway" may have been intended to denote a fugitive's unpredictable movements as they tried to avoid detection (*Cotillions &c.* 42–3). And yet, perhaps the most important deviation Cypess highlights is Sancho's unusual choice to notate French horn parts for five of his minuets (*Minuets Cotillons* 3–5 and *Minuets &c. &c.* 1, 10–11). Since notation for French horns was generally missing from eighteenth-century English dance music for small chamber ensembles – their inclusion was a matter of oral tradition, rather than written notation – and the instrument was often associated with Black performers, Cypess interprets this as Sancho's homage to Black musicianship.

Since nearly all of Sancho's compositions are for popular social dances, more than half of them are paired with dancing instructions. Writers associated with the Early Dance Circle, a UK-based charity dedicated to the study of historical dances, have done some of the best research to date analyzing and re-creating these instructions. Without any manuscript materials, it is not clear how the dance figures were composed. They may have been written by Sancho alone, in collaboration with his friends and family, or with an unnamed dancing master. The instructions are composed as simply as possible for people to reproduce, further evidence that his books were designed to function as teaching manuals for amateur dancers.[24] The pieces are all variations of couples' dances then in vogue at local balls and assemblies.[25] Roughly forty of them are "country dances," a catch-all term that references English folk dances in longways, or line, formations that originated in the seventeenth century. Another twenty or so are "minuets," an elegant and courtly dance that had its origins in France, but was commonly used to open balls in England in the eighteenth century. About seventeen are cotillions, also described as "French country dances," which were most often performed by four couples in a square formation. The figures, or dance notation, are basic, step-by-step instructions that describe each couple's movements and how they relate to the other dancers. The instructions are accompanied by symbols that indicate the bars and strains associated with each step so that couples can time their movements appropriately.[26]

Although dance steps tended to be standard, figures (how those steps were combined and mapped out in space) were always changing. As a result, the upper classes needed a dancing master to keep them informed of the latest and most fashionable dances. This makes it possible to analyze Sancho's figures for evidence of his creative contributions. For example, it is possible that Sancho was among the first composers to apply the terminology of the cotillion to English country dances.[27] In his piece "Ruffs and Rhees," Sancho used the term *pousette*, a cotillion figure that involved a dancer pushing their partner backwards while they joined hands and stood facing one another (*Twelve Country Dances* 3). This seems to be the first usage of the term in an English country dance. According to Cooper, Sancho was also one of the first to use the cotillion term *promenade* in an English country dance, and he was among the first composers to print and perhaps write cotillions when they first began being published in England during the 1760s (*Twelve Country Dances* 9). This evidence suggests that Sancho kept himself apprised of the evolving tastes of England's nobility, and that he was at the forefront of trends in popular dance culture. Along with numerous dancing masters and composers of his generation, Sancho published and possibly wrote figures that made the latest dances of the aristocracy accessible to non-nobles. Of course, this was a marketing decision as much as it was an artistic one. Sancho lived in Westminster at a time when it boasted a lively social dance culture. Aspiring socialites paid for dancing lessons at academies or at home to prepare for public events such as the annual ball held at Almack's Assembly Room on King Street in St. James's Square. Undoubtedly, Sancho knew that there was an active market for consuming aristocratic fashions, and he designed his music books in order to serve that demand.

Conclusion

Over the past several decades, there has been a great deal of theorizing about the limits of the historical archive. Scholars have lamented the fact that sources from the early-modern period contain abundant materials on racial violence and virtually nothing on Black peoples' perspectives. Within this context, it is exciting to study Ignatius Sancho, who probably left behind more letters in his own name than any other Black person from the early-modern era. However, those writing about Sancho today should understand that he does not survive only in his published correspondence. Sancho's letters continue to fascinate readers now, just as they had once fascinated Watson back in 1784. Yet these letters were not published by Sancho. They were arranged by his friends, after his death, and were printed without his involvement. By comparison, Sancho *chose* to publish his music in his life, not only once, but at least five times in a period of thirteen years. And while his contemporaries, for the most part, did not think of his music as noteworthy, modern readers need not make that same mistake. To put it simply, to write about Sancho but not about his music is to misrepresent him. Music was at the center of Sancho's world; it informed every aspect of his life. More broadly, to dismiss the role that music played in Sancho's life is to perpetuate an untenable bias: that prose sources are superior to music for understanding a person's world.

Notes

1. Watson, E., *Men and Times of the Revolution; or, Memoirs of Elkanah Watson. Including Journals of Travels in Europe and America, from 1777 to 1842* (New York, NY: Dana and Company, 1856), 233.
2. Sancho, I., *Minuets Cotillons & Country Dances for the Violin, Mandolin, German Flute, & Harpsichord Composed by an African Most Humbly Inscribed to his Grace Henry Duke of Buccleugh, &c, &c, &c.* (London: self-published,

c. 1767); A Collection of New Songs Composed by An African Humbly Inscribed to the Honble. Mrs. James Brudenell by her most humble Devoted & Obedient Servant (London: Printed for the Author, c. 1769); Sancho, I., *Minuets &c. &c. for the Violin Mandolin German-"ute and Harpsichord. Compos'd by an African. Book 2d. Humbly Inscribed to the Right Honble. John Lord Montagu of Boughton* (London: self-published, c. 1770); Cotillions &c. humbly dedicated (with permission) to the Princes's [sic] Royal, by Her Royal Highness's most obedient servant Ignatius Sancho (London: Printed for C. & S. Thompson, c. 1776); Sancho, I., *Twelve Country Dances for the Year 1779. Set for the Harpsichord By Permission Humbly Dedicated to the Right Honourable Miss North, by her most obedient Servant Ignatius Sancho* (London: printed for S. and A. Thompson, c. 1779).

3. *The Gentleman's Magazine* 50 (1780), 591; *The Kentish Gazette*, 20 December 1780; Jekyll, J., "The life of Ignatius Sancho" (1782), in Carretta, V. (ed.), *Letters of the Late Ignatius Sancho, an African* (Peterborough, ON: Broadview Press, 2015), 49–52; "Advertisements and notices," *Public Advertiser*, 16 April 1776; Gerber, E. L., Neus Historisch-*Biographisches Lexikon der Tonkunstler* 4:15.

4. Lee, S., "Sancho, Ignatius (1729–1780)," in Stephen, L. and Lee, S. (eds.), *Dictionary of National Biography* (London: Smith, Elder & Co., 1897), Vol. L, 243–4.

5. Scobie, E., "African composers in eighteenth-century London," radio broadcast, BBC Third Programme, 8 August 1958. Unfortunately, this broadcast no longer survives.

6. Wright, J. R. B., "Ignatius Sancho (1729–1780), African composer in England," *Black Perspective in Music* 7.2 (1979), 132–67; Wright, J. R. B., *Ignatius Sancho (1729–1780): An Early African Composer in England – the Collected Editions of his Music in Facsimile* (New York, NY: Garland, 1981); Wright, J. R. B., "Early African musicians in Britain," in Lotz, R. and Pegg, I. (eds.), *Under the Imperial Carpet: Essays in Black History, 1780–1950* (Crawley: Rabbit, 1986), 14–36; Girdham, J., "Black musicians in England: Ignatius Sancho and his contemporaries," in King, R. (ed.), *Ignatius Sancho: An African Man of Letters* (London: National Portrait Gallery, 1997), 115–25; Petchey, S. A. (ed.), *Dances for a Princess, humbly dedicated (with permission) to the Princess Royal by her Royal Highnesses Most Obedient Servant Ignatius Sancho, with additional research by P. Cooper* (London: Early Dance Circle, 2018); Hamilton, J., "Composing an African identity in 1770s Britain: Ignatius Sancho and antislavery music before abolitionism," in Hamilton, J., *Political Songs in Polite Society: Singing about Africans in the Time of the British Abolition Movement, 1787–1807*, PhD Thesis, New York, NY, Columbia University, 2021, 23–52; Cypess, R., "Notation, performance, and the significance of print in the music of Ignatius Sancho (c. 1729–1780)," *Journal for Eighteenth-Century Studies* 46.2 (2023), 185–211; Cypess, R., "The poetics of the wise fool in the music and letters of Ignatius Sancho," *Music & Letters* 104.2 (2023), 197–228; Cypess, R., Cartmill, C., Copeland, C. et al., "Antiracism and the arts in

eighteenth-century London: The life and world of Ignatius Sancho (ca. 1729–1780)" (Rutgers University, 2024), https://sancho.rutgers.edu.

7. Headlam, S. (soprano) and Cypess, R. (director and square pianist), The Raritan Players, "The music of Ignatius Sancho: The arts as Black resistance in eighteenth-century London," Lecture-recital presented at the 2021 annual meeting of the American Musicological Society, 12 November 2021 (online); Headlam, S. (soprano) and Cypess, R. (director and square pianist), The Raritan Players, *A Portrait of Ignatius Sancho: Music and Letters of an Eighteenth-Century Black Englishman, Featuring New Compositions by Trevor Weston*, CD, Centaur Label, 2024; Petchey, S. A., Thomson, M., and Cooper, P. of the Early Dance Circle, "Celebrating the Music and Dance of Ignatius Sancho (c. 1729–14.12.1780)" (research and dance presentation, 2020); www.youtube.com/watch?v=IOnjOprUWso; Copeland, C., Sargeant, K., and Petchey, S.-A., "Ignatius Sancho and dance" (research and dance presentations, 2024), https://sancho.rutgers.edu/dance.

8. Phillips, A., *A Collection of Old Ballads. Corrected from the Best and Most Ancient Copies Extant. With Introductions Historical and Critical* (London: J. Roberts, 1725), Vol. III, FitzWilliam Museum, Cambridge, old classmarks 721; 27.E.100. I am grateful to Libby Collard for bringing this archival find to my attention.

9. Cypess, "Notation, performance, and the significance of print," 209–10 n.35.

10. "London," *Middlesex Journal*, 17–19 January 1771.

11. *London Chronicle*, 16–18 February 1764.

12. Miller, M. L., *Slaves to Fashion: Black Dandyism and the Styling of Black Diasporic Identity* (Durham, NC: Duke University Press, 2009), 57–72.

13. Cypess, R., Cartmill, C., Copeland, C. et al., "Antiracism and the arts in eighteenth-century London."

14. Headlam and Cypess, The Raritan Players, "The music of Ignatius Sancho"; Hamilton, "Chapter 1: Composing an African Identity."

15. Headlam and Cypess, The Raritan Players, "The Music of Ignatius Sancho," 2:00–2:20, 44:00–46:00.

16. Hamilton, "Chapter 1: Composing an African Identity," 45–6.

17. Cooper, P., "A selection of ballads from 1808," *RegencyDances.org*, 22 July 2022, www.regencydances.org/paper058.php.

18. *Public Advertiser*, 27 June 1772.

19. Petchey (ed.), *Dances for a Princess*, 22.

20. "New Music," *Public Advertiser*, 16 April 1776.

21. *A Collection of New Songs Composed by An African Humbly Inscribed to the Honble. Mrs. James Brudenell by her most humble Devoted & Obedient Servant* (self-published, c. 1769), 11.

22. Hamilton, "Chapter 1: Composing an African Identity," 23–52.

23. Cypess, "Notation, performance, and the significance of print," 8–10, 12–16.

24. Petchey (ed.), *Dances for a Princess*, 74.

25. Wright, *Ignatius Sancho (1729–1780)*, 80–1.

26. Petchey (ed.), *Dances for a Princess*, 74, 80.

27. Cooper, P., "The Pousette figure in English Regency dancing," *RegencyDances .org.*, 7 November 2013, www.regencydances.org/paper002.php.

Further Reading

Cooper, P., "The Pousette figure in English Regency dancing," *RegencyDances .org.*, 7 November 2013, www.regencydances.org/paper002.php.

Cypess, R., "Notation, performance, and the significance of print in the music of Ignatius Sancho (c. 1729–1780)," *Journal for Eighteenth-Century Studies* 46.2 (2023), 185–211.

"The poetics of the wise fool in the music and letters of Ignatius Sancho," *Music & Letters* 104.2 (2023), 197–228.

"The musical community of Gainsborough's Portrait of Sancho," in Cypess, R., Cartmill, C., Copeland, C. et al., "Antiracism and the arts in eighteenth-century London: The life and world of Ignatius Sancho (ca. 1729–1780)" (Rutgers University, 2024), https://sancho.rutgers.edu.

Cypess, R., Cartmill, C., Copeland, C. et al., "Antiracism and the arts in eighteenth-century London: The life and world of Ignatius Sancho (ca. 1729–1780)" (Rutgers University, 2024), https://sancho.rutgers.edu.

Girdham, J., "Black musicians in England: Ignatius Sancho and his contemporaries," in King, R. (ed.), *Ignatius Sancho: An African Man of Letters* (London: National Portrait Gallery, 1997), 115–25.

Hamilton, J., "Composing an African identity in 1770s Britain: Ignatius Sancho and antislavery music before abolitionism," in Hamilton, J., *Political Songs in Polite Society: Singing about Africans in the Time of the British Abolition Movement, 1787–1807*, PhD Thesis, New York, NY, Columbia University, 2021, 23–52.

Headlam, S. (soprano) and Cypess, R. (director and square pianist), The Raritan Players, "The music of Ignatius Sancho: The arts as Black resistance in eighteenth-century London," Lecture-recital presented at the 2021 annual meeting of the American Musicological Society, 12 November 2021 (online).

A Portrait of Ignatius Sancho: Music and Letters of an Eighteenth-Century Black Englishman, Featuring New Compositions by Trevor Weston, CD, Centaur Label, 2024.

Lee, S., "Sancho, Ignatius (1729–1780)," in Stephen, L. and Lee, S. (eds.), *Dictionary of National Biography* (London: Smith, Elder & Co., 1897), Vol. L, 243–4.

Miller, M. L., *Slaves to Fashion: Black Dandyism and the Styling of Black Diasporic Identity* (Durham, NC: Duke University Press, 2009).

Petchey, S. A. (ed.), *Dances for a Princess, humbly dedicated (with permission) to the Princess Royal by her Royal Highnesses Most Obedient Servant Ignatius Sancho, with additional research by P. Cooper* (London: Early Dance Circle, 2018).

(ed.), *Twelve English Country Dances written by an erstwhile slave, with research by V. Webster, S.A. Petchey, and P. Cooper* (London: Early Dance Circle, 2014).

Petchey, S. A., Thomson, M., and Cooper, P. of the Early Dance Circle, "Celebrating the Music and Dance of Ignatius Sancho (c. 1729–14.12.1780)" (research and dance presentation, 2020), www.youtube.com/watch?v=IOnjOprUWso.

Phillips, A., *A Collection of Old Ballads. Corrected from the Best and Most Ancient Copies Extant. With Introductions Historical and Critical*, 3 vols. (London: J. Roberts, 1725).

Scobie, E., "African composers in eighteenth-century London," radio broadcast, BBC Third Programme, 8 August 1958.

Wright, J. R. B., "Ignatius Sancho (1729–1780), African composer in England," *Black Perspective in Music* 7.2 (1979), 132–67.

Ignatius Sancho (1729–1780): An Early African Composer in England – the Collected Editions of his Music in Facsimile (New York, NY: Garland, 1981).

"Early African musicians in Britain," in Lotz, R. and Pegg, I. (eds.), *Under the Imperial Carpet: Essays in Black History, 1780–1950* (Crawley: Rabbit, 1986), 14–36.

CHAPTER 12

Ignatius Sancho and the Theater

Atesede Makonnen

In eighteenth-century England, the hypervisibility of a Black minority, the popularity and proliferation of racist characters and caricatures, and a society increasingly concerned with racial boundaries created a complicated web around the idea of performance. Social "performance" could be an act of survival; performing respectability and deference could lead to opportunities, or, at least, a measure of safety, in a world eager to label Black people as savage, lacking in intelligence, and violent. These tropes were popularized by literal performances on stage, where blackness was portrayed by white playwrights and performed to great acclaim by white actors in roles like Mungo, Zanga, and Othello. Actual Black people found themselves associated with and often reduced to shadows of these fictional characters, while simultaneously being told that they lacked the ability to play these characters themselves.

The complexity of racial performance in the eighteenth century is especially evident in the life and career of Ignatius Sancho. Sancho grew up in servitude in England, eventually accessing an education through the patronage of the Duke of Montagu. After his time as a servant, he became a shopkeeper and one of the first known Black men to vote in a general election. Celebrated for his posthumously published correspondence, Sancho had a rich artistic life, from composing and publishing music to engagement with London's theatrical world. Unfortunately, very little is known about the latter – Joseph Jekyll's 1782 short biography of Sancho offers only a few sentences about what appear to have been failed attempts at playing the titular leads of William Shakespeare's *Othello* and Thomas Southerne's *Oroonoko*. Even this scanty evidence is suspect; as Brycchan Carey points out in Chapter 1 of this volume, "[Jekyll's biography] contains much that is unsubstantiated and some of which, on closer inspection, appears improbable, exaggerated, or even invented"[1] and, more specifically, "Jekyll's claim that Sancho attempted to act the parts of Othello and Oroonoko cannot be tested since the attempt came to nothing."[2]

However, Jekyll's biography offers an important window into eighteenth-century thinking about race and performance, in spite of (and, in part, because of) the text's factual limits. This chapter examines the story we have been given about (and have created around) Sancho's stage career against racial and theatrical conventions of the eighteenth century, and against his own self-perception. It begins with how Jekyll's stated reason for the end of Sancho's time on stage – what he calls Sancho's "defective and incorrigible articulation" – intersects with contemporaneous racial thinking about Black vocal performance (*Letters* 52). Brief as it is, Jekyll's biography starts a conversation about the performance of race that goes beyond skin color. Picking up that thread, this chapter focuses on the intersection of theories of Black vocal performance and the stories of Sancho and other Black individuals, including the professional actor Ira Aldridge (1807–67) and Dido Elizabeth Belle (1761–1804), the mixed-race niece of Lord Chief Justice Mansfield (1705–93), who was called to perform in private social settings. It ends with a consideration of how theater wound its way into Sancho's life in a number of documented ways besides the actual practice of acting, including references to Shakespeare in his letters, dramatic sources for his music, and a persistent identification with Othello in his everyday life and legacy.

"A Defective and Incorrigible Articulation": Race and Vocal Performance

Jekyll's biography prefacing the 1782 *Letters of Ignatius Sancho* is a complicated text, with perhaps warring racial impulses. At times, he appears to actively refute racial prejudice, using Sancho as proof that "the perfection of the reasoning faculties does not depend on a peculiar conformation of the scull or the colour of a common integument" (*Letters* 54). While this statement fits into a fairly progressive abolitionist narrative that challenges correlations between outward phenotypes and intellectual capacity, elsewhere, Jekyll seems to casually draw upon assumptions about racial difference. The paragraph referencing Sancho's attempt at theater stands out as one of the most explicitly racialist moments of the entire piece. In it, he details the ill-effects of "Freedom, riches, and leisure" which "naturally led a disposition of African texture into indulgences; and that which dissipated the mind of Ignatius completely drained the purse" (*Letters* 51).

Freedom and access to financial resources "naturally led" a man of "African texture" into ruin. Jekyll seems to suggest that a Black man can (theoretically) think and reason like a white one – however, when offered freedom and social privileges marked as "white," his "true" nature will inevitably emerge. Put another way, a Black man can perform proof of certain markers of humanity but cannot successfully step into the role of a privileged (white) man in society. Some of the vices Jekyll lists, including womanizing and gambling, fit neatly into contemporary racial stereotypes about the unmanageable excesses of Black desire. However, what strikes the final nail in Sancho's financial coffin is a fascination with (and failure at) literal performance:

> Ignatius loved the theatre to such a point of enthusiasm, that his last shilling went to Drury-Lane, on Mr. Garrick's representation of Richard. – He had been even induced to consider the stage as a resource in the hour of adversity, and his complexion suggested an offer to the manager of attempting Othello and Oroonoko; but a defective and incorrigible articulation rendered it abortive. (*Letters* 52)

While less obvious than womanizing and gambling, here the theater functions as another racial test that Sancho fails. It operates as both enticement and potential salvation; Sancho gives in to temptation but proves incapable of the performance necessary to achieve the latter. Ultimately, Jekyll tells us his failed attempt serves as a turning point back to a more respectable path: "He turned his mind once more to service" (*Letters* 52).

Crucial to Jekyll's explanation for Sancho's theatrical failure is a supposedly "defective and incorrigible articulation," most often read along the lines of disability. In a discussion of Sancho's links to the novelist Laurence Sterne (1713–68), one scholar writes that "[l]ike Toby, and like Sterne himself whose bout of tuberculosis affected his vocal chords and left him with a weak, cracked voice, Sancho suffered problems when it came to talking; Jekyll tells us that he had an ambition to perform on the theatrical stage but, 'a defective and incorrigible articulation rendered it abortive,'" while another scholar "has suggested that the lack of fluency or momentum created by the dashes is a faithful transcription of Sancho's vocal stutter."[3] Other scholars interpret the stutter as an inability to project: he was "offered the part of Othello, which he very much wanted to do, but was not able to project his voice sufficiently to act on stage"[4] and others suggest the issue was one of clarity: "he was not a clear enough speaker to play Othello and Oroonoko, though it seems he would have liked to."[5] From a single assertion about "a defective and incorrigible articulation" we are offered explanations of a stutter, issues with clarity, an inability to project, and a general vocal weakness.

It is entirely possible that Sancho did live with a speech impediment. However, "since hard evidence about Sancho's nativity and emancipation is unavailable, we can understand the stories we have been given only by reading both the *Life* and the *Letters* in the context of eighteenth-century literary conventions."[6] Following this suggestion to analyze Jekyll's biography as text rather than absolute, uninterpretable fact invites interesting questions about this episode of Sancho's life, especially when we bring Sancho's own words into play. For example, could we read "articulation" in the anatomical definition of the word – "a joint; *esp.* a joint that permits movement"[7] – in connection with Sancho's self-documented issues with mobility – "my stiff joint – my leg" (*Letters* 175)? Additionally, those who knew him and wrote about him make no mention of a speech impediment or a weakness in his voice, and indeed, at least one correspondent specifically highlights "a thundering voice" (*Letters* 361). What if, instead of a chronic difficulty with vocal articulation, the idea of formal performance triggered anxiety – what if he simply had stage-fright? Stepping away from Jekyll opens up a number of speculative avenues.

Perhaps most compelling is the avenue that leads back to Jekyll himself and his assumption that Sancho was compelled by "a disposition of African texture." Taking into consideration both contemporary theatrical conventions and racialism reveals that while Jekyll's few sentences tell us almost nothing about Sancho's engagement with the stage, they contain a wealth of immediate and obvious racial judgment. Jekyll's relation of Sancho's foray into the theater is rife with supposed "defects," becoming a locus for the faults of Black emotion, judgment, physicality, and performance. First, his "African texture" leads to the moral defect of unfettered indulgence. Then, Sancho proves unable to regulate his emotions, "lov[ing] the theatre to such a point of enthusiasm" that he cannot help but spend the last of his money on attending a performance. Finally, he appears to have "a defective and incorrigible articulation." If Jekyll's language about African dispositions is explicitly racialist, and his comment about unregulated enthusiasm a familiar racialist refrain, this last "defect" might be read as a subtly couched racial critique made more visible through intertwined theatrical and racial contexts. One scholar has suggested that "it more likely can be attributed to his speaking with an inflection or dialect connected to his origins and his very early years in New Granada."[8] Another explanation could be prejudice based on a racialism that focused on the body, rather than xenophobia: "The ability to speak was often a critical issue in determining the relative humanity or bestiality of Africans. Further, the word 'Hottentot,' sometimes a broad synonym for any African in the eighteenth century, derives from the Dutch words for 'stammer' and 'stutter.'"[9] Such explanations address an important context to Sancho's life: his society's investment in evidence of racial difference.

Both ideas are compelling, not because they definitively prove the existence of atypical linguistic markers in either his accent or his articulation, but rather because they consider the pervasiveness of racialism at the end of the eighteenth century. The idea of racialized vocal and linguistic ability, specifically the argument that Black people were physically incapable of pronouncing English, was a challenge to the very idea of Black humanity. The poet and philosopher James Beattie (1735–1803), writing against a belief in Black inferiority in 1790, recalls "I was once, about twenty years ago, engaged in this argument with a very eminent naturalist, who maintained that negroes are of a species inferior to the human; and gave this reason among others, that not one of them had ever learned to speak distinctly."[10] The question of who exactly this "very eminent naturalist" might have been is still a mystery (David Hume [1711–76], perhaps, or Lord Kames [1692–1782]?) but the sentiment echoes contemporary racial philosophy. This particular naturalist follows the more extreme polygenist opinion, believing not only in racial difference but also that Black people were not in fact members of the human species. His citation of distinct speech as a feature of personhood raises the stakes for those who might be judged to have "defective articulation" – in this paradigm of humanity, the inability to perform the act of speech to a certain standard casts doubt onto one's very species. Confronting the naturalist with a hypothetical that resembles the narrative of Sancho's life with which we are familiar, Beattie recalls

> [i]t was easy to answer, as I did, that such of them as were grown up to manhood before they conversed with our people, could not possibly acquire a good English pronunciation, even though pains were taken to teach them; because their organs had been too long inured to a different language; and that the children of our slaves could not learn to speak well, because they associated from infancy with people of their own condition, among whom a barbarous dialect had long prevailed, which their masters rather encouraged than endeavoured to rectify; but, if a negro from his earliest years were to keep company with English people, I did not see that any thing could hinder him from speaking as well as they did . . .[11]

Beattie acknowledges that "masters" purposefully opposed linguistic assimilation and that of course accent acquisition is a matter of where one learns to speak, and when. Balanced against this is his casual denunciation of the language of the enslaved as "a barbarous dialect" and unquestioning belief that the English speak "well" in contrast. Overall, he systematically challenges the assumption that the ability to speak distinctly is inherent, instead understanding it as learned and one's potential for learning universal.

Unfortunately, "This did not satisfy my opponent, who insisted, that negroes are naturally and utterly incapable of distinct articulation, and must therefore be of a race inferior to the human."[12] "Incorrigible articulation" marks racial inferiority, seemingly without proof, just as it appears to mark an inferior ability to act in Jekyll's account. Beattie goes on to relate how his side of the argument was shortly proven correct, through meeting Dido Elizabeth Belle, Lord Mansfield's mixed-race niece, who "not only spoke with the articulation and accent of a native, but repeated to me some pieces of poetry, with a degree of elegance, which would have been admired in any English child of her years ... She was in Lord Mansfield's family; and at his desire, and in his presence, repeated those pieces of poetry to me."[13] Beattie's evidence was obtained through performance, not only of Dido's recital but also in what seems to have been the conversation of every Black person Beattie subsequently crossed paths with; "[s]ince that time I have conversed with several African negroes, who spoke English well."[14] To be Black in eighteenth-century Britain was to be under the promise and threat of performance, to be called to perform blackness or to perform humanity at the mercy of a white audience.

While Beattie appears satisfied with his evidence, the idea that a Black person was physically unable to articulate English persisted well into the nineteenth century, with theatrical performance serving as a particularly public stage for the perpetuation of this myth. "[T]he complaint that black Othellos could not enunciate Shakespeare's text correctly because of inherited, 'incorrigible' flaws was to become a charge leveled repeatedly," including in reviews of Ira Aldridge, the most famous Black actor of the nineteenth century.[15] The reviews did not focus solely on Aldridge's accent as "unpleasantly, we would say, vulgarly, foreign," but also offered a more explicitly racialist version of "incorrigible defect of articulation," claiming that: "[o]wing to the shape of his lips, it is utterly impossible for him to pronounce English."[16] The obvious falsity of this racialism aside, there is a wealth of information about Aldridge's acting style that testifies to his power of articulation. Like Dido performing before Beattie, Aldridge's long career in both Britain and Europe refuted a challenge to Black articulation based in racialized (and racist) fictions.

It was not until decades after Sancho's possible attempt at the stage that Aldridge found success, decades filled with public debate about slavery, abolition, and racial relations. It's possible that the social landscape of the mid eighteenth century was too fraught to allow Sancho actorly agency; the act of acting was itself a type of threat, to more than one agenda. "White actors impersonating Othello could – and if we believe contemporary accounts, did – reinforce the stereotype of African passion. If Sancho had been able to portray Othello in the London theatres, his occupation of a speaking, subject position would have been too threatening."[17] Beyond the possibility of Black actors shifting stereotypes, there lingers, too, the uneasy idea that other identities could be assumed and altered. Acting itself presupposes that identity can, at least temporarily, be fluid, that one can momentarily inhabit a different race or gender, personality or emotional state, occupation, or relationship. To be able to act successfully is then a performance of power and freedom. The idea of a Black actor would certainly open questions of over who controls identity in a society reliant on firm boundaries.

Insistence on constrained notions of Black authenticity was one measure against boundary crossing. Here is a difference between acting or simply being displayed as an exhibition, with the latter emerging in critiques of Black actors – Aldridge, for example, often faced critics who said he was only expressing natural African savagery rather than acting in the role of Othello.[18] Both Jekyll's biography and the edited *Letters* themselves asked for a kind of exhibition, invested in the authenticity and sincerity of Sancho's own character in a posthumous performance. Jekyll and Frances Crewe, the editor, understood that the *Letters* would be examined by readers looking for cracks in this performance, searching for vulgarity, mockable offenses, or dangerous transgressions of identity.[19] While Sancho undoubtedly proffered a kind of private performance through his correspondence (and public, with those he chose to send to papers as Africanus), Jekyll and Crewe themselves also performed a version of "Sancho" for the world – a reassuringly "authentic" (yet marketable) Black man. Part of the reassurance seems to be the idea that Black acting, including vocal performance, was impossible, and not even actively desired. Jekyll appears to distance Sancho from both the ability and the *wish* to act. In the description of his venture into the theater, Sancho operates as a nearly passive figure; having been "induced to consider the stage" by others, it is his very blackness that speaks for him – "his complexion suggested an offer." It is his vocal performance that, perhaps reassuringly, ends the conversation, barring him from the stage and its potentially dangerously porous racial boundaries.

"Shakespeare Says": Confrontation, Composition, and Critique

While he lived, Sancho certainly understood that he was subject to a constant audience, even without a formal stage career. In one letter, he describes a night of entertainment with his family "three great girls – a boy – and a fat old fellow – were as happy and pleas'd as a fine evening – fine place – good songs – much company – and good music – could make them . . . We went by water – had a coach home – were gazed at – followed, &c. &c. – but not much abused (*Letters* 149)." This anecdote reveals a duality of experience – intimate family moments in public spaces and the awareness of being on a social stage, not as performers but still subject to a judging and abusive gaze. One of the most striking details about this anecdote is the normality of the first half. His description of himself, his family, his surroundings, the evening's entertainment – nothing seems out of the ordinary for a man of his economic status. What unsettles it all is the audience which refuses to let his everyday activity be something other than a spectacle to be commented on and critiqued. His etceteras are an almost casual acknowledgment of what must have been a regular event – being followed and watched and commented on as he went about his daily life.

Though denied the possibility of bringing them to life on stage, racialized theatrical characters added an extra layer to this surveillance of Black life. In 1814, Sancho's friend and correspondent William Stevenson offered more detail on the kind of abuse that could accompany this public scrutiny, articulated through Shakespeare:

> I have often witnessed his patient forbearance, when the passing vulgar have given vent to their prejudices against his ebon complexion, his African features, and his corpulent person. One instance, in particular, of his manly resentment, when his feelings were hurt by a person of superior appearance, recalls itself so forcibly to my mind that I cannot forbear mentioning it:
> We were walking through Spring-gardens-passage [near Charing Cross], when, a small distance from before us, a young Fashionable said to his companion, loud enough to be heard, "Smoke Othello!" This did not escape my Friend Sancho; who, immediately placing himself across the path, before him, exclaimed with a thundering voice, and a countenance which awed the delinquent, "Aye, Sir, such Othellos you meet with but once in

a century," clapping his hand upon his goodly round paunch. "Such Iagos as you, we meet with in every dirty passage. Proceed, Sir!" (*Letters* 360)

Again, this anecdote describes a moment full of duality, Sancho both accepting and rejecting identification with Shakespeare's character, a moment of imposition but also agency, with Sancho actively responding to his hecklers. He plays with the idea of being *an* Othello but a unique one, one capable of flipping a script. He names the "Fashionable" not only an "Iago," but a commonplace one, demonstrating both knowledge of the play and an ability to weaponize it. It is also quite the theatrical moment, with Sancho performing to a double audience – his heckler and his friend. He "blocks" the passage, deliberately placing himself center-stage to deliver his lines in a "thundering voice," acting with his face and body. He even provides stage directions to his "Iago" – "Proceed, Sir!" Clearly, he awes not only the "Fashionable" but Stevenson as well, who would go on to remember the moment "forcibly."

The world of theater, specifically Shakespeare, was a part of Sancho's life, whether invited or not. However, sometimes the theater *was* invited into his life – and indeed, deliberately invoked, from theatrical quotes in his letters to using Shakespearean characters to describe himself. Perhaps unsurprisingly, Othello numbered among the works he referenced. In one letter, he satirically contradicts the expression of his uniqueness articulated by the "Smoke Othello" encounter, joking that "Black-a-moors . . . from Othello to Sancho the big, we are either foolish, or mulish – all, all without a single exception" (*Letters* 236). However, he was also drawn to the character of Falstaff: in another letter he describes himself as "a man of a convexity of belly exceeding Falstaff" (*Letters* 251). Besides aligning himself with these fictional dramatic characters, he also understood how his familiarity and use of dramatists could allow him to "perform" for society as another kind of character. He opens another letter: "Young says, 'A friend is the balsam of life' – Shakspeare [sic] says, – but why should I pester you with quotations? – to shew you the depth of my erudition, and strut like the fabled bird in his borrowed plumage" (*Letters* 106). Sancho begins the letter with a reference to Edward Young (1683–1765), a poet and playwright perhaps best known for his 1721 play *The Revenge*, featuring the vengeful black character Zanga (eventually played by Aldridge). Then, teasing a follow-up quotation from Shakespeare, he interrupts the exercise to reflect on his myriad own motives – showing off his education is one, but so is a kind of assimilation reliant on that education.

His demonstration of learnedness here is punctured by the fact that he (purposefully or not) misquotes Young and is further undermined by another literary reference – the story of "The Vain Jack-daw" with his "borrowed plumage" in *Aesop's Fables*. Of the numerous translations available of the *Fables*, it seems likely that Sancho would have read the version about the Jackdaw who "[n]ot contented to live within his own Sphere" disguises himself with peacock feathers, fails to fit in, then fails to reassimilate with his own kind, who admonish him for having "disdain'd the Rank in which Nature had plac'd him."[20] The obvious lesson is that one cannot disguise oneself, physically or with an aura of erudition via literary quotation, and thus move out of one's assigned place in the world, socially, economically, or racially. To attempt to do so is to risk losing the place you do occupy. Another edition of the *Fables* which became popular in the late eighteenth century is more explicitly racialized. In it, the Jackdaw instead whitewashes his feathers; what gives him away, interestingly enough, is a defective vocal performance. "The pigeons, not distinguishing him as long as he kept silent, forbore to give him any disturbance. But at last he forgot his character, and began to chatter," and when he tries to return to the Jackdaws, they, "not knowing him and his discolored feathers, drove him away likewise."[21] The explanatory "Application" accompanying the fable reassures (or threatens) that while this attempted disguise "is a very base, vile thing,"

> let them but open their mouths, and . . . they immediately proclaim their kind. If they should deceive for a while, by appearing in an unquestionable place, or hanging out false colors, yet, if touched upon the right string, they would be discovered in an instant: For, when people are acting a wrong part, their very voice betrays them; They either cannot act their part sufficiently, or they overact it . . .[22]

The fable assures us that one's voice can serve as a gauge for one's status. Applying this to Jekyll's account, Sancho, appearing on stage, has been discovered as out of place, his "very voice" betraying him – he cannot act. The moral judgment here on those who would try to fit into roles they are not meant for is heavy, as is Jekyll's while portraying Sancho's time in the world of theater, a time of his life when he, like the Jackdaw, reached beyond his own sphere.

Sancho also quotes Shakespeare in a number of places – perhaps for pleasure or whatever benefits performing mastery over English literature might have afforded him – but he does so with an understanding that whatever assimilatory power quotation gives him is temporary and unstable. His own compositions, including his criticism, songs, and (possibly) his plays, might offer another perspective on his engagement with Shakespeare and the theatrical world at large. Jekyll claims that Sancho completed "two pieces [that] were constructed for the stage" (*Letters* 53). Again, a lack of textual or even anecdotal evidence beyond Jekyll throws this assertion into doubt. However, as Devin Leigh points out in Chapter 11 of this volume, we do have copies of Sancho's published musical compositions, which serve as tangible evidence of his artistic labor and theatrical influences. These compositions drew extensively from Shakespeare and from *the* Shakespearean actor of the moment, David Garrick (1717–79), who in 1769 organized the Shakespearean Jubilee.

In *A Collection of New Songs Composed by an African* (c. 1769), Sancho added music to the lyrics which open Act 4.1 of *Measure for Measure* (c. 1604). The selection is an interesting one, with the title ("The Complaint") and the choice to repeat the first line about lips ("Take, O take, those lips away") invoking a feeling of grievance centered on a vehicle for speech being taken away.[23] Adapting Shakespeare this way went beyond quotation – instead, he took Shakespeare's lines and made them his own. Similarly, he borrowed and exerted authority over the words of a Shakespearean actor when he set to music parts of Garrick's *An ode upon dedicating a building, and erecting a statue, to Shakespeare, at Stratford upon Avon*, which celebrates (and arguably establishes) bardolatry, a term used to describe the near worship of Shakespeare which emerged in part thanks to Garrick's efforts to canonize the author for the public. The poem includes lyrics referring to Shakespeare as a "demi-god" who "merits all our wonder, all our praise."[24] Rather than working with earlier lines in the ode that blatantly call to the general public to adore "[t]he lov'd, rever'd, immortal name!/ Shakespeare! Shakespeare! Shakespeare!" or later ones that cast Shakespeare as a master of "subject passions" who "[w]ith these his slaves ... can controul,/ Or charm the soul," Sancho chooses to highlight the complementary but not overwrought first Air:[25]

AIR.

I.
Sweetest bard that ever sung,
Nature's glory, Fancy's child;
Never sure did witching tongue
Warble forth such wood-notes wild!

II.
Come each Muse, and sister Grace,
Loves and Pleasures hither come;

Well you know this happy place,
Avon's banks were once your home.

III.
Bring the laurel, bring the flow'rs,
Songs of triumph to him raise;
He united all your pow'rs,
All uniting, sing his praise![26]

The resulting song, "Sweetest Bard," engages with the part of the ode that speaks to the Muses and Graces, and even Shakespeare himself. The first two lines are sung twice, the third three times, and the fourth another three times. Perhaps most striking, in light of his supposed difficulty with articulation, is the emphasis via repetition on "Never sure did witching tongue," a line partnered with a fast-paced tempo. The other part of the ode he sets to music is the second-to-last air, a reflection on the River Avon which inspired and sheltered Shakespeare's genius called "Thou Soft Flowing Avon" – here, the poem asks (and Sancho's song repeats) "Be the swans on thy bosom still whiter than snow."[27] Garrick uses his memorial to cloak the metaphorical source of Shakespeare's creativity in the whiteness of swans and even greater whiteness of snow; Sancho uses that very memorial to display Black creativity.

Later in his musical career, Sancho stepped away from Shakespeare. In *Twelve Country Dances for the Year* (1779), he included the song "Mungo's Delight," most likely referring to Mungo, a black character from Issac Bickerstaff's play *The Padlock* (1768). The character was popularized by the white actor Charles Dibdin (1745–1814), who wrote the music for *The Padlock* and played Mungo himself in blackface and with a put-upon "defective articulation." Some scholars theorize that the collection of songs was dedicated to Ann North, daughter of Prime Minister Lord Frederick North (1732–92), because of the personalized titles of some of the songs, but that, with his inclusion of "Mungo's Delight," "Sancho could not resist placing himself in the picture . . . More than likely [Mungo] was a role played by Sancho during his brief career as an actor. So Sancho had the last word, after all."[28] Though, again, that theatrical career may or may not have existed, Sancho used his *musical* career to speak back to a world that wanted to control where, when, and how his voice could be heard. By reclaiming Mungo in his artistic practice, as Aldridge would decades later, Sancho explicitly writes back to Bickerstaffe and Dibdin. Rather than substituting Sancho for Mungo and seeing this as "placing himself in the picture," we might read this as Sancho's decision to deliberately invoke Mungo, appropriating the character, and framing him in a composition of his own making. It is certainly an act of control, but one that demonstrates the power of a composer, or perhaps a director, playing with a character rather than using him to represent the self. In "Mungo's Delight," Sancho offers a playful critique based in knowledge of the theater and confidence in his own creative talent.

Besides adaptation and reference, he also offered theatrical commentary both on dramatic texts and on actors. In a letter to John Mehuex analyzing Voltaire's (1694–1778) *Tragedy of Semiramis* (c. 1746–9), he declares

> I have read, but have found nothing of the striking kind of sentimental novelty – which I expected from its great author – the language is good in most places – but never rises above the common pitch. – In many of our inferior tragedies – I have ever found here and there a flower strewn, which has been the grace and pride of the poetic parterre, and has made me involuntarily cry out, Bravo! – From dress – scenery – action – and the rest of play-house garniture – it may shew well and go down – like insipid fish with good sauce; – the Prologue is well – the Epilogue worth the whole – such is my criticism – read – stare – and conclude your friend mad . . .
> (*Letters* 134–5)

In these lines, Sancho wittily displays his familiarity with the language of dramatic texts and the effect of theatrical trappings on that rhetoric. While he seems to expect pushback from Meheux – perhaps because he is overly critical of Voltaire or, in contrast, overly accepting of the mediating effect of staging – this letter consciously and assertively makes a critical intervention: "such is my criticism." His comments and reduction of Voltaire's play to "insipid fish" feel particularly striking against Voltaire's own polygenic racial philosophy, which insisted on the mental inferiority of Black people. Through his analysis, Sancho also stakes a claim in his society's cultural world; almost casually, he refers to "*our* inferior tragedies" (emphasis mine), granting himself right of place in a dramatic landscape more comfortable with imitating a version of him than with celebrating his critique of it.

His knowledge and commentary went beyond the page to the contemporary stage. He personally knew actors such as Garrick and John Henderson (1747–85) and recalls witnessing others, including James Quin (1693–1766). In another letter to Meheux, he offers a judgment of one of Henderson's performances:

> I had an order from Mr. Henderson on Thursday night to see him do Falstaff; – I put some money to it, and took Mary and Betsy with me: – it was Betty's first affair – and she enjoyed it in truth – Henderson's Falstaff is entirely original – and I think as great as his Shylock; – he kept the house in

a continual roar of laughter: – in some things he falls short of Quin – in many I think him equal. – When I saw Quin play, he was at the height of his art, with thirty years judgement to guide him. Henderson, in seven years more, will be all that better – and confessedly the first man on the English stage, or I am much mistaken. (*Letters* 147–8)

Sancho confidently predicts Henderson's future success in part on the basis of his original take on a familiar character. In doing so, Sancho shows himself to be an assured theatrical commentator, with a deep knowledge not only of popular characters like Shylock and Falstaff, but also of a variety of interpretations, and knowledge of the careers of the actors themselves. Besides his review of Henderson, the letter also documents a remarkably ordinary moment of Black joy. Sancho documents treating his family to a night at the theater, the first of presumably others for Betsy (Elizabeth Bruce Sancho 1766–1837). Held up against Jekyll's image of an unreasonably enthusiastic theatergoer, Sancho's own words offer a picture of a man happy to introduce his children to a medium which he himself knew well and enjoyed greatly, passing his love of theater on to the next generation.

Ignatius Sancho's world intersected with that of the theater in a number of ways; so, too, does his legacy. I want to end by highlighting a moment in that legacy that underscores the liberating potential of theatrical composition and performance to our considerations of Sancho; actor Paterson Joseph's 2011 one-man play *Sancho: An Act of Remembrance*. Joseph explores what we know and don't know about Sancho through the medium of the stage and the idea of performance. In the monodrama, Paterson as Sancho recalls being forced to perform as a Black child cast in the role of plaything, talks through his encounters with the power of dramatic works such as *Oroonoko*, and acts out everyday encounters on the street, expressing how he feels along the way. Rather than trap him as a single-faceted character, Joseph's play leans into Sancho's complexity, ending with the political and emotional milestone of being one of the first Black men to cast a vote in a general election in Britain (in 1774). Like Sancho, Joseph references and questions theatrical works and culture and contemplates his own place in a theatrical landscape that, more than 200 years later, still resists Black interventions and innovation. *Sancho: An Act of Remembrance* stands out as a theatrical exploration and celebration of a man who deserves both.

As a racially marked "player," Sancho demonstrated both an awareness of and certain mastery over the-world-as-stage, as well as the influences of the theater and dramatic texts over his life. From his letters to his engagement with hecklers by deploying Shakespeare, he worked with and against stereotypes to style an image of himself that he had control over. He demonstrated a keen awareness of the power of literary appropriation in his letters, at once another form of performance and a way to make one's voice heard. In his work setting Shakespeare (and tributes to him) to music, Sancho superseded the circumstances (whatever they were) which kept him from the stage by engaging with the most famous English playwright of all time. Moreover, through his commentary on plays and actors, he passed judgment on the very theatrical world that judged him and found him wanting. Ultimately, Jekyll's posthumous biography reveals more about Sancho's society than it does about his theatrical career, offering an important reminder that complexities of racial performance do not begin or end on stage. The world around Ignatius Sancho demanded a constant performance; sometimes he played along; other times, he flipped the script.

Notes

1. Carey, B., Chapter 1 in this volume, XXX.
2. Carey, B. "'The extraordinary Negro': Ignatius Sancho, Joseph Jekyll, and the problem of biography," *Journal for Eighteenth-Century Studies* 26.1 (2008), 1–13, 1, 3.
3. Sandhu, S. S., "Ignatius Sancho and Laurence Sterne," *Research in African Literatures* 29.4 (1998), 88–105, 95, 98.
4. Levin, C., "From Leo Africanus to Ignatius Sancho: Backgrounds and echoes of Othello," in Trudeau, L. J. (ed.), *Literature Criticism from 1400 to 1800* (Detroit, MI: Gale Cengage Learning, 2013), 266–275, 273.
5. Fryer, P., *Staying Power: The History of Black People in Britain* (London: Pluto Press (1984), 94.
6. Carey, "'The extraordinary Negro,'" 1.
7. "articulation," *OED Online* (Oxford: Oxford University Press, 2022), www.oed.com/dictionary/articulation_n.
8. Nussbaum, F., *The Limits of the Human: Fictions of Anomaly, Race, and Gender in the Long Eighteenth Century* (Cambridge: Cambridge University Press, 2003), 220.
9. Ibid., 220.
10. Beattie, J. *Elements of moral science*, 2 vols. (London: printed for T. Cadell, 1790), Vol. ii, 202.
11. Ibid., Vol. II, 202–3.
12. Ibid., Vol. II, 202–3.
13. Ibid., Vol. II, 203.
14. Ibid., Vol. II, 203.
15. Iyengar, S., "White faces, blackface: The production of 'race' in Othello," in Kolin, P. C. (ed.), *Othello: New Critical Essays* (New York, NY: Routledge, 2002), 103–132, 106.

16. Ibid., 107.
17. Vaughan, V. M., "Race mattered: 'Othello' in late eighteenth-century England," *Shakespeare Survey* 51 (1998), 57–66, 63.
18. Callaghan, D., "'Othello was a white man': Properties of race on Shakespeare's stage," in Callaghan, D., *Shakespeare without Women* (London: Routledge, 2000), 89–110.
19. Saillant, J., "The invisible man of indecency: Profanity and the *Letters of the Late Ignatius Sancho, an African* (1782)," *Journal for Eighteenth-Century Studies* 43 (2020), 221–38; Pawluk, C. M., "'Almost a savage': The rhetoric of comic violence in Ignatius Sancho's *Letters*," *Eighteenth-Century Studies* 55.1 (2021), 1–19.
20. Aesop, *Fables of Æsop and others, translated into English, with instructive applications; and a print before each fable. By Samuel Croxall, D.D. Late Archdeacon of Hereford. The Ninth Edition, Carefully revised, and improved* (London: printed for W. Strahan, J. and F. Rivington et al., (1770), 7.
21. Aesop, *Fables of Æsop and others: Translated into English. With instructive applications; and a cut before each fable. By Samuel Croxall, D.D.* (London: printed for A. Millar, W. Law, and R. Cater, 1797), 173–4.
22. Ibid., 174.
23. Shakespeare, W., *Measure for Measure*, ed. Braunmuller, A. R. and Watson, R. (London: Bloomsbury, 2020), 4.1.1–6.
24. Garrick, D., *The Poetical Works of David Garrick, Esq. Now First Collected into Two Volumes. With Explanatory Notes* (London: printed for George Kearsley, 1785), 57.
25. Ibid., 58, 61.
26. Ibid., 59. See Cypess, R., "The poetics of the wise fool in the music and letters of Ignatius Sancho," *Music & Letters* 104.2 (2023), 197–228.
27. Ibid., 68.
28. Wright, J., "Ignatius Sancho (1729–1780), African composer in England," *The Black Perspective in Music* 7.2 (1979), 132–67, 139. See also Hamilton, J., *Political Songs in Polite Society: Singing about Africans in the Time of the British Abolition Movement, 1787 to 1807*, PhD Thesis, New York, NY, Columbia University, Columbia Academic Commons, https://doi.org/10.79 16/d8-16hc-gm90; Cypess, R., "Notation, performance, and the significance of print in the music of Ignatius Sancho (c. 1729–1780)," *Journal for Eighteenth-Century Studies* 46.2 (2023), 185–211; Cypess, R., "The poetics of the wise fool".

Further Reading

Couchman, D., "'Mungo everywhere': How Anglophones heard chattel slavery," *Slavery & Abolition* 36.4 (2015), 704–20.
Cypess, R., "Notation, performance, and the significance of print in the music of Ignatius Sancho (c. 1729–1780)," *Journal for Eighteenth-Century Studies* 46.2 (2023), 185–211.

Hamilton, J., *Political Songs in Polite Society : Singing about Africans in the Time of the British Abolition Movement, 1787 to 1807*, PhD Thesis, New York, NY, Columbia University, Columbia Academic Commons, https://doi.org/10.7 916/d8-16hc-gm90.

Gridham, J., "Black musicians in England: Ignatius Sancho and his contemporaries," in King, R. (ed.), *Ignatius Sancho: An African Man of Letters* (London, National Portrait Gallery, 1997), 115–26.

Pawluk, C. M., "'Almost a savage': The rhetoric of comic violence in Ignatius Sancho's *Letters*," *Eighteenth-Century Studies* 55.1 (2021), 1–19.

Saillant, J., "The invisible man of indecency: Profanity and the *Letters of the Late Ignatius Sancho, an African* (1782)," *Journal for Eighteenth-Century Studies* 43 (2020), 221–38.

CHAPTER 13

Ignatius Sancho and Visual Culture

Charlotte Grant

Ignatius Sancho is associated with two of Britain's most important eighteenth-century artists: the landscape and portrait painter Thomas Gainsborough (1727–88), who painted his portrait in 1768, and the painter, engraver, and graphic satirist William Hogarth (1697–1764), with whom he is variously, but tenuously, linked. In a period where the majority of images of Black people are of unfree individuals, often figured as commodities or objects, Gainsborough's portrait of Sancho stands out for its representation of his humanity. This chapter explores Sancho's relationship to visual culture not only through the images by Gainsborough and Hogarth, but also through Sancho's own rhetorical style, and the networks and relationships with artist correspondents that emerge through his letters. Sancho moved in circles where the visual was an important aspect of cultural life, and allusions to art and the language of art criticism permeate the letters. Read through this lens, Sancho emerges as an agent as well as a subject in eighteenth-century British visual culture.

The Letters: Sensibility, the Visual, and the Languages of Art

Sancho, like Laurence Sterne (1713–68), whose style and outlook so clearly influenced his letter writing, has a strong visual imagination. Like Sterne, he plays games with the material possibilities of his writing. In Letter XLIX to John Meheux (*Letters* 149), complaining about the effects of gout on his hand, he visualizes his writing practices – "You see I write, like a lady, from one corner of the paper to the other" – and brings his paper into the drama of the letter:

> confound the ink! What a blot! Now don't you dare suppose I was in fault—no, Sir, the pen was diabled—the paper worse, there was a concatenation of ill-sorted chances—all—all—coincided to contribute to that fatal blot—which has so disarranged my ideas—that I must perforce finish before I had half disburthened my head and heart. (*Letters* 149)

Scholars note that "at this point, the first edition reproduces the author's original black blot."[1] Nor is this the only blot: in a later letter to Meheux, Sancho complains of a "blot as big as both houses of parliament" (*Letters* 221). This level of performative self-consciousness of the writer's craft, embracing the material as well as the intellectual content of his letters, is a familiar move of sentimental writers. The letter form is already associated with sentimental fiction; many early sentimental novels were epistolary, including the first sentimental novel published in England, Samuel Richardson's *Pamela or Virtue Rewarded* (1740). Given that sensibility privileges feeling over reason, the letter, either in life or in fiction, which appears to offer the possibility of heartfelt communication, was an ideal mode. And, from the beginning of sensibility's adoption of the epistolary mode in fiction, its material and visual possibilities are exploited. Richardson has his heroine Pamela write in her very first letter to her parents "O how my Eyes run! – Don't wonder to see the Paper so blotted," suggesting that her tears, paradigmatic markers of feeling, are responsible for marking the page, simultaneously marring the text and providing a visual language which supersedes the written.[2] Like Richardson before him, and inspired by Sterne, Sancho exploits the evocative possibilities of a "fatal blot." Sterne himself famously enlisted typography and images in *Tristram Shandy* (1759–67), such as the narrative lines at the end of Volume VI and the marbled page of Volume III ("motley emblem of my work"), encouraging the reader to exercise their visual imagination at every stage.[3] Sancho's address to the reader, prolific use of dashes, the evocation of the drama of writing in the manner of Richardson's practice of writing "to the Moment,"[4] as well as the combined emphasis on the material (the ink, the paper, the pen, the blot) and the idea that the purpose of the letter is to "disburthen[ed] my head and heart" are all typically sentimental moves, many of which depend on the visual.

That Sancho draws attention to the visual and material qualities of his writing is particularly appropriate here, given that the recipient of this letter, John Meheux, was an amateur artist who submitted designs for prints to be etched or engraved by professional printers such as Matthew and Mary Darley from their print shop at 39 Strand (1767–80).[5] In Letter II we find Sancho trying to persuade Meheux to cut his hair, as he thinks it might alleviate the terrible headaches Meheux suffers from. Sancho encourages him to wear a wig, stating "Art, at this happy time, imitates Nature so well in both sexes, that in truth our own growth is but of little consequence. Therefore, my dear M, part with your hair and head-aches together;—and let us see you spruce, well shorn, easy, gay, debonnair—as of old" (*Letters* 79). Sancho's playful tone suggests how much attention he pays to visual and material culture, embracing painting, fashion, landscape aesthetics, and the vocabulary of connoisseurship. Here, talking about wigs, he alludes to the much debated relationship between art and nature. Later in the same letter, he turns to a more explicitly horticultural but no less visual simile: he reflects "real friendships are not hastily made— friendship is a plant of slow growth, and, like our English oak, spreads, is more majestically beautiful, and increases in shade, strength, and riches, as it increases in years" (*Letters* 79).

This awareness is not limited to the letters to artist friends. In writing to Jack Wingrave, his descriptions are strikingly visual and employ the terminology of contemporary writing on art: "the undaunted noble eye, enriched with innocence, and shining with social glee—peace dancing in the heart – and health smiling in the face" (*Letters* 73). This sensitivity to the visual also informs Sancho's references to his own appearance, driving the delicate terms he often employs to talk about his race, and how he might be seen or not seen by others in the predominantly white London he inhabits; he refers to "the miserable fate of almost all of our unfortunate colour" in a letter to Soubise (*Letters* 98). In drawing attention to the visual signifiers of his racial difference, Sancho employs a language which often seems to register that difference as chiefly aesthetic. Thanking Jack Wingrave for his letter, Sancho writes "I only meant in truth to thank you, which I most sincerely do, for your kind letter:—believe me, it gratifies a better principle than vanity—to know that you remember your dark-faced friend at such a distance" (*Letters* 73). Here "distance" seems both literal and figurative, as if Sancho is appearing as a distanced figure in a composition where his being "dark-faced" might risk him disappearing into the background, unseen and unremembered, were it not for Wingrave's "soul impressed with every humane feeling," his "honest friendly heart" (*Letters* 73), both strong signifiers of Wingrave's sensibility. Sancho seems to suggest that it is Wingrave's sensibility which guarantees his continued visibility. When we think about the ways the culture of sensibility not only motivates the rhetoric, but is also a key impetus behind the British anti-slavery campaign in which Sancho figures so crucially, it is perhaps unsurprising that Sancho here attributes his continued visibility to the capacity for feeling with which he credits his friend.

Sancho only occasionally writes directly about paintings; in a letter to Mr. Rush of 1775 (*Letters* 72), he records his gratitude for being sent a portrait of Mrs. Cocksedge by Mr. Gardner, who has "hit off her likeness exceeding well" (*Letters* 111), and later he thanks Mr. (William) Stevenson (a painter and miniaturist) for "the sweet and highly finished portrait of my dear Sterne" (*Letters* 225), but the language of art, connoisseurship, and his familiarity with the artists of the day informs his writing. For example, the last letter of the first volume, another letter to Meheux, contains an extended comparison between the writing styles of Laurence Sterne (1713–68), Jonathan Swift (1667–1745), and Henry Fielding (1707–54) couched in the language of visual connoisseurship. Sancho credits Meheux with the realization that "Sterne, it seems, stole his grand outline of character from Fielding" (*Letters* 180) and then continues

> Fielding and Sterne both copied Nature—their palettes stored with proper colours of the brightest dye—these masters were both great originals—their outline correct—bold—and free—Human Nature was their subject—and although their colouring was widely different yet *here* and there some features in each might bear a little resemblance—some faint likeness to each other—as for example—in your own words Toby and Allworthy—the external drapery of the two are as wide as the pole—their hearts—perhaps twins of the same blessed form and principles. (*Letters* 180)

In this bravura demonstration Sancho enacts a form of "ut pictoria poesis" (Latin, English translation: "as is painting so is poetry") in which he describes these well-known prose fiction writers as though what he writes about is visual art. This idea that poetry resembles painting is a classical trope employed by Horace in his *Ars Poetica* and central to the conception of the "sister arts"; it is their shared representation of nature that brings art and poetry together. Here Sancho talks of "colouring" and "keeping," and Sterne's ability to excel in the "distribution of his lights," claiming that Fielding and Sterne "were two great masters, who painted for posterity" (*Letters* 181). At the time Sancho wrote (1778), Fielding had died twenty years and Sterne only ten years earlier. Sancho claims that the reputations of these two great "masters" will last: he prophesizes that they "will charm to the end of the English speech" (*Letters* 181). Ironically, he foresees Sterne's longevity in a phrase which reads in retrospect like a rebuttal of Samuel Johnson's infamous 1776 statement that "Nothing odd will do long. *Tristram Shandy* did not last."[6]

Beyond the language and analogies which infuse the letters, Sancho also participated more directly as a viewer, subject, and patron in London's burgeoning art scene. His social mobility from child servant to paid butler, and from valet to shopkeeper, musician, and man of letters, gave him a series of different points of access to London's visual culture in addition to his status as an increasingly well-known Black Briton. Previous to the

period from which we have the published letters, when Sancho was
working as a butler and then valet within the Montagu household in
a variety of their grand houses in London, Richmond, Kettering, and
Dalkeith, Scotland, he would have been in daily contact with their extensive art collections. In the middle of the eighteenth century such visually
sumptuous houses as the Montagus' Boughton House outside
Northampton contained ornate furniture, Mortlake Tapestries, old
Masters, both Italian and Dutch, and a smattering of contemporary artists,
serving to cement and illustrate the family's status as cultured subjects and
patrons of the arts. Sancho also spent time in Windsor whilst the duke was
Sheriff of Windsor; Sancho had his own room at Windsor Castle and
would therefore presumably have known the Royal collections. Perhaps the
appreciation of visual art which informs Sancho's later letters was developed in these great houses.

London's Art Scene and Connections to Hogarth: A Family Portrait, a Satire, and a Trade Card

Alongside his exposure to visual culture in these great houses, Sancho was
also connected to London's developing art scene. One of the liveliest
contemporary accounts we have of Sancho comes from a description of
a visit by the sculptor Nollekens and his biographer John Thomas Smith to
Sancho's Westminster shop in 1780; according to Smith, Sancho "spake well
of art."[7] Joseph Jekyll notes in his *Life* that "Painting was so much within the
circle of Ignatius Sancho's judgement and criticism, that Mortimer came
often to consult him."[8] Sancho lived through a formative period in London's
art world, from the early eighteenth-century era of artists' academies, which
typically met in coffee houses, to the establishment of regular art exhibitions,
held from 1760 at the Society of Arts, Manufactures and Commerce (known
as the Society of Arts) and then, after 1769, at the Royal Academy. Founded
in the middle decades of the century, both institutions enjoyed Royal
patronage and permanent homes in prominent neo-classical buildings.[9]
Following a pattern set in the seventeenth century, the majority of those
making their way in the capital's art market in the Restoration period and
early eighteenth century had been European-born. For example, the
German-born Dutch painter Peter Lely (1616–80) became court painter to
Charles I (1600–49), survived the Revolution, and even painted Oliver
Cromwell (1599–1658). Following the Restoration of the monarchy in
1660, Lely became Painter in Ordinary to Charles II (1630–85). Lely's
successor, Godfrey Kneller (1646–1723), born in the free Hanseatic city of

Lübeck (now Germany), settled in London along with his brother in 1676. Between 1682 and 1702, Kneller lived at No. 16–17 The Great Piazza, Covent Garden, and from 1711 to 1716 he ran the Great Queen Street Academy of Painting and drawing nearby, often described as the first art school in Britain.[10] Both John, 2nd Duke of Montagu (1690–1749) and his wife Mary Montagu (née Churchill), Duchess of Montagu were painted on several occasions by Sir Godfrey Kneller.[11]

William Hogarth (1697–1764), born in London, set out to establish himself in contrast to this tradition. He enrolled in the drawing school run by Dorset-born Sir James Thornhill (1675–1734), one of the most successful artists of the early eighteenth century, best known for his monumental patriotic ceiling in the Old Royal Naval College in Greenwich (1707–26), close to Sancho's first known London home. Hogarth was instrumental in growing a community of artists and patrons in London, which included the Montagu family. Duke John lived in the Blackheath area of Greenwich and purportedly took an interest in Sancho and encouraged his reading when he was in the service of three ladies in Greenwich. It was to Duke John's widow Mary (1689–1751) that Sancho applied to join the Montagu household shortly after the duke's death in 1749. The Yale Centre for British Art has a small-scale group portrait or "conversation piece" attributed to Hogarth: *The Family of John, 2nd Duke of Montagu and an Attendant* (1730–5, Figure 13.1), which shows the 2nd Duke seated with his family in a domestic interior, and helps build a picture of the ways in which the family interacted with contemporary art.[12]

The painting shows three groups of figures. On the left, a seated gentleman appears to be speaking. Next to him a lady dressed in salmon pink turns toward him, momentarily turning her attention from the tapestry she's working on. A central group of three figures also seem to be listening, turning their attention from the tea table in front of them, and, closer to the foreground, a younger man sits with a pregnant-looking spaniel in his lap. Barely visible on the left edge of the image, a half-seen figure in green and red livery holds out a silver tray with an overturned teacup. The painting has been cropped and originally showed a full figure.[13] The small hands are black or brown, presumably belonging to a Black page boy, who could be Sancho, but is more likely a predecessor of his who worked in the Montagu household. In addition to employing several Black servants, Duke John was instrumental in providing patronage to other Black Londoners and African visitors, including Job Ben Solomon and Francis Williams. As was common in conversation pieces of the period, Hogarth's image shows the family in an opulent interior full of luxury

Figure 13.1   William Hogarth, *The Family of John, 2nd Duke of Montagu and an Attendant* (1730–5), oil on canvas, 21 × 29 1/2 inches (53.3 × 74.9 cm), B1977.14.58 (Yale Center for British Art, Paul Mellon Collection).

goods, many of which, like the blue and white Chinese vase standing in the ornate marble fireplace, and the lacquer cabinet in front of the green wallpaper, were imported. The young Black servant fits within that context. Many portraits from the seventeenth and eighteenth centuries such as Anthony Van Dyke's portrait *Princess Henrietta of Lorraine, Attended by a Page* (c. 1634) now in Kenwood House, London, show Black pages as visual accessories. In the Montagu family portrait, Hogarth plays with potential instability as he does in many of his group portraits; here a kitten has toppled a work basket as it pulls on a ball of wool, noticed, it seems only by the now edited figure of the child servant, and possibly the cause of the overturned cup he carries.

This family portrait was, at least ostensibly, a private image. Before the exhibitions held at the Society of Arts from 1760 onwards, one of the only places in London to see contemporary paintings by English artists in public was the Court Room of the Foundling Hospital in Bloomsbury. Granted a royal charter in 1739, the charitable institution founded by Sir Thomas Coram (1668–1751) became, thanks to the involvement of Hogarth, a key location in which to enjoy contemporary culture, both artistic and musical. Coram was born in the West Country and made his fortune in shipbuilding in America. A devout Anglican, he was horrified by the numbers of abandoned babies he saw in the streets of London on his return to the city, and campaigned for seventeen years to establish a home for them, finally enlisting the support of twenty-one "ladies of quality and distinction," all aristocratic ladies in waiting to Queen Caroline, to petition the king and promote his cause.[14] One of these ladies was Isabella Montagu, Duchess of Manchester (c. 1706–86), another was Elizabeth Brudenell, Countess of Cardigan (1689–1745), mother of George Brudenell (1712–90), who became the First Duke of Montagu of the new creation in 1766, and for whom Sancho subsequently worked as a valet. Whilst there is no record of Sancho visiting the Foundling Hospital, there are strong Montagu connections, both through Elizabeth Brudenell and through John, 2nd Duke of Montagu, who was a Foundling Governor. Both of the artists associated with Sancho, namely Gainsborough and Hogarth, contributed to the Hospital, Hogarth above all.

Hogarth supported Coram and the Foundling Hospital for over twenty-five years. In addition to his own magnificent 1740 portrait of Coram, Hogarth enlisted a group of artists to paint large- and small-scale paintings for the Court Room, where the governors held formal meetings, firmly allying contemporary British art with the emerging moral culture of civic duty and politeness. Hogarth, Francis Hayman (1708–76), Joseph Highmore (1692–1780) – grandfather to John Highmore, one of Sancho's correspondents and a subscriber to the *Letters* – and James Wills (c. 1705–76) all painted scenes from the Old and New Testaments. Hogarth, Hayman, and Highmore were members of the St. Martin's Lane Academy, organized by Hogarth in James Thornhill's house. Other artists, including the great Welsh landscape painter Richard Wilson (1714–82) and a young Thomas Gainsborough (1727–88), painted roundels showing prominent schools, hospitals, and charitable buildings in contemporary London. Hogarth's visual scheme in the Court Room, anchored by *An Allegory of Charity*, a magnificent bas relief over the fireplace by the Flemish sculptor Rysbrack (1694–1770), was designed to promote charity as a core Christian virtue, and to reassure prospective patrons of the Foundling Hospital that their support for the children was moral, rather than to be seen as inadvertently promoting vice through condoning the illicit sexual activity which led to so many unwanted babies.

The other place to see contemporary art in London was Vauxhall Gardens. These pleasure gardens, located on the south bank of the

Thames between Lambeth Palace and the modern Vauxhall station, were developed by Jonathan Tyers (1702–67). Sancho visited in 1777, as recorded in his letter to Mr. Rush of 27 August, where he notes "We went by water—had a coach home—were gazed at—followed, &c. &c.— but not much abused" (*Letters* 148). Previously suffering from a dubious reputation as a location for prostitution and vice, under Tyers the gardens became a hugely fashionable attraction from the 1740s. Hogarth was a key figure here, designing an admission ticket produced from 1732, and organizing the contribution of other artists, principally Francis Hayman, who painted a series of images to decorate the supper boxes which lined the main walks.[15] It was a place to be seen. A perfect place for people watching as visitors strolled along the "great walk" and listened to music; Markman Ellis writes about Sancho's own music being performed at Vauxhall in Chapter 7 in this volume. The back walls of the supper boxes at Vauxhall were decorated with domestic conversation scenes, such as Hayman's *Children building Houses with Cards* (c. 1743), which Gainsborough is reported to have helped paint.[16] This image, showing cards falling from a table, hints at the possibility of collapse or disruption, as do Hayman's other supper box paintings like the *Milkmaid's Garland*, now in London's Victoria & Albert museum, and his illustrations from Samuel Richardson's *Pamela*. Vauxhall's aesthetic was an eclectic and inclusive English Rococo, strongly linked to sentimental visual culture. It combined English sensibility with the playful fluidity of French Rococo, as well as garden buildings in the Chinese style, and promoted English music such as that by Sancho, though much of the music was composed by George Frideric Handel (1685–1759), who was resident in London between 1712 and his death in 1759. Handel had also been a key supporter of the Foundling Hospital, giving regular benefit performances of the *Messiah* in the Hospital Chapel and leaving the institution a fair copy of the score in his will.

Vauxhall and the Foundling Hospital were London's two main venues for the display of paintings prior to the exhibitions held at the Society of Arts and the Royal Academy. Many of Sancho's correspondents were members of the Society of Arts, and many had links to the artists' academies around Covent Garden, which predated the Society of Arts. In a letter of 22 May 1778 to Mr. J (identified as John Ireland, a watchmaker who sold prints, theater tickets, and books from his Maiden Lane house, who was also the publisher of the three-volume edition of Hogarth's prints published between 1791 and 1798 [see below]),[17] Sancho petitions Ireland to look at some drawings by a young artist (probably John Meheux), saying there are "some inaccuracies in both— which any regular artist will amend.—As my friend is self-taught, his errors must be excused" (*Letters* 177). Inspired by Laurence Sterne's novel *Tristram Shandy* (1759–67), Sancho uses the metaphor of the hobby horse to talk about the drawings, saying "The companions to this billet are the hobby horses of a young man that I respect" (*Letters* 177). Both Ireland and his lodger John Henderson were members of a Shandean Society (focused on the works of Laurence Sterne) in the late 1760s, as well as being members of a "society of artists, art collectors, and amateurs that for years met at the Three Feathers Public-House, in Leicester-Fields."[18] The artist John Hamilton Mortimer (1740–79) was another close friend of the Irelands, who himself ran an artists' academy on Maiden Lane. On the occasion of Mortimer's death in 1779, Sancho wrote: "He winged his rapid flight to those celestial mansions—where Pope—Hogarth—Handel—Chatham—and Garrick, are enjoying the full sweets of beatific vision—with the great Artists—Worthies—and Poets of time without date" (*Letters* 212). For Sancho, artists, writers, and actors formed an interwoven cultural fabric. Oliver Ayers notes in Chapter 3 in this volume how close London's theaters and many of its art institutions, such as James Barralet's art academy and Mortimer's academy in Covent Garden, were to Sancho's house in Charles Street, arguing that "this tight-knit urban geography played an active role fostering Sancho's social connections."[19]

A Satire: Hogarth's *Taste in High Life*

In his edition of Hogarth's engravings, *Hogarth Illustrated* (1791), John Ireland noted that Sancho was thought by some to have been the model for the Black boy in Hogarth's 1742 satirical painting *Taste in High Life* (Figure 13.2), but that he would have been too old.[20] *Taste in High Life*, like the Montagu family portrait described above, places a Black servant boy in a conversation piece setting, albeit in satirical mode.

The original painting was commissioned by an heiress, Mary Edwards of Kensington, but the image is well known through multiple engraved versions, including an etching of 1746 and a stipple engraving of 1798.[21] The unfounded but persistent link to Sancho serves to remind us that he was one of many young Black boys working as domestic servants in early eighteenth-century London whose names, unlike Sancho's, have been lost. Hogarth's satire, as requested by his patron Edwards, demonstrates how taste is perverted by fashion. The boy, dressed in a feathered turban style headdress, and seated on a high stool, is the object of attention from a fawning woman. She touches his chin with her right hand, an ambiguous chin-chuck gesture, whilst her left hand is out of sight beneath her petticoats in a typically suggestive pose. This pair is balanced by another, an

Figure 13.2   William Hogarth, *Taste in High Life* (1742), Lewis Walpole Library,
Yale University, 772.9.10.1, Kinnaird 74K(b) Box 115.
Courtesy of The Lewis Walpole Library, Yale University.

elderly woman dressed in an even more absurdly large hooped petticoat
entranced by a tiny china cup held by an exaggeratedly foppish elderly man
identified as Charles Colyear, 2nd Earl of Portmore. At the bottom right of
the image a partially dressed monkey "apes" or imitates the humans. On
the wall behind, Hogarth includes secondary smaller images, in one of
which we see a Venus de Milo statue labeled "*the Mode 1742*," where her
natural curves (as idealized elsewhere by Hogarth in his 1753 treatise *The
Analysis of Beauty*) have been corrupted by high heels, stays, and a half-
petticoat. Hogarth was trenchant in his aims for English culture to distance
itself from widespread French influence, as demonstrated in his 1748 *Calais
Gate* image and in the 1722 print *Masquerades and Operas*. In *Taste in High
Life*, as in the earlier Montagu family portrait, the Black servant boy is part
of a network of cultural figures and objects brought from around the world.
He is, as David Dabydeen put it, "as much a culture-object (a 'curiosity' or
'Exotick') as the statue of the Chinese mandarin he holds in his hand."[22]
The scene is one of domestic consumption infiltrated by New World

commodities (tea, sugar, china, Egyptian artifacts), where desire, specifically female desire, has been corrupted by luxury. The three mocked figures stand on a Persian carpet; to the boy's left is an Egyptian-style pyramid made of Chinese dominoes; in the foreground the monkey, dressed in fashionable clothing including a tricorn or "cocked" hat, holds up a French menu, another image of mimicry. The tiny cup which the right-hand couple fawn over may be for tea, another import from India or China, and the tiny cup itself references the appeal of Chinese porcelain as well as the growing taste for English ceramics. Whilst neither of the young Black servants represented in *Taste in High Life* and the Montagu family portrait can be securely identified as Sancho, they do suggest the world he lived in as a child, and some of the ways Black figures were visible and perceived in contemporary art.

The Trade Card

Another of Sancho's links to visual culture is the trade card (Figure 13.3) he commissioned for his Westminster shop. Copies of his trade card exist in both the British Museum and the Victoria & Albert Museum (V&A).

On the V&A's copy someone has written Hogarth's name. There is no evidence that the card was designed by Hogarth, and it is distinctly unlikely, since Sancho's shop was opened in early 1774 and Hogarth had died in 1764. However, the style is very much Hogarth's. One side of the card shows two young boys, both partially naked. The central figure, probably an Indigenous child, wears a feathered headdress and sits in front of a large barrel, relaxing and leaning on what may be a pile of tobacco leaves. Shown in profile facing left, he holds a long smoking pipe and a foaming tankard of beer. Behind him to his right is a Black boy who is shown working, gathering an armful of the leaves. The script above reads "Sancho's best Trinidado." The reverse depicts an encounter between two men. On the right a possible Kalinago or Caribbean Indigenous man with a feathered headdress gives his right hand to a European man wearing a tricorn hat who leans slightly forward to place his left foot on a shield displaying three Fleurs de Lis, presumably a representation of France, which he also pierces with the spear held in his left hand; the Indigenous man steps on the shield with his left foot. On the left, a barrel labeled "Sancho's Best Trinidado" and some boxes marked "No.19 Charles Street Westminster" are shown underneath a pulley used to transport goods from ships to the shore. A boat in the background and a ship's rigging frame the right-hand side of the image; in front we see from behind a sketchy figure

(a)

(b)

Figure 13.3 (a) and (b) Ignatius Sancho trade cards, two sides.
© The Trustees of the British Library.

carrying a large bundle on his back. This side is labeled "The Wish." The British Museum copy of the trade card is part of the Banks Collection of printed ephemera collected by Sarah Sophia Banks (1744–1818), sister to the botanist Joseph Banks. It is labeled in pencil "1779" and in pen "1801." The V&A dates the card 1772–1780. Sancho refers to a trade card in a letter sent from Charles Street on 1 November 1773 in which he plans his life as a grocer: "I have strong hope—the more children, the more blessings—and if it please the Almighty to spare me from the gout, I verily think the happiest part of my life is to come—soap, starch, and blue, with raisins, figs &c.—we shall cut a respectable figure—in our printed cards" (*Letters* 103). Whilst many trade cards and shop signs advertising goods imported from the Caribbean show enslaved Africans, there is a clear irony in Sancho's blatant employment of the iconography of the trade which relies on enslaved labor, and which might have been instrumental in his own displacement. With the celebration of "Sancho's Best Trinidado" he seems to have embraced that irony.

Sancho Represented: The Gainsborough Portrait (Bath, 1768)

The visual representation most clearly associated with Sancho is the Gainsborough portrait. Thomas Gainsborough was born in Suffolk and sent to London by his father in 1740, when he was aged thirteen, to receive art training. Initially he worked with a silversmith and then with the French engraver Hubert Francois Gravelot (1699–1773), a former pupil of leading Rococo painter Francois Boucher (1703–70). Gravelot, active in London between 1732 and 1745, was part of a group of artists who gathered in Slaughter's Coffee House in St. Martin's Lane, which then evolved into the St. Martin's Lane Academy, where the young Gainsborough was his pupil. It was probably through this connection that Gainsborough would have known Hogarth and been invited to contribute to the Foundling Hospital.

From 1744, Gainsborough had his own studio in London, but, having married in 1746, he moved back to his Suffolk birthplace, Sudbury, in 1748, and settled in Ipswich in 1752. Gainsborough's subsequent move to Bath in 1759 turned him from a provincial artist into a fashionable painter, and it was in Bath in 1768 that Gainsborough painted Sancho.[23] In the course of the eighteenth century, Bath had developed into a popular spa town with Royal patronage. Many of its Palladian-style buildings, such as Queen Square and the Circus, as well as the Royal Crescent and the Bath Assembly Rooms, were designed by father and son architects John Wood the Elder

(1704–54) and John Wood the Younger (1728–82); the movements of its
visitors were orchestrated by Richard "Beau" Nash, the master of cere-
monies of the Assembly Rooms, who presided over Bath social life between
1704 and 1761. When Sancho was painted in November 1768 whilst
working for the Montagus, Bath had a well-defined high season between
October and early June, and Gainsborough himself had become an attraction of Bath society.

Gainsborough's portrait of Sancho (Figure 13.4) measures 29 by 24 inches,
a common size for a portrait. A key detail is that "a note on the back of the
frame in William Stevenson's hand, which may have been copied from an
inscription on the back of the original canvas reads 'This sketch by Mr
Gainsborough, of Bath, was done in one hour and forty minutes,
November 29th, 1768.'"[24] However, it is also possible that this might not
have been the total amount of time spent on the painting, because "the
portrait seems too complex to have been achieved in a single sitting."[25] The
painting, now in the National Gallery of Canada at Ottawa, having been
bought in 1907, certainly appears more finished than the term "sketch" would

Figure 13.4   Thomas Gainsborough, *Portrait of Ignatius Sancho* (1768). Oil on
canvas, 73.7 × 62.2 cm, purchased 1907.
National Gallery of Canada, Ottawa. Photo: NGC.

imply. Rather the word hints at a kind of vibrant immediacy and sensibility – perhaps a "painting to the moment" analogous to Samuel Richardson's "writing to the *moment*." The painting's provenance comes through Sancho's daughter Elizabeth (1766–1837). Elizabeth had inherited it from her mother Anne when Anne died in 1817, and critics agree that the painting was "presumably commissioned by the Duchess of Montagu and given to the sitter."[26] Sancho was in Bath with the Montagus since the Duke of Montagu's account book records him going "to, From, & at Bath" from 9 November until December 1768, and Sancho, as his valet, would have accompanied him.[27] Gainsborough had painted the duke and duchess earlier in the spring of 1768, and payments are recorded for those portraits, but not for the Sancho portrait. This pair of Montagu portraits, now in the possession of the Duke and Duchess of Buccleuch and hanging at Bowhill House in Scotland, are a little larger than the Sancho painting. George Montagu's portrait is 49¼ × 39½ inches and that of his wife, Mary, Duchess of Montagu is 49½ × 39½ inches. Whilst Sancho is shown in a trompe l'œil roundel, the duke and duchess are shown in slightly more defined semi-domestic settings. The duchess sits facing to the right with her hands in her lap; we see a painting behind her, and the chair she sits on is in front of some drapery. Her husband stands in front of a barely delineated architectural form, his body angled slightly to the left as he gazes out at the viewer with his right hand tucked into his waistcoat. Whilst Sancho also has his right hand tucked into his waistcoat, we only see his head and shoulders and the top half of his chest.

Sancho's is a striking portrait with a coherent composition. His very dark blue coat with its gold buttons, and the gold braid on his fashionable red waistcoat, give a sense of a well-dressed and possibly slightly nonchalant and cosmopolitan figure. The hand-in-waistcoat pose, popular in English portraiture of the period, signals both strength and modesty and portrays Sancho as a gentleman.[28] Sancho seems comfortable with Gainsborough's attention and looks confident as he gazes to his left. The color palette is reminiscent of Alan Ramsay's (1713–84) 1766 portrait of the great Enlightenment philosopher David Hume (1711–76) now in the National Galleries of Scotland. Unlike Sancho, Ramsay's Hume looks straight out at the viewer, but he is also dressed in red, and the combination of Hume's rather more ornate gold braiding, his white cravat, and the warm brown background achieves a comparable glow. Incidentally, Ramsay's canvas is the same size as Gainsborough's portrait of Sancho. Sancho's pose is not dissimilar to the slightly larger Kit-Kat portraits by Sir Godfrey Kneller (1646–1723) from around 1705 now in the National Portrait Gallery, which also typically show the sitter against a plain dark brown background and crop the body at a similar point. Whilst there is no suggestion that Gainsborough is directly copying either Kneller or Ramsay, it is clear his portrait of Sancho fits available portrait conventions. Gainsborough clearly relishes the challenge of rendering Sancho's skin tones against a dark background. He modulates the warm brown behind Sancho with a subtle golden glow immediately behind the figure, almost a gentle halo, which gives the portrait a strong three-dimensional effect, to produce an extraordinarily nuanced representation of dark skin, creating perhaps the most successful portrait of a Black man in the period, as many have suggested.[29] Sancho looks wise and benevolent, possibly amused, or even slightly quizzical, with a fractionally raised right eyebrow, and perhaps a tiny bit weary since his left eye seems ever so slightly bloodshot. Gainsborough's lighting picks up on the iris and surrounding white part of the eyeball in Sancho's right eye, and then the white fabric of the cravat he wears at his neck above his waistcoat, as well as the white frill at his right wrist, and the gold buttons on his outer garment and gold brocade on the waistcoat. Sancho seems to have his hair drawn back into the shape of a bob-wig, whilst the duke had been painted in a full wig.

Gainsborough mentions his portraits of the duke and duchess in a 1768 letter to the actor David Garrick (1717–79), whom Sancho also counted amongst his friends and whose songs Sancho later included in his 1769 collection of *New Songs*. Gainsborough's letter is mostly about his proposed painting of Shakespeare, for which he intends to "supply a soul from his Works," but he suggests Garrick visit the duke to see his recent portraits of the Montagus:

> I could wish you to call *upon any pretence* any day after next Wednesday at the Duke of Montagu, because you'd see the Duke and Duchess in my *last manner*, but not as if you thought anything of mine worth that trouble, only to see his Grace's Landskip of Rubens, and the 4 Vandykes whole length in his Grace's dressing-room.[30]

Gainsborough's letter gives a good flavor of the kinds of works Sancho would have been familiar with in the Montagu collection, and it clearly gives Gainsborough pleasure to think that his own portraits are hanging in such good company.

In many ways Gainsborough was the ideal artist to paint Sancho. Unlike several other artists in the period, he liked to complete his portraits himself, in their entirety, whilst others often employed drapery painters like the Van Acken brothers, Joseph (1699–1749) and Alexander (1701–57), to finish off their works, with the named portrait painter completing the face and hands and the drapery being treated by a separate artist. Gainsborough makes full use of the expressive potential of fabrics, as seen in his splendid portrait of his wife Margaret Burr (1728–97) from c. 1778 now at the Courtauld Institute. This portrait, also of the same 29 × 24 inches canvas size as the portrait of Sancho, is remarkable for the vivid qualities of the painted fabric. Gainsborough's treatment of the black lace and gold and white fabrics of his wife's dress creates a subtle play of light and shade, evoking movement and depth from the canvas. It seems that Gainsborough and Sancho had shared tastes. Reading Gainsborough's letters, it is clear that he, too, was influenced by a sentimental mode of writing, employing dashes and exclamations. Gainsborough was also a musician and counted many professional musicians among his friends, including the virtuoso violinist Felice Giardini, whom Sancho also knew.[31] In a letter to William Jackson, a musician friend who lived in Exeter, Gainsborough wrote of his desire to escape the rigors of his life in Bath: "I'm sick of Portraits and wish very much to take my Viol da Gamba and walk off to some sweet Village where I can paint Landskips [sic: landscapes] and enjoy the fag End of Life in quietness & ease."[32] Critics suggest that Gainsborough "portrays Sancho as he did other creative men" and that "Sancho's gaze and expression suggest someone deep in contemplation."[33] Moreover, "the similarity to portraits of the artist's friends may mean that a sympathetic rapport was struck up by the two men, who both used charm and good nature to make their way."[34] Other critics suggest the possibility that "the hint of pathos [in the Sancho portrait] reflects the moment at which Africans in Britain were in process of transformation from objects of curiosity and romance to the focus of sentiment and pity."[35] Pathos and sentiment also drive Josiah Wedgwood's (1730–97) famous abolition medallion produced from 1787 onwards, which shows an enslaved African in chains beneath the words "Am I not a Man and a Brother." In retrospect, what is so moving about Gainsborough's portrait of Sancho is that he treats him not as an object of curiosity or pity, but as an individual and a gentleman.

Many contemporary portraits of people of color in the period tend to represent them as either borderline caricatures, as in many of Hogarth's images, or as distinctly "other" as in Sir Joshua Reynolds's impressive but stereotypical full-length 1776 *Portrait of Omai*, that depicts Mai (c. 1753–79), also known as Omai, who was brought to Paris in 1768 from Ra'iatea in the Pacific Islands. Another exception is the representation of a young Black boy playing drum and pipe in Hogarth's *Lord George Graham in his Ship's Cabin*

(c. 1742), "Hogarth's most considered representation of an apparently real African," "free of [. . .] physiognomic stereotyping"[36] and who, dressed in green livery, red scarf, and yellow waistcoat is "as colourful and variegated a figure as Lord Graham."[37] Perhaps the closest in feel to Gainsborough's portrait of Sancho is the sketch, thought to be by either Sir Joshua Reynolds (1723–92) or Sir James Northcote (1746–1831), which has traditionally been assumed to have been a portrait of Francis Barber, writer Samuel Johnson's (1709–84) servant, but has recently been suggested to represent another eighteenth-century Black man in London named John Shropshire.[38] This sketch is clearly individuated, but less finished than Gainsborough's portrait of Sancho. It is described as "a study in painterly technique rather than a portrait as such . . . the image embodies notions of the noble savage and is used to represent a type rather than an individual."[39] Similarly, the *Portrait of a Black Man identified as Olaudah Equiano* (c. 1745–97) (61.8 × 51.5 cm), also a roundel, is both a less sophisticated painting and less securely attributed to either artist or sitter.[40] There is no evidence to support recent suggestions that this painting might in fact represent Sancho.

Whilst the Sancho portrait itself remained with his family, the engraving after the portrait by Francesco Bartolozzi (1727–1815) had much wider currency as the frontispiece to Volume 1 of the *Letters* when it was first published in 1782. Francesco Bartolozzi's engraving (Figure 13.5), made in 1781, follows the portrait pretty faithfully and reproduces the oval rather than the full painting, as befitting a frontispiece. Gainsborough's brush-strokes are modified into Bartolozzi's stipple engraving, and they take on a monochrome tonality, giving the engraving a weightier feel. The engraving overall seems to bear more of the both literal and metaphorical weight that Sancho carried towards the end of his life. The confidence of Gainsborough's image translates well into a frontispiece, even if Bartolozzi's engraving gives Sancho a more seemingly melancholy expression and renders the image more overtly sentimental than Gainsborough's original. Sometimes engravings are mirror images of the original, but that is not the case here, as Sancho stares off to the left, gazing into the distance or even into the past, seeming to balance the title page, which reads: "Letters of the late Ignatius Sancho, an African. In Two Volumes. To which are prefixed, Memoirs of His Life. Printed by J Nichols and sold by J Dodsley in Pall Mall, J Robson in New Bond Street, J Walter Charing-Cross; R Baldwin, Paternoster Row; and J Sewell, Cornhill."

From Pall Mall and New Bond Street in the fashionable West End, to Charing-Cross, Paternoster Row further east near St Paul's, to Cornhill in the heart of the City, Sancho's letters and image were on sale in at least five

Figure 13.5   Francesco Bartolozzi, *Portrait of Ignatius Sancho, after Thomas Gainsborough* (1802).
© The Trustees of the British Museum.

key booksellers across London. James Dodsley (1724–97) in particular was a hugely influential bookseller, who published works by Frances Sheridan (1724–66), Oliver Goldsmith (1728–74), Samuel Johnson (1709–84), and James Boswell (1740–95) as well as Laurence Sterne's *The Life and Opinions of Tristram Shandy, Gentleman* (1759–67).

Gainsborough's fabulous portrait of Sancho and the subsequent Bartolozzi engraving cement Sancho's rare position as a named, visible man of color whose visual representation conforms to period conventions usually reserved for white subjects. Such a portrait of a servant would have been unusual, but not unique; as a butler, Sancho held an elevated position in the duke's household. But to have a secure and named portrait by Gainsborough, one of the most celebrated portraitists of the period, is a rarity and a fitting testimony to Sancho's visible standing in London's cultural scene. Complementing the Gainsborough portrait, through the letters Sancho emerges as a compelling agent of visual culture; Sancho's adept manipulation of the visual qualities of sentimental rhetoric, his patronage and support of younger artists like Meheux, and his manifest enjoyment of visual culture challenge the dominant representations of the period, which cast Black people as objects rather than agents.

Notes

1. Sandhu, S., "Ignatius Sancho: An African man of letters," in King, R. (ed.), *Ignatius Sancho An African Man of Letters* (London: National Portrait Gallery, 1997), 45–73, 54. See the first edition of Sancho's *Letters*, Sancho, I. *Letters of the Late Ignatius Sancho, an African*, 2 vols. (London: J. Nichols, 1782), Vol. I, 142.

2. Richardson, S., *Pamela; or, Virtue Rewarded*, ed. Keymer, T. (Oxford: Oxford University Press, 2001 [1740]), Letter I, 11.

3. Sterne, L., *The Life and Opinions of Tristram Shandy, Gentleman* (London: Penguin, 1997 [1759–67]), 391–2, 185–6.

4. Richardson, S., *The History of Sir Charles Grandison* (Oxford: Oxford University Press, 1986 [1753]), 4.

5. Carretta, V. (ed.), *The Letters of the Late Ignatius Sancho, an African* (1780) (Peterborough, Ontario: Broadview, 2015), 149n.1.

6. Boswell, J., *Life of Johnson*, ed. Chapman, R. W. (Oxford: Oxford University Press, 2008), 696.

7. Smith, J., *Nollekens and His Times*, ed. Stonier, G. W. (London: Turnstile, 1949), 14–15.

8. Carretta (ed.), *The Letters of the Late Ignatius Sancho*, 51, n.23 55.

9. Solkin, D., *Art in Britain 1660–1815* (New Haven, CT and London: Yale University Press, 2015); Bignamini, I., "Art institutions in London, 1689–1768: A study of clubs and academies," *The Volume of the Walpole Society*, 54 (1988), 19–140.

10. Solkin, *Art in Britain 1660–1815*, 80.

11. A full length portrait of John 2nd Duke is at Boughton, and a mezzotint dated 1740 after a painting by Kneller of his wife Mary is in the National Portrait Gallery: https://tinyurl.com/msuke332 along with a three-quarter-length Kit-Kat portrait of the duke: https://tinyurl.com/3uwu7wab.

12. Retford, K., *The Conversation Piece: Making Modern Art in 18th-Century Britain* (New Haven, CT: Yale University Press, 2017), 291, Figure 216; Einberg, E., *William Hogarth: A Complete Catalogue of the Paintings* (New Haven, CT and London, 2016), 83–5, cat. 47.

13. The Boughton Archive holds a letter recording payment to a John Rising for the cleaning of a Hogarth "family piece" in 1809, which may have been when the painting was cropped. I am grateful to Crispin Powell, Archivist of the Buccleuch Living Heritage Trust, for information about the Yale painting.

14. Howell, C., *The Foundling Museum: An Illustrated Guide* (London: Foundling Museum, 2014), 11.

15. Admission ticket, www.britishmuseum.org/collection/object/C_MG-678.

16. Vaughan, W., *Gainsborough* (London: Thames & Hudson, 2002), 73–81, 27.

17. Carretta (ed.), *Letters of the Late Ignatius Sancho*, 178n.1.

18. Carretta cites Smith, J. T., *Book for a Rainy Day* (London: Richard Bentley, 1845), 89.

19. All these locations can be explored at https://mappingblacklondon.org and are also discussed by Oliver Ayers in Chapter 3 in this volume.

20. Carretta (ed.), *Letters of the Late Ignatius Sancho*, 178n.1; King, R. (ed.), *Ignatius Sancho An African Man of Letters* (London: National Portrait Gallery, 1997), 30.

21. The painting is in a private collection, the V&A and Yale hold two of the many copies of the 1746 etching: https://interactive.britishart.yale.edu/slav ery-and-portraiture/297/taste-in-high-life and the stipple engraving is in the Met: www.metmuseum.org/art/collection/search/421469; Paulson, R., *Hogarth*, Vol. 11: *High Art and Low 1732–1750* (Cambridge: Lutterworth Press, 1992), 203–6.

22. Dabydeen, D., *Hogarth's Blacks: Images of Blacks in Eighteenth Century English Art* (Manchester: Manchester University Press, 1987), 128.

23. Vaughan, *Gainsborough*, 73–81.

24. Belsey, H., *Thomas Gainsborough: The Portraits, Fancy Pictures and Copies after Old Masters* (New Haven, CT and London: Paul Mellon Centre for Studies in British Art, Yale University Press, 2019), Vol. 11, cat. No. 796, 739–40.

25. Ibid., 739.

26. Ibid., 739.

27. Ibid., 739; Northamptonshire RO, Buccleuch papers x4573.

28. Meyer, A., "Re-dressing classical statuary: The eighteenth-century 'hand-in-waistcoat' portrait," *The Art Bulletin* 77.1 (1995), 45–63.

29. King, R., "Ignatius Sancho and portraits of the Black elite," in King, R. (ed.), *Ignatius Sancho An African Man of Letters* (London: National Portrait Gallery, 1997), 15–43, 30.

30. Woodall, M. (ed.), *The Letters of Gainsborough* (Bradford: The Cupid Press, 1961, 1963), 67.

31. Sancho mentions a ticket given by "the Great Giardini – to the lowly Sancho" in a letter of 1778 (*Letters* 170).

32. Woodall (ed.), *The Letters of Gainsborough*, 115.

33. Rosenthal, M., *The Art of Thomas Gainsborough: "A Little Business for the Eye"* (New Haven, CT and London: The Paul Mellon Centre for Studies in British Art, Yale University Press, 1999), 158–9.

34. Ibid., 158–9.
35. Bindman, D., Kaplan, P., and Weston, H., "The city between fantasy and reality," in Bindman, D. and Gates, H. L., Jr. (eds.), *The Image of the Black in Western Art: From the "Age of Discovery" to the Age of Abolition: The Eighteenth Century* (Cambridge, MA and London: Harvard University Press, 2011), Part III, 184–5.
36. Dabydeen, *Hogarth's Blacks*, 45, Figure 25. The painting is in the Maritime Museum.
37. Ibid., 45, Figure 25.
38. London Metropolitan Archives, *Unforgotten Lives: Rediscovering Londoners of African, Caribbean, Asian and Indigenous Heritage 1560–1860: A Guide to Documents on Display in the Exhibition* (London: London Metropolitan Archives, 2023), 9.
39. King, "Ignatius Sancho and portraits," 34–5.
40. Ibid., 34–5.

Further Reading

Bindman, D. and Gates, H. L. Jr. (eds.), *The Image of the Black in Western Art: From the "Age of Discovery" to the Age of Abolition: The Eighteenth Century* (Cambridge, MA and London: Harvard University Press, 2011).

Borg, A. and Coke D., *Vauxhall Gardens: A History* (New Haven, CT and London: Paul Mellon Centre, Yale University Press, 2011).

Dabydeen, D., *Hogarth's Blacks: Images of Blacks in Eighteenth Century English Art* (Manchester: Manchester University Press, 1987).

King, R. (ed.), *Ignatius Sancho: An African Man of Letters* (London: National Portrait Gallery, 1997).

Solkin, D., *Art in Britain 1660–1815* (New Haven, CT and London: Yale University Press, 2015).

CHAPTER 14

Sancho
On Belonging

Paterson Joseph

The bitter irony that Charles Ignatius Sancho was said to have been born on a slave ship, most likely crossing from the west coast of Africa to Colombia on the Caribbean Sea, is not lost on me. It makes him, by accident of birth, a person of neither here nor there, or, more positively, of everywhere. Sancho's story has always resonated most forcefully with me around this notion of belonging in the United Kingdom (UK), where I was born to St. Lucian parents. After all, in the streets of London where I grew up in the late 1960s and early 1970s, it was very common to see graffiti on walls declaring, "Wogs Out," "Keep Britain White," and the very direct, "N— Go Home." My school life was no more welcoming, as I was part of the cohort of African Caribbean children labeled "ESN," that is "Educationally Subnormal," and was treated accordingly by many of the teachers I encountered before I'd even opened my mouth.[1] I most certainly did not feel like I *belonged*.

My parents' generation had it even tougher, of course. They were the subsequently named Windrush Generation, aka British Colonial citizens, who arrived in Britain in large numbers, largely facilitated by the new Nationality Act, which gave people from the British colonies the right to live and work in Britain without the need for a visa and partly, fallaciously it turned out, to answer the fictitious call to aid the "mother country" in post-war ravaged Britain.[2] Named after the passenger ship *Empire Windrush*, these were not the first migrants from the colonies, of course, but the Pathé news reels of their arrival gave this ship an almost mythical status. When they arrived from the many British Caribbean possessions, like Jamaica, Trinidad, Barbados, St. Lucia, Grenada, and Antigua, they naively expected to be welcomed by the "mother country." They were instead met with hostility, negative discrimination, and ignorance by many in the white community. So-called "hostile environments" in housing, policing, law, and employment dogged their heels into the 2010s with the notorious Windrush Scandal,[3] an outrageous betrayal of these brave ex-colonial peoples, many of whom were "repatriated" to countries in the Caribbean that they had left either as young adults or as babes in arms, some even in their mother's bellies. The authorities claimed that their papers were "lost" in the system, therefore they were officially "undocumented aliens." This tragic and shameful episode in British history under successive Conservative Party governments, from David Cameron to Rishi Sunak, is still being felt by many today.

You may well wonder how the children and grandchildren of those British Caribbean people see themselves, given the struggles their antecedents had to be an accepted part of the country they came to aid. Back in 1999, when my research into a wider Black British history can officially be said to have started, I looked then at that generation of younger Black Britons around me, and asked them the question, "Who did they think they were?" – more forensically – "Who did they consider themselves to be?" "Are you British?" "Are you African or Caribbean?" And the even more provocative but pertinent question, "Do you feel you can call yourself English or Scottish, Northern Irish or Welsh?" Their answers were invariably prefaced with confused looks, as if they hadn't up to then asked themselves these profoundly important questions.

In England, the responses most commonly given by the young were, "Caribbean" or "African" – very rarely "British" – and certainly never "English." When you're constantly asked where you are from, and often made to feel a person of "elsewhere" in your own country, it is very difficult to fully embrace the nation that treats you in this way; even more so when your forerunners' part in that country's history has never been told you, aside from the negative context of slavery.

Like Sancho, those kids aren't really African in a purely cultural sense, not really Caribbean, since in reality in those places they would be considered, rightly, foreigners. Even their parents, who left those countries possibly decades earlier, are called "English Man" or "English Woman" in an African or Caribbean context: foreigners. For instance, when I walk the streets of St. Lucia, my whole person screams "Englishman." And that makes sense in every way, since in reality England was where I was born and raised. But that does not mean I feel I "belong" in the category of English. Nationhood, then, is much closer to an emotion than a logical–factual reality.

As offspring of the Windrush Generation, we can identify with – but never truly belong amongst – the powerful and globally influential African American culture, though we appropriate so much of it. Ways of speaking, views on history, music, fashion, and, more negatively, a disengagement from mainstream politics and culture are obvious signs of this deep connection with our US counterparts. I believe this identification, which is clearly seen across European communities of Black youth, is partly, perhaps subliminally, in order to empower ourselves in countries where we feel profoundly underrepresented in our nations' history, art, music, science, politics, and literature. This is true especially in those countries that deprecated our ancestral culture, initially, then exploited it shamelessly. In this transatlantic act of cultural appropriation, we might easily recognize the desire that sits in all of us, from the oldest to the youngest, the desire to belong.

When our sense of where we belong does not match the logic of where we are born and grew up, this must inevitably compound a form of cultural–national dysphoria. Dysphoria is defined as a condition equated with symptoms of depression, anxiety, and agitation. This sense of not knowing who you are and what shape, as it were, you might fit into, can lead to at least two states of being, as far as I can tell. The first is the kind of malaise that leaves you adrift, somewhere in the middle of the Atlantic Ocean, a person of no fixed origin. The other state? That might well be the appropriation of another culture that is not really, deeply, your own. For example, in the case of people with African- or Caribbean-born antecedents, it might be a connection to another culture through that parent or grandparent. But any attempt at making that connection foundational is surely a kind of reconstruction of an identity; motivated largely by the antagonism directed toward you in that very country of your birth and upbringing. I would never deny anyone the right to reconstruct an identity in this way. However, I would be wary of the deeper motivations behind the act. A feeling of *not belonging* can be a motivator in a negative sense, too.

Charles Ignatius Sancho, born in the middle of the Atlantic Ocean, is the natural forerunner for those of us Britain-born or Britain-raised children whose idea of ourselves might lie somewhere in the middle of the Atlantic. Neither here, nor there. I certainly think that is why this African Briton has been so important to me. Sancho is an African British figure who has often been overlooked. Indeed, from comments that I have garnered from British historian Professor David Olusoga when mentioning reactions to Sancho while teaching on him, younger people can tend to see him as a watered-down, perhaps even compromised, version of the more vociferous Olaudah Equiano, his younger contemporary.[4] He can easily be dismissed as irrelevant to today's discussions around the subject of who belongs and who does not in the UK.

As well as the notions of belonging that Sancho's life throw up for me, his quiet resistance to being left out of Britain's story strongly draws me to him. Sancho wanted to have his voice heard in the way any free man in the Britain of his day would want to be heard. He used the education he fought for and pursued, despite all obstacles, to help his fellow Africans suffering in the European-led slave world. He did this by making himself a visible and integral part of the Britain he had adopted. Belonging, for Sancho, meant a life lived in the spotlight. Through engagement with creative cultures such as music and literature and his confidence to speak out publicly on national and international politics, Sancho made an art of belonging that can only be marveled at, given his origins and lowly start in life. A flawed hero, without a doubt. The only kind of hero I truly believe in.

In order to confidently know that you belong, your story has to be found in your country's historical record, depicted in your country's art, too, and not just negatively, as is the case with the countless portraits of African children labeled simply "and negro slave" in European paintings from at least the Renaissance onwards. As African American writer Walter Mosley has said, "If people do not exist in literature, they do not exist at all."[5] Together with literature, I would, of course, include history. That my people were missing in the taught history of Britain was a vital component in giving my generation a sense that we did not belong, reinforcing the notion that we certainly did not matter.

Sancho: On Black British History

For Black Britons of my generation, the academic silence surrounding the topic of African chattel slavery, and its present links to our own history, was almost universal. Those of us fortunate enough to have had a grounding in Black History through after-school clubs organized by our elders are rare. Even today, the idea of Black British history is a mysterious subject to the general public. Eighty-five percent of British people are unable to name even one historical, Black British figure. Putting Black British history on the national curriculum is resisted by the educational establishment in the UK, on the grounds that it is a niche subject and not relevant to modern British life.[6] An outrageous statement, since without that brutal, exploitative, and vicious period of British acquisitive power, we Black Britons would not be living with our current, well-documented disadvantages. This was a period in the British and European story when millions of African souls were forcibly removed from their homelands to work in the colonies of the Americas for Britain, Spain, Portugal, France, Holland, and eventually the newly formed United States of America. We are descended from these people.

Apart from the obvious lack of honesty in this refusal to even acknowledge Britain's slavery past, there is also the dearth of information in the Black community in the UK about our own history. Discussions around the notion of reparations are also hamstrung by the general ignorance surrounding the modern resonances of Britain's former slave involvement, an involvement that is fundamental to the current geo-political status quo. Sancho, a man whose life played out during the very height of that cruel system of bondage, has now, more than ever, a vital role to play in our understanding of the place of African chattel slavery in European/ American global dominance.

My generation's painful ignorance of why we were even in the UK – why our presence was so problematic on the streets, in the classrooms, and amongst the debates of the political class that we witnessed on our television screens – Member of Parliament Enoch Powell's 1968 "Rivers of Blood" speech[7] being a good example of the kind of rhetoric we were living with on a daily basis – can be seen mirrored today in the inchoate indifference of young Black Britons who would baulk at calling themselves by the name of the country they are born and raised in.[8] The riots of 1981 were my generation's greatest public act of resistance to this notion of our alien status and Prime Minister Margaret Thatcher's government's attempt to reduce us to a silently suffering underclass. One wonders where the current generation's rage will manifest itself if their country continues to dismiss the need for them to become an integral part of the UK's story, especially in school, where this foundational learning should rightly be carried out.

Remounting my monodrama *Sancho – An Act of Remembrance* in a theater tour of North America from 2016 to 2018, the bizarre question "Did Britain ever have slavery?" was posed to me often, taking my breath away every time. The basis of this question comes from an historical misunderstanding bordering on propaganda. The idea that the law in Britain had always maintained that slavery could not exist in the pure, English air appears to be the established view of most Britons today. In actual fact, that inaccurate assessment is extrapolated from, amongst others, the Talbot *decision* of 1729[9] and the Somerset *opinion* of Lord Chief Justice Mansfield in 1772.[10] Contemporaneously with the latter announcement, it seemed to convey to many people, via a mix of grapevine, anecdote, and wishful thinking, that Britain was not a country that supported slavery. Today, despite the stark facts on offer about Britain's role in the wicked traffic of human souls, we lack visual and well-known depictions of Britain's role in the exploitation and transportation of captive Africans. Where is our version of Alex Haley's *Roots*, or Solomon Northup's *Twelve Years a Slave*, made into a Hollywood movie by African Caribbean British director Steve McQueen? Where, indeed, are our physical monuments to Britain's role in the "abominable trade"? No prominent memorials are to be found on UK soil, despite the campaigning work of Oku Ekpenyon and her long fight for an "Enslaved Africans Memorial."[11]

The failure to connect Britain to its colonial exploits and exploitations is not an accident. The idea that Britain was the land of the free, that it could "never, never, never" support slaves, is an insidious lie that has permeated thoughts on Britain and slavery for many centuries and continues to this day. This "forgetting" has been aided and abetted by teachers and the historians who have been instructing those teachers, from at least the time of Britain's first ventures into the role of colonizer in the 1600s, until today. The awful consequences of this "national amnesia" are that, when my parent's generation arrived in the 1940s, 1950s, and 1960s, the white British populace had no clue about these peoples' part in the building of the empire they were so very proud of exalting. For the white citizens, these "foreigners" simply did not *belong*.

When I explain to an American audience that Britain was the chief Western enslaving nation, that they had a license granted to them at the turn of the eighteenth century to procure African captives for the other European nations that traded in these souls, I am met with looks of shock. British audiences do not fare much better. I have had many people approach me after question-and-answer sessions to "confess" that, even though they had received first-class degrees in history at Oxford or Cambridge, they were totally unaware of a Black British history until the moment I introduced Sancho and his world to them. There's anger there, too, when they realize they have been sold a story that glossed over Britain's part in this foundational piece of human cruelty. It is foundational because slavery, African chattel slavery, is the basis of so much of not only Britain's, but the world's economy, from banking to insurance, stocks and shares, and education predicated on scientific racism. Indeed, any notions of white supremacy come directly from these pseudo-scientific justifications for the trade in human flesh.

At this point, I believe it is vital that we contextualize Sancho, how extraordinary his achievements were, and how significant his final act, the vote, truly was in the history of Black Britain. A decent starting point is to look at the world in which he was born and the stage on which his life was lived. In order to do that, we must begin at the beginning.

Britain and Slavery

From 1609 onwards, Britain began to acquire overseas territories in an ambitious attempt to expand the empire. Beginning in that year with Bermuda, British adventurers or buccaneers – aka "state-sanctioned pirates" – went on to grab Virginia and Massachusetts in North America and by 1632 had colonized Barbados, Antigua, Nevis, and Montserrat. The significance of these land grabs for Africans cannot be underestimated, for it was the need for cheap labor, laborers who could more readily support the brutal working conditions in those tropical climates, that led to the ramping up of Britain's trade in African captives.

It is true to say that Britain also "transported" white British criminals as well as the Irish, who were political opponents, and other "undesirables Oliver Cromwell wanted to see removed as far from the British Isles as possible."[12] As the brilliant Trinidadian historian Eric Williams stated, "White servitude was the historic base upon which Negro slavery was constructed."[13] However, the industrial trade in African captives was taken to another level altogether by Britain, France, Holland, Portugal, and Spain. To the evils of this European-led people-trafficking system, we must add the stripping of name, heritage, language, culture, and finally, horrifically, the very humanity from those African souls that was not mirrored in the terrible treatment of white indentured laborers. Theirs was a harsh life, no doubt, but the conditions Sancho's parents, had they lived, would have ended up in would have been more inhumane still.

In 1655, when England, under Cromwell, seized Jamaica from Spain, several state monopolies sprang up to more efficiently steal Africans to work on the plantations there, particularly the burgeoning sugarcane fields. Britain's consolidation of territories in West Africa followed, in order to facilitate the traffic of human souls across the Atlantic more readily to Britain's Caribbean and American possessions. One of these monopolies was The Company of Royal Adventurers Trading in Africa, which was established in 1660 after the restoration of the English monarchy, winning an exclusive charter to trade in African captives in 1663. The Royal Africa Company was established in 1672 after the original company ran into financial difficulties. This was a much-expanded operation including troops, forts, and factories in West Africa as well as the "right" to impose martial law in a grab for land, gold, silver, and humans. Even before 1663, however, it is estimated that Britain's state-sanctioned privateers (more commonly known as pirates) had already transported over 100,000 Africans across the Atlantic to supply free labor for Britain's slave-worked plantations. From 1663 to 1673, at least 10,000 Africans a year were brutally wrenched from their homes to work without pay or recompense in the cruel chattel slavery system.

So much wealth was being generated by this inhumane and criminal activity that a new coin was minted in 1663 – the Golden Guinea – made from African gold and stamped with the crest of the company, an Elephant and Castle.

In its many years of trading, the shareholders of the Royal African Company included Charles II and the royal family, over a dozen Lord Mayors of London, aristocrats, writers, composers, and philosophers, including Samuel Pepys, John Locke, and George Frideric Handel. Slavery was embedded into the very establishment of early empire building, commerce, and power. Those trading in captured Africans had only one faint qualm, perhaps, when a group of these men demanded to know whether Black captives could be considered mere goods. The legal opinion, from the Solicitor-General, was that "Negroes ought to be esteemed goods and commodities within the Acts of Trade and Navigation."[14] Professor Hakim Adi rightly assesses that this opinion dehumanized Africans and concludes that "The new business of Great Britain, formed by the act of union in 1707 was human trafficking."[15]

Asiento de Negros

When well-educated Americans question Britain's role in African chattel slavery by asking "Did Britain ever have slavery?" they are merely echoing the propaganda that has been prevalent ever since the first "adventurers," supported by the British crown, began to steal souls from the African continent. It may be helpful here to offer up some rarely heard facts to clarify the reality of Britain's role in this large-scale people-trafficking crime, a crime against humanity for which ex-Prime Minister Rishi Sunak declared in 2023 there would be no apology and no reparations.[16]

The Bank of England and the National Debt were created in 1694. These were established to raise finances to carry on the trade in captured Africans and to fund Britain's wars, mainly against that other slave-addicted superpower, France. These wars led to the famous Treaty of Utrecht, which granted Great Britain the rights that are known as the

Asiento de Negros. Signed between Queen Anne of England and King Phillip V of Spain, the Asiento de Negros pertains to Sancho's life story in a most significant way. Essentially, Sancho's history is intertwined with British history in ways I have only relatively recently discovered. His origin story, too, belongs to Britain's slave-trading story in real and surprising ways.

The Asiento de Negros, put into motion in 1713, just a decade or so before Charles Ignatius was born on a ship crossing the Atlantic Ocean carrying shackled African people across to European colonies in the Americas, granted Britain the exclusive monopoly of trading in African souls for the next thirty years. Since Sancho's slave ship landed in Colombia, I had presumed his life was connected not to the British slave economy, but to the rival Spanish one. However, the Asiento gave the UK the right to transport captive Africans to the many Spanish slave-reliant colonies as well as to its own possessions. *Britain is very likely to have had a direct hand in Sancho's life from the very beginning.*

It is vitally important to set the context when teaching about Sancho, lest our listeners or readers, seduced by the "*Bridgerton* Effect," fall under the misguided impression that Britain was an innocent party in the system that we have mostly seen perpetrated by the United States, via our screens and in our novels. The danger is that we as a nation smugly, if innocently in many cases, skip from the founding of the American and Caribbean colonies to William Wilberforce and British Quaker activism, then smoothly through to the blockading of the European nations' and the newly independent United States' shipping lanes to prevent them stealing Africans from their homelands.

This neat pseudo-history is seriously undermined with a few more little-known and rarely taught facts. Let's take Sancho's century, the eighteenth, for example. Between 1721 and 1730 alone, British ships transported an estimated 180,000 enslaved men, women, and children across the Atlantic. The estimate of stolen souls from 1701 to 1807 stands at 2.5 million Africans trafficked by Great Britain to the various European and British colonies of the Americas. Britain, then, was responsible for the human trafficking of a third of all Africans trafficked in the eighteenth century. The total throughout Britain's people-trafficking operations is estimated to stand at 3.1 million women, men, and children. Many more will have died, or been murdered, in the capture and brutal transportation system that preceded the life of toil that awaited those wretched souls who survived.[17]

There are many more examples of Britain's roots as a world economic super-power based on the evil institution of slavery, but let it suffice to conclude this section with the truth of a statement made by nineteenth-century economist Karl Marx, "Without slavery you have no cotton, without cotton you have no modern industry, it is slavery that gave the colonies their value, it is the colonies that created world trade, and it is world trade that is the pre-condition of large-scale industry."[18]

Sancho's Legacy

I was asked to write a chapter for this Cambridge Companion responding to the question, "How is Sancho seen today?" The answer is, naturally, multi-layered. It's worth beginning with a conversation had between myself and the brilliant British historian, author of the seminal book on Black British history *Black and British: A Forgotten History* (2016), Professor David Olusoga.

"A literary figure named after a literary character; Sancho is a man literally born in a liminal space."[19] David Olusoga's words echo in my mind long after he pronounces them. Professor Olusoga notes that children of the Windrush generation find that Sancho brings a sense of belonging and a reinforcement of our desire to be part of British history:

> Here is someone we can claim, here is someone who is a warrant for our existence that shows our story is not limited chronologically. He still has the "Wow Factor" for us. But he's not really made for a "Culture War" age. Sancho's a bad fit. I think some people, young and old, struggle with that. Younger Black Britons can see Sancho as weak and self-hating.[20]

They find it near-impossible, lacking context, to see how his strategy of rarely confronting white Britain head-on could have been effective. Professor Olusoga believes that

> Sancho isn't well understood because we're asking people who have no context for how he was using language – to attack without appearing to draw a weapon – to know what he was doing with that strategy. They haven't been taught about the way racism manifested itself in ages past. They have no idea of the terrain Sancho is negotiating . . . He just hints at what he's been through. And I think that some people struggle with the fact that he doesn't say more. But I like that he doesn't say more. As an historian I wish he'd said more. But I admire him for that strength of purpose . . . "but not much abused."[21]

Here, Professor Olusoga quotes from one of Sancho's letters, ". . . but not much abused" (*Letters* 148). Earlier, in this reserved entry in his letters, Charles Ignatius's words are suffused with a knowledge that whatever abuse he might suffer on the streets of London, it was negligible in comparison with what his Black brothers and sisters were suffering under the slavery system, elsewhere. One evening he takes his three daughters, Frances, Ann-Alice, and Betsy, and son Billy to Vauxhall Pleasure Gardens for an evening's entertainment. The treatment they receive on the way home and his chosen method of relating what happened are telling: "We went by water – had a coach home – were gazed at – followed, etc. etc. – But not much abused" (*Letters* 148). This restraint and his almost constant self-deprecating way of addressing himself to others are the source of much of our misunderstanding about Sancho. How he negotiated his sense of belonging, though, is vital to our comprehension of his world and the verbal–literary skill needed to navigate it. Context, then, is everything. These restrained words, "but not much abused," would have hit his more enlightened readers hard.

Sancho voted in at least two elections as far as the records show, in 1774 and 1780. I have been contacted recently by an historian who believes that Sancho may not have been the first person of African descent to vote in a British parliamentary election, an accolade we Sancho fans have always laid at his feet. It has been suggested that a publican by the name of John London or Loudon had that honor in 1749. The beauty of history, and of the gradually blossoming digital archives around Black British history in particular, is that new and important information is still to be teased out of the records. That is not to say that Sancho's vote is to be ignored or denuded of its power, pioneering or not. A man who was stripped of everything that would give him a sense of belonging, finally, literally – in the case of the public vote in Covent Garden Piazza – raises his hands to effect the outcome of two major elections in the country of his adoption and therefore becomes in this act a figure to be reckoned with, by anyone's judgment. In that public show of hands at the Westminster Hustings in 1774 and 1780, Sancho powerfully demonstrated to future Black Britons that, even though we might live in times of great oppression, we can, by whatever legal means necessary, make our voices heard.

Writer and educator Joanna Brown, who writes under the name J. T. Williams, is the author of the children's novel series *The Lizzie and Belle Mysteries* which re-imagines Dido Elizabeth Belle of Kenwood House and Elizabeth Sancho, Charles and his wife Anne's youngest daughter, solving mysteries in eighteenth-century London. These exciting tales for roughly nine- to twelve-year-olds were initially sparked by Joanna's introduction to Sancho through her work at the British Library. Having seen my play *Sancho – An Act of Remembrance* in 2018, Joanna was encouraged to write more creatively on the subject of Black British history, especially in the area of lesson plans and resources for primary school teachers. Joanna acknowledges the difficulty that young people have of accessing Sancho, when the language seems so far removed from their own. "I found it best to use fragments of his letters, some of which are so funny and quirky, with his made-up words and the detail of eighteenth-century life in London, but from the unusual angle of a Black person."[22] Joanna's novels in the *Lizzie and Belle* series achieve this viewpoint, nicely. We see eighteenth-century London through the lens of two young, Black women and note how different, fresh, and engaging it is to tell the story from a time we think we know from an angle with which we are not familiar. It's marvellous to think a generation of African- and African Caribbean-descended British pupils could be raised with an awareness of themselves in Britain's past, obviating any need to search too hard for a means to ground themselves in their country's history as our generation had to do.

Joanna notes, too, that the study of Sancho's life can lead us out of a male-centric Black history cul-de-sac, for we have to consider the powerful role that Anne Osborne played in his life; the woman who would root this rootless orphan in the Black community in a way that is often overlooked. Anne is a major figure in the life of Lizzie Sancho, and the Black matriarch is seen as the center of her family in a way that most Black people will relate to with ease. With young historians of British African and African Caribbean descent like Montaz Marché, Annabelle Gilmour, and Chiedza Mhondoro, to name but three of many, working in the field of Black British history, I feel confident that they will expand our knowledge of this long-neglected aspect of our national story, for a whole new generation of scholars and students. For example, Ms Marché is currently working on a theater piece around the life of Anne Osborne called *Mrs Sancho*. Sancho operas are being worked on on both sides of the Atlantic, and my new play *Sancho & Me – For One Night Only* is being performed to theater audiences in the UK and the United States as I write.

In the world of historical research, Crispin Powell is the archivist for the Buccleuch family, the aristocratic line that includes the Montagu dukedom amongst their many titles. Crispin had this to say about the future of Sancho studies: "I have been researching the Buccleuch archives for twenty years. And yet, I think I'm only about a third of the way through. I'm convinced that there is much more to discover about Sancho's role in the Montagu family's story."[23]

The work that is being undertaken at the London Metropolitan Archive, now called The London Archives, including their exhibition Switching the

Lens, where we meet with Black Britain in a way that has never been seen before, using installations, interactive websites, and a comprehensive archive that is accessible to all, is one of the most exciting contemporary ways in which our knowledge of Black Britain is increasing. Sancho's part in this resource is prominent, but his is by no means the only life we can investigate. Since so many African Americans turned up in London after fighting for Britain in its war against the American colonies in the late 1700s, those stories and peoples are featured there, too. These extraordinary lives, alongside countless ordinary tales of survival, are a rich source of history that has only just begun to be tapped. Any budding history student out there should be encouraged to pursue their studies as there is a lifetime's worth of ever-growing material available for the taking.

Curated brilliantly by Professors Nicole Aljoe and Oliver Ayres and their team of young history sleuths, Sancho's life is at the very center of Northeastern University London's Mapping Black London interactive archive.[24] Sancho's correspondence can be followed, and his spread of influence clearly traced and delved into in forensic detail. His letters continue to give us insights into eighteenth-century London life and beyond. More encouragingly still, several US-based universities are taking on the story of Sancho, finding a rich and untapped seam by which to open up the truth behind Britain's role in the transatlantic story of enslaved Africans.

The godmother of Black British history studies, for many of us who discovered our history through her work, Gretchen Holbrook Gerzina, has expanded her section on Sancho in the latest edition of *Black England*, which includes a powerful preface by author Zadie Smith, noting how seminal Professor Gerzina's work has been to our understanding of our own country's hidden Black past.

On 19 December 2023, I was privileged to be present at the unveiling of a new memorial celebrating the life of Sancho. A new plaque was set in St. Margaret's Church in Westminster, the church where he was married to Anne Osborne, his "hen," his "best self," and the love of his life, and where all his "Sanchonettas" were baptized, and three young ones buried in his lifetime. I was excited and moved to be present as the Ignatius Sancho Café opened its doors in Greenwich Park on 23 March 2024. It is a beautiful spot that boasts great food and great views, two things Sancho would have been happy to enjoy.[25] In the same park of his youth, a monument to Charles Ignatius will be unveiled shortly that will be a vibrantly colourful ceramic relief based on the Thomas Gainsborough Sancho portrait of 1768. It will be installed on the only surviving wall of Montagu House in Greenwich

Park and is being created by the artist Christy Symington, paid for largely through a public funding scheme and the kind permission of the Royal Parks and Greenwich council. A son of the borough will be celebrated in style.

Coda

A sad coda to these positive outpourings of interest in Sancho, and via him the wider Black British community in Britain's past, is the contrast with the struggles to ensure that Black British achievements and history are studied and respected.

Professor Deirdre Osborne, Distinguished Professor at Central China Normal University and Emerita Professor of Literature and Drama at Goldsmiths University, London was Programme Co-founder of the now defunct original MA in Black British Literature there. Professor Osborne believes that teaching Sancho is essential. She explains:

> It is important that perspectives from within the context of Britain are centralised as Black American experiences have historically overwritten those of Black Britons in publishing and cultural histories to become dominant points of reference. The MA Black British Literature followed diasporic and aesthetic routes in our study of Black literature and drama from the unique experiential viewpoints of being born and raised in Britain.[26]

She continues,

> In Sancho and Olaudah Equiano, for example, we have two contemporaries, eighteenth-century Black British writers who automatically contest the literary canon by exerting their authority in depicting Black people's lives as subjects and provide a cultural lineage for later historical drama and fiction. [I]n the [curriculum for the] MA Black British Literature contemporary writers were read interactively with voices from the past to enact a radical revision of literary history.[27]

The MA, co-founded with Emerita Professor Joan Anim-Addo, was under severe attack by higher-level administrators at Goldsmiths throughout its nine years of existence. Its interconnected research-led teaching, activism, and accompanying public events programmes have now been lost. Oddly, the university still headlines Professor Osborne's name and that of Dr. Suzanne Scafe, the pioneering Black British scholar who has not taught the course since 2023, to promote it. Student testimony on the website also relates to the degree as it was (2015–24).[28]

This lack of academic commitment to the study of the literature generated by Black Britons is an obvious mirror of the lack of respect these writers have constantly been plagued with, leaving us without any major consolidation of critical writing by Black academics about Black British writing. In terms of the effect of this course on students, the following exemplify student reactions: "I have never learnt so much in my entire education about the history of Black and Mixed people [. . .] until encountering this module" and "This module should be compulsory, it should trickle down into every level of education."[29]

So, we find ourselves where we began in some ways, struggling to have our voices heard and respected and still seeking a place of belonging, without having to force our way into our nation's story. Despite the great work that has been undertaken by Black Britons for hundreds of years, we currently find ourselves trying to make room for the Black British story in all its vibrant, creative, and innovative glory. Sancho and his contemporaries, both the famous and the obscure, will need advocates in the future if their stories, writings, and lives are not to be re-buried.

Charles Ignatius Sancho's legacy lives on. His great heart and bold engagement with life and the country of his adoption, despite all the obstacles that stood arrayed against him, his wife, and his children, allow us to continue to rely on him to help us tell the story of the long history of the Black presence in the UK. My journey of belonging started with my interest in Sancho. Today, to my surprise, I find that Sancho, a figure seen as innocuous for centuries, is now becoming a catalyst for the teaching of Black British history to a much broader audience than just those who belong to the African and African Caribbean British diasporas. Knowing where Sancho belongs in the landscape of British history will help us open up the habitually obscured annals of the cruel, brutal international trafficking of African bodies and its present-day consequences. The wonderful, surprisingly positive, by-product of this opening is the grounding it affords those of us who seek to see themselves in the fabric of British history. And it is largely in opening up this Black British history that I have found a personal and profound sense of belonging.

Epilogue: The Sancho Challenge

On 29 May 2023, the long-running quiz show University Challenge, first broadcasted on British television in 1962, had a season grand finale that featured three questions on Charles Ignatius Sancho. To most people watching this may have gone unremarked, as the questions posed on this highly competitive quiz are notoriously obscure. To those of us who had watched this program for decades and who are also Black British history enthusiasts, it was a remarkable moment. It marked the entering into mainstream quizzing of a figure so long forgotten by Britain that the mention of his name as recently in the past as 1998 would have had most Britons, of whatever ethnicity, scratching their heads in ignorance. I would have been one of them. Twenty-five years later and Jeremy Paxman, the show's outgoing host on his final episode, mentions Sancho as if he were posing a mildly tricky question about Florence Nightingale or Winston Churchill. That was no small moment. Not for me, at least.

Notes

1. Shannon, L., "Subnormal: A British scandal" (BBC, 2021), www.bbc.co.uk/programmes/m000w81h.
2. National Archives, "Empire Windrush: Caribbean migration," https://tinyurl.com/54vrc4yu; Hakim, A., *African and Caribbean People in Britain* (London: Penguin, 2023), 378–94.
3. Web Team/The Joint Council for the Welfare of Immigrants, "Windrush Scandal Explained" (June 2024), https://jcwi.org.uk/reportsbriefings/windrush-scandal-explained.
4. Conversation with David Olusoga, 4 September 2023.
5. Dukes, H., "Author Walter Mosley talks about creating, killing, and reviving Easy Rawlins," *South Bend Tribune*, 26 April 2017, https://tinyurl.com/3f5c2wzd.
6. Alberge, D., "Half of Britons can't name a Black British historical figure, survey finds," *Guardian*, 26 October 2023, https://tinyurl.com/4a4h9fwd.
7. Goodall, L., "Enoch Powell's Rivers of Blood: The speech that divided a nation," *Skynews*, 24 April 2018, https://tinyurl.com/bdfnbrtc.
8. Mohdin, A., "Less than half of black Britons feel proud to be British, Landmark survey says," *Guardian*, 28 September 2023, https://tinyurl.com/3c4fszh2.
9. "Yorke–Talbot Opinion, 1729," Northumberland Archives, www.northumberlandarchives.com/wp-content/uploads/2021/10/Yorke-Talbot.pdf.
10. Kaufman, M., "Black Tudors: The Somerset Case," *FutureLearn*, www.futurelearn.com/info/courses/black-tudors/0/steps/224795.
11. Memorial 2007, "Memorial 2007: Remembering enslaved Africans and their descendants" (2022), www.memorial2007.org.uk.
12. Veevers, D., "Irish people sent to the Caribbean were not enslaved," *Guardian*, 12 April 2023, https://tinyurl.com/bjhfkawm.
13. Williams, E., *Capitalism and Slavery* (London: Penguin, 2022).
14. Brewer, H., "Creating a Common Law of Slavery for England and its New World Empire," *Law and History Review* 39.4 (2022), 765–834.

15. Hakim, A., *African and Caribbean People in Britain* (London: Penguin, 2023), 31.
16. Adu, A., "Rishi Sunak refuses to apologise for UK slave trade or to pledge reparations," *Guardian*, 26 April 2023, https://tinyurl.com/ynd73ww6; Mohdin, A., "UK cannot ignore calls for slavery reparations says leading UN judge Patrick Robinson," *Guardian*, 22 August 2023, https://tinyurl.com/2jmctnbb.
17. Hakim, *African and Caribbean People in Britain*, 32.
18. Johnson, B., "Karl Marx: Intellectual father of the 1619 project?" *Religion and Liberty Online: Acton Institute*, 4 September 2019, https://tinyurl.com/dfx5n8zj.
19. Conversation with David Olusoga, 4 September 2023.
20. Ibid.
21. Ibid.
22. Conversation with Joanna Brown, August 2023.
23. Conversation with Crispin Powell, 2023.
24. https://mappingblacklondon.org.
25. Chamberlain, D., "New Greenwich Park café honours writer Ignatius Sancho," *The Greenwich Wire*, 13 March 2023, https://tinyurl.com/4287kxp8.
26. Personal correspondence with Professor Osborne, 28 September 2023.
27. Ibid.
28. McIntosh, M., Bernard, J., Busby, M., Johnson, L. K., and Sesay, G. K., "Letter to the Editor: Goldsmiths' redundancy plan shows a lack of commitment to Black British literature," *Guardian*, 12 July 2024, https://tinyurl.com/3nd59bjn.
29. Personal correspondence with Professor Osborne, 28 September 2023.

Further Reading

Hakim, A., *African and Caribbean People in Britain* (London: Penguin, 2023).
Gerzina, G., *Black England: A Forgotten Georgian History*, 2nd ed. (London: John Murray Press, 2022).
Olusoga, D., *Black and British: A Forgotten History* (London: MacMillan Press, 2016).
Williams, E., *Capitalism and Slavery*, 2nd ed. (Durham, NC: University of North Carolina Press, 2014).

A Manuscript Letter
Image of Sancho Autograph Letter, No. 1 (to William Stevenson, 26 November 1776)

Figure A.1 shows an image of a letter Sancho sent to William Stevenson.

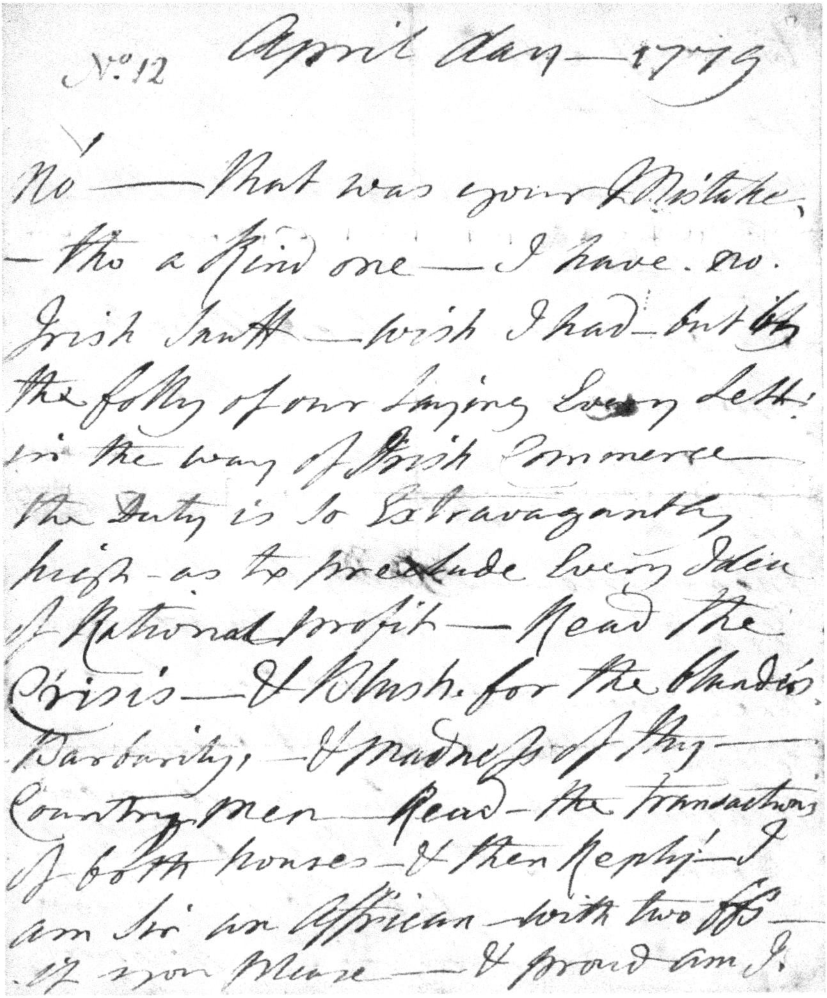
No. 12 April day—1779

No—that was your Mistake,
—tho a Kind one—I have no
Irish Snuff—wish I had—but thro'
the folly of our laying every Lett:
in the way of Irish Commerce—
the Duty is so Extravagantly
high—as to preclude every Idea
of National profit—Read the
Crisis—& blush for the Blunders
Barbarity,—& madness of thy—
Country men—Read—the transactions
of both houses—& then Reply—I
am Sir an African with two Ss—
if you please—& proud am I.

Figure A.1 Image of Sancho autograph letter, No. 1 (to William Stevenson, 26 November 1776) BL Add MS 89077, f. 1.

The Sancho Family Genealogy

Figure A.2 shows the Family Tree of the Sancho family.

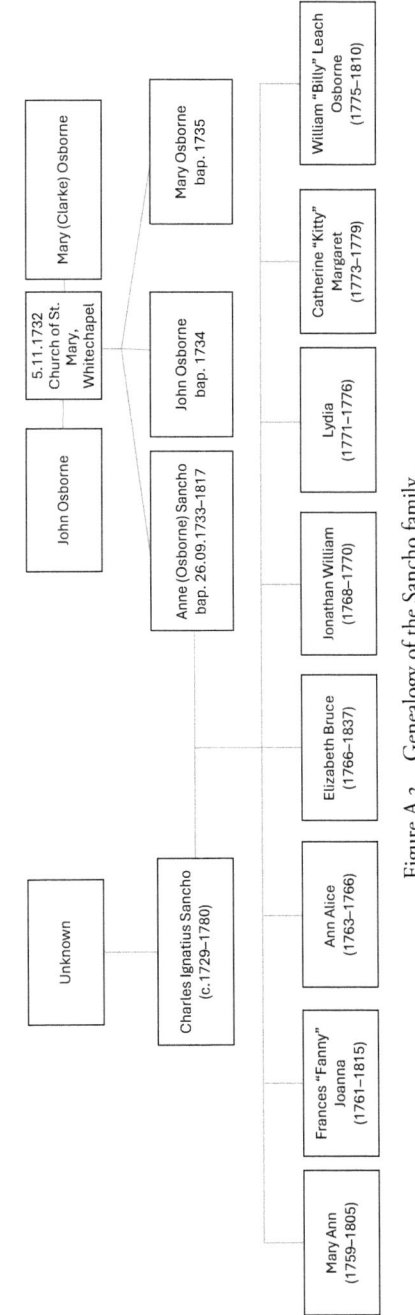

Figure A.2 Genealogy of the Sancho family.

Maps of Locations Associated with Sancho in London and the UK

The maps show key locations in London and its environs (Map A.1) and across the UK (Map A.2) in the life of Ignatius Sancho.

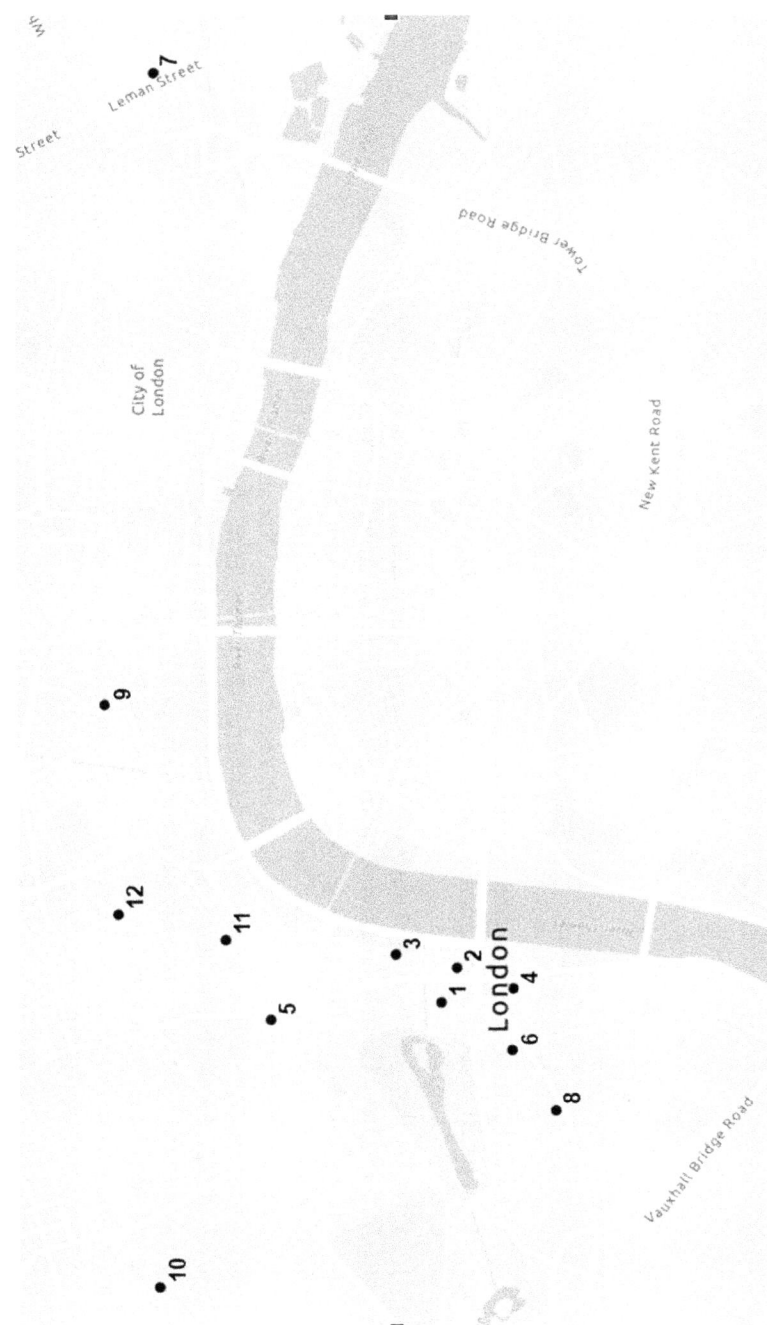

Map A.1   Key London and environs locations in the life of Ignatius Sancho. Based on data from www.mappingblacklondon.org

Caption for Map A.1 (cont.)

1. 19 Charles Street: Sancho's shop and family home.
2. Cannon Row: location of Ignatius and Anne Sancho's first home before moving to nearby Charles Street in 1773.
3. Privy Garden: London townhouses of the Montagu family and Sir (Thomas) Charles Bunbury.
4. St. Margaret's Church: location of marriage of Ignatius and Anne Sancho and baptisms of their children.
5. Mews Gate: bookselling premises occupied by William and Anne Sancho after 1806.
6. Tothill Street: residence of Elizabeth Bruce Sancho, the last surviving Sancho child, in the 1810s.
7. Lambert Street: the first home of Ignatius's future wife Anne Osbourne in 1733.
8. Christchurch Gardens: Ignatius's possible burial site following his death in 1780.
9. Red Lion Court: bookselling premises of correspondent John Wingrave.
10. Bond Street: residence of correspondent Lydia Leach.
11. Maiden Lane: commercial premises of correspondent John Ireland.
12. Drury Lane: longstanding heart of London's theater district, home to the Theatre Royal, where Sancho visited frequently with family and friends.

Map A.2   Key locations across the UK in the life of Ignatius Sancho. Based on data
from www.mappingblacklondon.org

1. Richmond Gardens: one of the many villas owned by Duke
    George and Duchess Elizabeth of Montagu, where Sancho
    worked as a valet.

2. Windsor Castle: records from 1763 show Sancho had a room in the
    Round Tower while employed in the Montagu household.

3. No. 17 The Circus, Bath: location where Sancho was painted by
    the renowned artist Thomas Gainsborough in 1768.

4. Tunbridge Wells: a spa town in Kent that was favored by royalty
    and the wealthy and visited by Sancho's friends and correspond-
    ents Lydia Leach and Margaret Cocksedge.

Caption for Map A.2 (cont.)

5. Retford: a market town in Nottinghamshire, where Sancho's correspondent Rev. Seth Ellis Stevenson was rector.

6. Deene Park: country estate of the Brudenell and Cardigan aristocratic families, where Sancho likely stayed while valet to Lord Cardigan (later Duke George Montagu).

7. Boughton House: Montagu family residence and current seat of the Duke of Buccleuch.

8. Barton Hall: country residence of Sir (Thomas) Charles Bunbury, whose household included many of Sancho's correspondents.

9. Bury St. Edmunds: Suffolk market town, where correspondent John Spink was a wealthy draper, banker, property owner, and influential citizen.

10. Dalkeith Palace: Scottish residence of the Montagu family visited by Sancho in 1770.

Index

Cambridge Companions To . . .

AUTHORS

Edward Albee edited by Stephen J. Bottoms

Margaret Atwood edited by Coral Ann Howells (second edition)

W. H. Auden edited by Stan Smith

Jane Austen edited by Edward Copeland and Juliet McMaster (second edition)

James Baldwin edited by Michele Elam

Balzac edited by Owen Heathcote and Andrew Watts

Beckett edited by John Pilling

Bede edited by Scott DeGregorio

Aphra Behn edited by Derek Hughes and Janet Todd

Saul Bellow edited by Victoria Aarons

Walter Benjamin edited by David S. Ferris

William Blake edited by Morris Eaves

Boccaccio edited by Guyda Armstrong, Rhiannon Daniels, and Stephen J. Milner

Jorge Luis Borges edited by Edwin Williamson

Brecht edited by Peter Thomson and Glendyr Sacks (second edition)

The Brontës edited by Heather Glen

Bunyan edited by Anne Dunan-Page

Frances Burney edited by Peter Sabor

Byron edited by Drummond Bone (second edition)

Albert Camus edited by Edward J. Hughes

Willa Cather edited by Marilee Lindemann

Catullus edited by Ian Du Quesnay and Tony Woodman

Cervantes edited by Anthony J. Cascardi

Chaucer edited by Piero Boitani and Jill Mann (second edition)

Chekhov edited by Vera Gottlieb and Paul Allain

Kate Chopin edited by Janet Beer

Caryl Churchill edited by Elaine Aston and Elin Diamond

Cicero edited by Catherine Steel

John Clare edited by Sarah Houghton-Walker

J. M. Coetzee edited by Jarad Zimbler

Coleridge edited by Lucy Newlyn

Coleridge edited by Tim Fulford (new edition)

Wilkie Collins edited by Jenny Bourne Taylor

Joseph Conrad edited by J. H. Stape

H. D. edited by Nephie J. Christodoulides and Polina Mackay

Dante edited by Rachel Jacoff (second edition)

Daniel Defoe edited by John Richetti

Don DeLillo edited by John N. Duvall

Charles Dickens edited by John O. Jordan

Emily Dickinson edited by Wendy Martin

John Donne edited by Achsah Guibbory

Dostoevskii edited by W. J. Leatherbarrow

Theodore Dreiser edited by Leonard Cassuto and Claire Virginia Eby

John Dryden edited by Steven N. Zwicker

W. E. B. Du Bois edited by Shamoon Zamir

George Eliot edited by George Levine and Nancy Henry (second edition)

T. S. Eliot edited by A. David Moody

Ralph Ellison edited by Ross Posnock

Ralph Waldo Emerson edited by Joel Porte and Saundra Morris

William Faulkner edited by Philip M. Weinstein

Henry Fielding edited by Claude Rawson

F. Scott Fitzgerald edited by Ruth Prigozy

F. Scott Fitzgerald edited by Michael Nowlin (second edition)

Flaubert edited by Timothy Unwin

E. M. Forster edited by David Bradshaw

Benjamin Franklin edited by Carla Mulford

Brian Friel edited by Anthony Roche

Robert Frost edited by Robert Faggen

Gabriel García Márquez edited by Philip Swanson

Elizabeth Gaskell edited by Jill L. Matus

Edward Gibbon edited by Karen O'Brien and Brian Young

Goethe edited by Lesley Sharpe

Günter Grass edited by Stuart Taberner

Thomas Hardy edited by Dale Kramer

David Hare edited by Richard Boon

Nathaniel Hawthorne edited by Richard Millington

TOPICS

For EU product safety concerns, contact us at Calle de José Abascal, 56–1°,
28003 Madrid, Spain or eugpsr@cambridge.org.

www.ingramcontent.com/pod-product-compliance
Ingram Content Group UK Ltd.
Pitfield, Milton Keynes, MK11 3LW, UK
UKHW022005080526
470874UK00009B/427